# Introduction to the Law of Austria

**General Editors of the Series: Prof. Tuğrul Ansay & Prof. Don Wallace, Jr.**

List of the Introduction books already published are as follows:

Introduction to the Law of Israel (1995)
Introduction to Hungarian Law (1998)
Introduction to Belgian Law (2001)
Introduction to Italian Law (2002)
Introduction to the Law of the United States (second edition 2002)
Introduction to the Law of South Africa (2004)
Introduction to Swiss Law (third edition 2004)
Introduction to German Law (second edition 2005)
Introduction to Polish Law (2005)
Introduction to French Law (2008)
Introduction to Greek Law (third edition 2008)
Introduction to Brazilian Law (2011)
Introduction to Turkish Law (sixth edition 2011)
Introduction to the Law of Kazakhstan (2012)
Introduction to the Law of Croatia (2014)
Introduction to the Law of Austria (2015)

# Introduction to the Law of Austria

Edited by

Christoph Grabenwarter
Martin Schauer

Wolters Kluwer
Law & Business

*Published by:*
Kluwer Law International
PO Box 316
2400 AH Alphen aan den Rijn
The Netherlands
Website: www.kluwerlaw.com

*Sold and distributed in North, Central and South America by:*
Aspen Publishers, Inc.
7201 McKinney Circle
Frederick, MD 21704
United States of America
Email: customer.service@aspenpublishers.com

*Sold and distributed in all other countries by:*
Turpin Distribution Services Ltd
Stratton Business Park
Pegasus Drive, Biggleswade
Bedfordshire SG18 8TQ
United Kingdom
Email: kluwerlaw@turpin-distribution.com

*Printed on acid-free paper.*

ISBN 978-90-411-4679-3



Printed and Bound by CPI Group (UK) Ltd, Croydon, CR0 4YY.

FSC
MIX
FSC® C103993

# Summary of Contents

# Table of Contents

# List of Editors and Contributors

Univ.-Prof. Dr Astrid Deixler-Hübner
Professor at the Department of European and Austrian Civil Procedure, Johannes Kepler University Linz
Univ.-Prof. Dr Constanze Fischer-Czermak
Professor for Civil Law, University of Vienna
Univ.-Prof. Dr Anna Gamper
Professor at the Department of Public Law, State and Administrative Theory, University of Innsbruck
Univ.-Prof. Dr Christoph Grabenwarter
Judge at the Constitutional Court, University professor for Public Law, Business Law and International Law, WU Vienna University of Economics and Business
Univ.-Prof. Dr Friedrich Harrer
Professor for Commercial Law and Civil Law, Paris Lodron University of Salzburg, attorney-at-law
Univ.-Prof. Dr Monika Hinteregger
Professor at the Department of Civil Law and Foreign Private Law and Private International Law, University of Graz
Univ.-Prof. Dr Susanne Kalss
Professor at the Department of Civil Law and Commercial Law, WU Vienna University of Economics and Business
Univ.-Prof. em. Dr Ferdinand Kerschner
Professor emeritus for Civil Law and Professor at the Department of Environmental Law, Johannes Kepler University Linz
Mag. Julia Kienast
Student Assistant at the Department of Civil Law, University of Vienna
Univ.-Prof. Dr Bernhard Alexander Koch, LLM (Michigan)
Professor for Civil Law, University of Innsbruck
Univ.-Prof. Dr h.c. Michael Lang
Professor at the Institute for Austrian and International Tax Law, WU Vienna University of Economics and Business
Univ.-Prof. Dr Peter Lewisch

Professor of Criminal Law and Criminal Procedure, University of Vienna, attorney-at-law
Univ.-Prof. Dr Brigitta Lurger, LLM (Harvard)
Professor at the Institute of Civil Law, Foreign Private Law and Private International Law, University of Graz
Univ.-Prof. Dr Franz Marhold
Professor at the Institute for Austrian and European Labour Law and Social Security Law, WU Vienna University of Economics and Business, attorney-at-law
Asst -Prof. Dr Kristin Nemeth, LLM (EUI, Florence)
Assistant Professor at the Department of Civil Law, University of Innsbruck
Univ.-Prof. Dr Paul Oberhammer
Professor at the Department of Civil Procedure, University of Vienna
Univ.-Asst Mag. Sebastian Reiter
Assistant at the Department of Civil Law, University of Vienna
Erich Schaffer, MSc LLB
Research Associate at the Institute for Austrian and International Tax Law, WU Vienna University of Economics and Business
Univ.-Prof. Dr Martin Schauer
Professor for Civil Law, University of Vienna
Univ.-Prof. Dr Erika Wagner
Professor for Civil Law and Professor at the Department of Environmental Law, Johannes Kepler University Linz
Univ.-Asst Mag. Katharina Windisch
Assistant at the Department of Civil Law, University of Vienna

# Preface

The purpose of this book is to provide foreign readers, be they practitioners, scholars or students, with an introduction to the most important areas of Austrian law. Each chapter has been prepared by leading experts in their respective field and presents an overview of the basic structure, principles and rules shaping Austrian law. In fifteen chapters the most important areas of public and of private law and of both substantive and procedural law are presented. Each contribution includes a bibliography referring to the most important literature for further reading.

As editors, we have left the content of the various chapters to the best judgment of the authors, who determined the structure, scope and emphasis of their contributions. With regard to terminology and style we confined ourselves to suggestions for revision and improvement. The final responsibility for the respective chapters lies entirely with their authors.

We are indebted to Sebastian Reiter and Gerlinde Winsauer for their help and patience with the editorial process.

Christoph Grabenwarter,
Vienna

Martin Schauer
Vienna
January 2015

CHAPTER 1

# Constitutional Law

*Christoph Grabenwarter**

## §1.01 INTRODUCTION

In Austria, there is no single document called 'the Constitution' but the constitution is spread among various legal documents. The main constitutional document is the Federal Constitution (*Bundes-Verfassungsgesetz*, in short: *B-VG*) of 1920. The Federal Constitution lays down the basic principles of the constitution; it regulates the organisational structure of the Austrian State, the constitution and the powers of its various institutions and bodies, and contains several fundamental rights. Apart from the Federal Constitution there are several other constitutional acts and constitutional provisions contained in various legal acts on a sub-constitutional level. Both must be expressly specified as constitutional law.

Austria consists of nine Federal Provinces, the so-called *Laender*. There are one federal Constitution and nine *Land* constitutions; the latter play a less important role.

From a comparative perspective, the approach to interpret the Constitution is a rather formalistic one (except for fundamental rights). The process of interpreting the Constitution encompasses the application of various methods of interpretation that may be summarised as textual interpretation (literal, grammatical and systematic interpretation), historical interpretation and teleological interpretation (i.e., the search for the objective purpose of a constitutional provision in the changing political and historical context). Each of the aforementioned methods constitutes a legitimate and equivalent principle of interpretation. Austrian legal scholars attach, however, particular importance to the historical development of the Constitution, which encompasses two facets: the subjective-historical interpretation and the objective-historical or historic-systematic interpretation. With the first the interpreter is looking for facts in

* I have to thank Mag. Eva-Maria Tos for her assistance in bringing the text into the English language.

the constitution's history of development that provides information on the meaning underlying the text (e.g., in legislative materials, such as Government Bills or Reports of the Parliamentary Committee). It is feigned that with the adoption of a bill, the meaning expressed in the related legislative materials has been adopted by all parliamentary representatives. This exegesis might lead to a rejection of certain interpretive results that were gained through the application of other methods of interpretation. In this context the question arises whether a corrective interpretation of the wording of the Constitution is permitted. The Austrian Constitutional Court holds the view that the constitution's wording is to be given priority.[1] The objective-historical or historic-systematic interpretation is also known as the 'theory of petrifaction' ('*Versteinerungstheorie*') and serves to interpret provisions on the distribution of competences between the central government *(Bund)* and the Federal Provinces *(Laender)*. The basic idea behind this theory is to establish the meaning of constitutional terms as they were understood at the time of their entry into force; this by taking into account the systematic context in which they were embedded and by drawing on the then existing legal order, in particular the sub-constitutional legal order.

Following the accession of Austria to the European Convention of Human Rights (ECHR) in 1958, the approach of interpreting the Constitution, in particular fundamental rights, has gradually changed during the last decades. In the 1970s the Constitutional Court started to incorporate the proportionality test established by the European Court of Human Rights[2] in a number of cases concerning different fundamental rights; amongst them the right to property and the freedom of expression. This development was influenced by two factors: First, the Constitutional Court referred to the necessity clauses of Articles 8-11 ECHR. Second, the Court implicitly took account of the German discussion on fundamental rights and their limits under the German Constitution. A third source influencing the interpretation of fundamental rights is the Charter of Fundamental Rights of the EU (CFR). In 2012, the Constitutional Court – in cases of a corresponding guarantee in the Constitution – incorporated the rights under the CFR as a standard of review in the proceedings before it and found that they were functionally equivalent to fundamental rights of the Federal Constitution.[3]

As to the structure of the Austrian legal system, there is a 'hierarchy of norms'; the concept was developed by *Adolf J. Merkl*. The hierarchy of norms is based on the idea that the law regulates its own creation. Both as regards the content and the formal aspects, every legal act must in general be enacted in accordance with another legal act. The law regulating the creation of another is considered to be of a superior rank in relation to the one whose creation it is regulating. The legislator, when enacting a legal act, must comply with the respective rules. In applying this concept to the Austrian legal system, the hierarchy of norms is as follows: The Federal Constitution and the

1. Cf. e.g., *Collection of Decisions of the Constitutional Court*, 11036/1986.
2. For references see Grabenwarter, *The European Convention for the Protection of Human Rights and Fundamental Freedoms*. Commentary, Article 8, m.n. 51 et seq.
3. Cf. *Collection of Decisions of the Constitutional Court*, 19632/2012.

constitutions of the *Laender* authorise the legislators to enact ordinary laws. Constitutions and laws authorise administrative authorities to enact ordinances. Laws authorise authorities to issue rulings or judgments. There is even a hierarchy among constitutional law depending on the requirements for its creation: There is ordinary constitutional law and the basic principles of the Constitution that can be derived therefrom; the latter are on top of the hierarchy of norms as the strictest rules of enactment and amendment of all apply to them (for further details see section §1.02). No legal act of subordinate rank must contravene a legal act of superior rank. The hierarchy of norms depending on the rules of enactment and amendment is interrelated with the hierarchy according to the superseding power of norms. According to the latter, the rank of a legal act in the hierarchy of norms depends on the question whether it can supersede or whether it is superseded by another legal act. This concept does not say anything about the legal consequences in case a subordinate legal act contravenes a superior one. However, the legal order may provide with the possibility that legal acts of subordinate rank that contravene superior norms can be quashed in particular proceedings.

## §1.02 THE BASIC PRINCIPLES OF THE AUSTRIAN FEDERAL CONSTITUTION

The basic principles of the Austrian Federal Constitution enjoy a special position among the rest of the constitutional law. They are not expressly laid down in the Constitution but they can be derived from the overall context of the Constitution. The basic principles inherent in the constitution are the democratic, the republican, the federal and the liberal principle, the principle of the separation of powers and the principle of the rule of law.

The basic principles are subject to special rules of enactment and amendment. Their abolition and fundamental amendment or a fundamental change of their interrelationship is considered to be a 'total revision of the Federal Constitution' ('*Gesamtänderung*') within the meaning of Article 44(3) Federal Constitution. On such changes the legislator can vote only in the presence of at least half the members and by a two-thirds majority of the votes cast. Furthermore, a referendum among the Austrian people must be held.

If an amendment of ordinary constitutional law or provision conflicts with one of the basic principles, it is in violation of the Constitution ('unconstitutional constitutional law'). This view is confirmed by the Austrian Constitutional Court.[4]

The basic principles of the Constitution must be distinguished from so-called *state objectives* ('*state* objectives'; e.g., permanent neutrality, comprehensive national defence and comprehensive environmental protection). State objectives are neither basic principles nor do they grant any subjective right to individuals. They reflect basic decisions of the Austrian State on the political system and values and have to be implemented by the legislator of sub-constitutional law, to whom they are addressed.

4. Cf. e.g., *Collection of Decisions of the Constitutional Court*, 16327/2001.

In the case law of the Austrian Constitutional Court, state objectives mainly serve as a criterion in the interpretation and application of constitutional law.[5]

### [A] Democratic Principle

Article 1 Federal Constitution reads: '*Austria is a democratic republic. Its law emanates from the people.*' According to the democratic principle, the people subject to the legal order are the ones to enact the law.

Austria is an *indirect parliamentary democracy*. Unlike in a direct democracy, in an indirect democracy the law is enacted solely by representatives who are elected by the people of Austria. On the federal level, nationals elect the members of the *National Council* (the legislative period lasts five years); in the federal provinces, nationals elect the members of the respective *Diet* (*Landtag*).

The right to vote the members of the National Council is granted to every Austrian citizen provided that they have reached the age of 16 on the day of the election (*universal suffrage*; Article 26(1) Federal Constitution provides for a constitutionally granted subjective right). Each citizen has one vote (*equal suffrage*) and elects the candidate standing for election directly (not indirectly through the election of an electoral college as, for instance, in the US – *direct suffrage*). The voters have to cast their vote in person (no representation by another person: *personal suffrage*). The election must be secret (*secret ballot* in order to protect the electoral freedom). Canvassing must not be restricted or be supported by the State in a discriminating manner (*free suffrage*). The National Council is elected based on the principle of proportional representation (as opposed to *majority representation*); thus, all political forces that enjoy the support of a not insignificant number of citizens are represented in Parliament according to their political strength.

The elected *representatives* have a free mandate and are thus free from instructions from the voters and, in principle, from their political parties. Freedom from instructions from political parties means that it is contrary to the Constitution if a political party obliges representatives to vote in a certain manner. It is, however, considered to be in compliance with the Constitution if they voluntarily follow the opinion of their parliamentary group. Moreover, the representatives enjoy immunity in particular with a view to their speeches and their voting in Parliament (so-called professional immunity).

Every act of the executive branch (jurisdiction and administration) must be based on law (*principle of legality*; cf. Article 18 Federal Constitution); the highest administrative authorities are responsible to the legislator in matters pertaining to the administration. There are certain instruments to make this responsibility effective (Parliament committee of inquiry, vote of no confidence, proceedings against members of the Government before the Constitutional Court).

5. Compare e.g., *Collection of Decisions of the Constitutional Court*, 12009/1989, 13109/1992, 18114/2007.

The Constitution contains certain elements of a direct democracy which modify the principle of an indirect democracy:

- In case of a 'total revision of the Federal Constitution' or if the National Council so decides a *referendum* must be held on an act of parliament.
- If the National Council so decides, a so-called '*consultation of the people*' must be held on matters of fundamental and overall national importance for whose settlement the legislature is competent. The result of the consultation of the people is not legally binding (but of great political significance).
- 100,000 voters may take a so-called '*popular initiative*'. With this motion, they may initiate the passing of a law that concerns a matter to be settled by federal law. However, the National Council is not obliged to comply with it.

### [B] Republican Principle

The Federal President is the highest executive body of the Austrian State. He is elected by all Austrian citizens who are entitled to vote. The term of office is *six years*, re-election being possible once. Before the expiry of the term of office, the Federal President may be impeached by referendum; there has not been a single impeachment procedure in the history of Austria. The Federal President carries the title of the 'head of state'; this is owing to his typical functions, such as commander-in-Chief of the Federal Army, acts of grace, representation of the Republic. Further competences of the Federal President are, for instance, that he can dissolve the National Council or that he appoints and dismisses the Federal Chancellor, the other members of the Federal Government and State Secretaries. Due to the legal position of the Federal President, his political responsibility and the limited term of office, Austria is a republic.

### [C] Federal Principle

Article 2(1) Federal Constitution stipulates that '*Austria is a federal state*'. Compared to federal states, the degree of decentralisation of legislation and judicial powers is relatively low.

Apart from the federal legislation and administration, the *Laender* have relatively autonomous legislators and administrations. Jurisdiction is exclusively a matter of the Federation (cf. Article 82(1) Federal Constitution).

All competences which are not expressly allocated to the Federation fall within the competences of the *Laender* (*taxative enumeration by way of a general clause;* Articles 10-15 Federal Constitution). In fact, most competences lie with the Federation (e.g., external affairs, civil law affairs, matters pertaining to trade and military affairs). Matters remaining within the competence of the *Laender* (legislation and administration) are, for instance, building and regional planning law, law on environmental protection, hunting and fishing law (Article 15 Federal Constitution). However, the *Laender* may influence federal legislation and administration in two ways: First, in the *Federal Council* (the second chamber of Parliament), whose members are elected by the Diet, mainly by way of a temporary veto, and, second, by way of the *indirect federal administration* (see section §1.04 below).

The federal element of the Austrian State is rather weak since most competences lie with the Federation and the influence of the Federal Council (in which the *Laender* are represented) is very limited.

### [D] Principle of the Separation of Powers

The principle of the separation of powers is reflected in the separation of the state powers in a legislative body (National Council and Federal Council, Diets), administration and jurisdiction. This principle is supplemented by numerous *rules on incompatibility* according to which one person cannot, at the same time, exercise a function within the three branches of the state (it may be permitted, however, to exercise a function within the same branch of the state at the same time). An exception to this principle is, for instance, the possibility that it is possible that a member of the Government is, at the same time, a member of Parliament (or the Diet). Moreover, between the branches there exist powers of appointment and of dismissal, rights of participation and rights of control (e.g., the Federal Government is under the control of the National Council, of the Constitutional Court and the Supreme Administrative Court; the Federal President can dissolve the National Council).

### [E] Liberal Principle

A central element of the Austrian Constitution is the self-restraint of the State in the sense of a separation of the State and society. This is reflected in *fundamental rights and freedoms*, which shall grant a *'freedom from the State'* (e.g., freedom to exercise every kind of gainful activity (Article 6 Basic Law on the General Rights of Nationals: StGG), inviolability of property (Article 5 StGG, Article 1 of Protocol Number 1 to the ECHR), freedom of opinion (Article 13 StGG, Article 10 ECHR), principle of equality (Article 7 Federal Constitution)).

### [F] Principle of the Rule of Law

States under the rule of law are characterised by a certain legality and foreseeability of the legal order, and by institutions which shall guarantee the implementation of these two elements. The difference between a state under the rule of law and a police state lies exactly in the certainty and foreseeability of existing rights and obligations. A state under the rule of law is thus a *constitutional state*, in which constitutional law governs the legislation and laws govern the administration.

A main element of the principle of the rule of law is the *principle of legality*, which requires that every administrative act must be based on law. In the Austrian Constitution, the principle of legality is laid down in Article 18 Federal Constitution. Another central element of the principle of the rule of law is the existence of institutions which guarantee compliance with the constitution and the law; the individuals concerned may thus seek remedies against acts of the state. The principle of the rule of law is particularly reflected in the possibility to subject decisions of administrative courts to a review by the Constitutional Court (Article 144 Federal Constitution, '*Entscheidungsbeschwerde*') and the Supreme Administrative Court (Article 130 Federal Constitution; '*Bescheidbeschwerde*'); they examine compliance of these acts with the constitution and the law. The principle of the rule of law is further reflected in the possibility of having legal acts, regulations and international treaties examined for their compliance with the constitution and legal acts respectively (Articles 139-140a Federal Constitution).

## §1.03 THE LEGISLATURE

### [A] Federal Legislation

Article 24 Federal Constitution stipulates that the legislative power of the Federation is exercised by the Parliament, i.e., the *National Council* jointly with the *Federal Council* (the Federal Parliament thus consists of two chambers). The 183 members of the National Council are directly elected by the Austrian people; the members of the Federal Council are elected by the Parliaments of the Federal Provinces.

Legislation is *initiated* by way of a *legislative proposal*, thus by way of a 'request' directed at the National Council for passing a law. A legislative proposal can only be made by members of the National Council, by the Federal Government (Government Bills), by the Federal Council or by way of popular initiatives.

In general, *ordinary laws* can only be adopted in the presence of at least one-third of the members of the National Council and an absolute majority of the votes cast. *Constitutional laws* require the presence of at least half the members of the National Council and a two-thirds majority of the votes cast; furthermore, they must be expressly specified as constitutional laws.

After an enactment has been adopted by the National Council the president of the National Council has to transmit it to the *Federal Council*, which generally has a *suspensive veto*. The Federal Council can reject the enactment by means of a reasoned objection within eight weeks. If it does not object to the enactment, the law is authenticated by the Federal President as having been passed in compliance with the constitution; this act is countersigned by the Federal Chancellor. Finally, the law is published in the Federal Law Gazette (*Bundesgesetzblatt*, in short: *BGBl*). If the Federal Council does, however, raise a reasoned objection within eight weeks, the National Council has to deliberate on the enactment again. The National Council may (in the presence of at least half its members) *insist* on the enactment being adopted as a law. In this case, the Federal Council cannot raise an objection again but the enactment is authenticated and published as described above.

### [B] *Land* Legislation

The Federal Constitution provides that a *Land* law to enter into effect requires that a *Diet* passes a law which is then authenticated and countersigned in accordance with the provisions of the *Land* concerned, and *published* by the Governor in the *Land* Law Gazette.

According to Article 99(2) Federal Constitution, a *Land constitutional law* can be passed only in the presence of half the members of the Diet and with a two thirds majority of the votes cast. According to Article 99(1) Federal Constitution the *Land* Constitution must not contravene the Federal Constitution; ordinary federal laws do not, however, enjoy precedence over ordinary *Land* laws.

## §1.04 THE EXECUTIVE

The highest executive bodies of the Austrian State are the *Federal President*, the *Federal Government* (Federal Chancellor, Vice-Chancellor and Federal Ministers) and the *Federal Ministers*.

The executive power of the Federation is exercised in two ways: First, through federal authorities (*direct federal administration*, e.g., security police, financial administration); second, through the Governor and the *Land* authorities subordinate to him (*indirect federal administration*). In the latter case, the acts of the *Land* authorities are considered to be acts of the federal authorities.

### [A] Federal Government

The Federal Chancellor, the Vice-Chancellor and the other Federal Ministers are entrusted with the highest administrative business of the Federation in so far as it is not assigned to the Federal President (Article 69(1) Federal Constitution). The Federal Chancellor and, on his recommendation, the other members of the Federal Government are appointed by the Federal President. No recommendation is requisite to the dismissal of the Federal Chancellor or the whole Federal Government; the dismissal of individual members of the Federal Government ensues on the recommendation of the Federal Chancellor. The Federal Government or the Federal Minsters can also be removed from office by an explicit vote of no confidence taken in the National Council or if they so wish.

It has to be distinguished between the individual Federal Ministers and the Federal Government. The Federal Ministries and the authorities subordinate to them perform the business of the federal administration. A Federal Minister is entrusted with the direction of a certain Federal Ministry. Certain businesses are entrusted with the Federal Government as a collegiate body (e.g., adoption of Government Bills which are submitted to the National Council as legislative proposals) under the chairmanship of the Federal Chancellor.

### [B] Federal President

The legal status and functions of the Austrian Federal President are discussed in section §1.02[B] above. From a comparative perspective, the Austrian Federal President has only limited powers.

## §1.05 JUDICIARY

Articles 82-94 Federal Constitution contain rules on the organisation, authorities and the constitutional principles of the ordinary jurisdiction as well as the administration of justice.

### [A] Organisation of Ordinary Courts

According to Article 82(1) Federal Constitution, the Federation is the source of all jurisdiction. Administrative courts, the Supreme Administrative Court and the Constitutional Court are courts, too; however, special rules apply to them (Chapter VII Federal Constitution), which in certain respects refer to the rules governing ordinary courts (e.g., Article 135(4) Federal Constitution).

The constitution and *competence of ordinary courts* is laid down by federal law (Article 83(1) Federal Constitution). The competences of the courts are further determined by the 'allocation of cases' within a certain court. The *principle of the 'allocation of cases'* is laid down in Article 87(3) Federal Constitution. It requires that business shall be allocated in advance among the judges of a court. This principle is a special form of the principle of legality and is complemented by the *right to a lawful judge* pursuant to Article 83(2) Federal Constitution. This subjective right grants to everyone the right that the allocation of competences is complied with.

According to Article 92(1) Federal Constitution, the Supreme Court (OGH) is the court of final instance in civil and criminal matters; it does not, however, require that the parties of each civil or criminal case must be provided with a remedy to the Supreme Court.

Article 94(1) Federal Constitution contains an essential principle typical for the principle of the separation of powers: Judicial and administrative powers must be separated at all levels of proceedings. This principle prohibits that an authority is both a judicial and an administrative authority; it prohibits remedies between ordinary courts and administrative authorities and instructions between administrative authorities and ordinary courts (cf. VfSlg 19.281/2010). Different rules apply under Article 94(2) Federal Constitution, according to which federal or *Land* laws may provide that in certain matters (instead of the remedy of a complaint to an administrative court) there is a remedy from an administrative authority to an ordinary court. The legislator has availed him/herself of this opportunity in various fields of law, e.g., in social legislation. These cases are excluded from the jurisdiction of administrative courts (Article 130(5) Federal Constitution).

Articles 83 and 84 Federal Constitution provide for guarantees for professional judges, such as independence. According to Article 91(1) Federal Constitution, under certain circumstances the people shall participate in the jurisdiction. The participation of *lay judges* in criminal proceedings is further determined in Article 91(2) and (3) Federal Constitution: A jury returns a verdict upon the guilt of the accused in crimes entailing severe penalties, to be specified by law, and in all cases of political felonies and misdemeanours; together with professional judges they decide on the degree of punishment. In criminal proceedings for other punishable offences *lay assessors* take part in the administration of justice if the penalty to be imposed exceeds a limit to be determined by law. Lay assessors also enjoy judicial independence.

*Public prosecutors* are functionaries of the jurisdiction (Article 90a Federal Constitution). They represent the investigation and prosecution in cases for acts carrying a penalty by court. Federal law determines the detailed regulations on their being bound to instructions of their superior functionaries. Acts of the criminal police implemented on the basis of an order of the prosecution constitute an act of jurisdiction.[6]

### [B] Administrative Jurisdiction

The principle of the rule of law does require not only that the public administration must be based on law (Article 18(1) Federal Constitution) but also that an entity examines whether the laws have in fact been complied with. The latter function is exercised by administrative courts and the Supreme Administrative Court, the parties before which are a person subject to the legal order on the one hand and an administrative authority on the other. Administrative courts examine whether administrative acts comply with the law; the Administrative Court is the court of final instance in administrative matters. Furthermore, it may be appealed to in case an administrative court defaults on passing a decision by way of an application for setting a time limit. The Supreme Administrative Court is also competent to resolve a conflict of jurisdiction between administrative courts or between an administrative court and the Supreme Administrative Court (Article 133(1) Federal Constitution).

In Austria, there are nine administrative courts of the *Laender* and two of the Federation (the Federal Supreme Administrative Court and the Federal Finance Court), with whom the legal protection against acts of administrative authorities lies (with few exceptions). Decisions are usually taken by a single judge or a judicial officer. The law may, however, stipulate that it is to be taken by a senate consisting of a number of professional judges or of professional and lay judges. The *principle of the 'allocation of*

6. *Collection of Decisions of the Constitutional Court*, 19281/2010.

*cases'* also applies to administrative courts (Article 135(2) and (3) Federal Constitution).

Administrative courts are not competent to deal with matters of the ordinary jurisdiction (even in cases of a successive competence, cf. Article 94(2) Federal Constitution) or with matters falling within the competence of the Constitutional Court (Article 130(5) Federal Constitution).

In matters pertaining to the municipality's own sphere of competence, municipalities generally perform their business to the exclusion of legal redress to administrative authorities outside the municipality, except this is barred by law (Article 118(4) Federal Constitution).

## §1.06 FUNDAMENTAL RIGHTS

Fundamental rights are subjective rights of individuals that are granted to them on a constitutional level. Article 144 Federal Constitution refers to them as 'constitutionally guaranteed right[s]'. Fundamental and human rights are laid down, in particular, in the Basic Law on the General Rights of Nationals of 1867 ('*Staatsgrundgesetz*'), Federal Constitution and the European Convention on Human Rights and the Protocols thereto; they all have constitutional rank.

*Citizen's rights* differ from *human rights* in that human rights are granted to everyone, while fundamental rights are granted only to citizens. However, different rules apply in respect of EU citizens. EU law stipulates that any discrimination of EU citizens on grounds of their nationality shall be prohibited. Thus, EU citizens may rely on fundamental rights as well.[7]

*Persons subject to fundamental rights* are both natural persons (humans) and legal persons (e.g., stock companies, limited companies).

Fundamental and human rights can be divided into the following groups:

- *Civil rights and liberties*: They grant to individuals certain freedoms (e.g., Article 7 Federal Constitution, right to life, freedom of religion, artistic freedom, freedom to exercise every kind of gainful activity).
- *Rights of equality*: They shall prevent discrimination (e.g., general principle of equal treatment; federal constitutional law prohibiting racial discrimination).
- *Procedural guarantees*: They guarantee the enforcement of rights (e.g., right of access to a court, right to a fair trial, right to a judge).
- *Political rights* (e.g., right to vote, right to petition).
- *Social fundamental rights*: The Austrian Constitution does not enshrine social fundamental rights (e.g., right to work, right to housing). Such claims may possibly be derived from existing fundamental and human rights. The application of the CFR may lead to the implementation of further social rights into the Austrian Constitution.

7. Cf. *Collection of Decisions of the Constitutional Court*, 19077/2010, 19118/2010, 19568/2011.

## §1.07 THE CONSTITUTIONAL COURT

The Constitutional Court is the central institution to guarantee the precedence of the constitution, to guarantee that all state acts comply with the constitution and to safeguard fundamental and human rights ('guardian of the constitution'). The most important competence of the Constitutional Court is the competence to review the constitutionality (or lawfulness) of general norms, in particular the constitutionality of laws. It may do so in the course of pending proceedings (*concrete norm control proceedings*) in *abstract norm control proceedings*. In norm control proceedings, the Constitutional Court examines both federal and *Land* laws, including the Federal Constitution and the constitution of the *Laender*. Federal laws are examined for their compliance with the Federal Constitution, *Land* laws for their compliance with the *Land* constitution and Federal Constitution and sometimes federal laws (Article 12 Federal Constitution). The constitutions of the *Laender* are examined for their compliance with the Federal Constitution and the basic principles of the Federal Constitution; the Federal Constitution is examined for its compliance with the basic principles derived therefrom. EU law with the exception of the CFR is not a standard of review in norm control proceedings.

Another function of the Constitutional Court is, for instance, that it resolves conflicts of competences between the Federation and a *Land* or between the *Laender* themselves, and that it pronounces upon challenges to elections.

## §1.08 NEUTRALITY

Austria's peaceful relations with other States are determined by its status as a "permanently neutral" state. Neutrality was declared unilaterally by Austria under international law in 1955 and notified to a number of States which explicitly recognised the declaration. Unlike the Scandinavian 'neutral' States (Sweden and Finland), Austria is legally bound to remain permanently neutral. On a national constitutional level, this is laid down in a special constitutional law entitled 'Federal Constitutional Act on the Neutrality of Austria' (*Bundesverfassungsgesetz über die Neutralität Österreichs*; henceforth: BVG Neutrality) of 1955. Article I(1) stipulates that Austria 'of her own free will declares herewith her permanent neutrality' '[f]or the purpose of the permanent maintenance of her external independence and for the purpose of the inviolability of her territory'. In order to secure these purposes, another constitutional provision prohibits Austria from ever acceding to any military alliances or agreeing to the establishment of military bases of foreign States on its territory (Article I(2)).

The content of the legal status of neutrality is determined by international law. The classical legal rules of neutrality under international law are laid down in the Fifth and Thirteenth Hague Convention and are, however, determined by customary international law.[8] In times of war, these rules must be observed by any State not

8. See Bindschedler, *Permanent Neutrality of States*, in Bernhardt (ed.), *Encyclopedia of Public International Law*, Instalment 4 (1982) 133 (136 et seq.); Miehsler, *Permanent Neutrality and*

taking part in a particular conflict; they apply both to temporarily and permanently neutral States. A neutral State is not allowed to supply belligerents with any war material, to grant loans or financial aid directly for the purposes of warfare or to permit belligerents either the transport of war material across its territory or the installation and use of telephone and telegraph devices upon its territory for purely military purposes. If a neutral State is maintaining economic and financial relations with belligerents, it must observe strict impartiality to both sides.

In times of peace the obligations of neutrality apply only to States committed to permanent neutrality under international law. A State bound to permanent neutrality must observe indirect or 'secondary' legal obligations.[9] It must not act in a manner or accept obligations under international law which might destroy the trust of other States in its neutrality in case of war. The respective duties emerge from those applying in times of war. Accordingly, a permanently neutral State has to shape its foreign relations with a view to preventing possible violations of its neutrality and protecting itself against involvement in future wars. In short, the conduct of foreign relations must enable the permanently neutral State to fulfil its duties in times of war. The concrete conduct of foreign relations, however, is to some extent left to the discretion of the State.

There are different positions on the content of Austria's permanent neutrality. This is mainly due to rapidly changing conditions in international relations. Following the developments in Eastern Europe since 1989 and the Gulf war in 1990/91 a new approach to permanent neutrality was discussed. The new approach proceeds from the assumption that the expectations of other States towards neutral ones have changed following the emergence of a potentially more effective system of collective security within the United Nations. Such changes would also modify the expectations of the international community regarding neutral States.[10] Furthermore, it has been suggested that the concept of permanent neutrality has been reduced to its military core.[11]

In a common declaration with the EU of April 1994 annexed to the Document of Accession, Austria confirmed to accept the rights and obligations under EU law and its institutional framework ('*acquis*'), in particular the principles and the political goals of the EU. As a consequence of this declaration, a special provision confirming Austria's participation in the Common Foreign and Security Policy of the EU was introduced into the Constitution. This provision covers participation in actions by which economic relations with one or more third parties are suspended, restricted or entirely

*Economic Integration*, in Bernhardt (ed.), *Encyclopedia of Public International Law*, Instalment 8 (1981) 431 (432); Zemanek, *The Changing International System: A New Look at Collective Security and Permanent Neutrality*, AJPIL 1991,277 (278 et seq.); *ibid.*, ÖJZ 1992, 179 et seq.; very critical *idem*, *The Chaotic Status of the Laws of Neutrality*, Schindler-FS (1989) 443 et seq.

9. See Schindler, *Die Lehre von den Vorwirkungen der Neutralität*, Bindschedler-FS (1980) 536 (577 et seq.).
10. Cf. among others Zemanek, AJPIL 1991, 277 et seq.
11. On the parallel discussion in Switzerland see Schindler, *Changing Conceptions of Neutrality in Switzerland*, AJPIL 1992, 107.

discontinued.[12] The amendment to the Constitution is intended to ensure that no conflict arises between participation in the Common Foreign and Security Policy and other constitutional requirements, especially those arising from the 1955 Constitutional Neutrality Act.[13]

On the international level, the Austrian Government has not taken any further steps in this respect. They obviously concurred in the opinion that changed expectations towards neutral States have also modified the status of permanent neutrality, which was in their view no longer in conflict with participation in the Common foreign and Security Policy. In particular they proceeded from the assumption that there was no contradiction between the obligations of membership to the EU and the 'military core' of neutrality.[14]

## §1.09 THE FEDERAL CONSTITUTION AND INTERNATIONAL LAW

The Austrian Constitution contains explicit rules on generally recognised rules of international law and on the incorporation of international treaties.

The generally recognised rules of international law form an integral part of federal law. That means that *customary international law* is *ipso iure* transformed into federal law. However, its rank in the national legal system is disputed. According to the case law of the Constitutional Court it has the quality of an ordinary federal law,[15] whereas according to the constitutional law doctrine customary international law is of a higher rank (or may at least be of a higher rank) than ordinary law.[16] The main approach among legal scholars is that it ranks between the Federal Constitution and ordinary federal laws. If a rule of customary international law emerges, it supersedes older ordinary federal laws.

*International treaties* have to be transformed into domestic law in order to become legally binding. However, their identity as internationally binding legal instruments is not altered by their incorporation into national law. The Austrian Constitution does not contain a rule granting international treaties a superior rank over

12. For economic sanctions in the framework of the Common Foreign and Security Policy see Stein, *Außenpolitisch motivierte (Wirtschafts-) Sanktionen der Europäischen Union – nach wie vor eine rechtliche Grauzone?*, in Bernhardt-FS (1995) 1129 (1136 et seq.).
13. For further details see Zemanek, *Österreichs Neutralität und die GASP, Vorträge, Reden und Berichte aus dem Europainstitut der Universität des Saarlandes*, 315 (1995) 10 et seq.
14. For a detailed discussion on this position see Griller, *Verfassungsfragen der österreichischen EU-Mitgliedschaft*, ZfRV 1995, 89 et seq.; and Cede, *Österreichs Neutralität und Sicherheitspolitik nach dem Beitritt zur Europäischen Union*, ZfRV 1995,142 et seq.
15. VfSlg 1375/1931, 2680/1954, 3950/1960; Seidl-Hohenveldern, *Völkerrecht*[7] (1992) 597.
16. Rill, *Der Rang der allgemein anerkannten Regeln des Völkerrechtes in der österreichischen Rechtsordnung*, 10 ÖZÖR (1959/60) 439 (446 et seq.); Thienel, *Österreichische Staatsbürgerschaft II* (1990) 50 et seq.; Köck, *Das allgemeine Völkerrecht*, in Schambeck (ed.), *Das österreichische Bundes-Verfassungsgesetz und seine Entwicklung* (1980) 739 (763); Walter, *Bundesverfassungsrecht 170*; Walter/Mayer, *Grundriß 220*; Öhlinger, *Verfassungsrecht*[2] (1995) 64.

domestic laws in general. The legal quality of treaties varies depending on their content and the procedure followed in the process of ratification.[17]

All political treaties and other treaties, in so far as they modify or complement existing laws, and treaties by which the TEU and TFEU are modified may only be ratified with the approval of the National Council; the necessary majorities are subject to the type and content of the treaty involved (Article 50 and Articles 42 and 44 Federal Constitution). International treaties concluded by the Federal Government which concern a matter falling within the *Laender's* autonomous sphere of competence have to be approved by the Federal Council.

Treaties not falling within the scope of Article 50 Federal Constitution do not need to be approved by Parliament; they enter into force with expiry of the day of their publication in the Federal Law Gazette (BGBl) (*general transformation* as opposed to *special transformation*). Whether a treaty is directly applicable depends on whether its content is sufficiently precise. The legal quality of a generally transformed international treaty depends on whether it is approved by the National Council within the meaning of Article 50 Federal Constitution (which – for treaties not falling within the scope of Article 50 Federal Constitution – is possible but not mandatory) or not. If it approved by the National Council, it has the rank of an ordinary law. All other treaties have the rank of ordinances. All international treaties that have been concluded before a constitutional amendment in 2008, and which modified or complemented the Constitution have the rank of a constitutional law.

The *Laender* are accorded a limited power to conclude treaties with neighbour States and their provinces. However, this power does not encroach upon the Federal Government's treaty-making power. This competence of the *Laender* is not exercised in practice.

The legislator has the power to prevent an international treaty from being directly applicable in domestic law even if it could – due to its content – be directly applicable. On giving its approval to a treaty the National Council may vote that the treaty in question shall be implemented by the issue of law or laws (reservation of implementation). Such a vote has the effect that the treaty is not directly applicable in national law regardless of whether it is self-executing or not.

In the field of approving human rights treaties the practice of the Austrian Parliament is diverse.[18] The ECHR, for instance, was originally considered to be a non-self-executing treaty, which ranked only as an ordinary federal law;[19] in 1964, however, it was raised to the rank of a constitutional law (with effect of the year 1958). Since then, it has not been disputed that the Convention is directly applicable in domestic law. All Protocols to the ECHR also have the rank of constitutional laws.

---

17. For further details on the process of incorporation of treaties see Holzinger, *International Human Rights Instruments and National Law* (Austria), in Matscher/Karl (eds), *Austrian-Soviet Round-Table on the Protection of Human Rights* (1992) 15 (20 et seq.).
18. Cf. Morscher, *Die Hierarchie der Verlassungsnormen und ihre Funktion im Grundrechtsschutz in Österreich*, EuGRZ 1990, 471.
19. See the case law of the Constitutional Court beginning with the *Collection of Decisions of the Constitutional Court* 3767/1960.

Today, the guarantees of the ECHR form the most important source of human rights in Austrian constitutional law.

Whereas, other international human rights treaties were ratified with a reservation of implementation and thus not directly applicable in domestic law. The Convention on the Elimination of All Forms of Racial Discrimination (CERD) was ratified with a reservation of implementation.[20] It was therefore not directly applicable under Austrian law. However, in 1973, a specific Constitutional Law on the Implementation of the CERD was adopted.[21] Its Article 1 prohibits any form of racial discrimination and puts the legislative and executive powers under an obligation to refrain from discriminatory measures.[22] The same applies to the Convention on the Rights of the Child (CRC). It was ratified by Austria with a reservation of implementation. In 2011 a special constitutional law, the Federal Constitutional Law on the Rights of the Child,[23] was adopted in order to implement the rights contained in the CRC.

The UN Covenant on Civil and Political Rights (CCPR) was also ratified with a reservation of implementation and ranks only as an ordinary federal law.[24] No law on the implementation of the treaty has been adopted so far. However, the guarantees of the CCPR are to a large extent covered by the ECHR.

## §1.10 AUSTRIA AND INTERNATIONAL OR SUPRANATIONAL ORGANISATIONS

Until 1982, the Federal Constitution did not contain explicit provisions on the participation of Austria in international organisations. In 1981, a provision allowing the transfer of jurisdiction to international institutions,[25] and in 1994, a new chapter on the participation in the decision-making process in the EU were introduced into the Constitution.[26]

The Austrian Constitution contains a special provision for the *transfer of sovereign powers* to an international organisation. According to Article 9(2) Federal Constitution, single competences may be transferred to other states or intergovernmental institutions by federal law or state treaties that have been approved by the National Council. However, the authorisation applies only to competences of the Federation. Moreover, a general transfer of large areas of sovereign powers cannot be based on this provision as a transfer under Article 9 Federal Constitution is limited to 'specific'

20. BGBl 1972/377.
21. Federal Constitutional Act on Elimination of Racial Discrimination (*Bundesverfassungsgesetz zur Durchführung des Internationalen Übereinkommens über die Beseitigung aller Formen rassischer Diskriminierung*), BGBl 1973/390.
22. See Okresek, *Development* 40 et seq.
23. BGBl I 4/2011.
24. BGBl 1978/591; for the position of the CCPR in the Austrian legal system cf. Fioretta/Öhlinger, *Die Menschenrechtspakte der Vereinten Nationen* (1978); Ermacora, *Die UN-Menschenrechtspakte - Bestandteil der österreichischen Rechtsordnung*, JBl 1979, 191 et seq.; Nowak, *Erfüllt Österreich seine Verpflichtungen nach dem UN-Pakt über bürgerliche und politische Rechte?*, EuGRZ 1981, 513 et seq.
25. BGBl 1981/350.
26. BGBl 1994/1013.

('single') competences.[27] Decisions by intergovernmental institutions have to respect the limits set by human rights. In addition, the obligation of permanent neutrality must be observed in decisions on the transfer of competences.

The most important transfer of sovereign powers in the history of the Federal Constitution took place when Austria *acceded to the EU*. However, the transfer was not based on Article 9(2) Federal Constitution as the scope of that provision was too narrow for being the basis of a transfer of sovereign powers to that extent. Therefore, the Government introduced a special constitutional law authorising the competent authorities to ratify the treaty on accession. This law (and not the treaty itself) was subject to a referendum before the ratification of the treaty. The amendment constituted a total revision of the Constitution within the meaning of Article 44(3) Federal Constitution.[28]

Various provisions of the Federal Constitution concern the *participation of Austrian organs in the EU* (Articles 23a–23k).[29] Article 23a Federal Constitution deals with the election of Austrian members to the European Parliament. Unlike in other Member States, an Austrian member of the European Parliament may not simultaneously be a member of the federal legislative bodies (Article 59 Federal Constitution).

Another Article provides for the procedure of participation of the *Laender* and *Land* Governments in the decision-making process of the EU (Article 23d Federal Constitution). The Federation is obliged to inform the *Laender* without delay regarding all projects within the framework of the EU which affect their autonomous sphere of competence or could otherwise be of interest to them. The same applies to municipalities in so far as their own sphere of competence or other important interests of the municipalities are affected. *Laender* and municipalities have the right to present their views on these projects. In case the *Laender* make a 'uniform comment' on a project where legislation is their business, the comment is binding upon the Federation. The Federal Government may deviate from such an opinion only for compelling integration and foreign policy reasons. These reasons have to be communicated to the *Laender* immediately.

If a project of the EU concerns at least in part matters falling within the legislative power of the *Laender*, the Federal Government may confer on a member of the *Land* Government nominated by the *Laender* the right to participate in the decision-making process of the Council. This authority is exercised in cooperation and coordination with the competent Federal Minister.

The federal legislative bodies (National Council and Federal Council) are, too, accorded the right to participate in the decision-making process of the EU (Article 23e Federal Constitution). The competent Federal Minister is obliged to inform these two

27. Constitutional Court, 16/3/2013, SV 2/12.
28. BGBI 1994/77 4; for the procedure and its legal problems in detail see Schäffer, *The Accession of Austria to the European Union. Constitutional problems and solutions*, Förvaltnings-Rättslig Tidskrift 1994, 237 et seq.
29. For further details see Grabenwarter, *Änderungen der österreichischen Bundesverfassung aus Anlaß des Beitritts zur Europäischen Union*, ZaöRV 1995, 166 et seq.; Seidl-Hohenveldern, *Constitutional Problems involved in Austria's Accession to the EU*, CMLR 1995, 727 (731 et seq.); Neisser, *Verfassungsreform im Lichte des EU-Beitrittes*, in Rill-FS (1995) 335 (342 et seq.).

bodies without delay of all projects within the framework of the EU and afford them opportunity to express their opinion. The opinion of the National Council is binding upon the Federal Minister if the project is aimed at passing a binding legal act which would affect the issuance of a federal law within the ambit of that EU legal act. The Federal Minister may deviate from such an opinion only for imperative integration and foreign policy reasons. In case the Federal Minister intends to deviate from the opinion of the National Council, the latter must deal with the issue again. If the project is aimed at passing a binding legal act which either needs to be implemented by a federal constitutional law or which contains rules that can only be adopted following the adoption of constitutional provisions, a deviation is permissible only if the National Council does not object to the deviation within reasonable time. The Federal Council may adopt binding opinions on projects which encroach on the competences of the *Laender* and have to be transformed by a constitutional act, or which contain rules that can only be adopted following the adoption of constitutional provisions.

Finally, there is also a special provision confirming Austria's participation in the Common Foreign and Security Policy of the EU. This includes participation in tasks by which economic and financial relations with one or more third countries are suspended, restricted or entirely discontinued (Article 23j Federal Constitution).[30]

30. See § 1.08 above.

CHAPTER 2

# Administrative Law

*Anna Gamper*[*]

## §2.01 HISTORICAL BACKGROUND

Embedded in a civil law system, administrative law emerged in Austria both as a branch of law and as an academic legal subject, as state administration transformed into a separate and distinct form of public power from the eighteenth century onwards.[1] In its early phase, administrative law was seen as part of *Polizeyrecht* that laid focus on public policy principles, while it still took some time until it matured into its specific character in the second half of the nineteenth century. When, after the breakdown of the Austro-Hungarian Empire, the Austrian Republic was founded in 1918, administrative law had already reached the stage of the *Rechtsstaat*, since the administration was seen not only as a power distinct from the legislative and the judicial power, but also as a power bound to the rule of law. Courts exercising 'strong-form'[2] judicial review both with regard to the constitutionality of administrative acts and the laws upon which they were based were increasingly considered vital for the reconciliation of the administration with individual rights. The legalisation and even constitutionalisation of the administration thus became predominant concerns of Austrian administrative law in the twentieth century.[3]

* Thanks go to Univ.-Asst Dr Maria Bertel for her assistance in editing the footnotes of this chapter.

1. Adamovich et al., *Österreichisches Staatsrecht*, vol. 4 (2009) 18 f, Wiederin, *Staat, Verwaltung und Verwaltungsrecht: Österreich*, in von Bogdandy/Cassese/Huber (eds.), *Handbuch Ius Publicum Europaeum*, vol. 3 (2011) 187 (197 and 202).
2. Tushnet, *The rise of weak-form judicial review*, in Ginsburg/Dixon (eds.), *Comparative Constitutional Law* (2011), 321 (321 f).
3. Adamovich et al., *Staatsrecht* 3 ff., Leitl-Staudinger, *Wissenschaft vom Verwaltungsrecht: Österreich*, in von Bogdandy/Cassese/Huber (eds.), *Handbuch Ius Publicum Europaeum*, vol. 4 (2011) 195 ff., Wiederin, *Staat* 197 ff.

Today, administrative law in Austria faces different challenges: First and foremost, perhaps a growing tendency towards a 'judicial administration' is visible. This development culminated in the very recent establishment of administrative courts[4] that replaced administrative authorities as a second instance in administrative matters.[5] It is remarkable that, while the administration in continental Europe had historically received its distinctiveness through the very fact that it became a domain separate from the ordinary judiciary,[6] modern procedural guarantees of the ECHR and EU Charter of Fundamental Rights demand a return to the (ordinary or specific) judiciary in many administrative matters.

Being challenged by new and complex branches, the administration is moreover situated in a context of multilevel governance: While EU membership requests Austria to implement and apply EU law in a wide range of administrative matters, Austria is also a federal state where administrative competences are shared between the federal government and the nine constituent states (*Länder*) as well as, at a second stage, the municipalities. At the same time, the public administration undergoes severe outsourcing processes and is exposed to the growing influence of private-sector-related concepts such as new public management. Whereas the nineteenth century was held to be the 'century of administration',[7] a growing disintegrative tendency is thus discernible at the beginning of the twenty-first century.

## §2.02 DEFINITIONS

### [A] What Is 'Administration'?

While the first leading handbooks on (republican) Austrian administrative law, which were written by *Adolf J. Merkl* and *Walter Antoniolli* in the earlier part of the twentieth century,[8] widely reflected on the question how the administration could best be defined as a distinct power of its own, more recent works[9] rather avoid rigid definitions, in particular because the multifaceted process of disintegration of the administration entails repercussions on the question of definition.

4. In order to distinguish these administrative courts (*Verwaltungsgerichte*) from the *Verwaltungsgerichtshof* – the Supreme Court that regularly decides in administrative matters – the latter court's name is here translated as 'Administrative High Court'.
5. BGBl I 2012/51.
6. Sordi, *Révolution, Rechtsstaat, and the Rule of Law: historical reflections on the emergence of administrative law in Europe*, in Rose-Ackerman/Lindseth (eds.), *Comparative Administrative Law* (2010) 25.
7. Sordi, *Révolution* 27 with reference to Stolleis, *Geschichte des öffentlichen Rechts in Deutschland*, vol. 2 1800-1914 (1992) 229.
8. Merkl, *Allgemeines Verwaltungsrecht* (1927), Antoniolli, *Allgemeines Verwaltungsrecht* (1954).
9. Adamovich et al., *Staatsrecht* 2 f, Raschauer, *Allgemeines Verwaltungsrecht*[4] (2013) 14 f, Kahl/Weber, *Allgemeines Verwaltungsrecht*[5] (2015) 31 ff, Leitl-Staudinger, *Wissenschaft* 216, Wiederin, *Staat* 216.

Traditional definitions of administration focus on the separation of powers: The administration is defined as the branch of state power that remains after the 'subtraction'[10] of the legislative and the judicial branch. Such a negative definition requires, of course, a definition of what the legislative and judicial branches consist of; in any case, however, we do not learn from this definition what the agenda of administration or administrative law positively is. And yet, positive definitions[11] that describe the administration as the entirety of activities of public officers bound to instructions neglect important aspects: Administrative functions delivered by supreme administrative authorities as well as by independent administrative authorities are excluded by this definition, while activities of office-holders within parliamentary or judicial bodies, where they are atypically bound to instructions, are included. As the use of instructions was drastically reduced over the last years due to the increase of independent administrative authorities and, most recently, administrative courts, they became a less and less significant parameter.

A main problem lies in the distinction between the organisational and the functional meaning of administration: When, for instance, the new administrative courts decide *in merito* on appeals against administrative acts issued by instruction-bound administrative authorities, they functionally serve as an administrative instance,[12] while they belong to the judiciary in an organisational sense. Similarly, it will be difficult to properly accommodate certain administrative functions performed by, e.g., Parliaments' presiding officers or by single (ordinary) judges. Although 'administration' is a term explicitly used by the Austrian Federal Constitution, the constitutional context suggests either an organisational or, in turn, a functional meaning.[13] Where the Federal Constitution uses the term 'execution', this comprises both the judiciary and the administration as a branch of state power distinct from the legislative power, but this neither entails a clear definition between the judicial and the administrative branch.

### [B] What Is 'Administrative Law'?

Administrative law, as an academic subject, traditionally comprises three traditional parts which are called general administrative law (*Allgemeines Verwaltungsrecht*), special features of administrative law (*Besonderes Verwaltungsrecht*) and administrative procedural law (*Verwaltungsverfahrensrecht*).

General administrative law comprises the principles that are inherent in Austrian administrative law. They are not entrenched in a single codified law, but to a large extent derive from the Federal Constitution or can else be found as a recurring context of many administrative laws. Main themes of general administrative law deal with

10. Mayer, *Deutsches Verwaltungsrecht*[3], vol. I (1924) 7.
11. On positive definitions and their limited scope, Merkl, *Verwaltungsrecht* 42 f, Antoniolli/Koja, *Allgemeines Verwaltungsrecht*[3] (1996) 19 f, Kahl/Weber, *Verwaltungsrecht* 32 ff.
12. See already De Pansey, *De l'autorité judiciaire en France* (1818) Chapter XXVII: '*Juger l'administration c'est encore administrer*'.
13. Raschauer, *Verwaltungsrecht* 5 f, Kahl/Weber, *Verwaltungsrecht* 33 ff., Wiederin, *Staat* 226 f.

definitions and categories of the administration, organisational aspects of the administration, constitutional determinants and legal sources of administrative behaviour, the different legal shapes of administrative acts, relations between the administration and the citizen, channels of legal protection against administrative action, state liability, but also general trends such as electronic government or the 'right to good administration'. The fact that the Austrian Federal Constitution governs these general aspects of administrative law in such high degree shows the importance that it attributes to the administrative branch; it does so with a focus on the administration's democratic legitimacy as well as the observance of legality and fundamental rights.

In contrast, the part which is called 'special features of administrative law' comprises a plethora of laws that refer to single administrative issues. Being enacted either at federal or *Land* level, their different contents cover a vast deal of administrative fields whose number, not the least due to EU legislation and technical developments, steadily increases. Some of the diverse fields of administrative law, such as health and social welfare law, environmental law or public economic law, have reached an almost independent status in academic teaching and research. Others can roughly be divided into the law regulating natural resources and infrastructure, safety law and education law,[14] but this list is not exhaustive.

In a narrow sense, administrative procedural law comprises a couple of ordinary laws that were enacted under a federal competence 'on demand' (Article 11 paragraph 2 B-VG[15]). Accordingly, administrative procedures, including procedures in case of administrative offences, may be regulated by an ordinary federal law, provided that the federal law-maker recognises the need for a uniform enactment; this was the case in as early as 1925.[16] Digressive legal provisions may only be enacted by the federal or *Land* law-maker, if this is strictly necessary. In a wider sense, the federal Service of Documents Act (*Zustellgesetz*), but also the Administrative High Court Act (*Verwaltungsgerichtshofgesetz*) and the new Proceedings of Administrative Courts Act (*Verwaltungsgerichtsverfahrensgesetz*) are relevant, too, although, in the latter two cases, this depends on whether judicial proceedings in administrative (appeal) matters can be treated as part of administrative procedural law. It is also remarkable that general principles of the law on administrative offences are part of administrative procedural law, while the more specific provisions on administrative offences are entrenched in the laws on single administrative issues.

## §2.03 CATEGORIES OF ADMINISTRATION

The administration – and, thus, also the relating administrative law – can be classified in different ways that are either concerned with the sphere of competence in which administrative tasks are performed or with the purpose and function of an administrative task. According to the former category, the administration can be distinguished

14. Wiederin, *Staat* 210 ff.
15. B-VG is the abbreviation of *Bundes-Verfassungsgesetz* which is the main document of the strongly fragmented Austrian Federal Constitution.
16. BGBl 1925/273.

into federal and constituent state (*Land*) administration. According to the allocation of powers, which is mainly entrenched in Articles 10-15 B-VG, both the federation and the *Länder* are responsible for (different) administrative tasks. Federal administrative tasks are enumerated explicitly, while *Land* administrative tasks are either enumerated or entrenched in the residuary competence of the *Länder*. However, many federal administrative tasks are carried out by authorities of the *Länder* on behalf of the federation according to a system which is called 'indirect federal administration' (Article 102 B-VG).[17] While these tasks formally remain allocated at federal level, they are nevertheless administrated by *Land* authorities which lessens the need for federal administrative authorities in the *Länder* and at the same time increases the administrative scope of the *Länder* ('executive federalism'). The *Land* Governors have been the traditional bodies responsible for indirect federal administration and are, though only in that very function, bound to instructions of the federal government or one of its members. Recently, however, the new administrative courts have replaced the *Land* Governors in their capacity to decide on appeals in matters falling into the sphere of indirect federal administration – part of this function had already been exercised by the former Independent Administrative Senates instead of the *Land* Governors –, so that only fragments of the overall responsibility in indirect federal matters remain with the *Land* Governors. Moreover, a wide range of federal administrative matters may be retained by the federation and thus be performed directly by federal administrative authorities, which is the case in fiscal matters or matters pertaining to security, asylum or monument protection. As regards their own sphere of competences, the *Länder* are responsible for all remaining matters under their residuary competence as well as for a range of enumerated competences. The same division of competences applies with regard to the implementation and execution of EU law. As EU law often regulates matters that involve both the federation and the *Länder* according to the Austrian distribution of competences, there is much need for internal cooperation during the implementing and executing phase.[18]

Another distinction can be drawn between state administration (*staatliche Verwaltung*) and autonomous administration (*Selbstverwaltung*): According to the classical concept of federalism as a dual system, competences are shared between the federation and the *Länder*. Nevertheless, also the municipalities that constitute the third territorial tier in Austria are competent for a wide range of administrative tasks, even though their competence must always be based on a federal or *Land* law that delegates this task to the municipality. Where these tasks, however, are considered to fall into the municipality's autonomous sphere – along lines that are drawn by the Federal Constitution in accordance with the principle of subsidiarity (Article 118 paragraph 2 B-VG; some examples are given in Article 118 paragraph 3 B-VG) –, laws

17. Raschauer, Art. 102 B-VG, in Korinek/Holoubek (eds.), *Österreichisches Bundesverfassungsrecht*, 4. rev. (2001), Bußjäger, Art. 102 B-VG, in Kneihs/Lienbacher (eds.), *Rill-Schäffer-Kommentar. Bundesverfassungsrecht*, 14. rev. (2014), Kahl/Weber, *Verwaltungsrecht* 177 f.
18. Ranacher, *Bezüge zur Europäischen Union*, in Pürgy (ed.), *Das Recht der Länder* (2012) 87 (143 ff.).

must vest the municipalities with administrative competences and will be unconstitutional if they omit doing so. Apart from their autonomous sphere, where they cannot be bound to instructions of the federation or the *Länder*, even though they are subject to supervisory measures, the municipalities are also responsible for a range of delegated matters where municipal bodies are bound to federal or *Land* instructions; it is up to federal or *Land* legislation to determine in accordance with general constitutional principles such as reasonability and efficiency which non-autonomous administrative matters are delegated to the municipalities.

Apart from the municipalities being entities of territorial autonomous administration, other types of autonomous administrative entities exist (Article 120a-c B-VG):[19] Typical examples are the professional chambers or social insurance agencies. All of these bodies constitute legal persons under public law and must be organised democratically. They are responsible for administrative matters that are assigned to them by the laws either as an autonomous or as a delegated competence. Only in the latter case, administrative matters are carried out under the umbrella of 'state administration', where they are bound to instructions issued by federal or state authorities, whereas all other tasks are performed autonomously.

The administration can also be classified according to the purpose or specific functionality of administrative activities. Usually, a distinction is drawn between administration that seeks to grant protection against threats to the public through precepts and prohibitions, management of public services, social welfare and other types of state sponsorship, management of administrative resources and fiscal administration where the state acts as a private entrepreneur; many administrative activities, moreover, refer to more than just one of these four sectors.[20] Another distinction can be drawn between authoritative administration (*Hoheitsverwaltung*) and private-sector-oriented administration (*Privatwirtschaftsverwaltung*): In the first case, the state acts with authority (*imperium*), through the enactment of rules and, if necessary, the use of force, when it carries out administrative tasks. In the second case, the state acts as a private person, using the forms and instruments of private law as any private person might do. While the state has to observe fundamental rights even as a person dealing under private law, it is neither bound to the distribution of competences nor to the legality principle, which are crucial constitutional determinants in case of authoritative administration. This means that, e.g., a *Land* government will be able to sponsor scientific research, although the universities, from an authoritative viewpoint, fall into the federal competence. While it is possible for the federation and the *Länder* to enact self-binding laws in order to determine their private law activities, they are not required to enact legislation in this case, whereas authoritative administration regularly needs to be based on a law.

19. Eberhard, *Nichtterritoriale Selbstverwaltung*, JRP 2008, 91 ff.
20. Adamovich/Funk, *Allgemeines Verwaltungsrecht*³ (1987) 2 ff, Kahl/Weber, *Verwaltungsrecht* 38 ff.

## §2.04 CONSTITUTIONAL DETERMINANTS

Within the hierarchy of the Austrian legal system, all kinds of administrative law must observe superior law, in particular constitutional law. A selection of the most important constitutional determinants of administrative law shall be mentioned here.

As already noted, authoritative administration is bound to the distribution of powers which allocates the competence to enact laws regulating the administration and the competence to execute them respectively to the federation or the *Länder*. In a wider context, constitutional rules on power-sharing also apply with regard to self-governing bodies such as the municipalities.

Another highly important determinant, entrenched in Article 94 paragraph 1 B-VG, is the separation of the administration from the judiciary. While the Federal Constitution does not expressly stipulate which matters fall into the administrative and, *vice versa*, judicial sphere, it is mainly left to ordinary legislation to determine this question.[21] Nevertheless, it would derive from Article 94 paragraph 1 that administrative issues only had to be dealt with by administrative authorities and not by judicial bodies. The Federal Constitution itself, however, provides some exceptions from this general rule. One is mentioned in Article 94 paragraph 2 B-VG which establishes that 'in single issues' a federal or *Land* law may provide that appeals against administrative acts can be lodged at an ordinary court instead of an administrative court. As this 'constitutional breach' of the separation of powers is limited to 'single issues', it appears that the separation of powers as a leading principle of the Federal Constitution is not seriously violated. Still, however, the very fact that administrative *courts* are normally responsible to decide appeals against legal acts originally set by administrative authorities demonstrates that administrative issues are not only dealt with by genuine administrative authorities, but, at remedy stage, by judicial bodies. Previous to 2014, this had only been possible in the context of an extraordinary appeal to the Administrative High Court or the Constitutional Court (for a limited period between 2008 and 2014 also the Asylum Court). There had been no other courts under public law, even though several types of administrative tribunals had served as quasi-judicial bodies, but still formed part of the administrative organisation. The need for such bodies had become pressing due to the European Court of Human Rights' wide interpretation of Article 6 ECHR which required the establishment of courts or, at least, quasi-judicial tribunals in many fields, where, according to the Austrian tradition, 'mere' administrative authorities had previously been responsible as second instances.[22] As the possibility to appeal against their decisions before the Constitutional Court and the Administrative High Court, due to the limited reviewing powers and cognizability of these courts, had been considered inadequate to meet the demands of

21. Pernthaler, *Österreichisches Bundesstaatsrecht* (2004) 168.
22. Grabenwarter/Holoubek, *Demokratie, Rechtsstaat und Kollegialbehörden mit richterlichem Einschlag*, ZfV 2000, 207, Öhlinger, *Abschied von den UVS, Die UVS: Gestern – heute – morgen*, ZUV 2012, 51 (52), Pabel, *Verwaltungsgerichtsbarkeit – Wesen und Wandel*, ZÖR 2012, 61 (68 ff).

Article 6 ECHR,[23] the establishment of quasi-judicial, though still formally administrative, tribunals had become necessary. After all, this solution lasted more than two decades, but was accompanied by an intense discussion on how these tribunals could be replaced by genuine administrative courts.[24] In 2012, finally, this purport was realised though a federal constitutional amendment,[25] so that, as of 1 January 2014, 9 *Land* and 2 federal administrative courts took responsibility to decide on appeals which had hitherto been either the responsibility of administrative tribunals or higher administrative authorities, such as governments or members thereof. Although the new courts do not belong to the ordinary judiciary (which decides in civil and criminal matters), they are genuine courts. Formerly, the judiciary had been solely vested in the federation so that the *Länder* could at best establish independent administrative tribunals, but no genuine judicial bodies. This is one reason why the recent reform was ultimately approved, since the principle of federalism appears to be strengthened by this new judicial power of the *Länder*; at the same time, however, the *Länder* lost political influence, because appeals are now decided by independent courts instead of their governments (or members thereof). The reform had also been instigated by the wish to establish courts that decide before the Administrative High Court and thus help reduce the mass of cases to decide which this Court had traditionally been called upon. Moreover, Article 6 ECHR and Article 47 EU Charter of Fundamental Rights require courts or tribunals with the power of full cognizability, which the administrative courts largely are endowed with.

Preventing the administration from arbitrary decisions that lacked the democratic legitimacy which could only be conferred by law was the most prominent aim with regard to administrative law in the nineteenth century,[26] and it still remains a most important pillar of good (in the sense of lawful) administration. Thus, another constitutional principle that governs the administration is the legality principle which is enshrined in Article 18 paragraph 1 and 2 B-VG. According to this principle which constitutes the formal entrenchment of the rule of law, administrative action must always be based on a law. Administrative acts execute laws, but they must neither change nor supplement them. The laws themselves, however, must be sufficiently accurate in order to convey a clear idea to administrative authorities how they are expected to act. It would therefore either violate the legality principle if an administrative authority acted against, outside or without a law or if the content of a law itself was phrased in too vague a manner. At the same time, it is admitted that the degree of accuracy demanded from a law varies from subject-matter to subject-matter. According

23. Grabenwarter, *Civil rights – neuere Entwicklungen*, in Achatz et al. (eds.), *Steuerrecht Verfassungsrecht Europarecht – FS Ruppe* (2007) 154 (154 ff.), Pabel, *ZÖR* 2012, 73.
24. Pernthaler (ed.), *Unabhängige Verwaltungssenate und Verwaltungsgerichtsbarkeit* (1993), Jabloner, *Die Entwicklung der Verwaltungsgerichtsbarkeit in Österreich*, ÖJZ 1994, 329 ff, Grabenwarter, *Auf dem Weg zur Landesverwaltungsgerichtsbarkeit*, JRP 1998, 269 ff.
25. BGBl I 2012/51. For a general discussion on the reform Holoubek/Lang (eds.), *Die Schaffung einer Verwaltungsgerichtsbarkeit erster Instanz* (2008), Lienbacher, *Allgemeines zur Einrichtung einer Verwaltungsgerichtsbarkeit 1. Instanz*, JRP 2011, 328 ff, Öhlinger, *ZUV* 2012, 54 ff.
26. Pernthaler, *Bundesstaatsrecht 553*, Kahl/Weber, *Verwaltungsrecht* 45, Wiederin, *Staat* 205 ff.

to the notion of 'differentiated legality',[27] planning laws, for instance, need not be worded as precisely as, for instance, taxation laws, even though laws with a less accurate wording need to compensate this deficit by the exact formulation of their purposes and the procedures regulated by them.

There are, however, some exceptions to this rule: One exception is the rare type of 'emergency regulation' which empowers supreme executive bodies at federal or *Land* level to change laws in case of state emergency, even though they are thereby submitted to several restrictive conditions.[28] Another, much more common exception is the regulation against nuisances at municipal level (*ortspolizeiliche Verordnung*).[29] This kind of regulation may only be enacted within the autonomous sphere of a municipality in order to prevent imminent or combat existing nuisances that disturb the local population. While these regulations must not change laws that already regulate such nuisances, they may enact complementary rules, provided that the nuisance had not yet been regulated by a law. Moreover, the Federal Constitution uses the phrase 'within the framework of laws' – instead of the phrase 'on account of laws' (Article 18 paragraph 1 and 2 B-VG) – in the context of municipalities and other self-governing bodies as well as of the universities.[30] While, with regard to municipal self-government, the Constitutional Court interprets this phrase in the sense that regulations need to have a legal basis,[31] even though they may be less precise, it does not ensue from the prevailing case law which meaning the Court attaches to the phrase in the other cases. It is hardly reasonable, on the one hand, that the Federal Constitution should use two different phrases and yet mean the same, namely that administrative acts must be based on a law, which may be more or less accurate according to the idea of 'differentiated' legality. On the other hand, it would be detrimental to both the rule of law and the democratic principle if regulations might be enacted as complementary quasi-laws on a large scale.

Due to the principle of efficiency, moreover, the administration is bound to observe the principles of thrift, economy and expediency as far as they are compatible with other constitutional principles. For instance, neither the federal distribution of powers nor fundamental rights could be ignored by the administration with reference to the efficiency principle.

Constitutionally guaranteed fundamental rights bind the administration both when it acts authoritatively and under private law. If a person feels violated in such rights by an administrative act, it will ultimately be possible to gain protection from the Constitutional Court. The Constitutional Court equalises rights granted under the EU Charter of Fundamental Rights with rights granted under the Austrian Federal Constitution, provided that the Charter is applicable and that Charter rights have the same

27. Novak, *Das 'differenzierte Legalitätsprinzip' in der verfassungsgerichtlichen Rechtsprechung*, in Funk et al. (eds.), *Staatsrecht und Staatswissenschaften in Zeiten des Wandels – FS Adamovich* (1992) 491.
28. Article 18 paragraphs 3-5 and Art. 97 paragraphs 3-4 B-VG.
29. Article 118 paragraph 6 B-VG.
30. Article 81c paragraph 1, Art. 118 paragraph 4 and Article 120b paragraph 1 B-VG.
31. Cf. e.g., VfSlg 19.559/2011.

normative structure, wording and determination as the respective national right.[32] While many aspects of 'good administration' are protected by the Federal Constitution, not all of them embody a subjective constitutional right, although Article 6 ECHR and other procedural rights enjoy the rank of federal constitutional law. It is thus impossible to directly claim a constitutional right to legality before the Constitutional Court, whereas it will be possible to claim a violation in fundamental rights by a decision of an administrative court that lacks a proper legal basis. Neither does the 'right to good administration' as granted by Article 41 EU Charter (which is targeted at the EU administration and thus not applicable at national level) enshrine all imaginable standards of good administration, but focuses on procedural rights. It is obvious, however, that exactly because of the principle of legality 'good administration' will need 'good legislation'.[33] With a view to the administrative courts, moreover, 'good administration' will also imply a right to 'good (administrative) adjudication'.

## §2.05 ADMINISTRATIVE ORGANISATION

Administrative organisation is basically regulated by the Federal Constitution, but implemented in detail by both federal and *Land* ordinary laws as well as the *Land* Constitutions that, in accordance with the Federal Constitution, govern the administrative organisation of the *Länder*.

Traditionally, Austrian administration had consisted of diverse administrative authorities that were bound to the instructions of the supreme administrative authorities: The latter include the Federal Government or its individual members and the Federal President at federal level, and the *Land* Government or its individual members, including the *Land* Governor, at *Land* level. While all supreme administrative authorities enjoy an equal position with respect to each other (except for the *Land* Governor when he carries out federal administrative tasks), the so-called 'subordinate' administration consists of authorities that cannot only be bound to instructions of the supreme administrative authorities, but whose individual rulings could formerly also be examined by these supreme authorities according to the various appeal stages provided by law. Their accountability – to the supreme administrative authorities and, through them, to the Federal Parliament or the *Land* Parliaments – endows these subordinate administrative authorities with democratic legitimacy. An increasingly large number of administrative authorities, however, had not met these criteria in so far as they had either been tribunals according to Article 6 ECHR – in particular, Independent Administrative Senates or collegiate bodies part of whose members had to be judges – or bodies that were in some degree accountable to Parliament, though they could not be bound to instructions; the establishment of the latter category had been largely facilitated by an Amendment of Article 20 paragraph 2 B-VG in 2008.[34] It thus became less and less adequate to describe the administrative organisation as a

32. This has been the case law of the Constitutional Court since the decision VfSlg 19.632/2012.
33. Gamper, *Das 'Gute' in der Verwaltung – und außerhalb?*, in Ennöckl et al. (eds.), *FS für Bernhard Raschauer zum 65. Geburtstag* (2013) 99 (112 ff).
34. BGBl I 2008/2.

homogeneous body of instruction-bound authorities on the one hand and apex authorities at supreme executive level on the other.

With the Federal Constitutional Amendment of 2012, however, which applies as of 1 January 2014, the structure of administrative organisation underwent massive changes. While subordinate authorities that are bound to instructions of either federal or *Land* supreme executive authorities remain responsible for administrative issues at first instance, appeals can be lodged at the newly-established administrative courts (Articles 129 et seq. B-VG). These courts replaced the former tribunals, other instruction-free administrative agencies as well as the Asylum Court as appeal bodies; they also replaced the supreme executive bodies with regard to their functions as last administrative instances, even though these latter bodies retain their other functions, such as general policy-making, issuing regulations, preparing legislative drafts or giving instructions to the administrative authorities at first instance.

The administrative authorities at first instance mainly consist of the district administrative authorities (*Bezirksverwaltungsbehörden*) that are *Land* authorities as regards their organisation, even though they carry out not only *Land* administrative tasks, but also a vast majority of federal administrative tasks. A special situation applies in the context of self-governing bodies, such as the municipalities, as their administration is carried out by their own authorities at first instance. It is only with regard to the self-governing sphere of municipalities, however, that appeals against first-instance-decisions may still be dealt with by another municipal authority (and not yet by an administrative court that can nevertheless be appealed afterwards), but this possibility may be excluded by law. Another exception applies in the context of federal administration, since the general rule that federal administration is carried out by the *Länder* on behalf and in the name of the federation ('indirect federal administration') allows numerous exceptions where federal administration is carried out directly by federal administrative authorities. Further to that, the Federal Constitution still explicitly provides for several special types of administration, namely in the fields of schools, security police or national defence. Article 20 paragraph 2 B-VG, moreover, empowers ordinary legislation to establish certain categories of administrative authorities that cannot be bound to instructions, but that are to some extent accountable both to the supreme administrative authorities and to Parliament; *Land* constitutional laws are authorised to establish further categories of such instruction-free authorities.

As regards the remedy stage, most administrative issues where legal protection is sought for fall into the competence of the new administrative courts. Only with regard to municipal self-government will it be possible for an ordinary law to endow a municipal authority with the functions of a second instance.[35] In the field of indirect federal administration, the traditional role of the *Land* Governor as the responsible body to carry out indirect federal administration (even though this role had been challenged even previous to 2014 by the empowerment of the former Independent Administrative Senates to replace the *Land* Governor as a second instance in many indirect federal administrative issues) has now been reduced to issuing regulations or

35. Article 118 paragraph 4 B-VG.

giving instructions to the district administrative authorities as administrative authorities at first instance. Also other members of the *Land* Government and the *Land* Government as a whole that, with regard to bureaucratic services, rely on the Office of the *Land* Government, retain their political and administrative functions as far as this, roughly speaking, does not involve appeals against administrative rulings, against direct administrative compulsory or forceful measures or remedies against administrative delay. Hierarchical relations between subordinate and supreme administrative authorities thus no longer imply the existence of appeal stages from one authority to the other. However, even after the introduction of administrative courts, which by and large made legal protection in administrative matters uniform, the administrative organisation remains rather complex. This is not only due to the multilevel governance of a small state, but also to the fact that some fields of administrative law are considered as something particular and accordingly still provided with their own structures.

However split the organisation of the administration thus may appear, it features some very general characteristics. One concerns the distinction between monocratic and collegiate bodies. The Austrian administration is familiar with both types, and it is remarkable that such a Janus-faced character sometimes even applies to the (seemingly) same body: The Federal or *Land* Government, for instance, may exercise certain powers as a collegiate body, while single members of these governments, as monocratic bodies, may exercise other powers. While administrative monocratic bodies can be found both at first instance (e.g., mayors, heads of district administrative authorities) and at top level (e.g., single members of the Federal or a *Land* Government, Federal President), the collegiate system of decision-making, in the form of senates or chambers, is more usual (and desirable) for higher courts.[36]

A central reference term with regard to administrative organisation is the 'organ' (*Organ*) that the state needs in order to exercise its administrative activities. The Austrian terminology distinguishes the abstract organ (*Organ*) from the physical office-holder (*Organwalter*). Authorities (*Behörden*) are organs that are empowered to act authoritatively, while auxiliary organs only support the administrative activity of organs, e.g., a police officer who acts on behalf of a security authority. Quite often, moreover, Austrian law refers to the *Amt* which is a rather ambivalent term that is sometimes used as a synonym for an authority, but frequently stands just for the office staff that supports an administrative authority bureaucratically.

It is not only possible for administrative authorities to act as private persons under private law and to co-operate with private persons under the 'public private partnership' model,[37] but also to outsource administrative tasks to other legal persons. If the task is outsourced to a private law person, the outsourcing process will be called a privatisation. It is possible to empower private persons either to carry out authoritative administrative tasks or merely to support the administration as auxiliary bodies. However, the Constitutional Court defined certain limits[38] so that only selected tasks

36. See also VfSlg 18.632/2008.
37. See Wimmer, *Dynamische Verwaltungslehre*³ (2013) 163 ff, Weber/Kahl, *Verwaltungsrecht* 167.
38. An overview is given by Adamovich et al., *Österreichisches Staatsrecht*³, vol. 2 (2014) 100 f, Pabel, *Verfassungsrechtliche Grenzen der Ausgliederung*, JRP 2005, 221 (222 ff).

that do not belong to the core sector (e.g., security police or national defence) of state activity may be outsourced. Moreover, the outsourcing of an administrative task must be reasonably justified and serve the purposes of efficiency. Finally, the state is required to retain its legal influence on the outsourced terrain, e.g., through a certain percentage of shares in a capital company.

## §2.06 LEGAL SOURCES OF ADMINISTRATIVE LAW

Among the legal acts affiliated with administration, regulations (*Verordnungen*), administrative rulings (*Bescheide*), direct administrative compulsory or forceful measures (*Maßnahmen unmittelbarer verwaltungsbehördlicher Befehls- und Zwangsgewalt*) or instructions (*Weisungen*) are the most important.

Like laws, regulations have a general nature insofar as their content normally addresses not an individual, but an indefinite group of persons who can only be described according to general characteristics. A distinction is drawn between external regulations that are directed at persons outside the administrative organisation and internal regulations that are general instructions directed at a collective of administrative organs. Due to the principle of legality, regulations may only be enacted on account of a law that, explicitly or implicitly, empowers an administrative authority to enact a regulation. The law itself must determine all relevant elements in a sufficiently precise manner, while the implementing regulation puts them into more detail. Regulations that lack a proper legal basis or go beyond their legal empowerment will be unconstitutional and risk being repealed by the Constitutional Court. Only in exceptional cases, which have already been mentioned, may regulations complement or even amend laws. Referring to the case that EU directives need to be implemented in Austria, the Constitutional Court held that an implementing regulation might only be enacted by an Austrian administrative authority, if it had a sufficiently determinate basis in an Austrian law according to the Austrian principle of legality.[39] Unconstitutional regulations may be challenged before the Constitutional Court either under the umbrella of 'abstract' judicial review, by courts or by individual persons who claim that the unconstitutional regulation directly and actually violates their rights.

In contrast to regulations, administrative rulings have an individual nature, since they are decisions addressed to external individual persons or individual groups of persons in almost innumerable fields of administration. Administrative rulings have a formal, though not necessarily written character and must regularly include some essential components such as the tenor and the name of the issuing administrative authority, moreover the legal reasoning and an instruction on the right to appeal. They can be distinguished either as to whether they exact certain performances from their addressees, shape legal positions or just decide on a controversial legal status. Another distinction, moreover, can be drawn between rulings that are issued in general administrative proceedings (e.g., a permission to build a house or a plant) and rulings that are imposed as a consequence of criminal offences.

39. See, most recently, VfSlg 19.569/2011.

Administrative rulings are subject to appeals so that their conformity to the law can be examined by another authority, which will regularly be an administrative court, before extraordinary appeals can be lodged against the appeal decisions at either the Constitutional Court or the Administrative High Court.

Direct administrative coercive and forceful measures share their individual and external character with administrative rulings. However, they can be distinguished from administrative rulings with regard to the fact that while the latter have to meet several strictly formal requirements, measures are largely form-free, since they are taken in a context where promptness and efficiency are requisite; the arrest of persons or the confiscation of objects on account of supposed administrative offences are illustrative examples. At the same time, the very lack of formality when the coercive and forceful measure is taken suggests the need for a remedy wherefrom legal protection can be gained. Accordingly, the new administrative courts are now responsible to decide on complaints against such measures.

Instructions are administrative acts that may have a general or individual nature: In the first case, they can be classified as an 'internal' subspecies of the regulation, whereas, in the second case, they constitute an administrative species of their own. In either case, they are not directed at external addressees, but at administrative organs, which allows them to be distinguished from other administrative acts. As mentioned before, the instruction has lost much of its weight as a typical attribute of the administration, not only because it never applied to supreme administrative authorities, but also on account of the establishment of independent administrative agencies and, ultimately, administrative courts. Where, however, administrative authorities are still subject to instructions, the instruction will have to be carried out, unless the organ that issued the instruction acted *ultra vires* or unless abidance by the instruction implied a criminal offence.[40] Complaints against instructions can be lodged at the administrative courts if this is provided by an ordinary law in accordance with Article 130 paragraph 2 subparagraph 1 B-VG; the Federal Constitution itself requires such a remedy only in case of certain instructions within the framework of school administration.

Apart from these diverse legal instruments, there are some other types of legal acts bearing an administrative character. On the one hand, this concerns the possibility for administrative authorities to act under private law, since they may thus use the same legal instruments as any private person. On the other hand, some special types of administrative legal acts exist, among which the 'administrative contract' should be mentioned.[41] This contract is concluded between a private person and a public body within the sphere of authoritative administration. Such contracts may only be concluded if they are provided by an ordinary law; if the contract is controversial, its issue must ultimately be regulated by an administrative ruling. Other categories include the transnational administrative act which, being an act set by an administrative authority of an EU Member State, binds the administration of another Member State; or acts

40. Article 20 paragraph 1 B-VG.
41. Eberhard, *Der verwaltungsrechtliche Vertrag: ein Beitrag zur Handlungsformenlehre* (2005).

pertaining to 'simple' administration which so far could not be challenged independently, but where some change is to be expected by the introduction of the administrative courts in accordance with Article 130 paragraph 2 subparagraph 1 B-VG. Administrative acts will thus either need to be enacted as form-bound legal acts according to the classical 'canon',[42] against which certain constitutionally entrenched remedies apply; or as administrative acts outside this canon – where they are authoritative, however, it is plausibly argued that the law-maker will have to provide access to the new administrative courts.[43]

## §2.07 LEGAL PROTECTION IN ADMINISTRATIVE MATTERS

### [A] Judicial Control over the Administration

#### *[1] The Administrative Courts*

Previous to 2014, it had been typical of the Austrian administration that appeals against administrative rulings or direct administrative coercive and forceful measures could be heard by administrative authorities. Accordingly, appeals usually went from one administrative authority to another. While the respective appeal authority varied according to the respective administrative issue, it was nevertheless an administrative authority that was appealed to; often, the appeal was lodged at a quasi-judicial administrative tribunal. One-stage administrative appeals were usual, whereas, in rarer cases, there were either two stages of appeal or no possibility to appeal at all. After the administrative appeal channels were exhausted, an extraordinary appeal could be lodged at the Constitutional Court or the Administrative High Court. At this stage, however, the appeal was filed before courts that, in organisational terms, clearly did not form part of the administrative organisation.

The introduction of administrative courts has largely changed this system, since these courts are now responsible to hear complaints against administrative rulings, direct administrative coercive and forceful measures, certain instructions in the context of school administration as well as complaints on account of administrative delay (Article 130 paragraph 1 B-VG); the exception with regard to municipal self-government has already been mentioned. As regards other administrative acts, Article 130 paragraph 2 B-VG empowers ordinary legislation to allow complaints to the administrative courts in further cases, including, e.g., the case of 'illegal behaviour of administrative authorities when they execute laws' (as far as this behaviour is not already absorbed by the aforementioned acts under Article 130 paragraph 1). The complaints can be lodged either by persons who allege a violation of their rights by the

42. On the alleged 'closeness' of this canon Eberhard, *Altes und Neues zur 'Geschlossenheit des Rechtsquellensystems'*, ÖJZ 2007, 679 ff.
43. Holoubek, *Handlungsformen, Legalitätsprinzip und Verwaltungsgerichtsbarkeit*, in Ennöckl et al. (eds.), *FS für Bernhard Raschauer zum 65. Geburtstag* (2013) 181 (195); see also § 53 Proceedings of Administrative Courts Act (*Verwaltungsgerichtsverfahrensgesetz*).

appealed act or administrative delay or, in certain cases, by a Federal Minister against a *Land* administrative ruling or in school matters. Ordinary laws may provide the appellants in case that Article 130 paragraph 2 B-VG is invoked.

The Federal Constitution provides a residuary competence of the *Land* administrative courts. As regards the two federal administrative courts, one is a special court dedicated to hear complaints in financial issues, while the other hears complaints in matters for which a federal administrative authority takes direct responsibility (e.g., asylum cases), possibly also in matters pertaining to public procurement and in conflicts with regard to federal public employees, if this is provided by an ordinary law.[44] Moreover, ordinary federal legislation may extend the competence of the latter federal administrative court in matters pertaining to ecological audit or in other matters pertaining to *Land* administration or indirect federal administration; if it does so in the latter case, however, the consent of the *Länder* is requisite.[45] The same will apply, if federal legislation vests the *Land* administrative courts with competences that would normally fall into the competence of one of the two federal administrative courts.[46] *Vice versa*, if *Land* legislation provides the responsibility of a federal administrative court in *Land* administrative matters, this will need the consent of the Federal Government.[47] Otherwise, the *Land* administrative courts are always competent.[48]

When it comes to the scope of decision-making by the administrative courts, it is striking that they may regularly decide on the merits of a case in a reformatory way, i.e., not just repeal an administrative act and refer it to the authority of first instance for a renewal, but replace it by their own decision. A reformatory decision, however, requires that the complaint was made against a ruling on account of an administrative offence; or with regard to other complaints against administrative rulings provided that the relevant facts of the case are certain or that it is more efficient or cheaper if the administrative court itself investigates these facts.[49] However, if a law leaves a margin of appreciation to a respective administrative authority and if this authority uses this margin in conformity with the law, this will not be considered illegal, even if the administrative court would have used it differently; administrative offence cases and financial issues which fall into the sphere of the federal administrative court of finances are exceptions to this rule, though.[50] Nevertheless, the question whether a margin of appreciation is used in a manner conform to the law or not, often allows some scope of interpretation so that this restriction does not appear as perfectly rigid.[51]

In case of complaints on account of administrative delay, the administrative court may restrict its own decision to the relevant legal questions and order the defaulting administrative authority to enact the ruling in accordance with the administrative

44. Article 129 and Article 130 paragraph 2 B-VG.
45. Article 131 paragraph 4 B-VG.
46. Article 131 paragraph 4 B-VG.
47. Article 131 paragraph 5 B-VG.
48. Article 131 paragraph 1 B-VG.
49. Article 130 paragraphs 1 and 4 B-VG.
50. Article 130 paragraphs 3 B-VG.
51. Raschauer, *Verwaltungsrecht* 232.

court's legal opinion; if the administrative authority does not do so within a set period of time, the administrative court will itself decide the issue in its entirety.[52]

### [2] The Administrative High Court and the Constitutional Court

Appeals against decisions taken by administrative courts can be lodged at the Administrative High Court or the Constitutional Court which extends the stages of judicial appeal in administrative matters.

As regards the Administrative High Court, an appeal (*Revision*) against the decision of an administrative court at first instance will only be admissible if the legal issue is of fundamental significance, in particular because the administrative court at first instance differed from the case law of the Administrative High Court, or if this case law was inconsistent or if the Administrative High Court had never yet treated this issue.[53] Further, an ordinary federal law can exclude an appeal if the decision imposed only a small fine. This reduces the enormous charge of cases which the Administrative High Court had to deal with hitherto. An appeal may claim the illegality of the administrative court's decision and be lodged either by a person who feels violated in rights or by the administrative authority whose act had been appealed to the administrative court or by certain authorities in school matters; other appellants may be defined by ordinary legislation.[54] Again, it will not be considered illegal if an administrative court just used its margin of appreciation in conformity with the relevant law.[55] The admissibility of an ordinary appeal will be first judged by the challenged administrative court itself; if this court denies the admissibility, the appellant may lodge an extraordinary appeal where the Administrative High Court itself examines the question of admissibility.[56]

Apart from the competence to decide on appeals, the Administrative High Court is also responsible to decide on appeals made in order to set a deadline for decision in case of the delay of an administrative court and to decide on competence conflicts between the administrative courts or between an administrative court and the Administrative High Court.[57]

Another possibility to appeal a decision of an administrative court is the complaint to the Constitutional Court under Article 144 B-VG. Such a complaint is only possible if either the appellant feels violated in constitutionally guaranteed rights or if the violation concerns any subjective right provided that the violation was caused by the application of certain illegal general norms, such as unconstitutional laws or illegal regulations. The Constitutional Court and the Administrative High Court thus complement each other by and large, even though appeals to the Administrative High Court are not always possible, while they can neither be decided by the Constitutional Court

52. § 28 paragraph 7 Proceedings of Administrative Courts Act.
53. Article 133 paragraph 4 B-VG.
54. Article 133 paragraph 8 B-VG.
55. Article 133 paragraph 3 B-VG.
56. §§ 25a ff, 30a, 30b and 34 Administrative High Court Act.
57. Article 133 paragraph 1 B-VG.

unless they pose constitutional questions in the aforementioned sense. Although the administrative courts, the Constitutional Court and the Administrative High Court are genuine courts, the manner in which they decide is different: Whereas the administrative courts may decide on the merits of a case, the Constitutional Court may only repeal the decision, but not replace it by its own decision, while the Administrative High Court could decide on the merits under certain conditions.[58] In all cases and despite their organisational nature as judicial bodies, however, they perform an administrative function inasmuch as they take pivotal influence on the original act set by an administrative authority.

### [B] Informal Legal Protection and Other Control Channels

Legal protection cannot only be sought from these courts, though, and neither is it always a strictly legal issue that is contested. Accordingly, the Parliaments both at federal and *Land* level may review the supreme administrative bodies as well as subordinate administration. Instruments of parliamentary control range from the rights of interpellation, resolution, investigation to the vote of no confidence or the accusation of supreme administrative authorities before the Constitutional Court. The introduction of the new administrative courts that, being judicial bodies, are excluded from parliamentary scrutiny is in line with a previous process where certain independent administrative authorities, due to the fact that they could not be bound to instructions, had been subject to no or to only marginal parliamentary control.[59] This reduces democratic legitimacy from the viewpoint of parliamentary control, but at the same time heightens the potential to protect the constitution as the legal source with the highest level of democratic legitimacy on account of the administrative courts' independent character.[60]

Additionally, the institution of parliamentary ombudsman helps protect the interests of persons who feel aggravated by nuisances for which administrative organs are responsible. As a consequence of the Austrian federal system, the Federal Ombudsman who is an auxiliary body of the Federal Parliament controls the administration at federal level as well as the administration of the seven *Länder* that volunteered to empower the Federal Ombudsman at their own level, while the remaining two *Länder* established their own similar *Land* Ombudsmen as auxiliary bodies to the respective *Land* Parliament.[61] Persons can appeal to the Federal Ombudsman free of charge and in an unbureaucratic manner, but previous to that they have to exhaust all formal remedies that are applicable with regard to their respective concern. While 'nuisance' includes more issues pertaining to maladministration than just illegality (e.g., 'mere' impolite behaviour of administrative officers), so that the Ombudsman may be approached in a wider range of cases (only marginally, in judicial cases, too), the

58. §§ 42 paragraph 4 Administrative High Court Act allows that Court to decide on the merits of a case provided that it is ready for decision, if it simplifies matters, is practical and saves costs.
59. Lienbacher, *JRP* 2011, 328 (334).
60. Grabenwarter/Holoubek, *ZfV* 2000, 205 ff.
61. Article 148i B-VG.

Ombudsman is at the same time restricted to a limited choice of measures. Apart from the right to challenge regulations before the Constitutional Court, to report before Parliament and to investigate human rights' violations in the context of administrative behaviour, the Ombudsman can also give recommendations to the authority against which the complaint was directed. The administrative authority can either follow the recommendation or, within eight weeks, explain why it omits doing so. Apart from the parliamentary ombudsmen, there are plenty other ombudsmen that are established by ordinary laws and are responsible to assist certain groups of citizens, e.g., disabled people, or to represent certain public interests, e.g., nature protection, in administrative procedures.[62]

Courts of auditors constitute another type of auxiliary body that supports the respective parliament with regard to the financial control of the administration. The Federal Court of Auditors as well as the *Land* Courts of Auditors do not only control whether the administration of public finances is in line with the law and numerically correct, but also whether the constitutional efficiency principle is observed. However, neither the parliamentary ombudsmen nor the courts of auditors can themselves impose sanctions on account of maladministration, even though they report it to Parliament and even though parliamentary ombudsmen may give recommendations or invoke the Constitutional Court in case of illegal regulations.

## §2.08 AREAS OF 'SPECIAL' ADMINISTRATIVE LAW: SELECTED EXAMPLES

Larger perhaps than any other field of law in Austria, administrative law consists of not only a plenitude of laws enacted at federal or *Land* level, but also of innumerable other pieces of law. The distribution of competences serves as constitutional navigator through the mass of possible administrative fields, since the Federal Constitution enumerates lengthy lists of exclusive federal or shared subjects-matters. In many cases, administrative laws are enacted alongside these subject-matters: For instance, as 'water law' is an exclusive federal competence, the federal 'Water Act' is the ordinary law that by and large regulates administrative matters pertaining to water. Frequently and increasingly, however, subject-matters are fragmented into numerous piecemeal administrative laws. This is particularly so in case of 'complex subjects', such as spatial planning or environmental protection, where not only all territorial tiers participate to some extent, but also where even at federal or *Land* level a multitude of different laws apply. Administrative law has thus grown into a huge domain that governs all possible real life contexts, as far as they do not fall into the sphere of the ordinary courts (such as, roughly speaking, cases with regard to civil law, criminal law, labour law or commercial law).[63]

Particular branches of administrative law have gained an almost independent status in legal teaching. Social welfare law, including health issues, and tax law,

62. Gamper, *FS Raschauer*, 109 f.
63. Wiederin, *Staat* 226 f.

although administrative in nature, largely pass as legal subjects of their own. Under the aegis of EU law, moreover, other fields have almost reached a similar status: Public economic law, for instance, does not only encompass a vast amount of different laws that range from the law on public procurement to the law on the delivery of infrastructural services such as public transport, electricity or telecommunication, but also accommodates regulatory authorities as a specific type of an administrative authority. With regard to liberalised public services, regulatory authorities have been frequently established over the last years in order to control the free market with regard to fair competition and an adequate delivery of services to the public.[64] With the establishment of the administrative courts these regulatory authorities lost their competences as appeal authorities, as far as they had exercised such functions previously.

Another important field is environmental law that, e.g., comprises federal laws on air pollution control, waste management or eco-audit as well as *Land* laws on nature protection. The same goes for spatial planning that is regulated at *Land* and, with regard to local planning, at municipal level, as regards the more general aspects, whereas either the federation or the *Länder* are competent for specific issues of spatial planning as they arise from the administration of a subject-matter.

Modern administrative law also centres on issues of the media, data protection and telecommunication. Technical developments, in particular with regard to the internet, have moreover had great impact on the administration in general: Over the last years, electronic government became widely established throughout administrative law, in order to make the administration not only more citizen-friendly and service-oriented, but also more efficient, while at the same time data security and protection is an important issue at stake.[65]

Another sensitive branch of Austrian administrative law comprises matters pertaining to security police as well as to the law relating to foreigners and to asylum seekers. These matters are largely influenced by international and supranational law as well as by the Federal Constitution, since they are particularly concerned with the issue of human rights. Embedded in a difficult context of highly controversial social and political developments, watched over by not only the Austrian Constitutional Court, but also the European Court of Human Rights in Strasbourg, these laws undergo frequent amendments, which rather augment than decrease their complexity and very often raise critical questions on their compatibility with the rule of law and rights protection.

A last field to be mentioned here refers to the legislation on schools and education. The basic rules on school administration are laid down in the Federal Constitution itself, but have been much contested in recent times. Also the law on universities offers a controversial issue, since the 'full' autonomy and new management concepts that Austrian universities were endowed with more than a decade ago raise many questions that are, as yet, left unanswered.

64. Wimmer/Müller, *Wirtschaftsrecht*[2] (2012) 551 ff.
65. Berka, *Das Grundrecht auf Datenschutz im Spannungsfeld zwischen Freiheit und Sicherheit*, 18. ÖJT vol. I/1, (2012).

In a large majority of administrative fields, EU law widely determines administrative policy-making at both federal and *Land* level and often influences the respective legislation in great detail.[66] How subject-matters are conceived and regulated at EU level poses a particular problem, since the Austrian distribution of powers is not streamlined to EU legislation. In many cases, therefore, only a cooperative course of action between the federation and the *Länder* allows an adequate implementation and execution of 'administrative' EU law. The term 'administration' in the EU context diverges, moreover, from the Austrian (and, even there, heterogeneously used) term 'administration'.[67]

The introduction of the administrative courts entailed also modifications of the special administrative laws in order to adapt them to the new terminology and substantive alterations. In 2012 and 2013, therefore, federal and *Land* legislation on all administrative fields underwent massive adaptation amendments. Still, however, the very structure of special administrative laws has not undergone severe changes. Typically, they define their scope of applicability, enclose legal definitions on account of their often highly technical character, determine the relevant administrative authorities, establish the criteria of administrative permits and penalise offences against the precepts they entrench. The various demanding purposes they should comply with – clarity and determination of language, citizen-friendliness, efficiency, compatibility with superior law – constitute a great challenge. Failings of the 'administration' thus often are, in truth, failings of the legislature.

## §2.09 ADMINISTRATIVE PROCEDURAL LAW

Procedural law, in Austria, has a highly heterogeneous nature. Civil or criminal procedural law that applies with regard to civil or criminal cases stands quite apart from administrative procedural law. Moreover, and increasingly so with the establishment of the administrative courts, administrative procedural law consists of procedural law that pertains to proceedings before administrative authorities and procedural law that pertains to judicial proceedings in administrative matters. As described before, the judicial control exercised on the administration by administrative courts, by the Administrative High Court and the Constitutional Court entails a 'judicialization' of the administration which also bears on procedural law: It is judicial insofar as it is linked to judicial bodies, while at the same time the issue at stake is an act which was originally set by an administrative authority.

Proceedings before the Constitutional Court, Administrative High Court and the administrative courts are regulated by three different federal laws, while proceedings before the administrative authorities are regulated by other pieces of federal legislation. As a consequence, procedural law in Austria became still more complex, as these laws, despite structural similarities with regard to recurring procedural elements, differ not

66. Merli, *Die Zukunft der Verwaltung* (2010) 17 ff.
67. Kahl/Weber, *Verwaltungsrecht* 130.

only with regard to the question whether the proceedings refer to an administrative authority or to a court, but also which kind of court they refer to.

Considering that the early and highly systematic codification of administrative procedural law in 1925 earned Austrian public law much international reputation,[68] these latter developments, justified though they are with regard to the new institutional structures, produce a rather cumbersome mass of norms that are applicable in the various stages of 'administrative administration' and 'judicial review of the administration'. This neither facilitates the academic teaching of administrative law nor follows up the Austrian tradition of a clear, orderly and altogether rather homogeneous set of rules that are, by and large, applicable for all kinds of administrative proceedings.

The main body of laws on proceedings before administrative authorities, first enacted in 1925 and re-enacted in the 1990s, consist of the Introductory Act to the Administrative Procedure Acts (*Einführungsgesetz zu den Verwaltungsverfahrensgesetzen*),[69] the General Administrative Procedure Act (*Allgemeines Verwaltungsverfahrensgesetz*),[70] the Administrative Penal Act (*Verwaltungsstrafgesetz*)[71] and the Administrative Enforcement Act (*Verwaltungsvollstreckungsgesetz*).[72] They are still applicable with regard to administrative proceedings led before administrative authorities; the General Administrative Procedure Act is even referred to as a subsidiary legal source by other pieces of law, including the new Proceedings of Administrative Courts Act.

The Introductory Act to Administrative Procedure Acts mainly includes references to which kind of administrative authorities and administrative proceedings the three aforementioned laws on administrative proceedings apply. Most important of these is the General Administrative Proceedings Act, as it entrenches the basic rules on the proceedings before administrative authorities which, with regard to their chronological stage, can be classified as introductory proceedings, investigative proceedings or completion proceedings. The main contents of this Act refer to competences and requirements of administrative authorities, parties, other concerned persons and their representatives, provisions relating to the communication between administrative authorities and concerned persons, time limits, service of process, administrative penalties and costs. Particularly detailed provisions refer to the elements and instruments of preliminary proceedings as well as of administrative rulings. The chapter on legal protection against administrative rulings or direct administrative compulsory or forceful measures was severely abridged, since the complaint to the administrative courts has now been established as the regular remedy against such acts, while only some provisions on certain extraordinary remedies and appeals in municipal matters remain.

The Administrative Penal Act includes general provisions on administrative offences, specific procedural requirements that diverge from the general procedural

68. Leitl-Staudinger, *Wissenschaft* 218, Wiederin, *Staat* 206.
69. BGBl I 2008/87 as amended by BGBl I 2013/33.
70. BGBl 1991/51 as amended by BGBl I 2013/161.
71. BGBl 1991/52 as amended by BGBl I 2013/33.
72. BGBl 1991/53 as amended by BGBl I 2013/33.

requirements as entrenched in the General Administrative Procedure Act as well as provisions on safety measures and enforcement. Again, due to the introduction of the new administrative courts, the provisions on legal protection were largely eliminated, since the former appeal against administrative rulings on account of administrative offences was replaced by the complaint to the administrative courts. Still, however, the remonstrance remains part of this law: It constitutes a type of appeal against a fine imposed in case of certain minor offences and is directed at the same administrative authority that had imposed the fine in an abbreviated procedure requiring it to start full proceedings on the same issue. The Administrative Penal Act, however, does not itself determine what the administrative offences are, as this is left to the laws that regulate the special administrative fields.

In contrast to the aforementioned laws, the scope of the Administrative Enforcement Act was extended: It does not only govern the enforcement of administrative rulings or the execution of certain payments, but also the execution of the decisions of all administrative courts, except the federal administrative court on financial matters.

As mentioned before, the federal or *Land* law-maker may only diverge from these uniform federal laws if this is indispensable. Altogether, therefore, the federation holds the basic competence for the administrative proceedings. The Proceedings of Administrative Courts Act (*Verwaltungsgerichtsverfahrensgesetz*),[73] too, is a federal law that applies to all administrative courts, except the federal administrative court on financial matters.[74] This Act also regulates the possibility for an administrative authority of first instance to pre-decide an appeal against its own ruling, which entitles the respective authority to some kind of self-monitoring, even though the appellant may lodge an appeal against the pre-decision at the administrative court.[75] The administrative authority of first instance is also entitled to prevent a reformatory decision by the administrative court, unless – but this will largely be the case – a reformatory decision is imperative according to Article 130 paragraph 4 B-VG.[76]

The proceedings before the Administrative High Court and the Constitutional Court are regulated by the federal Administrative High Court Act (*Verwaltungsgerichtshofgesetz*)[77] and the Constitutional Court Act (*Verfassungsgerichtshofgesetz*)[78] respectively. There are many parallels both with regard to terminology and certain structural elements, e.g., concerning extraordinary remedies such as the renewal of the procedure or the reinstatement, but still there is a visible difference between procedures led by these two supreme courts and those led by administrative authorities or administrative courts either.

73. BGBl I 2013/33.
74. According to § 24 Administrative Court on Financial Matters Act (*Bundesfinanzgerichtsgesetz*, BGBl I 2013/14 as amended by BGBl I 2014/105), several prevailing laws on financial proceedings apply.
75. §§ 14 and 15 Proceedings of Administrative Courts Act.
76. § 28 paragraph 3 Proceedings of Administrative Courts Act.
77. BGBl 1985/10 as amended by BGBl I 2013/122.
78. BGBl 1953/85 as amended by BGBl I 2015/23.

## §2.10 TRENDS

Administrative Law in Austria has recently undergone one of its most radical changes. The introduction of a new order of courts did affect not only several leading constitutional principles,[79] but also entailed huge amendments of the ordinary law in force. The establishment of administrative courts was largely influenced by the dynamic extension of procedural rights at the European level. This is not the only case, though, where administrative innovation does not just emerge from internal developments, but is influenced by processes which originate at international or supranational level.[80]

It is a striking characteristic of Austrian administrative law that it is in such high degree – and increasingly so – determined by sources of superior law both inside and outside the nation state. While the general principles of Austrian administrative law have always been governed by constitutional law and thus been 'constitutionalized' to a great deal,[81] the protection of procedural rights not only at constitutional, but also at international and supranational level triggered off far-reaching changes in general and procedural administrative law. Moreover, many fields of special administrative law are widely determined by EU law which has altogether led to an 'Europeanization' of administrative law as well as to an expansion of administrative tasks.[82]

The complexity and technicality of administrative law have also increased, which is partly due to technical developments, globalisation and new possibilities of electronic government. There are also other reasons, though. One may be that the highly technical and casuistic character which is typical of EU law is reflected in the implementing administrative law of the Member States. Another significant factor is the unusually high degree of 'constitutional' administrative law which encumbers the Federal Constitution with provisions whose detail is surprising also from a comparative perspective. A recent example is the provision regarding the professional qualification of the judges of the administrative courts, which is a matter that many constitutions do not even regulate with regard to supreme justices. Thus, administrative law may be partly 'constitutionalized', but the question rather is whether constitutional law is not getting more 'administrized' simultaneously.[83]

New technical developments pose threats to administrative law, but they can also be conducive to administrative innovation. One example is the internet which on the one hand raises serious questions on the rights of data protection and private life, while on the other hand electronic government aims at making the administration more open, transparent and citizen-friendly; presently, even the remaining stronghold of

79. Gamper, *Landesverwaltungsgerichte im Spannungsfeld der Bauprinzipien der Bundesverfassung*, in Bußjäger et al. (eds.), *Die neuen Landesverwaltungsgerichte* (2013) 1 (10 ff).
80. Potacs, *Einfluss des EU-Rechts auf das nationale Verwaltungsrecht*, in Hummer/Obwexer (eds.), *10 Jahre EU-Mitgliedschaft Österreichs* (2006) 241 (244 ff), Morscher, *Art 6 voll implementiert*, JBl 2012, 681 ff.
81. Leitl-Staudinger, *Wissenschaft* 209, Wiederin, *Allgemeines Verwaltungsrecht: Auf der Suche nach dem Sinn*, in Ennöckl et al. (eds.), *Über Struktur und Vielfalt im Öffentlichen Recht – FS Raschauer* (2008) 281 (282 ff).
82. Merli, *Zukunft* 15 ff.
83. Wiederin, *FS Raschauer*, 282 ff, Merli, *Zukunft* 41.

official secrecy, which had long been one of the holy grails of the Austrian administration until the end of the 1980s, is being challenged by further demands for more public transparency. It is not the least due to the reconciliation of these divergent aims, spelt out in so many details, that administrative law grows more and more complex.

On the whole, however, 'good' administration has not only been regarded as a value manifest in many facets of formal Austrian administrative law, but also been largely realised in practice.[84] The natural complexity of multilevel legal systems that can be found in all federal states and which also Austrian administrative lawyers have long been familiar with, the well-established doctrines and theories on Austrian administrative law as well as the paramountcy of the rule of law and human rights as governing principles of the administration significantly enhance the chance for meeting present and future challenges successfully.

## SELECTED BIBLIOGRAPHY (IN ENGLISH)

Herbert Hausmaninger, *The Austrian Legal System* (2011).
Nigel Foster, *Austrian Legal System and Laws* (2003).
Anna Gamper, *Legislative and Executive Governance in Austria* (2004).
Manfred Stelzer, *An Introduction to Austrian Constitutional Law*[3] (2014).

## SELECTED BIBLIOGRAPHY (IN GERMAN)

Ludwig K Adamovich et al., *Österreichisches Staatsrecht*[3], vol. 2 (2014).
Susanne Bachmann et al. (eds.), *Besonderes Verwaltungsrecht*[10] (2014).
Ronald Faber, *Verwaltungsgerichtsbarkeit neu* (2013).
Johannes Fischer et al. (eds.), *Handbuch der Verwaltungsgerichtsbarkeit* (2014).
Peter Bußjäger et al. (eds.), *Die neuen Landesverwaltungsgerichte* (2013).
Christoph Grabenwarter/Mathis Fister, *Verwaltungsverfahrensrecht und Verwaltungsgerichtsbarkeit*[4] (2013).
Christoph Grabenwarter/Michael Holoubek, *Verfassungsrecht. Allgemeines Verwaltungsrecht*[2] (2014).
Stefan Hammer et al. (eds.), *Besonderes Verwaltungsrecht* (2012).
Johannes Hengstschläger/David Leeb, *Verwaltungsverfahrensrecht*[5] (2014).
Michael Holoubek/Michael Lang (eds.), *Das Verfahren vor dem Bundesverwaltungsgericht und dem Bundesfinanzgericht* (2014).
Gerhart Holzinger/Peter Oberndorfer/Bernhard Raschauer (eds.), *Österreichische Verwaltungslehre*[3] (2013).
Gerhart Holzinger, *Zum gegenwärtigen Stand der Verwaltungslehre in Österreich*, in Siegfried Magiera/Karl-Peter Sommermann/Jacques Ziller (eds.), *Verwaltungswissenschaft und Verwaltungspraxis in nationaler und transnationaler Perspektive – FS Heinrich Siedentopf* (2008) 779 ff.

84. Kahl/Weber, *Verwaltungsrecht* 287.

Clemens Jabloner, *Merkls Verwaltungsrechtslehre und die heutige österreichische Dogmatik des Verwaltungsrechts*, in Robert Walter (ed), Adolf J. Merkl – *Werk und Wirksamkeit – Ergebnisse eines internationalen Symposions in Wien* (22.-23. März 1990) (1990) 37 ff.

Andreas Janko/David Leeb (eds.), *Verwaltungsgerichtsbarkeit erster Instanz* (2013).

Arno Kahl/Karl Weber, *Allgemeines Verwaltungsrecht*[5] (2015).

Barbara Leitl-Staudinger, *Wissenschaft vom Verwaltungsrecht: Österreich*, in Armin von Bogdandy/Sabino Cassese/Peter Michael Huber (eds.), *Handbuch Ius Publicum Europaeum*, vol. 4 (2011) 195 ff.

Adolf Merkl, *Allgemeines Verwaltungsrecht* (1927).

Franz Merli, *Die Zukunft der Verwaltung* (2010).

Österreichische Juristenkommission (ed.), *Justizstaat: Chance oder Risiko. Verwaltungsgerichtsbarkeit NEU* (2014).

Bernhard Raschauer, *Allgemeines Verwaltungsrecht*[4] (2014).

Irmgard Rath-Kathrein/Karl Weber (eds.), *Besonderes Verwaltungsrecht*[8] (2013).

Dieter Kolonovits et al., *Grundriss des österreichischen Verwaltungsverfahrensrechts*[10] (2014).

Ewald Wiederin, *Staat, Verwaltung und Verwaltungsrecht: Österreich*, in Armin von Bogdandy/Sabino Cassese/Peter Michael Huber (eds.), *Handbuch Ius Publicum Europaeum*, vol. 3 (2011) 187 ff.

Gerhart Wielinger, *Einführung in das österreichische Verwaltungsverfahrensrecht und das Recht der österreichischen Verwaltungsgerichtsbarkeit* (2014).

Norbert Wimmer, *Dynamische Verwaltungslehre*[3] (2013).

CHAPTER 3

# The Law of Persons

*Martin Schauer & Julia Kienast*

## §3.01 INTRODUCTION

The first part of this chapter will give a brief overview of the scope and duration of the legal capacity of natural persons and associations. Whereas the second part will explain the system of the various associations under Austrian law and set out the specifics of the most important forms of associations. However, the description is not to be understood as an exhaustive list, but a comprehensive overview of the most significant aspects of Austrian law of persons.

The English translations of the Austrian legal acts and the names of associations will only be used at the first time mentioned. Afterwards, for the ease of reading and in order to facilitate further research of the reader, the German titles and abbreviations will be used.

Amongst others, law has the function to distribute goods (rights and obligations) among persons. On the one hand there are legal subjects and on the other hand there are legal objects, which are assigned to a certain legal subject. Legal subjects are attributed with legal capacity, the ability to carry rights and obligations. Only natural and legal persons have legal capacity.

## §3.02 LEGAL CAPACITY OF NATURAL PERSONS

### [A] Scope

The term legal capacity describes the ability of a person to carry rights and obligations. Every natural person has indispensable legal capacity, since there is no distinction made on the basis of e.g., citizenship, religion or gender. Instead the principle of equal treatment confers legal capacity to everyone, also legal persons (section §3.03[A]).

The legal capacity is to be distinguished from the capacity to act. Being able to carry rights and obligations, does not automatically provide the ability to acquire rights or undergo obligations by acting on his or her own behalf. For instance, a minor might act through representatives instead. The capacity to act is further divided into the capacity to perform a legal act, such as conclude a contract, and the capacity to be liable for torts. Every natural person has by nature of his or her existence full legal capacity.

### [B] Beginning and End

The legal capacity of individuals begins with birth. Even if the child only lives for few seconds, it obtains full legal capacity. In unclear situations § 23 of the Austrian Civil Code (*Allgemeines Bürgerliches Gesetzbuch – ABGB)* provides for the assumption of live birth. Especially in inheritance cases this provision can quickly become relevant.

Moreover, Austrian law recognises the legal capacity of an unborn individual (*nasciturus*) in § 22 *ABGB* from the moment of its conception. However, the legal capacity is restricted as it only includes the ability to carry rights (e.g., inheritance and personal rights), not obligations and it is conditioned by the later live birth.

The legal capacity of a natural person ends with his or her death. The moment of death is nowadays agreed to have entered, when the individual does not show brain activity anymore. A physician usually determines the moment of death.

In the case of a disappeared person the Austrian Death Declaration Act (*Todeserklärungsgesetz – TEG*) provides the possibility to declare a person as dead. According to § 1 *TEG* the declaration of death is subject to three conditions: the person's unknown residence over a longer period of time, no information whether the person is alive or dead and serious concerns about the person's survival in view of the circumstances. Additionally, certain periods of time must have passed since the person's disappearance depending on the circumstances (§ 3 et seq. *TEG*).

### [C] Personal Rights

§ 16 *ABGB* states that all humans have inherent and self-evident rights and thus are to be regarded as persons. Thereby § 16 *ABGB* grants certain rights to all natural persons, which do not need to be acquired but are attributed to a person by the mere fact of his or her existence. Although the provision only mentions natural persons, i.e., individuals, according to the principle of equal treatment those personal rights, which do not require natural characteristics of a person, are conferred to legal persons as well (§ 26 ABGB; section §3.03[C]). These rights protect the personality and are as such absolute which means they have to be respected by everyone else. However, § 16 *ABGB* only provides for a general recognition of personal rights, which needs further concretisation in specific provisions. Furthermore, a balance between the conflicting rights and freedoms of persons must be found, since they might interfere with each other. For instance, when one person has the freedom to smoke, but another person has the right to protection of his or her health, a balance of interests must be found in specific regulations.

The most important personal rights include the following:

- The right to *life, health and protection against physical harm* (§§ 1325 et seq. *ABGB*), which arises from criminal law provisions as well (§§ 75 et seq. *StGB*); Also medical treatments might interfere with these rights and thus requires the consent of the person concerned.
- The right to *sexual self-determination* (§ 1328 *ABGB*).
- The right to *freedom* (§ 1329 *ABGB*); exceptions can be made in the case of a judicial prescribed imprisonment, psychiatric hospitalisation or placement in a nursing home.
- The right to protection of *honour and reputation* (§ 1330 *ABGB*), which protects the person from defamation, slander and the dissemination of untrue statements that endanger the person's credit, earnings or advancement, especially in the case of qualified publicity (Media Law, *MedienG*).
- The right to the use of a *name* (§ 43 *ABGB*), as the most important tool for the identification of a person; It also includes aliases and pseudonyms. The right can be interfered by the denial or the arrogation of a name.
- The right to *privacy* (§ 1328a *ABGB, MedienG, DSG*), which protects the privacy of a person and facts which are not intended for the public; infringements of this right are e.g., wiretapping, the publication of private pictures, the disclosure of private facts and the exploitation of private circumstance by a third party with financial benefit.
- The right to *data protection* (Data Protection Act; *Datenschutzgesetz – DSG*).

Personal rights may be invoked even after the death of a person by relatives and spouses (e.g., protection of honour).

### [D] Capacity to Perform Legal Acts

In contrast to legal capacity, which is the ability to carry rights and obligations, the capacity to perform legal acts stands for the ability to acquire such rights and obligations by one's own action. Not everyone who has legal capacity automatically has the capacity to perform legal acts. This kind of capacity mainly depends on two aspects of the ability to self-determination: the age and the sanity of the individual. Legal persons in contrast, only are able to act represented by their organs and other representatives (section §3.03[D]).

Every sane, full-aged person has the capacity to perform legal acts and is responsible for his or her own actions. Full capacity to perform acts is acquired at the age of 18.

#### *[1] Age*

In Austria, there are four kinds of the capacity to perform legal acts:

- Children: 0-7 years

- Under age minors: 7-14 years
- Minors: 14-18 years
- Adults: above 18 years.

In principle, children and other minors cannot undergo obligations or acquire rights without the consent of their legal representative (§ 170(1) *ABGB*).

Moreover, *children* under 7 years are generally incapable to perform legal acts. Their actions are void and cannot even be validated by the subsequent consent of the legal representative (§ 865 *ABGB*). There is just one exception: A child, regardless his or her age, may enter into a contract which refers to a small matter of everyday life and which is generally concluded by children of the same age (such as buying a soft drink). Such a contract becomes effective by the child's fulfilment of its obligations (e.g., payment).

In contrast, *under age minors*, from 7 to 14 years, only have *limited* capacity to contract. They can accept offers, which are solely for their own benefit, such as accepting a gift. However, minors can acquire property. All other contracts are not void, but *suspended* (§ 865 *ABGB*). This provision involves that the minor's contract partner is bound to the agreement in first instance. The legal representative of the minor can subsequently decide to give his or her consent, which leads to the validity of the contract, or to reject the contract. However, the contractual partner may determine a period of time for the decision of the legal representative. The legal representative may also give his or her consent beforehand, for instance by giving pocket money to the minor.

*Minors* from 14 to 18 years have all the aforementioned capacities. Additionally, emancipated minors may dispose of property which had been given to them to their free disposal; and they may dispose of their own earnings, provided it does not endanger the satisfaction of their fundamental needs.. Nevertheless, minors from 14 to 18 years can only conclude an employment contract, provided it does not constitute an apprenticeship. Furthermore, the legal representative may terminate the contract for important reasons. After reaching the age of *legal majority* of 18 years, any restrictions on the capacity to perform legal acts come to an end.

Furthermore, persons, who are under age, require representatives to perform legal transactions. For minors, usually the parents (or the mother, if the child is born out of wedlock) will function as legal representatives as part of their duty of care. In principle, every parent is allowed to represent the child on his or her own. However, for certain acts the agreement of both parents is required (§ 167(2) *ABGB*), e.g., the change of name, religion or citizenship or the termination of an apprenticeship. For extraordinary financial decisions, like the disposal of properties or the acquisition of other than gilt-edged investments, in addition to the consent of the parents approval by court is required.

### *[2] Sanity*

A full-aged person, who is not capable of the use of reason, does not have capacity to perform legal acts either. This situation might be permanent due to mental illness, or temporary due to drugs, for example. They may either be represented by a special guardian, appointed by court, or a proxy, which the person chooses for such a case in advance. This provision is only to be used restrictively: only when necessary and only in so far as necessary (principle of subsidiarity).

The guardian or proxy takes care of personal and financial affairs, concludes contracts and handles communication with administrative authorities. In many cases, relatives take the position of a guardian or proxy. Apart from that, an association of guardians, an attorney or notary may be appointed. The appointment must be entered in public registers (e.g.,: commercial register, land register) and brought to the attention of third parties with legal interests by the court.

The affairs assigned to the guardian depend on the grade of sanity of the person. They might be assigned for only single tasks, a certain kind of tasks or all affairs of the person. Within the field assigned to the guardian, the person cannot enter into a contract without the guardian's consent. If the person permanently recaptures his or her sanity, the guardian must be relieved from office by a judiciary decision. The tasks of a guardian also include the personal care and contact (at least once a month) and to ensure social and health care for the disabled.

For the supervision of the guardian, he or she must report to the court on the disabled person's mental and physical condition, living situation and contact to the guardian in regular periods (maximum three years). Moreover the guardian must render account to the court after the first year and then on a regular basis (maximum three years). Even if the court approves of the account, the guardian stays liable.

### *[3] Special Affairs*

Special regulations on the capacity to contract exist for the ability to enter into a marriage, to make a will and for medical treatments. It is not possible to enter into a *marriage* without any capacity to perform legal acts (children under 7 years and persons which are incapable of reason). However, when there is limited capacity, the consent of the legal representative allows for the person to enter into a marriage. Furthermore, under age minors are not capable of *making a will*. In contrast, minors over fourteen may make their own will, but only verbally before the court or a notary. A mentally disabled person may make a will insofar as he or she is capable of reason. The court may impose that the will is to be made verbally before court or a notary. It is not possible to use a representative to make the will.

*Medical treatments* (§ 173, 283 *ABGB*): When a child is sufficiently capable to reason it may take the decision itself. However, for treatments that usually come with a severe or permanent impairment of the body or personality, the consent of the legal representative is required in addition. If the child lacks the aforementioned capacity, the decision always requires the legal representative's consent. In a situation of imminent danger, neither the child's nor the guardian's consent is necessary. It is never possible to agree to a medical treatment that leads to permanent infertility. For mentally disabled persons there are similar provisions as for minors (§ 283 *ABGB*).

### [E] Capacity to Be Liable for Torts

The capacity of being liable for torts means that the tortfeasor is liable for his or her own unlawful action. This capacity depends on the age and the sanity of the person. The capacity for tort liability begins when the person reaches the age of 14 years (§ 176 *ABGB*). However, in case of mental illness or disability, where the person is not capable of controlling his or her will and action, in principle no capacity for tort liability exists.

The lack of capacity for tort liability may result in the liability of the person responsible for the custody of the child or the minor (§ 1309 *ABGB*). However, this person may only be held liable, if there is negligence from his or her side. Only in very few exceptional cases may the judge hold the tortfeasor himself liable for the damage on grounds of equity (§ 1310 ABGB).

## §3.03 LEGAL CAPACITY OF ASSOCIATIONS

In Austrian law as in other legal systems, legal capacity means the ability of a person to hold rights and obligations. For instance, this capacity includes the ability to be a contracting partner, to be employer, to be plaintiff or defendant in a court procedure, to be the owner of chattel or real estate and to hold intellectual property. Not only natural persons, but also legal persons are granted this legal capacity, i.e., legal personality, by law. The purpose to establish a legal person in distinction to a natural person can either be a collective pursuit of interests, the limitation of liability, the dedication of assets for a special purpose or the execution of public interest.

A *legal person* is defined as an entity, which is not a natural person, but holds full legal capacity. Nevertheless, not all associations automatically also constitute legal persons; it depends on whether the law grants the association the status of a legal person and thus its full legal capacity. Most of the associations in the Austrian system are also legal persons. However, there are certain associations in the Austrian system, which lack such legal capacity and constitute mere partnerships. In these cases, the partners behind the association are the carriers of the rights and obligations, not the partnership as such. The few cases of associations without legal capacity include the civil-law partnership (*Gesellschaft bürgerlichen Rechts – GesBR*) and the 'silent' partnership (*stille Gesellschaft*). All other forms of associations have legal personality. Thus, when referring to the legal capacity of associations in the following chapters, these two forms are meant to be excluded.

However, the recognition of *registered partnerships* under the term 'legal person' is highly disputed amongst Austrian scholars. Despite, just like legal persons, i.e., corporate bodies, registered partnerships have all-encompassing legal capacity provided for in § 105 of the Austrian Commercial Act (*Unternehmensgesetzbuch – UGB*). A more comprehensive illustration of this issue will be given in section §3.04[B][1].

### [A] Scope

Pursuant to the second sentence of § 26 *ABGB*, associations are granted the same rights as individuals. This sentence constitutes a general *principle of equal treatment*: The legal capacity of individuals and associations is basically equal and thus unlimited. As aforementioned, this applies for corporations, foundations and registered partnerships, which have full legal personality.

The legal capacity not only includes the ability to carry rights and obligations in the commercial sphere, but also fundamental and personal rights as provided for in § 16 *ABGB*. However, the inherent natural differences of legal and natural persons implicate certain restraints. Thus, a legal person cannot have such rights and obligations, which require a natural person: such as in family law and certain parts of inheritance law.

Furthermore, for certain associations the law provides only a *partial legal capacity* (*Teilrechtsfähigkeit*). One example thereof is the condominium owner's association (*Wohnungseigentümergemeinschaft*), whose legal capacity is exclusively restricted to matters of management of its property (§ 18(1) *WEG*).

Most important, in Austrian law, the legal capacity of associations is not limited by their objects and functions as laid down in their constitution (*Ultra-vires-doctrine*). Hence, the association might be held liable for actions exceeding the object of the company. The purpose of this regulation is to take the burden off potential contracting partners, who otherwise would have to review the memorandum of associations or statute every time before entering into a contract.

#### *[1] 'The Separation Principle'*

The legal person's legal capacity leads to a phenomenon, which is called 'separation principle' (*Trennungsprinzip*), because it distinctly separates the legal spheres of the legal person and its members. The rights and obligations achieved and entered into by the association, form the assets of the legal person, not its members. Hence, creditors of the legal person in general only have access to the assets of the association. The important exceptions hereof constitute registered partnerships, where the personal liability of the partners applies in addition to the liability of the association (§§ 128 et seq., 171 et seq. *UGB*). This construction builds one of the reasons for the aforementioned exclusion of both forms of incorporated partnerships from the term 'legal person'.

However, exceptions of the separation principle can be found. In some situations, it is possible to 'pierce the corporate veil' and reach through the legal person and out to its members. This specific issue (*Durchgriffsproblem*) leads to the imputation of acts of the legal person to its members and *vice versa*. For instance, in very rare cases the shareholders might be liable for the debts of the corporation.

### [B] Beginning and End

Basically, the legal capacity of an association begins with its formation and ends with its liquidation. The formation of Austrian associations follows the so-called 'normative system' (*Normativsystem*): When the association fulfils the prerequisites set out by law, it will receive its legal personality and therewith its legal capacity. The most essential requirement is always the formation of the memorandum of associations or statute of the association, which is equally the constitution and the internal contract of the members of the association. The formation of the memorandum or statute constitutes the incorporation (*Errichtung*) of the association. For many types of associations (e.g., *GmbH, OG, KG,* foundations) the registration in the Austrian commercial register (*Firmenbuch*) is the last requirement of the formation. For some types of associations, such as those running a bank or an insurance, further requirements exist (see § 21 *AktG*, § 31 *VAG*).

The legal personality of the association ends with the association's complete liquidation. Legal persons usually require an entry of liquidation in the commercial register in addition.

### [C] Personal Rights

§ 16 *ABGB* grants certain inherent personal rights, which according to the principle of equal treatment provided in § 26 *ABGB* apply not only to individuals but also to legal persons (including incorporated partnerships). These rights are absolute and subjective. However, as mentioned above (section §3.02[A]), the scope of personal rights granted to legal persons is limited by their nature.

Among the personal rights which also legal persons may claim, there are the following:

- The right to protection of their *honour and reputation* (§ 1330 *ABGB*), which protects the association of defamation and slander, especially in the case of qualified publicity (*MedienG*).
- The right to the use of a *name* (§ 43 *ABGB*) and prevent others from unauthorised use; A common example hereof is the unauthorised use of a company's name in Internet domains.
- The right to a *sphere of privacy* (§ 1328a *ABGB, MedienG*).
- The right to *data protection* (*DSG*).

Nonetheless, conditioned by the essence of their nature, legal persons cannot carry such rights that require the subject to have natural personality. Particularly, this applies to the right to life, health and physical integrity (§§ 1325 et seq. *ABGB*)

### [D] Capacity to Contract

Even though legal persons have full legal capacity under Austrian law, it is impossible for an association to undergo obligations or exercise rights without individuals acting for it. In other words, they only can act through *representatives*. Hence, any association has a representative (executive) organ (*organschaftliche Vertreter*) to exercise its legal capacity. Furthermore, this organ may appoint other contractual representatives (*rechtsgeschäftliche Vertreter*). The organs of incorporated partnerships generally consist of the partners themselves, whereas in corporations non-shareholders may be appointed as a member of the representing organ. (e.g., executive directors).

Generally, the authority of the organ to represents the association is unlimited and may not be restricted by the statutes. In order to ensure legal certainty and facilitate the conclusion of contracts (§ 74(2) *AktG*, § 20(2) *GmbHG*, § 19 *GenG*, § 6(3) *VerG*). Any restriction imposed by the statutes, such as the requirement of seeking the approval of another organ (e.g., the supervisory board or the shareholders assembly) have only an internal effect and, in case of noncompliance by the representative organ, do not prevent the conclusion of a valid contract. However, this principle does not apply in a case of an obvious abuse of the power to represent. In order to facilitate market activities, the members of the representative organ and other qualified representatives have to be registered in the commercial register.

### [E] Capacity of Being Liable for Tort

The principle of equal treatment of legal and natural persons also provides for the capacity for tort liability of associations. However, there is no general principle of vicarious liability in Austria. Instead legal persons can be held responsible for wrongful actions of their executive organs and for other representatives with an extended sphere of authority (*Machthaber*), such as branch managers and other executives (§ 337 *ABGB m.m.*)

The actions of other individuals, who do not fall within these definitions of representatives, might be accounted to the association through the construct of '*liability for agents*' (*Gehilfenhaftung)* stated in §§ 1313a and 1315 *ABGB (*see *the chapter on tort law)*.

Moreover, the association might face criminal prosecution according to the Austrian Act on Criminal Prosecution of Legal Entities (*Verbandverantwortlichkeitsgesetz – VbVG*).

## §3.04 SYSTEM OF ASSOCIATIONS IN AUSTRIAN LAW

The Austrian law only provides for certain types of associations to be formed ('*numerus clausus of associations*'). Individuals who want to start a business have to choose one of the types of association. The rationale behind this system is the protection of market participants. Every form of association is regulated by an elaborated complex of type-specific provisions. Hence, it is important for all parties to know the type of association they are dealing with. Furthermore, not all types of associations are eligible for any kind of undertaking. However, it is possible to modify the configuration of the association within the boundaries of mandatory law. Moreover, the opportunity to combine different types of associations is given. For instance, a very common form of a mixed association is the so-called *GmbH & Co KG*, where one of the general partners of the limited partnership is a limited liability company.

Since Austria's accession to the European Union, further types of associations were added to the closed system of associations: According to the ECJ Member States are required to recognise all types of associations, which were set up in another Member State. Furthermore, supranational forms of associations were introduced by European Union law (i.e.,: EEIG, SE, SCE). Due to their limited significance on the Austrian market and the introductory character of this chapter, these types of associations will not be further discussed.

The types of associations to be discussed in this chapter are the following:

(1) Corporate Bodies:
  (a) Corporate Bodies under Public Law.
  (b) Corporate Bodies under Private Law.
    (i) Corporations (*Körperschaften*):
      - Limited Liability Company (*Gesellschaft mit beschränkter Haftung – GmbH*).
      - Joint Stock Company (*Aktiengesellschaft – AG*).
      - Association (*Verein*).
      - Cooperative Society (*Genossenschaft*).
    (ii) Foundations (*Stiftungen*):
      - Foundations according to the Federal Foundation and Fund Act (*Stiftungen/Fonds nach dem Bundesstiftungs- und Fondsgesetz*).
      - Private foundations (*Privatstiftungen*).
(2) Partnerships:
  (a) Partnerships with Legal Personality:
    (i) General Partnership (*Offene Gesellschaft – OG*).
    (ii) Limited Partnership (*Kommanditgesellschaft – KG*).
  (b) Partnerships without legal personality:
    (i) Civil-law Partnership (Gesellschaft Bürgerlichen Rechts – GesBR).
    (ii) Silent Partnership (*Stille Gesellschaft*).

### [A] Corporate Bodies

A corporate body under Austrian law is defined as an entity with full legal capacity that is not a natural person. According to the type of formation and powers, corporate bodies are separated into corporate bodies under public law and corporate bodies under private law.

#### [1] Corporate Bodies under Public Law

Corporate bodies under public law are constituted by an act of legislation such as for instance, regional administrative bodies (such as the republic of Austria, the federal states [provinces] and the municipalities), institutions providing social insurance and the legal representative bodies of interests (Economic chamber, chamber of labour, bar association, chamber of notaries, med).

#### [2] Corporate Bodies under Private Law

In contrast to corporate bodies under public law, corporate bodies under private law are created by a private act, i.e., a contract or declaration. Their object is of a private nature, usually the pursuit of a specific purpose or the dedication of assets.

##### [a] Corporations

Corporate bodies are legal persons and thus have full legal capacity; typically its members are not liable for the corporation's obligations due to the separation principle (see above). Furthermore, members of the representative organ do not have to be members of the corporation. The limited liability company and the joint stock company form specific types of corporations, so-called 'capitalized corporations' (*Kapitalgesellschaften*). In contrast to other forms of associations, capitalised corporations have to be capitalised by its members in cash or in kind the value of which must reach the amount set up in the statutes and must not be below the minimum capital as provided by law. Since there is no personal liability of shareholders for debts of the corporation, strict principles of capital maintenance apply.

For the kinds of capitalised corporations under private law see the chapter on company law.

###### [i] Association *(Verein)*

Generally the term 'associations' is used as a collective term for various kinds of corporations. Nevertheless, the practical use of 'associations' is more specific – usually it means non-profit (incorporated) associations (*Idealverein*). The legal terms for non-profit associations are set out in the Austrian Association Law 2002 (*Vereinsgesetz 2002 – VerG*) which deals both with the organisation of an association and the control of associations by the state.

For the *formation* of an association two steps are necessary: The first step is the formation of the memorandum (*Errichtung*) of the association. The seconds step is the approval by the state authority ('invitation to commence the association's operation') which may be refused only if the purpose, the name or organisation of the association is unlawful. The association requires two *mandatory organs*: an executive organ, the board, which consists of at least two persons; and the general assembly (*Mitgliederversammlung*) or its representative, a delegate assembly. Voluntarily, the association can add a supervisory organ. Additionally, it requires at least two auditors (*Rechnungsprüfer*), or in the case of a 'large' association (having more than 3 million turnover and expenditures in two consecutive years, or donations of more than EUR1 million per year), a certified auditor (*Abschlussprüfer*).

For *public disclosure* associations need to be incorporated in the local register of associations (*Vereinsregister*), which is transferred to the central register of associations, where every association is assigned an identification number (*ZVR-Zahl*). In general, everyone is entitled to retrieve information from these registers. However, in certain matters a 'disclosure-ban' may be imposed (*Auskunftssperre*).

#### *[b]* *Foundations* (Stiftungen)

For the understanding of Austrian foundations, it might be useful to draw a comparison to common law trusts. The functions of foundations are widely similar to those of trusts. Nevertheless, there are some distinctions; most importantly, foundations have legal personality, whereas trusts only constitute a specific legal relationship between the parties.

Two types of Austrian foundations can be distinguished: Foundations according to the Federal Foundation and Fund Act on the one hand and private foundations on the other hand. Due to the liberal regulation of private foundations (especially regarding the flexibility of their purpose and the rights of the founder to reserve special rights vis-à-vis the foundation) private foundations enjoyed a great popularity after their introduction in 1993. Despite, after some recent changes in tax law, they are now on the decline. Nevertheless, with above 3,000 private foundations, they are still forming by far the greater part of Austrian foundations. The total value of assets held by private foundations is estimated at EUR 70 billion.

##### [i] Foundations According to the Federal Foundation and Fund Act (*Stiftungen/Fonds nach dem Bundesstiftungs – und Fondsgesetz – BStFG*)

According to the *BStFG*, foundations are set up to pursue their purpose permanently. In contrast, funds are not permanently invested, since the consumption of their assets is possible. Apart from that, the same rules apply to both foundations and funds. The Austrian *BStFG* refers only to *charitable* foundations and funds; for other objects private foundations (see below) may be considered.[1]

For the *formation* of a foundation or fund according to the *BStFG* a deed (a unilateral act) and a permission by the supervisory authority for foundations and endowments (usually the governor of the federal state or otherwise the federal minister) is required. Moreover, foundations are subject to regularly monitored by the supervisory authority for foundations and endowments (*Stiftungsbehörde*).

1. If the object of the foundation is limited to the interests of one of the Austrian Federal States, the Federal States Foundation Act (*Landes-Stiftungs- und Fondsgesetz*) applies.

#### [ii] Private Foundations (*Privatstiftungen*)

Private foundations are laid down in the Austrian Private Foundations Act 1993 (*Privatstiftungsgesetz 1993 – PSG*). In contrast to foundations according to the Federal Foundation and Fund Act, private foundations can be formed for *any legal purpose*; in other words, private foundations can be formed for other than charitable objects. Still, the foundation must have what may be called an external effect. It is not possible that the sole purpose of a foundation is the management of its own assets (*Selbstzweckstiftung*). Frequently, private foundations are used for similar purposes as a trust; for instance, the foundation could be an instrument to provide maintenance for the family members of the founder.

There are only few *excluded activities*: A private foundation may conduct a commercial activity only if it is ancillary (*Nebentätigkeit*). Furthermore, it is not allowed to take over the management of a company or to be a general (unlimited) partner of an incorporated partnership. However, holding shares of a company and even being the majority shareholder of a company which engages in commercial activities is permitted provided that the private foundation does not actually manage this other company.

Private foundations can be set up *inter vivos* and *mortis causa*. Generally, the formation requires a foundation deed (*Stiftungserklärung*), a minimum capital of EUR 70,000 and the registration in the commercial register (*Firmenbuch*). Furthermore, the foundation needs certain statutory organs: A board of directors of at least three persons and an auditor. In some cases there has to be a supervisory board. Other facultative organs, like an advisory board, can be established. The beneficiaries of the foundation might be stated in the deed or can be chosen by the board or by another organ of the foundation as provided by the statutes of foundation. In general, these beneficiaries do not have an enforceable claim.

The duration of the foundation may be determined or undetermined. However, as many trust jurisdictions, the Austrian Private Foundation law knows the concept of 'rule against perpetuities': A foundation with the (prevailing) purpose to ensure the supply of individuals (e.g., family foundations; *Versorgungsstiftung*) automatically ends after a duration of 100 years, unless the final beneficiaries (who would receive the proceeds of the liquidation) unanimously decide for its renewal. The rationality of this rule against perpetuities is to prevent the tie-up of great amounts of assets over centuries.

### *[c] Group of Affiliated Companies* (Konzern)

Groups of companies do not constitute separate legal persons, but an aggregation of independent enterprises under a common economic administration (§ 15 *AktG*, § 115 *GmbHG*). However, in certain aspects, groups are treated like as an organisational whole. For instance, in consolidated group accounting (§§ 244 et seq. *UGB*) and antitrust law, where the group might be treated as one entity and hence be excluded from the prohibition of cartels.

### [B] Excursus: Entrepreneur – Consumer

In Austrian law the protection of consumers plays an important role and various regulations exist for this matter. These provisions only become applicable in the interaction of entrepreneurs and consumers (B2C). Thus, it is necessary to distinguish between both. § 1 *UGB* provides a definition of the term entrepreneur in accordance with § 1 of the Austrian Consumer Protection Act (*Konsumentenschutzgesetz – KSchG*). According to these provisions an entrepreneur is a person who runs an enterprise which is every permanent organisation for self-determined economic activity, even when it is not for profit. Furthermore, § 1 *KSchG* states that for the matter of consumer protection an entrepreneur is the person who concludes the contract for the pursuit of his business. In contrast, a party merely acting in his or her private sphere is considered to be a consumer, also regarding actions taken for the preparation of the commencement of a business.

# Chapter 4
# Contracts

*Monika Hinteregger**

## §4.01 INTRODUCTION

Contract law is part of the law of obligations. The ABGB regulates the law of obligations as part of property law which comprises the regulation of the rights in rem (Part 2, subdivision 1) and the obligatory rights (Part 2, subdivision 2: 'About personal property rights'). This broad concept of property has its roots in the three-part 'Institution System' developed by the Roman jurist Gaius who divided his commentary on the institutes of the civil law into the law of the person (*personae*), the law of property (*res*) and the procedural rules (*actiones*). The ABGB follows this three-part system. Part 1 of the ABGB contains the rules regulating the rights of the person ('*Von dem Personenrechte*'), Part 2 the rules concerning the law of property ('*Von dem Sachenrechte*') and Part 3 the rules common to the law of persons and property ('*Von den gemeinschaftlichen Bestimmungen der Personen- und Sachenrechte*'). In doing so the ABGB draws a fundamental distinction between the law regulating the rights of the person as the holder of legal rights (*Rechtssubjekt*) and the property as the object of legal transactions (*Rechtsobjekt*). The ABGB thereby achieves a high level of abstraction and flexibility which has enabled it to cope with new legal and technological developments over the centuries.

According to § 859 ABGB, obligatory rights may be derived directly from the law, a legal transaction or an incurred damage. On this basis modern doctrine now distinguishes between statutory and contractual obligations. Statutory obligations

* University of Graz.

comprise non-contractual liability for incurred damages (tort law),[1] the law of unjust enrichment,[2] *negotiorum gestio*[3] and the law concerning creditor's avoidance.[4]

The law of contracts is regulated in the ABGB itself and in several specific statutes. The main source for the regulation of contracts is Part 2, subdivision 2 of the ABGB which comprises Chapters 17-30 of the ABGB. Chapter 17 contains general rules for contracts and legal transactions, and Chapters 18-29 regulate the specific types of contracts, such as donation, deposit, gratuitous loan for use, loan, mandate, barter, sale, tenancy etc. Chapter 30 provides for the rules on compensation for damages which comprise both contractual and non-contractual liability. Important fields of contract law are regulated outside the ABGB in specific statutes. The Consumer Protection Act (*Konsumentenschutzgesetz, KSchG*) contains specific rules for contracts between enterprises and consumers. The Consumer Protection Act also contains many of the provisions for the implementation of the EU consumer protection directives.[5] Several EU consumer protection directives, however, were implemented by way of specific statutes.[6] § 343 - § 454 Commercial Code (*Unternehmensgesetzbuch*, UGB) provide for specific rules for business related contracts, especially sales contracts, and regulate special types of commercial contracts (commission, forwarding business, warehousing and freight business). The CISG applies to the international sale of goods.[7] Housing law is regulated by the Tenancy Act (*Mietrechtsgesetz*), the Law of Condominiums (*Wohnungseigentumsgesetz*), and the Limited Profit Housing Act (*Wohnungsgemeinnützigkeitsgesetz*).

---

1. See the contribution by Kerschner & Wagner (see chapter 6).
2. § 1431 - § 1437 ABGB, § 877, § 921, § 1174 and § 4 Consumer Protection Law.
3. §§ 1035 et seq. ABGB.
4. § 1409 ABGB, §§ 27 et seq. *Insolvenzordnung* and *Anfechtungsordnung*.
5. Package Travel Directive 90/314/EEC: § 31b - § 31f KSchG; Unfair Contract Terms Directive 93/13/EEC: § 6 (1) nos 5, 9, 13, 14, 15 and (2) no 6 KSchG; Consumer Sales Directive 1999/44/EC: §§ 8 et seq. KSchG (but see also § 922, § 924, § 932 - § 933b, 1167 ABGB and the Consumers Protection Directive 2011/83/EU: § 3 (revision), § 5a, § 5b, § 6b, § 6c, § 7a, § 7b KSchG and the '*Fern- und Auswärtsgeschäfte-Gesetz*' (provisions concerning distance and off-premises contracts).
6. Directive 2002/65/EC of distance marketing on financial services: *Fern-Finanzdienstleistungs-Gesetz*, BGBl I 2004/62; Consumer Credit Directive 2008/48/EC: *Verbraucherkreditgesetz*, BGBl I 2010/28; Timeshare Directive 2008/122/EC: *Teilnutzungsgesetz* 2011, BGBl I 2011/8; Unfair Commercial Practices Directive 2005/29/EC: *Kartell- und Wettbewerbsrechts-Änderungsgesetz* 2012, BGBl I 2013/13; EU Directive 2006/114/EC on misleading and comparative advertising: amendment of the UWG, BGBl I 2007/79; Services Directive 2006/123/EC: 39 implementation acts on national and federal state law level; Digital Signatures Directive 1999/93/EC: amendments to *Signaturgesetz*, BGBl I 2000/137 and *Signaturverordnung*, BGBl II 2000/30; Directive 2000/31/EC on electronic commerce: amendments to *Signaturgesetz* and *Zivilprozessordnung*, BGBl I 2001/152; Credit Transfer Directive and Payment Services Directive 2007/64/EC: *Zahlungsdienstegesetz*, BGBl I 2009/66 and numerous amendments to other laws and Product Liability Directive 85/374/EEC: amendments to *Produkthaftungsgesetz*, BGBl 1993/95.
7. UN-Convention on the International Sale of Goods, effective in Austria since 1 Jan. 1989.

## §4.02 GENERAL PRINCIPLES OF CONTRACT LAW

### [A] Private Autonomy and Freedom of Contract

The most important fundamental principle of contract law is the principle of freedom of contract which derives from the general notion of private autonomy according to which a person is free to decide on his or her own affairs. The freedom of contract comprises the freedom to determine all aspects and stages of the conclusion of a contract, namely whether or not to conclude a contract, the choice of the person with whom the contract is concluded and the contents of the contract within the limits of *ius cogens*. Unlike the law of property, the law of obligations does not provide for a *numerus clausus* of available types of contracts. Accordingly, the freedom to decide on the contents of the contract also includes the freedom to create new types of contracts that are not provided in the ABGB and to conclude contracts that contain elements of different types of contracts established by law ('mixed contracts').

Freedom of contract requires consensual parity of the parties. The ABGB therefore provides for a series of rules to safeguard the freedom of the will of the contracting party (see under section §4.04) and to ensure the equality of the bargaining position of the parties (see under section §4.03[B]).

### [B] Form Requirements

In Austrian law there is no general form requirement for the conclusion of contracts. This principle of *freedom of form* can be derived from § 883 ABGB, which states that 'a contract can be concluded orally or in writing, at court or out of court, with or without witnesses.' While most contracts are consensual contracts which are concluded through the concurrent declarations of the parties' will, there are still some types of contracts which require, in addition to the concurrent declaration of wills, performance by one party. Examples for such 'real-contracts' are deposit (§ 957 ABGB), gratuitous loan for use (§ 971 ABGB) or sale on commission (§ 1086 ABGB). Parties are also free to provide for a specific form requirement by contractual stipulation. According to § 884 ABGB, it is then assumed that the parties do not intend to be bound unless this formal requirement is satisfied. Moreover, several specific provisions provide for *specific form requirements, in concreto* written form and notarial form. Stipulation in written form requires also the signature of the stipulator (§ 886 ABGB). An important example for the requirement of the written form is the declaration of suretyship by the surety guarantor (§ 1346 Abs 2 ABGB). A notarial deed (*Notariatsakt*) is required for the donation agreement without actual transfer of the donated object, matrimonial property agreements or sales, barter or credit agreements between spouses (§ 1 *Notariatsaktsgesetz*). In implementing Directive 1999/93/EC on a Community framework for electronic signatures, § 4 Digital Signature Act (*Signaturgesetz*) provides that advanced electronic signatures satisfy the legal requirement of a handwritten signature. Exceptions apply for legal transactions in the area of family and succession law and for the declaration of suretyship by a consumer.

The violation of the required form leads to the nullity of the contract or declaration, but, dependent on the purpose of the form requirement, an *obligatio naturalis* may be established which cannot be enforced, but be effectively fulfilled by the debtor.

### [C] The Concept of the Legal Transaction

Austrian doctrine follows the theoretical concept of the legal transaction (*Rechtsgeschäft*) which covers all declarations of intention, given effect by the law, through which one seeks to change legal relations. Under the generic term of the legal transaction, doctrine distinguishes between different types of legal transactions, such as unilateral and bilateral, gratuitous and non-gratuitous legal transaction, or private and business transaction. A contract is, accordingly, a bilateral (or multilateral) legal transaction which creates legal obligations for one party, as is the case with respect to donations, or for both parties. If the contract creates reciprocal rights and obligations for both sides, doctrine speaks of a 'synallagmatic contract' (e.g., barter or sales contract) for which § 1052 ABGB provides for the application of the *do ut des*-principle (performance upon counter-performance). According to the principle of causal tradition, Austrian law distinguishes between disposition (*Verpflichtungsgeschäft*) and executory agreement (*Verfügungsgeschäft*).

### [D] Interpretation of Contracts

A declaration of intention may be expressed explicitly, through words and generally accepted gestures, or indirectly by way of actions or other behaviour. In order to have legal effect and to amount to a declaration of intention such actions must be executed in a way which leaves no reasonable doubt considering all circumstances. Customs and practises applicable in honest dealings must be thereby considered (§ 863 ABGB). It is a general rule that silence does not constitute assent.

Declarations of intentions must be understood according to the objective meaning that the other party would, in the given context, reasonably attribute to the declaration. In order to establish the objective meaning of a declaration, § 914 ABGB provides that one shall not adhere to the literal meaning of an expression but has to determine the intention of the parties. This must not be decided according to the subjective will of the declaring party, but in an objective way according to the receiver's viewpoint. If this is not sufficient to establish the meaning of a declaration, it must be construed in accordance with the customs of honest dealings (*Übung des redlichen Verkehrs*). § 914 ABGB refers explicitly to contracts, but this rule extends also to the interpretation of unilateral declarations of intention with the exception of testamentary dispositions for which special rules apply (§§ 655 et seq. ABGB). For commercial transactions § 346 UGB provides that for the meaning of actions and omissions of entrepreneurs the established customs and usages must be considered. If a problem arises that cannot be solved by reference to the contract or dispositive law, one can refer to the method of 'supplementary interpretation' (*ergänzende Auslegung*). It must then be asked what honest and reasonable parties would have stipulated if they had known of the problem. In addition to these methods, § 915 ABGB provides for two special rules. In case of a unilaterally binding contract it is presumed that the obliged party wanted to assume rather the less than the more cumbersome burden, and in case of contracts which are obligatory for both parties, an unclear expression must be interpreted to the detriment of the party who has used it. Contractual provisions included in general business terms and conditions that are unclear or unintelligible are void (§ 6(3) KSchG implementing Council Directive 93/13/EEC on unfair terms in consumer contracts).

## §4.03 CONCLUSION OF THE CONTRACT

### [A] Offer and Acceptance

Contracts are concluded by mutual consent of the parties (§ 861 ABGB) through offer and acceptance. The consent to a contract must be declared freely, seriously, precisely and clearly (§ 869 ABGB). The *offer* must be sufficiently specific and indicate the offeror's intention to be bound. The invitation to start negotiations, the submission of proposals, catalogues or price lists thus do not constitute an offer but an invitation to make an offer. In order to be sufficiently specific the offer must contain the essential terms of the contract, such as asset and price for a sales contract, whereby it is sufficient that the terms are determinable.[8] The offer becomes binding on *receipt* by the offeree. Unless the offeror has not excluded this binding effect, the offer becomes irrevocable. The offeree must accept the offer within the period of time explicitly specified by the offeror. In lack of an explicit deadline § 862 ABGB applies which provides that an offer made to a person who is present or via telephone must be accepted immediately. An offer made to a person who is not present must be accepted within a reasonable period of time.

The *acceptance* must correspond to the offer in all terms. If the acceptance deviates from the offer, this is regarded as a new offer which in turn needs acceptance by the other party. Only if offer and acceptance are congruent, mutual consent is achieved. The acceptance takes effect on receipt by the offeror within the time of acceptance, and the contract is concluded. The contract is also concluded, when the acceptance is delayed, if the offeror who could see that the declaration of acceptance

8. See § 1056 ABGB which allows the parties of a sales contract to leave the determination of the price to a third party or § 354 (1) UGB which provides that an appropriate price is stipulated if the parties agreed that there should be consideration without specifying the price. The same is provided for the employment contract: If not stipulated in the contract the employer owes the employee a reasonable remuneration (§ 1152 ABGB) and the employee is obliged to render services reasonable in relation to the circumstances (§ 1153 ABGB).

was sent in good time did not notify the other party immediately from his rescission (§ 862a ABGB). The acceptance can be given by explicit or implicit declaration of intent. In cases where it is unusual to give an explicit declaration of acceptance, the contract is concluded if the offeree actually complies with the offer (§ 864(1) ABGB).

*Special rules* apply for the conclusion of contracts by way of distance communication, such as mail, telephone or email, and for off-premises contracts,[9] for distance marketing contracts on financial services between an entrepreneur and a consumer,[10] the conclusion of contracts by way of e-commerce[11] and for calls for tenders by public entities.[12]

### [B] Standard Terms and Conditions

Special rules apply for the formation of contracts under standard terms and conditions. It is today generally accepted that standard terms and conditions must be incorporated into the contract by way of mutual agreement of the parties (*contractual theory*). This may be done by an explicit or implied declaration of intent by the parties. The customer must at least be aware that the other party is only willing to conclude the contract under these standard terms and conditions and must have the opportunity to obtain knowledge of their contents prior to the conclusion of the contract. Standard terms and conditions are construed according to the general rules governing the interpretation of contracts provided by §§ 914 et seq. ABGB.

The fact that standard terms and conditions are pre-formulated unilaterally by one of the parties impairs the consensual parity between the parties and leads to a legal and economic imbalance between the user of the standard terms and conditions, usually an enterprise, on the one hand and the customer on the other hand. In order to protect the customer as the typically weaker party the ABGB provides for two mechanisms to control and restrict the validity of such clauses which also apply to contracts between merchants, private persons as well to consumer contracts. § 864a ABGB regulates that clauses with unusual content do not become part of the contract if they are detrimental and, in particular due to the formal appearance of the contract, surprising to the other party, unless the party who used the standard terms and conditions has expressly drawn attention to them (so-called '*incorporation test*', *Geltungskontrolle*). § 879 Abs 3 ABGB contains a validity test with respect to the *content* of the clause (*Inhaltskontrolle*). According to § 879 Abs 3 ABGB, a contractual provision contained in general terms and conditions or contractual forms, which does not determine one of the main obligations of the parties, is void, if it is, considering all circumstances of the case, grossly detrimental to one party.

---

9. § 4 - § 9 Distance and Off-Premises Contract Act, BGBl I 2014/33, implementing the Consumers Protection Directive 2011/83/EU.
10. § 5 - § 7 Distance Financial Services Act, BGBl I 2004/62, implementing Directive 2002/65/EC of distance marketing on financial services.
11. § 9 - § 12 E-Commerce Act, BGBl I 2001/152, implementing Directive 2000/31/EC on electronic commerce.
12. See Federal Public Procurement Act, BGBl I 2006/17, and the Procurement Acts of the Provinces.

For *consumers* the types of clauses that are inadmissible within the meaning of § 879 ABGB are specified in § 6 KSchG. § 6(1) KSchG contains a comprehensive, albeit not exhaustive list of clauses that are not binding for the consumer, and § 6(2) KSchG provides for a list of clauses that are only binding for the consumer, if the entrepreneur proves that they were individually negotiated. § 6(3) KSchG implements the transparency rule of Article 5 of Council Directive 93/13/EEC on unfair terms in consumer contracts by providing that unclear or unintelligible clauses are void. § 28 - § 30 KSchG grant specific public entities and consumer associations[13] the right to bring an injunction against any business operator who uses general terms and conditions which contravene a statutory prohibition or which are contrary to public policy.

The ineffectiveness of an individual clause does not affect the validity of the remaining contract. Possible loopholes may be closed by way of construction, if necessary also by the use of 'supplementary interpretation' (see section §4.02[D]).

### [C] Pre-contractual Obligations and *Culpa in Contrahendo*

Already with the commencement of contract negotiations parties assume certain pre-contractual duties even when in the end no contract is concluded. These duties encompass on the one hand the (genuinely delictual) duty to observe due care for the health and property of the other party during the negotiation period which may entitle to a claim for damages, and, on the other hand, the obligation to conduct the contractual negotiations in a fair and honest way. Accordingly, each party must inform the other party of the properties and condition of the object of the contract and disclose legal obstacles to the validity of the contract, or any matter that may endanger the performance of the contract. It may also be a breach of duty, if one party cuts off contractual negotiations for no obvious reason after inducing the other party to incur expenses or miss other opportunities in the reasonable expectation that the negotiations would succeed.

The party who intently or negligently breaches such a pre-contractual duty is liable to the other party on the basis of the rules of contractual liability. This means that he is fully vicariously liable according to § 1313a ABGB instead of § 1315 ABGB for the culpable behaviour of his employees and agents, that he bears the burden of proof for the establishment of fault (§ 1298 ABGB) and may even be liable if the other party suffers merely pure economic loss. Liability covers damage to person and property and reliance damages (negative contractual interest, *Vertrauensschaden*) of the other party. Contributory negligence reduces the amount of damages (§ 1304 ABGB).

13. § 29(1) KSchG: Austrian Economic Chamber, the Federal Chamber of Labour, the Council of Austrian Chambers of Agricultural Labour, the Presidential Conference of Austrian Chambers of Agriculture, the Austrian Trade Union Federation, the Consumer Information Association and the Austrian Council of Senior Citizens. § 29(2) KSchG extends this right to organisations from other EU Member States as provided by Directive 98/27/EC on injunctions for the protection of consumers' interests, Official Journal L 166 of 11 Jun. 1998, p. 51.

## §4.04 DEFECTS OF VALIDITY AND DEFECTS IN THE CONTRACTING PROCESS (DEFECTS OF THE WILL)

### [A] Defects of Validity

A contract must meet some basic requirements in order to be valid. The parties must have sufficient legal capacity,[14] there must be mutual consent (§ 861 ABGB) and the contract must not violate the law or be against *bonos mores* (§ 879 ABGB). Such defects make a contract void *ab initio*. The same applies to a contract which violates form requirements (see above section §4.02[B]). Most of these defects make a contract absolutely void (e.g., lack of legal capacity, violation of form or of a legal provision that is in the public interest). However, if the defect affects only the private interest of one party, as for instance in case of a usurious contract according § 879(2) no. 4 ABGB, nullity is only relative, and avoidance by the affected party is necessary.

### [B] Defects of the Will

Declarations of intent must be free from defects in the will of the party. Accordingly, a contract can be avoided, if a declaration of intent was made by reason of mistake, deceit or duress. Avoidance has retroactive effect, but – unlike in cases of absolute nullity – it must be invoked by the aggrieved party.

*Mistake* is regulated in §§ 871 et seq. ABGB. The party who, at the time of the conclusion of the contract, is in the mistaken belief about the main object of the contract, or about a significant condition of the main object of the contract, is allowed to avoid this contract, if the mistake was (i) caused by the other party, or (ii) the other party had to be aware of this mistake, or (iii) the mistake was clarified in due time (§ 871 ABGB). If the mistake was only an insignificant one, because it related only to a minor matter of the contract, the contract is not avoidable, but may be judicially modified according to the will of the parties free from mistake (§ 872 ABGB). This relates to errors in expression (*Erklärungsirrtum*), mistakes of fact (*Geschäftsirrtum*) and errors concerning the person to whom a promise is made (§ 873 ABGB, *Irrtum in der Person*). If the error was caused by a third person, avoidance is only permissible if the other party participated in the actions or obviously had knowledge thereof (§ 875 ABGB). An error in motivation does not allow for the avoidance of a contract with consideration, but would be enough for the avoidance of donations or testamentary dispositions (§ 570 - § 572, § 901 ABGB), consumer contracts (see § 3a KSchG), in case of deceit (§ 870 ABGB), or if the parties declared the motive expressly to be a condition of the contract (§ 901 ABGB).

*Duress*, which requires that unjust and reasonable fear was caused, and *deceit* allow for avoidance or judicial adaptation of the contract, if the party had not concluded the contract at all or in a different way (§ 870 ABGB ).

---

14. § 21 and § 865 ABGB: Full legal capacity to act is reached with the age of 18 years.

The statute of limitation for mistake is three years and for deceit thirty years from the conclusion of the contract. In case of duress it is three years from the end of the coercive situation (§ 1487 ABGB).

### [C] Other Defects in the Contracting Process

If one party receives from the other party less than 50% of the market value of the own performance in return, he or she may rescind the contract. The other party, however, may preserve the contract by paying the full market value (*laesio enormis*, § 934, § 935 ABGB).

Although not expressly provided by law, doctrine and jurisprudence allow avoidance or adaptation of a contract in case of unforeseeable or unconsidered changes of circumstances which form the basis of the contract (principle of frustration of contract, *Wegfall der Geschäftsgrundlage*).

## §4.05 PERFORMANCE DEFAULTS

### [A] Non-performance (*Leistungsstörungen*)

The rules concerning remedies for the breach of contract are highly fragmented. The ABGB distinguishes between impossibility of performance, delay and warranties. They apply only to *contracts with consideration*, such as sale, barter or contract for work.

#### *[1] Impossibility of Performance*

With the conclusion of a contract the creditor is entitled to claim performance from the debtor. However, such a specific performance cannot be claimed, if the debtor's obligation has become impossible because performance is impeded by a permanent and insurmountable obstacle, but also if the performance is unreasonable or economically inefficient. The law distinguishes between several scenarios for *impossibility of performance*. The obstacle may have already existed at the time of the conclusion of the contract (initial impossibility) or may occur afterwards (subsequent impossibility). Initial and subsequent impossibility have the same legal consequences (unless something was stipulated that is outright impossible, be it that it is factually absurd or legally impossible, which would lead to the absolute nullity of the contract according to § 878 ABGB).

If the impossibility of performance was caused by *coincidence* before the performance is due, the contract will be terminated without any further notice, and the parties will be obliged to return everything they received as performance of the obligation (§ 1447 ABGB). The contract, however, remains valid, if the impossibility occurs after the due date and the debtor is not in default. In this case, the creditor bears the economic risk of the transaction and must effect performance without receiving the stipulated counter-performance, e.g., in case of a sales contract pay the purchase price without receiving the merchandise.

If the performance is impossible due to the debtor's fault, or due to specific circumstances attributable to the debtor, like fault of his agents or representatives or accidental perishing of the stipulated object while the debtor is in default, the creditor has the choice either (i) to perform his own obligation and to claim the value of the stipulated counter-performance, or (ii) to rescind the contract and to claim damages for the non-performance of the contract. The debtor then owes the expectation interest which means that the compensation must be equivalent to the benefit which the creditor would have received from the fulfilment of the contract. In case of slight negligence the debtor must compensate the creditor for the actual loss deriving from the non-performance (*damnum ermergens*), while, according to § 1324 ABGB, a debtor who acted intentionally or with gross negligence owes also the loss of profit (*lucrum cessans*). In business to business contracts the claim for compensation always includes the loss of profits (§ 349 UGB). In case of partial impossibility the creditor may rescind the whole contract, if it is evident, either from the nature or the purpose of the transaction, that the partial performance is of no interest for the creditor.

### *[2] Default*

If the *debtor* does not perform at the due date or the due place or in the stipulated way, the creditor has the choice either to (i) request performance and, if the debtor is at fault, compensation for the damage caused by the delay, or (ii) to declare rescission of the contract and, in case of fault on behalf of the debtor, to request the expectation interest (§ 918, § 921 ABGB). The declaration of rescission becomes only effective if the creditor grants the debtor the chance to deliver performance within a further reasonable period of time. This additional respite must be granted together with the declaration of rescission, but can be omitted if the business had to be settled on a fixed date (§ 919 ABGB), or when the debtor has definitely refused to perform, or is apparently not able to perform even within this additional period of time. In case of partial delay the creditor may rescind only part of the contract if partial performance is of interest to him. Delay with the performance of a contract that shall be fulfilled by both parties in portions may entitle the aggrieved party to declare rescission only with respect to the specific delayed or to all the outstanding partial performances (§ 918(2) ABGB).

Rescission of the contract has retroactive effect. Both parties have the duty to return to each other what they have received on the basis of the contractual agreement (§ 921 ABGB). When restitution in kind is not possible, money for the value received must be paid. Delay of payment of a monetary claim obliges to the payment of default interest (§ 1333, § 1000 ABGB). The debtor who is at fault is, in addition to the obligation to pay legal interest, liable for any further damage, including the necessary costs for extrajudicial debt collection.

Delay of acceptance by the *creditor* makes him responsible for the negative consequences (§ 1419 ABGB). The creditor must deliver his own performance (e.g., pay the price for the bought object) and bear the economic loss if the stipulated object perishes after the agreed time of performance because of a coincidence or the debtor's slight negligence. The debtor may also be entitled to court deposit of the debt in order to be released from the obligation (§ 1425 ABGB).

### *[3] Warranty*

The rules on warranty are provided by § 922 - § 933b ABGB. They relate to the transfer of goods for consideration and are of high practical importance for the sale of goods. Special rules apply for the lease of goods (§ 1096 ABGB), the assignation (§§ 1397 et seq. ABGB) and for business to business sales contracts (§ 377 UGB). Consumers enjoy special protection. § 8 KSchG contains specific rules in favour of consumers, and § 9 KSchG provides that the rules on warranty cannot be excluded or limited by the entrepreneur prior to the knowledge of a defect. In 2002, the law of warranty was comprehensively amended in order to implement the Consumer Sales Directive 1999/44/EC.

Warranty relates to defects that are present at the *time of delivery*. This is assumed if the defect appears within six months after delivery (§ 924 ABGB).[15] According to § 922 ABGB, the debtor must warrant that the transferred good *conforms to the contract*. He is liable that the good has the, expressly or implicitly, stipulated or generally assumed qualities, that it is in conformity with the description, sample or model and that it can be used according to the nature of the transaction or the concluded agreement. Defects comprise physical shortcomings regarding quality or quantity as well as legal deficiencies when the transferor is not able to grant the transferee the promised legal position (e.g., acquisition of ownership in case of a sales or barter agreement). No warranty applies for defects which are obvious or apparent from public books (land register, commercial register), provided that there is no express guarantee or fraud on behalf of the debtor (§ 928 ABGB).

Claims for warranty comprise, according to § 932 ABGB, primarily the right to *improvement* (repair or supplement of the missing quantity) or the *replacement* of the good. If, however, improvement or replacement are not possible or would require unreasonable efforts by the transferor, the transferee may claim a *reduction of the price* or, provided that the defect is not only a minor one, the *rescission* of the contract ('*Wandlung*'). Rescission of the contract is also available if the transferor refuses improvement or replacement of the good, or if he does not provide it within a reasonable period of time, or if these remedies are not legitimately acceptable to the transferee. In business to business contracts, but not in general civil law, the transferee is required to inspect the goods immediately after delivery and to notify the transferor of the defect (§ 377 UGB).

Warranty claims must be filed in court and lapse after two years counted from the day of delivery of the good when they concern movable goods and three years for claims with respect to immovable goods. For legal defects, however, the time period commences on the date when the transferee became aware of the defect.

15. Special rules apply for the transfer of animals (§ 925 - § 927, § 932a, § 933(2) ABGB).

Claims for warranty are irrespective of fault. If the transferor was at fault the transferee may also claim for compensation in *damages* according to § 933a ABGB. This applies for the loss caused by the defect itself and for consequential damage.

### [B] Rescission Rights of the Consumer

Specific rescission rights are provided in the Consumer Protection Act[16] and in a number of special statutes aiming at the protection of the consumer.[17]

## §4.06 MODIFICATION OF CONTRACTS

The law recognises various instruments to alter an already concluded contract. Instruments to change the *contents of a contract* are the novation agreement by which the legal basis or the main object (§ 1376 ABGB) or only an ancillary provision (§ 1379 ABGB) is modified, the settlement (§ 1380 ABGB) and the admission, by which disputed or uncertain rights are determined. The parties to a contract can also agree with a third person that one party may transfer his contractual position as a whole to a third person (*Vertragsübernahme*).

Instruments to change the *position of the creditor* are the assignment, the transfer of a claim by the creditor to a new creditor, and the assignation, by which the creditor allows the debtor to deliver the owed performance to a third person (see §§ 1400 et seq.).

The *assignment* can be made by way of contract between the old and the new creditor (contractual assignment, § 1392 - § 1399 ABGB) or can occur by way of law ('legal assignment') which is usually provided when somebody pays the debt of another person whether he is liable for the debt (as is the case for the surety guarantor or the pledger, § 1358 ABGB), or not (§ 1422 ABGB). Legal assignment is also provided for private and social insurance companies, if they make payments to a customer who was harmed by the tortious act of another person. They acquire the customer's damage claim against the liable tortfeasor by way of law.[18]

Section 1393 ABGB provides that all rights that are tradeable may be the object of an assignation. Strictly personal rights, like the right to claim alimony or the employer's right to claim services from the employee (§ 1153 ABGB), cannot be transferred. The transfer of rights in rem, such as ownership or a pledge, cannot be performed by way of assignation, but follows special rules in property law (§§ 426 et seq., §§ 451 et seq.).

---

16. § 3, § 3a, § 26d, § 27, § 30a, § 31c KSchG.
17. See § 12 Consumer Credit Law, BGBl I 2010/28; § 8 Distance Financial Services Act, BGBl I 2004/62; § 11 Distance and Off-Premises Contract Act, BGBl I 2014/33; § 8 Timeshare Act, BGBl I 2011/8; § 63 Federal Act on the Supervision of Securities-Related Services, BGBl I 2007/60; § 54 (3) Trade, Commerce and Industry Regulation Act, BGBl 1994/194; § 5b(2) and § 165a Insurance Contract Act, BGBl 1959/2; § 5(1) and (2) Capital Market Act, BGBl 1991/625; § 6 Investment Funds Act, BGBl I 2001/77; § 5(2) and (3) Commercial Developer's Act (*Bauträgervertragsgesetz*), BGBl I 1997/7 or § 4 Dating Agency Regulation, BGBl 1987/434.
18. See § 67 Insurance Contract Law (*Versicherungsvertragsgesetz*) or § 332 General Social Insurance Law (*Allgemeines Sozialversicherungsgesetz*).

The parties of a contract may agree to prohibit the assignation of a claim, but the validity of such contractual clauses is rather restricted (§ 1396a ABGB).

The assignment needs an effective title which can be a donation[19] or the purchase of the claim by the new creditor. In case of a purchase and in all other cases, when an assignment is with consideration, the old creditor must warrant that the claim is correct and that it can be collected on maturity (§ 1397 ABGB). There is no special form requirement for the assignment, except for the assignment for security which must meet the same publicity requirements as is provided for the pledge of a claim (namely notification of the debtor or entry in the creditor's accounting records). Since the assignment does not alter the debtor's position (§ 1394 ABGB), notification to the debtor is not necessary for the validity of the assignment. It is, however, only after notification that the debtor is not entitled any more to pay the first creditor or to settle the claim with him. Even after notification the debtor retains the right to raise all the objections which he has against the first creditor also against the new creditor, unless the debtor has acknowledged the validity of the claim towards the honest new creditor (admission, § 1396 ABGB).

Legal practise has developed many different types of assignation, such as silent assignment (assignation without notifying the debtor) and global assignment (assignment of multiple claims), or assignment of accounts receivable for collection and factoring.

Instruments to change the *position of the debtor* are the assumption of an obligation (§ 1404 ABGB, *Erfüllungsübernahme*), when a person promises the debtor to procure performance to the creditor, or, according to §§ 1405 et seq. ABGB, the assumption of debt (*privative Schuldübernahme*), when the debtor is replaced by a new debtor (either by contract between the new debtor and the creditor or by contract between the old and new debtor with the creditor's consent), and the cumulative assumption of debt (*Schuldbeitritt*), when the creditor gets another debtor who is jointly and severally liable together with the old debtor.

## §4.07 END OF AN OBLIGATION

Usually an obligation is terminated with the *performance* of the debtor. Performance requires that the debtor pays the creditor at the time, the place and in the way as provided by the contract. The creditor is not obliged to accept something else than was agreed on in the contract (§ 1413 ABGB). He, for instance, does not need to accept payment of a debt in instalments or subject to a discount. If more than one debt must be paid and debtor and creditor do not agree which debt shall be terminated, the payment will be taken into account first for interest and then for the principal and, if more than one principal is owed, then for the principal which has already been claimed or is due, and then for the principal which is most burdensome for the debtor (§ 1415, § 1416 ABGB).

19. Which must fulfil the form requirement provided in § 943 ABGB (actual transfer or notarial deed).

In certain circumstances, for example if a debt cannot be paid because the creditor is unknown, absent or refuses to accept the performance, the debtor may be entitled to *court deposit* of the debt (§ 1425 ABGB). The debtor is also released from his obligation, if the creditor accepts *performance in lieu of payment* (§ 1414 ABGB), or if the parties agree on a set-off. *Set-off* by unilateral declaration of one party is only permissible, if both debtor and creditor have reciprocal claims which are homogenous, correct and due (§§ 1438 et seq. ABGB). Further reasons for the termination of an obligation are the *merger* of the position of creditor and debtor (§ 1445 ABGB) and *waiver* by the creditor (§ 1444 ABGB). The debtor's or the creditor's *death* usually do not terminate an obligation, except those which are of a strictly personal character.

*Continuing obligations*, such as lease or the employment contract, end with the lapse of the stipulated time (§ 1449 ABGB), with the mutual agreement of both parties that the contract shall be terminated, or by notice of one party of ordinary or due to important reasons, extraordinary termination.

## §4.08 SPECIAL TYPES OF CONTRACTS

### [A] Donation

A donation is a contract by which an asset is transferred to another person without remuneration (§ 938 ABGB). It can relate to a thing, a claim or the waiver of a claim. The economic background for a donation is the donor's generosity, not the exchange of performances, which distinguishes the donation from a low paying sales or service contract or from an admission where one party waives an uncertain right. The promise to donate a thing in order to receive a donation by the other party is not a donation. It is, however, not detrimental to the qualification of the contract as donation that the donation is given out of gratitude or in consideration of the services rendered by the donee (§ 940 ABGB, rewarding donation). A person may donate the entire present, but only half of the future fortune (§ 944 ABGB).

A valid donation requires actual transfer of the donated object or it must be made by notarial deed (§ 943 ABGB in connection with § 1 *Notariatsaktsgesetz*) If the donation is effected, the donor, however, has no right to claim it back (§ 1432 ABGB).

The donation agreement is concluded by offer and acceptance (section §4 03[A]) and is subject to the general rules concerning the defect of validity of contracts and defects of the will (section §4.04) with the exception that the donor may avoid the donation because of an error in motivation (§ 901 ABGB). The rules on performance defaults (see under section §4.05) do not apply to donations. The donor is, however, liable for damage caused to the donee by fault which is restricted by doctrine in application of § 915 ABGB to gross negligence and intent. This restriction does not apply, if the donor knowingly donates a thing that belongs to another person (§ 945 ABGB). If a thing is transferred partly for consideration and partly as a donation (*gemischte Schenkung*), then the rules on donation or sale are applied, whatever is more appropriate for the issue in question.

A donation is not freely revocable (§ 946 ABGB), but there are several exceptions. The donor may revoke the donation due to poverty (§ 947 ABGB) or gross ingratitude on behalf of the donee (§ 948 ABGB). A person whose right to alimony or right to a compulsory portion of the donor's estate is violated by the donation may also claim the loss from the donee (§§ 950 et seq.). Special rules apply for donations that are given with respect to a future marriage or donation between spouses (§ 1247, § 1266 ABGB).

### [B] Sales Contract

The sales contract is governed by § 1053 - § 1089 ABGB. Special rules apply to sales contracts between enterprises and consumers (KSchG and various other consumer protection laws),[20] commercial sales (§§ 373 et seq. UGB) and to the international sale of goods (CISG).

In the sales contract one party, the seller, agrees to transfer ownership of a thing to another person, the buyer, for the payment of money (§ 1053 ABGB). According to the principle of *causal tradition*, the buyer acquires with the conclusion of the contract only the right to claim the transfer of possession and ownership of the thing from the seller. The acquisition of ownership requires additionally for movables the transfer of possession from the seller to the buyer (§ 380, § 426 et seq. ABGB) and, with respect to the transfer of ownership of land, the registration of the new owner in the land register (§ 431 ABGB).

All sorts of things, including rights and claims,[21] may be the object of a sales contract. The purchase price must always, according to the wording of § 1054 ABGB, consist of 'hard cash' which is, however, constructed by legal doctrine as to include also bank money and payment in foreign currencies. The money-requirement distinguishes the sales contract from the *barter*[22] where the counter-performance consists of another thing. If the counter-performance is composed partially of another thing and partially of money, § 1055 ABGB provides that the contract will be a barter if the value of the thing exceeds that of the money, or a sale, if the counter-performance in money at least amounts to the value of the thing owed.

The effective conclusion of a sales contract requires that the object of the sale and the purchase price must be certain or at least *determinable* (§ 1054 ABGB, *essentialia negotii*). For the determination of the price it is sufficient that the parties agree to contract at the market price or to leave the specification of the price to a third person (§§ 1056 et seq. ABGB). The specific determination of the form, the measures or other qualities can be left to the buyer (§ 1063b ABGB, sale by buyer's specification). It is also possible to agree on a purchase of a future object, of someone else's asset (§ 923 ABGB) or a specified share of a future profit (§ 1275 ABGB).

The main obligation of the buyer lies in the payment of the price (§ 1062 ABGB), while the seller is obliged to transfer possession and ownership of the thing to the buyer

20. See for instance § 13 Consumer Credit Law (*Verbraucherkreditgesetz*) which protects consumers in case of sales contracts financed by third parties.
21. Which are transferred by way of subrogation, see above.
22. Regulated in § 1045 - § 1052 ABGB.

in the way as stipulated in the contract (§ 1061, § 1047 ABGB). The seller must also take care of the sold object until the time of the transfer of possession and observe any explicit or implicit duties provided in the contract (to warn of risks or to provide information concerning the functioning of the sold machinery etc.).

Until the stipulated time of delivery, or if no time of delivery is set until actual delivery, the seller bears the economic risk of accidental loss, destruction or deterioration of the stipulated goods (§ 1064, § 1048 - § 1051 ABGB).[23] In a contract involving delivery by mail the risk (and ownership) passes onto the buyer at the moment the seller hands over the goods to the carrier, if the method of consignment is in accordance with the contract, or if the seller uses a usual method of carriage, like postal or railway services.[24] However, if the buyer is a consumer, § 7b KSchG provides that the risk passes only when the goods are actually received by the buyer. Even if the price is credited by the seller, § 1063 ABGB provides that ownership passes onto the buyer upon transfer of possession (or registration in the land register). This consequence is, however, usually avoided by the stipulation that the seller retains ownership until the actual payment of the purchase price. To be effective, this condition of reservation of title requires explicit contractual agreement between the parties.

The parties are free to shape their contract according to their wishes. The ABGB defines and regulates some typical supplements to sales contracts, like the right of pre-emption (§§ 1072 et seq. ABGB),[25] the option to repurchase (§§ 1068 et seq. ABGB),[26] the buyer's right to resell the object to the original seller (§ 1071 ABGB), sale on approval (§ 1080 - § 1082 ABGB) and the option to resell at a higher price to another purchaser within a specified period of time (§ 1083- § 1085 ABGB).

### [C] Loan and Credit Agreement

The rules on the loan and the credit agreement were comprehensively amended in 2010.[27] The loan agreement is regulated in § 983 - § 987 ABGB and the credit agreement in § 988 - § 991 ABGB. In the *loan agreement* the lender stipulates to transfer the ownership of a certain amount of fungible things, usually money, to the borrower. The borrower is then obliged to return an equal amount of the same kind and quality after the termination of the contract (§ 983 ABGB). A loan may be with or without consideration. When in doubt, the law presumes that it is for consideration. A loan agreement without consideration and without transfer of the things is only effective if the lender's declaration is in writing (§ 984 ABGB). Loan agreements can be concluded for a specified or indefinite period of time. A contract that is not limited in time can be terminated by each party subject to a notice period of one month. Each party may,

23. For the consequences of delay see section §4.05[A][2].
24. § 905(3) in connection with § 429 ABGB.
25. Obliges the purchaser to offer the object first to the seller in case of resale. The right of pre-emption may, however, also be stipulated outside a sales contract or may constitute an independent legal transaction.
26. Grants the seller the right to repurchase the sold object.
27. BGBl I 2010/28.

however, terminate the contract, be it limited by time or not, at any time, when the continuation of the contract becomes unbearable due to important reasons (§ 987 ABGB, extraordinary termination).

The *credit agreement* is a specific form of the loan agreement, the loan agreement for money, which also includes credit-opening contracts by which the lender is ready to provide an amount of money on the borrower's demand. The consideration usually consists of interest to be paid by the borrower. The level of interest rates is subject to the contractual stipulation between the parties, who, however, have to observe some limits, namely the prohibition of usury (§ 879(2) no. 4 ABGB), the prohibition of the laesio enormis (§ 934 ABGB) and the rules of the Exploitation Regulation (BGBl 1933/66 last amended by BGBl I 2001/98). In the absence of a contractual agreement the interest rate amounts to 4% per year (§ 988, § 1000(1) ABGB). This also applies to compound interest which the lender is entitled to claim, if especially provided in the contract or with the commencement of legal action in order to enforce the payment of interest that is already due. For consumer contracts there are limits for the permissible level of interest rates in standard terms and conditions (§ 6(1) no. 13 KSchG).

Section 989 ABGB provides that the limitation of a contract period can, not only be derived from the set maturity date, but also from the agreements regarding the credit amount as well as the way of repayment of the credit and the interest. According to § 991 ABGB the lender can reject the payment of the loan, if circumstances arise after the conclusion of the contract which threaten the repayments (deterioration of the borrower's financial situation, devaluation of securities).

At the end of the contract period the borrower has to repay the credit amount including the outstanding interest (§ 989(2) ABGB). The lender may only reserve the right of early termination of a credit agreement, which was concluded for a certain period of time and has already been performed by the lender, when this is justified for objective reasons (§ 990 ABGB; for consumers contracts: § 6(2) no. 1 KSchG).

For consumers the Consumer Credit Statute (*Verbraucherkreditgesetz*, VKrG), by which the Consumer Credit Directive 2008/48/EC was implemented, applies. It covers credit agreements and other forms of crediting between enterprises and consumers with a total amount of at least EUR 200 (§ 2, § 4, § 26 VKrG) and subjects the lender to comprehensive information obligations (§ 6 VKrG), documentation requirements (§ 9 VKrG) and the performance of a strict credit check (§ 7 VKrG). In addition, the consumer has a special rescission right (§ 12 VKrG) and the right of early repayment of the credit (§ 16 VKrG).

### [D] Mandate and Power of Attorney

#### *[1] The 'Contract of Power of Attorney'*

The ABGB regulates the mandate and the power of attorney together in § 1002 - § 1034 ABGB under the title of 'contract of power of attorney' (*Bevollmächtigungsvertrag*). Modern doctrine, however, distinguishes between the mandate and the power of attorney. The *mandate* is a contract by which one party, the agent, agrees to procure a legal action or transaction for the other party, the principal. It concerns the relationship between the agent and the principal and constitutes mutual obligations between the parties. The *power of attorney* relates to the legal power of the agent to act in the principal's name and to create legal obligations for him. A mandate may be combined with a power of attorney. If this is not the case, the agent acts in his own name but on account of the principal.

### *[2] Mandate*

The mandate may be directed at one specific action (e.g., the conclusion of a specific contract) or it may constitute a continuing obligation. It can be with or without consideration. Special rules apply for attorneys,[28] notaries[29] or architects.[30]

The *agent* is obliged to procure the transaction diligently and honestly. He must protect the principal's interests and follow the principal's orders (§ 1009 ABGB). The agent must transfer all benefits arising out of the transaction to the principal (§ 1009 ABGB) and to render account whenever requested from him (§ 1012 ABGB) and is not allowed to accept donations from third parties in relation to the management of the execution of the mandate (§ 1013 ABGB). The agent is liable to the principal for any damage caused by fault (§ 1012 ABGB). The agent must carry out the mandate in person and is not entitled to pass the mandate on to another person ('substitution'), unless in case of emergency or if allowed by the principal. In case of substitution special liability rules apply. If the substitution was admissible, the agent is only liable for negligence with respect to the selection of the substitute. When it was not admissible, the agent, however, is liable for any damage that would not have occurred without the substitution (§ 1010 ABGB).

The *principal* is obliged to pay the agent the remuneration stipulated in the contract or provided by law (§ 1004 ABGB), to reimburse the agent for all necessary and useful expenses made in connection with the procurement of the mandate, to grant him a reasonable advance payment and to pay the agent any damage incurred because of the procurement of the mandate (§ 1014 ABGB). This liability is irrespective of fault on behalf of the principal. For an agent who took over the mandate without consideration, the principal is also liable for damage that was caused by pure coincidence. The liability is limited with the highest possible amount which the agent would have received if he had acted with consideration (§ 1015 ABGB).

The principal is free to revoke the mandate at any time (§ 1020 ABGB) subject to the agent's right to claim proportional reimbursement of costs, incurred damages and remuneration. This also applies if the completion of the mandate is frustrated by coincidence. The agent is likewise entitled to terminate the contract, but must compensate the principal for any damage caused by the untimely termination (§ 1021 ABGB). The principal's or the agent's death usually terminate the contract

28. §§ 8 et seq. RAO (*Rechtsanwaltsordnung*); see also RATG (*Rechtsanwaltstarifgesetz*).
29. § 5, § 36 et seq. NO (*Notariatsordnung*); see also NTG (*Notariatstarifgesetz*).
30. § 4, § 13 et seq. ZTG (*Ziviltechnikergesetz*).

(§ 1022 ABGB) (unless it is agreed that the mandate shall also extend to the principal's death). The agent, however, is obliged to continue any transaction which cannot be delayed until another disposition is made by the principal's heirs (§ 1025 ABGB). The mandate is also terminated with the commencement of insolvency proceedings against the principal (§ 1024 ABGB).

### *[3] Power of Attorney*

The power of attorney is conferred onto the agent by way of unilateral declaration of intention by the principal and comes into effect on receipt by the agent. According to the general rule of § 863 ABGB, the declaration may be explicit or implicit. It may be declared directly to the agent (internal power of attorney) or to the public or to the other party of the intended transaction (external power of attorney). In principle, the declaration of power of attorney does not require any specific form (§ 1005 ABGB). There are, however, some exceptions to this rule[31] and, in addition, it is held that the power of attorney for transactions that are subject to form requirements must fulfil the same form requirements.

There are different types of power of attorney. They may comprise only one or a series of transactions, or one or several types of transactions, or only to court or out of court matters (§ 1006 ABGB). Some transactions require a specific type of power of attorney. According to § 1008 ABGB, a power of attorney comprising the specific type of transaction is necessary in order (i) to sell or buy an asset in the name of someone else, (ii) to grant or borrow a loan, (iii) to initiate legal proceedings or (iv) to conclude a settlement. A specific power of attorney relating to the specific transaction is needed for the acceptance or unconditional rejection of an inheritance, to establish an association or to make a donation. The scope of a power of attorney is determined by the declaration. For the construction of such declarations § 1029 ABGB provides that its extent must be determined in accordance with the subject and the nature of the transaction. If not explicitly specified, it is assumed that the power of attorney comprises the power to undertake everything that is usual and necessary to perform the entrusted activity. Certain employees are presumed by law to possess power of attorney (e.g., the cashier in a shop, § 1027 ABGB). Commercial law regulates specific types of power of attorney (power of attorney for managing directors of companies etc.).

The power of attorney terminates as provided in the specific case, for example, with the procurement of the specific transaction or the lapse of the time for which it was granted. The rules concerning the termination of the mandate also apply for the termination of the power of attorney. In order to protect third parties § 1026 ABGB provides that contracts are valid if the third party did not know of the termination without fault.

31. See § 30 ZPO, § 48 et seq. UGB, § 284f et seq. ABGB, § 16, § 114(3) AktG; § 4(3), § 39(3) GmbHG, § 78, § 180(2) EO, § 10 AVG, § 83 BAO.

### [E] Contract for Work

In a contract for work the contractor agrees to take over the manufacturing of a work for remuneration (§ 1151 ABGB). The contractor owes the successful performance of the work and is obliged to perform the work in person or under his personal responsibility (§ 1165 ABGB). This distinguishes the contract for work from the labour contract and the independent service contract where the employee owes only an effort and is obliged to perform services for a certain period of time in person (§ 1151 and § 1153 ABGB).

The definition of the *work* is very broad and comprises all sorts of physical actions, like the construction of a building as well as the creation of a piece of art or a computer program. For actions of a legal nature the rules concerning the power of attorney must be observed (§ 1151(2) ABGB). For the distinction between the contract for work from the sales contract it is, according to § 1166 ABGB, essential that the contractor also provides the material for the object that shall be constructed, or that the object must be constructed according to the customer's specific needs. For business to business relationships § 381(2) UGB, however, provides that the rules for sales contracts are also applicable to contracts for work and barter contracts aiming at the manufacturing of tangible movable things.

The customer is obliged to pay the stipulated or, if nothing is provided by the parties, a reasonable remuneration (§ 1152 ABGB). The remuneration must be paid in general upon completion of the work, but the parties may also agree on advance or partial payment (§ 1170 ABGB) and the contractor of building constructions may claim a special security from a customer who is not a consumer or a legal person governed by public law (§ 1170b ABGB). For contracts for work that are based on a cost estimate § 1170a ABGB provides that the contractor may not demand an increase of the remuneration, if the cost estimate is with warranty which is, according to § 5(2) KSchG, presumed in case of a consumer contract. If the cost estimate is without warranty the contractor must promptly notify the customer that a considerable increase of the remuneration will be necessary who then has the right to rescind the contract subject to a reasonable remuneration for the services already provided by the contractor. Omission of this notification leads to the loss of all claims for the excess works.

The contract for work is subject to the general rules on performance defaults (see under section §4.05). Moreover, § 1168a ABGB provides that the contractor has a *duty to warn* the customer if the material provided by the customer is apparently unsuitable for the construction of the work or if the customer's instructions are apparently incorrect. The contractor who violates this duty is liable for the damage caused to the customer.

The contractor may still claim the remuneration, subject to a reduction for spared expenses, if the performance of the work remains undone due to reasons attributable to the customer and may claim the additional cost if the work is delayed due to such circumstances ('sphere theory'). If the contractor cannot construct the work because of the lack of the customer's cooperation, the contractor is entitled to rescind the contract after an additional respite (§ 1168 ABGB). The risk for the accidental destruction of the already constructed work before delivery lies with the contractor, while the accidental loss of the material must be borne by the party who provided it (§ 1168a ABGB).

The contract for work is terminated upon completion and delivery of the work. The customer's death only terminates the contract when the work becomes useless. The contractor's death only affects a contract that was concluded because of the individual qualities of the contractor (§ 1171 ABGB).

### [F] Loan for Use and Lease

#### *[1] General Classification*

Loan for use and lease are contracts which allow one party to use a non-consumable good of another person for a certain period of time. If the contract is without consideration, it is a loan for use. A contract with consideration constitutes a lease. The loan for use is a 'real contract' which needs the transfer of the thing in order to be effective, the lease is a consensual contract (section §4.02[B]). Both contracts are concluded for a limited or unlimited period of time and are thus continuing obligations.

#### *[2] Loan for Use*

The loan for use is regulated in §§ 971 et seq. ABGB. The borrower is allowed to use the object in the way as provided by the contract or, in absence of such provision, in an ordinary way. He is liable for damage caused by fault and even for damage caused by pure coincidence, if he allows a third person to use the thing without the lender's authorisation, or if he uses the thing in another way as agreed, or if he delays the return of the thing (§§ 978 et seq. ABGB). In such cases the lender is also entitled to immediately demand the return of the thing. If the thing is lost and the borrower pays the lender the value of the thing, he is nevertheless not entitled to keep the thing when it is found again, if the lender is willing to return the money (§ 980 ABGB). The lender's liability is analogous to the liability of the donor. The rules on performance defaults (see under section §4.05) do not apply to the loan for use, and the lender's liability is restricted to gross negligence or intent, except when he lends the thing of another person without authorisation (§ 945 ABGB).

The borrower must bear the ordinary expenses for the use of the thing. If extraordinary expenses become necessary the borrower may return the thing to the lender, or he must bear these cost, but is allowed to demand reimbursement from the lender (§ 981 ABGB).

Upon expiry of the specified time the borrower must return the thing (§ 972 ABGB). The duration of the contract may be determined explicitly or implicitly according to the circumstances, for instance the purpose of the contract. The lender is not entitled to claim the thing before the expiry of the contract, even if he urgently needs it for himself (§ 976 ABGB). The borrower, however, may return the thing anytime, unless the earlier return is burdensome for the lender (§ 979 ABGB). The lender loses his claim if he does not notify the borrower of the misuse or excessive use within thirty days upon return of the thing. The same applies for the borrower with respect to his claim for reimbursement of extraordinary expenses (§ 982 ABGB). The lender's right to claim the return of the thing expires after thirty years (§ 1478 ABGB).

### *[3] Lease*

The ABGB regulates the lease in §§ 1090 et seq. ABGB under the title of '*Bestandvertrag*' which comprises the *tenancy agreement* (*Mietvertrag*) and the *lease contract* (*Pachtvertrag*). The difference between these contracts lies in the fact that the tenancy agreement allows the tenant to use a non-consumable thing (apartment, house, car) without further work, while the lease contract comprises the right to use a thing (piece of land, farm, enterprise) and to draw fruits from the thing (§ 1091 ABGB).

Austrian law provides for several statutes in order to protect lessees and tenants. Statutes for the protection of the lessee of farm land are the *Landpachtgesetz* 1969, for the lessee of allotments the *Kleingartengesetz* 1959 and for specific lessees of pieces of land for the operation of sporting premises the *Sportstättenschutzgesetz* 1990. Tenants of buildings (apartments or business premises) enjoy comprehensive protection by the *Mietrechtsgesetz* 1981 (MRG, Tenancy Act) which is of very high practical importance. The MRG restricts the landlord's rights concerning the termination of the contract and, together with some other statutes,[32] provides for comprehensive rules on rent control. The rules of the MRG are usually compulsory and cannot be altered to the detriment of the tenant. They are very detailed and subject to frequent amendments.

The ABGB regulates the mutual obligations of lessor and lessee as following.[33] The lessor is obliged to transfer and maintain the leased thing at his own cost in a usable condition and must not disturb the lessee in the agreed use or enjoyment (§ 1096(1) ABGB). The lessee is, according to § 1096(2) ABGB, however, obliged to bear the ordinary repair cost of the business premises, as far as he can cover them with the materials or services provided by the leased good. Section 1096(1) ABGB constitutes a special warranty obligation for the lessor. If the lessor does not comply with these obligations, the lessee is allowed to reduce the rent or may even be relieved from the obligation to pay rent for the duration of the deficiency. This relief cannot be waived in advance by the lessee of land (and by the consumer only within the narrow limits of § 9 KSchG). If the leased thing cannot be used at all because of an extraordinary coincidence, such as fire, war, plague or extensive floods, the lessor is not obliged to restore the leased object.

The lessee is entitled to use object according to the contract (§ 1098 ABGB). He must notify the lessor without delay that repairs which must be conducted by the lessor are necessary. If the lessee makes an expense which must be borne by the lessor or which is useful for the lessor, he may claim reimbursement according to the rules on

32. The MRG is supplemented by the *Richtwertgesetz* 1993 and its regulations which regulate the determination of the rent and the *Heizkostenabrechnunggesetz* 1992 which contains detailed rules on the calculation and settlement of the water and heating costs.
33. For the tenancy agreement on buildings which fall under the scope of application of the MRG, however, specific and quite different rules apply.

*negotiorum gestio* (§§ 1035 et seq. ABGB) within six months upon return of the leased object (§ 1097 ABGB). With respect to tenancy, the lessor, and in case of lease, the lessee usually bears all burdens and levies (§ 1099 ABGB). The lessee is obliged to pay the agreed rent (§ 1100 ABGB). In order to secure the payment of the rent, § 1101 ABGB grants the lessor of an immovable object a special statutory right of pledge on the other party's movable assets. Tenant and lessee are entitled to sublet the object, unless this is explicitly prohibited in the contract or detrimental to the lessor (§ 1098 ABGB). Upon termination of the contract they must return the object to the lessor (§§ 1109 et seq. ABGB). They must compensate the lessor for damage caused by fault, including fault of their sub-lessee, which must be claimed by the lessor within one year after the return of the thing (§ 1111 ABGB).

The contract is terminated by agreement of the parties or by the lapse of the stipulated period of time (§ 1113 ABGB) or, if no such time period is stipulated, by notice of termination by one party (§ 1116 ABGB). Such notice is subject to a certain time period and may only be declared at certain dates (see § 560 ZPO, 'ordinary notice of termination'). A lease contract, whether time limited or not, can be terminated immediately due to important reasons as follows ('extraordinary notice of termination'): According to § 1117 ABGB, the lessee is entitled to terminate the contract if the leased object is unfit for the agreed purpose, or if, due to a coincidence, a substantial part of the object cannot be used for a longer period of time. The tenant is entitled to terminate the contract, if the rented accommodation is hazardous to health even if he waived this in the contract or was aware of the condition of the rooms at the conclusion of the contract. The lessor may terminate the contract, if the lessee uses the leased object in a materially detrimental way, or if the lessee does not pay the rent even after notice or if the leased building must be newly constructed (§ 1118 ABGB).

Destruction of the leased object usually terminates the contract (§ 1112 ABGB). Death of one party does not terminate the contract, but if the tenant of an accommodation dies, the tenant's heirs and the landlord may terminate the contract subject to a period of notice (§ 1116a ABGB).

### [G] Deposit

A deposit contract is established if one party takes another person's assets into custody (§ 957 ABGB). The deposit contract is a '*real contract*' (section §4.02[B]) which requires transfer of the deposited object in order to be effective. The object of the deposit can be a movable or immovable thing. The deposit contract may be with or without consideration (§ 969 ABGB) and because of the time element constitutes a continuing obligation.

The *depositary* is obliged to keep the entrusted object safe for the specified period of time and to return it to the depositor upon the expiry of this period in the same state as the thing was taken over, including all accession (§ 961 ABGB). The depositary is not entitled to use the deposited object. In general, the depositary is liable for damage caused by fault, and even when the deposited object is more valuable than his own, the depositary is not obliged to save the entrusted object by sacrificing his own thing

(§ 964 ABGB). If he does so, he is entitled to demand reasonable reimbursement (§ 967 ABGB). Under certain circumstances, however, the depositary is even liable for harm caused by pure coincidence, namely when he used the object, or when he deposited it with a third person without the depositor's consent, except in case of an emergency. If he delays the return of the thing, the depositary is liable for any damage which would not have occurred had it been in the depositary's possession (§ 965 ABGB). For the keeper of accommodation facilities, such as hotels, inns or guest-houses, special liability rules apply (§§ 970 et seq. ABGB).

The depositor is obliged to pay the depositary the remuneration if provided (§ 969 ABGB), must reimburse the depositary the incurred necessary and useful expenses and is liable for damage caused by fault (§ 967 ABGB). If the deposited object is a movable thing, both depositor and depositary must made their claims within thirty days upon return of the object.

The deposit contract ends with the expiry of the specified period of time or, if no such time limit is provided, by notification of one party (§ 963 ABGB). The depositor is entitled to request the return of the thing at any time from the depositary who may only demand compensation for damages caused to him by the early return. The depositary, however, is not allowed to return the deposited thing before the specified period of time, unless an unexpected event prevents him from keeping the thing safe or without negative consequences for him (§ 962 ABGB).

## SELECTED BIBLIOGRAPHY

### Textbooks

Apathy Peter/Riedler Andreas, *Bürgerliches Recht III: Schuldrecht – Besonderer Teil*[4]. *Springers Kurzlehrbücher der Rechtswissenschaft, Bürgerliches Recht*, hrsg von Apathy Peter (Wien 2010).

Bydlinski Peter, *Bürgerliches Recht I: Allgemeiner Teil*[6]. *Springers Kurzlehrbücher der Rechtswissenschaft, Bürgerliches Recht*, hrsg von Apathy Peter (Wien 2013).

Bydlinski Peter, *Grundzüge des Privatrechts für Ausbildung und Praxis*[9] (Wien 2014).

Dullinger Silvia, *Bürgerliches Recht II: Schuldrecht – Allgemeiner Teil*[4]. *Springers Kurzlehrbücher der Rechtswissenschaft, Bürgerliches Recht*, hrsg von Apathy Peter (Wien 2010).

Hausmaninger Herbert, *The Austrian Legal System*[4] (Wien 2011).

Koziol Helmut/Welser Rudolf /Kletečka Andreas, *Grundriss des bürgerlichen Rechts: Allgemeiner Teil, Sachenrecht, Familienrecht I*[14] (Wien 2014).

Koziol Helmut/Welser Rudolf (bearbeitet von Welser Rudolf), *Grundriss des bürgerlichen Rechts: Schuldrecht Allgemeiner Teil, Schuldrecht Besonderer Teil, Erbrecht II*[13] (Wien 2007).

Perner Stefan/Spitzer Martin/Kodek Georg, *Bürgerliches Recht*[4] (Wien 2014).

Riedler Andreas, *Zivilrecht I: Allgemeiner Teil*[5] (Wien 2010).

Riedler Andreas, *Zivilrecht II: Schuldrecht Allgemeiner Teil*[4] (Wien 2010).

Riedler Andreas, *Zivilrecht III: Schuldrecht Besonderer Teil, Vertragliche Schuldverhältnisse*[4] (Wien 2010).

**Commentaries of the ABGB**

Kletečka Andreas/Schauer Martin (Hrsg), *ABGB-ON*[1.01]*: Kommentar zum Allgemeinen bürgerlichen Gesetzbuch* (Wien 2014, www.rdb.at).
Klang Heinrich (Hrsg), *Kommentar zum Allgemeinen Bürgerlichen Gesetzbuch (§ 897 - § 916)*[3] (Wien 2011).
Koziol Helmut/Bydlinski Peter/Bollenberger Raimund, *Kurzkommentar zum ABGB*[4] (Wien 2014).
Schwimann Michael (Hrsg), *Praxiskommentar zum Allgemeinen Bürgerlichen Gesetzbuch IV*[4] (Wien 2014).
Schwimann Michael (Hrsg), *ABGB-Taschenkommentar*[2] (Wien 2013).
Rummel Peter (Hrsg), *Kommentar zum Allgemeinen bürgerlichen Gesetzbuch I*[3] (Wien 2000).

**Translation of the Austrian Civil Code**

Eschig Peter Andreas/ Pircher-Eschig Erika, *Das österreichische ABGB – The Austrian Civil Code* (Wien 2013).

CHAPTER 5

# Commercial Contracts

*Friedrich Harrer*

## §5.01 INTRODUCTION

Commercial law or company law played a substantial role in the history of codification.[1] In Germany, the Civil Code was enacted only after the conception of the General German Commercial Code.[2] The Austrian codification of civil law (General Civil Code (*ABGB, Allgemeines Bürgerliches Gesetzbuch*)) took place already in 1811. However, in Austria commercial law has also been closely connected with the idea of codification. In light of this, it would be possible to assume that the legal basis for every contract concluded by entrepreneurs could be found in a clearly and systematically arranged collection of laws. This is, nevertheless, not the case.

The sale of goods is deemed as the traditional legal transaction of the entrepreneur (*Rechtsgeschäft des Unternehmers*). In past centuries, the entrepreneur was denominated as 'merchant' (*Kaufmann*),[3] a term that is no longer appropriate for several reasons. However, the importance of commercial law for many entrepreneurs is certainly beyond doubt. The statutory basis for the sale of goods is regulated in the

1. The decisive impulse for the codification and standardization of private law came from commercial law. (*Unternehmensrecht*); see Zöllner, in Harrer/Mader, *Die HGB-Reform in Österreich* (2005) 2 et seqq. About 40 commercial codes emerged in the 19th Century (documented bei Müller-Freienfels, *Zur 'Selbständigkeit' des Handelsrechts, FS v Caemmerer* [1978] 583, 601).
2. The ADHGB was recommended on 31 May 1861 by the Bundestag of the German federal states for adoption without change. The enactment was carried out by state law (Saxony: 1 Mar. 1862, Bavaria: 1 Jul. 1862). The Civil Code (BGB) came into force on 1 Jan. 1900 (together with the German Commercial Code).
3. Germany still holds the traditional *Kaufmann* term (see §§ 1 et seqq. dHGB). In Austria, the Commercial Code reform (HaRäG, BGBl I 120/2005) replaced the term merchant with entrepreneur. The 'commercial transactions' term (§§ 343 et seqq.) was renamed to 'corporate-related transactions' (*Unternehmensbezogene Geschäfte*), see Winkler, Kaufmann quo vadis? *Zur geplanten Reform des Kaufmannsbegriffs* (1999) 25 et seqq.; Kalss/Schauer, *Allgemeines Unternehmensrecht*[2] *(2014)* Rz 2/1 et seqq.

Civil Code.[4] The Commercial Code (*UGB, Unternehmensgesetzbuch*) only provides company-specific supplements. Additionally, it should be mentioned that neither the Civil Code (*ABGB*) nor the Austrian Commercial Code (*UGB*) apply when goods are exported by an Austrian entrepreneur.[5]

Aside from the sale of goods, another form of exchange may be established – lease. This form of exchange is treated as an addition and often as an alternative, to the sale. However, a legal regulation on the subject is missing. It is important to mention nonetheless, that leasing is an impressive demonstration of the power of economic life for legal innovation.[6]

Many entrepreneurs are concerned with the law of service contracts.[7] Building contractors and construction-oriented entrepreneurs (electrical contractors, plumbers, painters, carpenters, tillers, etc.) purchase products which are subsequently used in the course of their economic activity. However, the basis of their business is constructed around service contracts with their customers. Traditionally, commercial law excludes this type of contract. This is a strange phenomenon that cannot be objectively justified, but instead, only historically explained by the fact that the legal basis of service contracts has been provided by the Civil Code (*ABGB*).

Commercial law or *Unternehmensrecht* barely deals with rental agreements. This is a reality that contrasts with the significant practical relevance of these agreements for many entrepreneurs. An example of this can be seen in the phenomenon of accommodation establishments, which is characterised by a great variety, ranging from hostels to luxury hotels. Additionally, professional rental of holiday homes and apartments is becoming increasingly important. Finally, it is relevant to point out that companies that provide parking areas and garages should also be considered as landlords.[8]

Other contracts are also regulated in the Commerce Code *UGB* (former *HGB*). These contracts are regarded by the legislator as typical and important variations of entrepreneurial activity, such as the Commission, the shipping business, the warehousing business and the freight business.[9] The practical relevance of these categories

4. See Krejci, *Unternehmensrecht*[5] (2013) 316, 397 et seqq.
5. Export transactions are always import transactions under the condition that the supplier belongs to a member country of the 'Vienna Sales Convention' (United Nations Convention on Contracts for the International Sale of Goods, Federal Law Gazette 1988/96).
6. See Koziol/Welser, *Bürgerliches Recht II*[13] (2006) 244 et seqq.; Apathy/Riedler, *Bürgerliches Recht III, Schuldrecht Besonderer Teil*[4] (2010) 119 et seqq.; see on the development and importance of leasing, Martinek in Martinek/Stoffels/Wimmer-Leonhardt, *Leasinghandbuch*[2] (2008) § 1 Rz 7 et seqq.; Krejci in Egger/Krejci, *Das Leasinggeschäft* (1987) 1 et seqq.
7. See Koziol/Welser, *Bürgerliches Recht II* 254 et seq.; Apathy/Riedler, *Bürgerliches Recht III, Schuldrecht Besonderer Teil* 29 et seqq.; Riedler, *Zivilrecht III, Schuldrecht Besonderer Teil – Vertragliche Schuldverhältnisse*[4] (2010) 133 et seqq.
8. The legal bases for this are the Civil Code (§§ 1090 et seq.) and the Tenancy Act (MRG).
9. The sale on commission is regulated in §§ 383 UGB. The commission on goods is found mostly in relation to the sale of art and antiquities. The securities commission (*Effektenkommission*) is economically important; see on this Büchele, in U. Torggler, *UGB* [2013] § 383 Rz 3). §§ 407 et seqq. deals with the freight forwarding business. In this regard, however, important additions and changes have been introduced by the General Austrian Forwarder's terms and conditions (AÖSp), published by the Austrian Chamber of Commerce (comments on this are offered by Csoklich, in Jabornegg/Artmann, *UGB*[2]). In the case of warehousing businesses (§§ 416 et seqq. UGB) the General Austrian Forwarder's terms and conditions (AÖSp) are also applicable (Rauter, in U.

(e.g., shipping, freight) is significant even today. Nevertheless, it is evident that this traditional collection should be understood primarily as based on historical reasons.

Organising and structuring distribution are key issues for many entrepreneurs. However, legal regulations on the subject are only partially available. Commercial agents are traditional in Germany and Austria and are defined as those 'entrusted with the operation or conclusion of transactions, in the name and on the behalf'[10] of other entrepreneurs. The most important forum, in which agents develop their mediation, is in the setting of large trade fairs.

The commercial agent is an important marketing intermediary. However, other marketing channels – so to speak beyond the *lex lata* – could be established. Particular mention should be made of the franchising system. The peculiarity of a franchising organisation is that the franchise partner, (the hotel, the fast food restaurant, the salesroom, etc.) conducts the business independently, in a legal and in an economic sense. However, the integration into the franchising organisation is so strong that – for third parties – the legally independent entrepreneur seems to be a branch or a subsidiary. The attractiveness of the model – from the perspective of the franchisor – is obvious: the costs of establishing and maintaining these marketing channels are not borne by the franchisor but instead by the franchisee.[11]

Another marketing intermediary is the authorised dealer.[12] So-called 'distributorship agreements' have gained great importance, especially concerning the distribution of motor vehicles. The manufacturer establishes a subsidiary (GmbH), in a particular country (e.g., in Austria), which imports the vehicles, but the distribution is performed by selected entrepreneurs known as authorised dealers. The dealers sell the vehicles to (professional or non-professional) customers in their own name and on their own account. They are, as previously noted, independent entrepreneurs. However, the integration into the distribution system of the manufacturer usually features strict guidelines. Consequently, the power relations are (according to experience) unequal. The manufacturer is, in a similar fashion to the franchisor, the dominant party.

These distribution systems can also cause competition-problems. No further justification is required to affirm that coordinated distribution can reduce competition at the dealer level or may even eliminate it. In this regard, competition law and competition policy seek to find a compromise.[13]

Another key issue not only for banks and lending institutions is the subject of **pledging transactions**; every entrepreneur deals with pledging strategies. The legal situation is confusing and not easy to fathom. The relevant regulations are contained in

---

Torggler, *UGB* § 416 Rz 1). The freight law of the Commerce Code (UGB §§ 425 et seqq.) is superimposed through a large variety of general terms of business and international agreements; for an up-to-date summary on this see Steyer, in U. Torggler, *UGB* § 425 Rz 1 et seqq.

10. See under section §5.03[D][2].
11. C.f. section §5.03[D][4].
12. See Krejci, *Unternehmensrecht* 474 f.
13. See Regulation (EC) of 20 2010/330 April 201, on the application of Art. 101 para. 3 of the Treaty on the Functioning of the European Union to categories of vertical agreements and concerted practices ABl EU 2010 L 102/1; for details see Immenga/Mestmäcker, *EU-Wettbewerbsrecht*[5] (2012) fourth chapter, on block exemption Regulations (*Gruppenfreistellungsverordnungen*).

the Civil Code (*ABGB*), while commercial law offers only selective approaches to the subject. Also, the *ABGB* does not provide for a chapter that regulates hedges. The civil law differentiates (systematically) between in rem and in personam security.

Unfortunately, it should be admitted that the *ABGB* hardly regulates, or mostly indirectly a means of security that is particularly important. The retention of title[14] is a common phenomenon. Almost every supplier of goods, who sells on credit, retains property in the goods until the full payment of the purchase price is received. This legal right (the property) gives the seller a privileged position in case of insolvency of the buyer.

The classic security instrument **according real** (in rem) rights is the lien. In present business practice, the lien on movable property plays a subordinate role [15] This is explained by the so-called principle of publicity (*Publizitätsprinzip*). The formation of a lien presupposes that the *lienee* transfers the item to the *lienor,* this situation is in most cases not an option. A constructor cannot transfer his truck, crane or steamroller to the bank to collateralise a loan, because these items were purchased for the purpose of performing an economic activity. Therefore, the lien over means of production is generally (for economic reasons) not possible.

In Austria, the lien on real estate has special importance.[16] The requirements of publicity are fulfilled by the registration in the land register. The *lienee* can continue to use the land. However, for entrepreneurs the relevance of mortgages or liens over real estate is rather limited. Many companies do not own real estate. In addition, financial securing by mortgages is attained regularly only in the case of long-term funding (e.g., as collateral for a bank loan that serves the financing of a production line, or the construction of a cable car). For the collateralisation of day-to-day businesses mortgages do not qualify.

Another kind of lien worth mentioning is the lien on receivables. These security interests are particularly important for companies that do not have real estate and cannot pledge production resources (for the reasons set out before). Consequently, instead of pledging property, the loans are secured by the pledging of claims or the assignment for the purpose of security. As in several others types of liens, this type of collateral require that certain disclosure steps are fulfilled.[17]

The surety (*Bürgschaft*)[18] and the joint liability (*Schuldbeitritt*)[19] are legal strategies for the securing of credits. These transactions have legal relevance, especially in the collateralisation of loans required by corporate entities in which non-liable partners

14. About the retention of title Riedler in Apathy/Iro/Koziol, *Österreichisches Bankvertragsrecht IX*[2] (2012) 243 et seqq.; Koziol/Welser, *Bürgerliches Recht II* 169; Apathy/Riedler, *Bürgerliches Recht III, Schuldrecht Besonderer Teil* 5 et seqq.
15. See Harrer, *Sicherungsrechte* (2002) 55 et seqq.
16. On this matter, for example Iro in Apathy/Iro/Koziol, *Österreichisches Bankvertragsrecht X* 69 et seqq.; Koziol/Welser, *Bürgerliches Recht I*[14] (2014) 417 f; Apathy/Riedler, *Bürgerliches Recht IV, Sachenrecht* 193; Riedler, *Zivilrecht V, Sachenrecht*[3] (2010) 186.
17. C.f. Koziol/Welser, *Bürgerliches Recht I* 418 f; Apathy/Riedler, *Bürgerliches Recht IV, Sachenrecht* 250; Riedler, *Zivilrecht V, Sachenrecht* 187.
18. §§ 1346 et seqq. ABGB.
19. §§ 1404 et seqq. ABGB.

participate (limited liability companies, limited partnerships). The traditional example would be the corporate entity that seeks the extension of the credit line but has no available real estate assets, the means of production cannot be pledged and the assignment of future receivables for security purposes has already occurred. In this situation, a shareholder may agree to personally assume any obligation of the corporate entity as surety.

Probably, the most important pledging instrument for entrepreneurs is not regulated by law but developed through practice. As part of a bank guarantee[20] an entrepreneur instructs his bank to pledge a specific receivable. The bank emits a guarantee for a third party (business partner of the company). In this guarantee the guaranteed event is described in detail. In case the event does occur, for example, if the entrepreneur does not fulfil his obligation to deliver a particular payment, then the bank will execute the guarantee. The entrepreneur cannot contest the existence of the obligation. The bank only checks whether the formal requirements of the guarantee are met. If this is the case, the bank complies with the duties set out in the guarantee.

The advantages of this pledging strategy are manifold. A bank guarantee is handled discretely. The public remains – unlike in the creation process of a mortgage – excluded. The risk that customers will be concerned with the processes does not exist. Defences are not possible. The entrepreneur cannot be freed from the original obligation. Thus, the bank guarantee differs from the surety. It should be remarked that there is still some degree of insolvency risk. Complete security against potential insolvency of the bank does not exist, however, the risk of insolvency is considered very low.

## §5.02 FORM

Legal transactions can be conducted in a form free fashion. There are, however, several exceptions that should be noted and that hold some importance for business practice.

The donation contract is in contrast to the purchase contract bound to a specific legal form.[21] Donation contracts require a notarial act. Also bound to specific legal formalities are the surety[22] and the joint liability acts.[23] The binding of the parties requires a written document. Other formalities are also required for the partnership agreement of a corporation (notarial deed[24]) and for the resale of the shares in a limited company, which can also be transferred through a notarial deed (e.g., sold or given away).[25]

20. See Koziol/Potyka, Bankgarantie in Apathy/Iro/Koziol, *Österreichisches Bankvertragsrecht* $V^2$ (2009) 225 et seqq.; Koziol/Welser, *Bürgerliches Recht* II 152, insb 153 et seqq.
21. § 1 Abs 1 d) Notariatsaktsgesetz.
22. § 1346 Abs 2 ABGB.
23. OGH 20.4.2010, 4 Ob 205/09i, SZ 2010/38, JBl 2010, 509 (Faber, Lukas), RdW 2010, 570 (Bruchbacher).
24. § 16 Abs 1 S 1 AktG; § 4 Abs 3 S 1 GmbHG.
25. § 76 Abs 2 S 1 GmbHG.

## §5.03 SELECTED EXAMPLES

### [A] Preliminary Comment

The Austrian Commercial Code (*UGB*) regulates the 'business-related transactions' in its Fourth Book. The catchy wording of the reform to the German Commercial Code (*HGB, Handelsgesetzbuch*) was 'commercial transactions' (*Handelsgeschäfte*). Enterprise-related transactions (*Unternehmensbezogene Geschäfte*) are the sale of goods, the sale on commission, the shipping business, the warehousing business and the freight business.[26] However, it does not make sense to limit the **enunciation** enumeration to these types of contracts. The focus point of the Fourth Book should, as already indicated, be explained historically. The reality of economic life is not reflected or very imperfectly reflected in this collection.

Consequently, the following selection is not based or not mainly based on the Fourth Book of the Commercial Code (*UGB*), but rather on the practical importance of the legal transactions for enterprises.

The list of the enterprise-related transactions begins with a brief segment on the sale of goods.[27] The overview below also provides information about sale contracts. These types of transactions are revised first, taking into consideration the large role they play, primarily in industry and commerce.

### [B] Sale of Goods (*Warenkauf*)

The title of the second section is 'sale of goods'. However, the Commercial Code (*UGB*) does not regulate the sale of goods, it is rather a guideline on the subject and only provides some additional special norms.[28]

The provisions of the Civil Code (*ABGB*) also apply for the sale of goods. The civil law governs the basic questions of corporate law decision-making (legal capacity, consent, form). The Twenty-third section ('on the purchase contract') is dedicated to the purchase (Civil Code (*ABGB*) §§ 1053 et seq.). The law regulates, the obligations of the seller (Civil Code (*ABGB*) § 1061) and the buyer (Civil Code (*ABGB*) §§ 1062 et seq.), the transfer of risk (§ 1064 Civil Code (*ABGB*)). Moreover, the law distinguishes between different types of sales of goods (resale, pre-sale, sale on trial).

Warranty law for the entrepreneur is regulated in the Civil Code (*ABGB*), not in the context of sales law, but under the 'General provisions on pecuniary contracts and enterprises' (*Allgemeinen Bestimmungen über entgeltliche Verträge und Geschäfte* §§ 922 et seq. Civil Code (*ABGB*)). For movable property (sale of goods), the warranty period is two years (§ 933 Abs 1 Austrian Civil Code (*ABGB*)). In addition, claims for damages are possible, however, the fault of the 'transferor' is required (§ 933 Civil Code (*ABGB*)).

26. See above fn. 9.
27. S §§ 343 et seqq. UGB.
28. Krejci, *Unternehmensrecht* 389.

The most significant special regulations of the Code of Commerce (*UGB*) are those related to the warranty right. The entrepreneur, who has purchased an item, should reveal the flaws, 'which he has discovered or should have discovered in the ordinary course of business by inspection of the goods after delivery, within a reasonable time' (§ 377 paragraph 1 *UGB*).[29] Otherwise, the buyer can present warranty claims, claims for damages affecting the goods and claims seeking contract rescission due to vitiated consent (§ 377 paragraph 2 *UGB*).

Another subject may be important in relation to the marketing of goods. According to the Product Liability Law (*ProdukthaftungsG, PHG*)[30] the manufacturer of defective products (§ 1 paragraph 1 no. 1 PHG) and the entrepreneur that introduces them to the European Economic Area (§ 1 paragraph 1 no. 2 PHG) are liable for their marketing. This liability is based not on a contract and does not require culpability. However, the entrepreneur must be familiar with the requirements of the PHG. An entrepreneur who has sold a commodity is liable as a manufacturer or importer if the manufacturer or importer, are not known and he does not identify the supplier 'within a reasonable time frame'.

### [C] Service/Work Contracts (*Werkvertrag*)

According to the Austrian Commercial Code (UGB), the service contract does not belong to the 'business-related transactions' (*Unternehmensbezogene Geschäfte*). A factual justification for this is not possible, because, just to name a prominent example, the construction industry is at the forefront of this type of contract.[31]

The legal foundations of this type of contract are contained mainly in the Civil Code (*ABGB*) (§§ 1165 et seqq.).[32] Special mention should be given to the provisions on cost estimates (§ 1170 a)[33] and those on the guarantee of construction contracts (*Sicherstellung bei Bauverträgen* § 1170 b).[34] Pointedly formulated, it is possible to speak of an entrepreneur legal standard in general civil law.

Significant importance can also be attributed to the so-called right of retention. For which a legal basis can be found both in the Civil Code (*ABGB*) (§ 471) and in the Commerce Code (*UGB*) (§§ 369 f). The right of retention is an important tool, especially for those enterprises that conduct repair work (e.g., owner of motor vehicle workshops). In case the commissioning party contracts improvement or repairs, but fails to pay the compensation, the entrepreneur can decline the claim for the return (*Herausgabeanspruch*) of the item based on the right of retention.

29. See Krejci, *Unternehmensrecht* 396 et seqq.
30. On this, Koziol/Welser, *Bürgerliches Recht* II 378 et seqq.
31. In the reality of economic life companies that execute repairs play ('workshops') a significant role. The legal relationship between the owner of the shop and the customer is the work contract.
32. Literature on work contract see above fn. 7.
33. Koziol/Welser, *Bürgerliches Recht* II 258 f.
34. Koziol/Welser, *Bürgerliches Recht* II 259 f.

### [D] Distribution Agreements (*Vertriebsverträge*)

#### *[1] General Overview*

Each producer is faced with the question of the appropriate distribution system for his products. In general, it is possible to distinguish two models: direct marketing and indirect marketing. Direct marketing is conducted via the branches or subsidiaries of the manufacturer. However, it is unusual in entrepreneurial practice to create fully owned distribution channels. Instead, distribution is commonly conducted through wholesale and retail trade.

In the case of indirect distribution, the producer supplies the dealer and the dealer sells the goods on his own responsibility to the end costumer. Where this approach is taken, the question arises as to the manner in which the contact with the dealers is achieved and maintained. In this context, the business relationship is a mere postal one. The producer writes to the dealer in question and then provides the corresponding orders. As a rule, however, more intensive business cooperation will be required.

Usually, it is not enough that the producer provides brochures, catalogues, etc. Instead, it is often procured that the goods are physically presented. The fora for these presentations are mainly trade fairs that take place around the world throughout the year. In case the manufacturer chooses to present his products physically, two variants are possible, the use of his own employees or the commissioning of third parties, usually referred to as commercial agents.

#### *[2] Commercial Agency Agreements (***Handelsvertreterverträge***)*

The activity of the commercial agent is a legally regulated form of indirect sale of goods.[35] In the course of economic life different manifestations of the commercial agency have been developed. The range extends from the representative large agency, on whose support a manufacturer can almost be dependent, to the small-scale entrepreneur that handles just one client and whose position is similar to that of an employee. In general, the economic importance of the commercial agent is viewed (in Austria and Germany) as considerable.

The commercial agent is an independent entrepreneur operating for another party, **formerly** known as the 'principal' (*Geschäftsherr*). The object of the activity of the agent is the arrangement or conclusion of transactions for the entrepreneur 'in his name and on his behalf.'

In the field of operations of the agent, different kinds of businesses are included especially merchandise sale transactions. Nonetheless, transactions over immovable property are excluded.

A commercial agent is 'continuously entrusted'. Agents and entrepreneurs are parties in a continuing obligation. This peculiarity distinguishes the agent particularly,

35. See Krejci, *Unternehmensrecht* 436 et seqq., with further references.

from the broker. Therefore, 'continuously entrusted' means that the agent is integrated in a distribution system and, therefore, is also dependent on instructions.

The commercial agent must 'seek the arrangement or conclusion of transactions'.[36] In the course of his activity he has to look after 'the interest of the entrepreneur' with 'the care of a prudent entrepreneur' providing any required reports.[37]

The law does not contain a non-competition prohibition. However, when derived from the general 'duty to protect interests' (*Interessenwahrungspflicht*) the agent shall not commercialise competing products. Nonetheless, a divergent contractual agreement is allowed.

The entrepreneur has to support the commercial agent in its activities. He must take into account the legitimate interests of the other contractual party. The extent of these duties depends on the contractual terms. Intensive involvement in the sales organisation makes increased consideration seem appropriate.

Usually, the contractor owes the agent a commission.[38] The compensation claim (*Entgeltanspruch)* leads to the assumption that the transaction (as a result of the activities of the agent) has come to fruition. The mere identification of the party is generally insufficient. Other important provisions included in the law relate to the compensation for expenses, the settlement date, the limitation period and the right of retention.

The right to indemnity has a significant practical importance under § 24 of the Law on Commercial Agents (*Handelsvertretergesetz*). The agent is entitled to this right after the termination of the contractual relationship, if he has brought in new customers or has significantly expanded the already existing business connections in a way that it is possible to assume that the entrepreneur will further benefit, even after the termination of the contract. The relevance of the indemnity right for other distribution systems is considerable.[39]

### *[3] Distributorship Agreements* (**Vertragshändlerverträge***)*

In recent decades, new forms of indirect sale of goods have been created. One of these is the selling of goods through authorised dealers. The dealer buys and sells – like other principals – in his own name and on his own account.[40] The special feature is that the dealer is part of a distribution system. It represents and promotes the products of a particular manufacturer; it arranges its operation in a specific way subordinated to the interests of the manufacturer.

The dealer has to take care of storage, transportation, sales financing, etc. (unlike the commercial agent). He exercises these functions, however, in accordance with the manufacturer's instructions, acting as the 'executive body' (of the manufacturer). The

36. Krejci, *Unternehmensrecht* 441.
37. Krejci, *Unternehmensrecht* 440 f.
38. § 8 para. 2 HVertrG.
39. Following examples from the case law of the Supreme Court: 30 Aug. 2006, 7 Ob 122/06a (franchising); 30 Apr. 2012, 9 Ob 32/11p, ecolex 2012, 1067 (dealer).
40. Krejci, *Unternehmensrecht* 475; *K.* Schmidt, *Handelsrecht*[5] (1999) § 28 II.2.

dealer is involved in the distribution system of the manufacturer, but it also bears the sales and credit risk.

The rights and obligations are regulated in the distributorship agreement. This contract does not only organise the buyer-seller relationship; the contract specifies the integration of the dealer in the sales model of the manufacturer. In distributorship agreements, it is often possible to find clauses that are typical for commercial agency agreements. The dealer must follow the manufacturer's instructions, provide information and he shall also not market competing products without the prior approval of the manufacturer.

From the distributorship agreement, several obligations for mutual safeguarding of interests arise. The scope of these obligations can only be concretised on a case-by-case basis in accordance with the contractual stipulations. An exclusivity right obliges the dealer to additional measures beyond those of a non-exclusive agreement. But even if the manufacturer does not give the dealer exclusive distribution rights, the dealer is required to take into consideration the legitimate interests of the manufacturer.

### *[4] Franchising Contract (***Franchisingverträge***)*

The dealer is integrated into the sales organisation of the manufacturer, but the independence of the dealer is nevertheless beyond doubt. From the perspective of a manufacturer, it may sometimes seem desirable that the sales intermediary places the product or brand even more in the foreground so that manufacturers and sellers are perceived as merged into one identity. This objective would correspond to the creation of an own distribution system (branches, subsidiaries). However, the creation of an own distribution system is cost intensive.

In view of this, it was natural to consider marketing possibilities that would not be borne by private intermediaries but largely organised according to the manufacturer's instructions. The result of these efforts was the invention of a new system of contracts, namely the franchise.[41] Franchisees are legally independent entrepreneurs. Therefore, franchising is not an own distribution model of the manufacturer.

However, **the franchisor** seeks to have broad powers granted in the contracts. This option has been used extensively in practice. Evidence of this is the fact that courts often had to evaluate the close similarity of franchisees with employees. The individual contracts of a franchise organisation have nearly identical content. This aspect contributes primarily to the homogeneous appearance of the distribution system. This system is also attractive for the franchisee, his advantage consists in benefiting from the image of a known name. A consequence of the latter is that the risk of business failure in franchises is unusually low.

Franchising was established in the beginning of the twentieth century in the United States. Subsequently, this distribution system was tried in France and England. Today, the paramount importance of franchising is, also for Austria, beyond doubt.

41. Krejci, *Unternehmensrecht* 476 f; *K.* Schmidt, *Handelsrecht* § 28 II.3.

The peculiarity of franchising resides in the fact that the franchisor entrusts a particular entrepreneur to provide goods or services in a manner specific to the franchise. The franchise-specific presentation is a differentiating factor between the operation of the franchisees and that of a dealership. The business establishments are equipped and set up according to accurate and uniform criteria. The focus is solely the product, while the individual entrepreneur stays in the background. The general use of language illustrates this aspect. It is common to hear: 'There is a new Benetton store.' But nobody says: 'A dealer opened a new store, which will sell Benetton products'.

The franchising agreement is a continuing obligation, in which elements of different contracts are connected. The contract entitles the franchisee to participate in the marketing system developed by the franchisor. He may use the trade mark or other designations of the franchisor and is, however, committed to promoting the name through its sales and promotional activities. These aspects relate to the licensing or regulatory elements of the contract.

In franchising the sales law is added. The law of the commercial agency should not be neglected in this context; in the field of distribution of services, revenues based on contract of service law and agency law play important roles.

The question, which type of contract dominates the franchise, cannot be answered on an abstract level. Also, the proposal to assign license agreements to franchising has not been adopted for good reasons. The license aspects can gain importance in the assessment of conflict of laws issues.

The franchise agreement creates mutual duties of loyalty. The extent of these duties, regarding the scope and intensity, requires case-specific analysis. The close relationship between the franchise contract and the regulated types of contracts should be observed. On this basis, one can investigate whether and to what extent such an addition according to sales law, tenancy law, agency law, company law, etc. can be considered.

### [E] Service Contracts (*Dienstleistungsverträge)*

The broad field of providing services is hardly approached in statutory law. An objective explanation of this situation is not possible. Nonetheless, service contracts have gained great importance in entrepreneurial practice.[42]

Each enterprise uses a tax consultant. The preparatory and supportive role of these advisors is indispensable in general, even though, it is the job of the executive bodies to prepare the financial statements. The tax consultant performs a service and consequently the legal relationship between him and the company is shaped in the form of a service contract.

The variety of legal problems to which enterprises are subjected in the course of their economic activity can often only be overcome with the help of lawyers. Obvious topics in this regard include administrative law (commercial law, environmental law,

42. K. Schmidt, *Handelsrecht* § 35 V.1.

etc.), civil law (purchase contracts, cooperative agreements, or partnership agreements) and competition law. Additionally, it is important to point out that even the advisory activities of the lawyer are based on service contracts.

Not less important for this overview is the management consultant, who provides valuable support in establishing an enterprise or advises in time of economic crisis. Also, the development of new markets often requires the assistance of a management consultant.

Service contracts can hardly be classified into different types, since most service contracts differ in the different projects and areas of responsibility. The work contract is characterised by the result-oriented point of view. The lawyer owes the client meticulous, quality service, however, he is not required to succeed or attain a specific result. Service contracts can be of different types concerning the *lex lata* (business management, order), but a comprehensive statutory scheme in this regard, is still lacking.

### [F] Bank Guarantee

The economy has gone in new ways in the field of security rights. An important result is the bank guarantee.[43] Its peculiarity lies in the fact that the secured claim (in civil law terminology: the main obligation) should generally play no role in the legal relation between the creditor and the debtor.

Three parties are generally involved in bank guarantees. The debtor instructs the bank to guarantee the creditor for a particular obligation. The agreement between the debtor and the bank is based on a contractual relationship (according to the Civil Code (*ABGB*) §§ 1002 et seq.). By virtue of this agreement, the bank is obliged in the interest and on behalf of the debtor (its customer) to complete a guarantee contract with the beneficiary. In general, the bank has to execute the order itself. This process is referred to as issuance (*Hinauslegung)* of the guarantee to the beneficiary. Following the issuance of the guarantee, the debtor (customer) is denied any further influence. In particular, it may not instruct the bank not to pay. The exclusion of such influence is an essential element of the bank guarantee. Only because the customer counter-instructions are denied, does the beneficiary acquire the desired secured position.

The guarantee-obligation, the obligation of the Bank to act upon the occurrence of the guaranteed event is based on a contract with the beneficiary. Special features surround the conclusion of these contracts; explicit acceptance of the beneficiary is uncommon. The beneficiary of a bank guarantee generally does not communicate the acceptance to the bank guarantee. Since the guarantee only creates advantages for the beneficiary, there are no objections to qualify the silence as a conclusive agreement.

After the occurrence of the guaranteed event (retrieval of the guarantee) the bank will first inform the client. The possible presentable objections of the guarantor are limited, nonetheless, the interests of the client require, however, that he will be

43. See the literature in fn. 20 especially Koziol/Potyka in Apathy/Iro/Koziol, *Österreichisches Bankvertragsrecht V*, 225 et seqq.

informed of the execution of the guarantee. The bank is also obliged to notify the beneficiary immediately about the nature and form of execution. The beneficiary should retain the possibility of a renewed (error-free) retrieval of the guarantee.

From the abstractness of the bank guarantee follows an exclusion of liability. This objection relates to the exclusion on a substantive level. The formal requirements, however, have to be considered by the bank. The guarantee contract determines which documents or statements are to be presented. The bank has to determine whether prima facie these documents comply with the terms of the guarantee, if authority to represent is given and whether the agreed form and deadline were met.

There are in principle no substantive requirements. The bank has to pay if the agreed formal requirements are met. The payment obligation of the bank is, however, subject to claims for abuse of law. This occurs when the guarantee is demanded despite the obvious and provable lack of grounds. In this case, the bank of the client is required to raise the objection of abuse of law and refuse payment.

CHAPTER 6

# Tort Law

*Ferdinand Kerschner & Erika Wagner*

In Austria's tort law the principle of a fault-based liability is still hegemonic. Its basic structure can be portrayed in the following way:

*Figure 6.1*

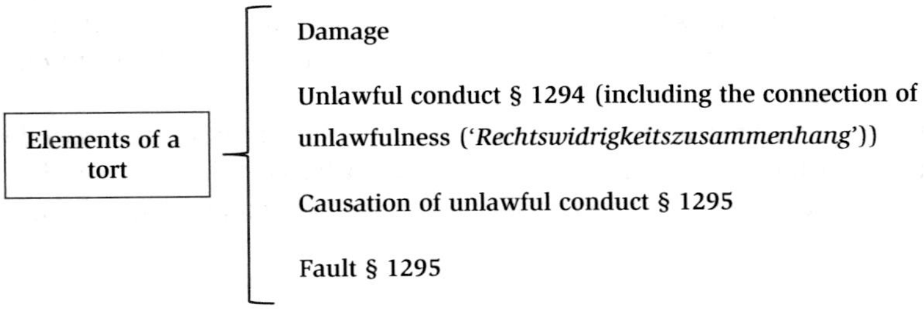


Since it is mainly about the causation of unlawful conduct, it is factually required to investigate causation after it has been determined that the conduct is unlawful.[1]

The distinction between the liability due to a breach of contract and a tort (compare generally § 1295 paragraph 1 *Allgemeines Bürgerliches Gesetzbuch*, abbreviated ABGB (General Civil Code of Austria; provisions quoted without source refer to the ABGB), is especially significant with regard to who carries the burden of proof, vicarious liability and the ability to compensate the pecuniary loss.

1. Compare *Reischauer* in Rummel (ed.), ABGB$^{3}$ § 1295 rc 1; *Kerschner*, Amtshaftung statt Kundmachung? JBl 1984, 359; aside from other opinions see the predominant jurisdiction and *Karollus*, Funktion und Dogmatik der Schutzgesetzverletzung (1992) 391 ff., which are content with a 'natural' causation (behavioural causation); compare also *Harrer*, Schadenersatzrecht (1999) 13.

In the ABGB and especially in supplementary laws there are principles of liability in addition to fault-based liability which show other stricter grounds for attribution of liability.

An increase of liability – still in the context of a fault-based liability – results in a shift of the burden of proof (compare especially § 1298 on obligations to guarantee for a result (*'Erfolgsverbindlichkeiten'*)). The liability for someone else's fault (vicarious liability §§ 1313a, 1315, see below) departs from the pure fault principle. Special provisions of liability (§§ 1318, 1319, 1320) are close to strict liability. However, their classification on its own is controversial.[2] Even being in possession[3] of a very dangerous object or placing a potential dangerous product on the market falls within the strict liability (e.g., *Eisenbahn- und Kraftfahrzeughaftpflichtgesetz* (EKHG; Railway and Motor Vehicle Liability Act), *Rechnungshofgesetz* (RHG; Court of Audit Act), *Atomhaftpflichtgesetz* (Atomic Liability Act), *Produkthaftungsgesetz* (PHG; Product Liability Act), *Gentechnikgesetz* (GTG; Act on Genetic Engineering), etc.). A strict public law liability for environmental damage is provided for in the *Bundesumwelthaftungsgesetz* (B-UHG; Environmental Liability Act).[4] If cases of damage by particularly dangerous objects are not regulated then a single-analogy according to the expressly regulated instances of strict liability has to be considered.[5]

If unlawful and culpable conduct is not a requirement for strict liability then an intervention in a foreign legally protected interest will be prohibited. Acts intending to cause certain damage are allowed in cases of *'Eingriffshaftung'*. Although the damage is permitted, one is liable for it. The following are examples of *'Eingriffshaftung'*:

Liability for (permitted) immissions of (especially industrial) facilities which are officially approved;[6] liability of someone who inflicts harm in a state of emergency referred to § 1306a; liability of the owner of water rights referred to § 26 *Wasserrechtsgesetz* (WRG; Water Act).[7]

If there are indications for more grounds of liability in a specific case, it is possible that they coexist (according to the principle of the concurring basis of claims).[8] This has its practical importance: Strict liabilities often show a limit of liability. Any further

2. For further information see below.
3. Holder is someone, who uses the object for his own account and who has the actual power of disposal, e.g. a car holder; compare *Koziol*, Haftpflichtrecht² II 529 ff.
4. For further information see *Hinteregger/Kerschner* (eds.), Kommentar zum Bundes-Umwelthaftungsgesetz (2011).
5. Compare *Koziol*, Umfassende Gefährdungshaftung durch Analogie? FS Wilburg (1975) 173 ff.; who assumes an analogy to several provisions (*'Gesamtanalogie'*); more restrictive *Kerschner*, Kausalitätshaftung im Nachbarrecht? RdU 1998, 10 ff.
6. See *Jabornegg*, Bürgerliches Recht und Umweltschutz, Gutachten zum Neunten Österreichischen Juristentag 1985 (1985); *Rummel*, Erfolgshaftung im Nachbarrecht? JBl 1967, 120 ff; *Kerschner*, in Stolzlechner/Wendl/Bergthaler (eds.), Die gewerbliche Betriebsanlage (2008) rc 278 ff; *Wagner*, Die Betriebsanlage im zivilen Nachbarrecht (1997); lately *Kerschner/Wagner* in Fenyves/Kerschner/Vonkilch/Klang (eds.), Kommentar zum ABGB³ to § 364a.
7. See *Kerschner*, Zur Haftung nach § 26 Wasserrechtsgesetz und zum Deliktsstatut im IPR, JBl 1983, 337 ff.; for an appropriate classification of the strict liability see *Jabornegg*, Bürgerliches Recht und Umweltschutz 78 ff.
8. Compare *Koziol/Welser* (edited *Kletečka*) I¹³ 35 f.

damage has to be compensated if the wrongdoer acted unlawfully and culpably. Furthermore, the periods of prescription can be different. The burden of proof may also differ.

One can distinguish as follows with respect to the 'strength' of the grounds of liability (measured according to the basis of fault liability):

(1) *'Eingriffshaftung'*
(2) Strict liability
(3) Fault liability where the burden of proof shifts
(4) Fault liability.

In matters of fault liability not only the own fault of the wrongdoer (defendant) can be attributed to him, but also the fault of his assistants (at least resulting from an objectively careless conduct) can be attributed to him under certain circumstances. The vicarious liability pursuant to §§ 1313a and 1315, but also the other cases of extended vicarious liability (e.g., § 1319a; § 19 paragraph 2 EKHG (Railway and Motor Vehicle Liability Act); § 2 RHG (Court of Audit Act); § 10 paragraph 2 *Rohrleitungsgesetz* (Act on Pipelines), 'representative's liability', etc.) and the liability of the juristic person for the acts of its organs and executive employees (§ 337) always demands the fulfilment of certain criteria.

It further applies that *special provisions take precedence over general provisions*. This principle only applies if there are indications in the facts that speak for the applicability of a special provision. If, for example, someone is harmed by an animal, then § 1320 will primarily be applied; if a roofing tile falls on a parked car, then § 1319 will firstly be looked at. If a person is bodily injured, then § 1325 is applicable. § 1327 is relevant if a person is killed.

The precedence of the special provision is explained by the fact that for its scope of application in either the conditions of liability (especially the type of the damage, the type of the harmful act) or in the legal consequences of the general rules the diverging applies.

According to general methodical rules it then needs to be determined whether the special provision displaces the general provision. According to § 1300 sentence 2 one is only liable if one knowingly gives wrong advice, provided that one has not been remunerated for the advice (sentence 1). Hence, negligence establishes – contrary to general rules – no liability.

Mostly, the general fault liability is not displaced, but only supplemented or modified; special provisions require either an increased liability (e.g., §§ 1319, 1320) or special obligations to compensate (e.g., §§ 1325, 1327).

In the following the most important special liability provisions are pointed out. These are fewer special provisions than one might assume.

## §6.01 OVERVIEW OF SPECIAL LIABILITY PROVISIONS OF THE ABGB[9]

§ 19: Liability for Unauthorised Self-Help

A citizen has to rely on the help of the state for the protection of his rights. Self-help in a broader sense (self-defence, emergency relief and emergency situation) is only allowed under strict conditions (especially if help provided by the state would come too late). If self-defence (necessary defence, compare § 3 Criminal Code (*Strafgesetzbuch*, StGB)) or acceptable self-help is exceeded, compensation for damage will have to be paid.[10]

§ 335: Liability of the Possessor in Bad Faith

The possessor in bad faith is liable in a very strict sense for every disadvantage resulting from his possession solely as a consequence of being in bad faith (in certain circumstances including even cases of force majeure). Not only must the positive damage (*damnum emergens*) be compensated, but also the loss of profit.

§ 933a: Liability of the Person Obligated to Provide the Warranty

If the transferor has caused a defect at the transfer of the goods for payment, the transferee will have a claim for compensation.[11] The specific feature of § 933a lies in the legal consequence of deficiency damage. While according to general rules (§ 1323) a change from restitution in kind to monetary compensation is already possible, if the former is not physically possible,[12] then according to the compensation claim in terms of § 933a one of the following conditions (§ 933a paragraph 2) must be present to be able to claim monetary compensation:

- impossibility of rectification and replacement;
- disproportionately high effort for the transferor;
- refusal of rectification or replacement by the transferor;
- no action taken within a reasonable period of time;
- considerable inconvenience for the transferee;
- unacceptability for the transferee due to weighty reasons lying in the person of the transferor.

Therefore, unison with the warranty law exists. The shift of the burden of proof for deficiency damage and consequential damage caused by defect referred to in § 1298 is limited to ten years according to § 933a paragraph 3.

§ 1300: Liability when Giving Advice

An expert is liable for wrong advice/information, which concerns his special field or activity area. Such a person is only liable if he does not gratuitously (but for reward)

9. This is not a closed list.
10. *Reischauer* in Rummel (ed.), ABGB[3] § 19 rc 13.
11. *Ofner* in Schwimann (ed.), ABGB[3] § 933a rc 1.
12. For further information see *Reischauer* in Rummel, ABGB[3] § 1323.

give advice.[13] He is also liable for pure pecuniary loss, where a contractual relationship between him and the injured person is assumed, but which is not mandatory. If someone knowingly gives wrong advice, the adviser will be liable in terms of § 1300 sentence 2 even if he did so without asking for remuneration.[14] In this case also non-expert advisers are liable for giving advice.[15] The prevailing opinion[16] demands the existence of intent to cause damage.

§§ 1301 f.: Damage caused by Several Persons

If several wrongdoers participate intentionally, they will be jointly and severally liable. This needs to be distinguished from negligent participation. If the damage of each wrongdoer can be determined separately they will only be liable for their damage. If the determination of their part of the damage is not possible, the wrongdoers will be jointly and severally liable. In order to achieve an internal settlement between the wrongdoers it is stated in § 1302, that a wrongdoer, who has satisfied the damage may demand restitution from the others corresponding to their internal relationship.[17]

§ 1306a: Liability in an Emergency Situation

If somebody has acted due to an emergency, the judge needs to determine 'if and to what extent' the damage has to be compensated. (Criteria: omitted defence, proportionality, assets of the wrongdoer and the injured person)[18]

§ 1309: Liability of the Custodian

If a minor (or a mentally disabled person) causes damage to someone, it needs to be determined with priority whether the custodian has objectively neglected his duties of care. The court needs to consider which measures would have been necessary in that circumstance according to the measures which would have been set by 'reasonable parents'. If the liability of the custodian has been confirmed, the minor will principally not be held liable.[19]

§ 1310: Liability of the Incapable Wrongdoer

If the custodian is not held liable, the incapable wrongdoer can be held liable if exceptional circumstances exist. The decision of the court needs to be based on equity and thus the court can use its own discretion.[20]

13. *Reischauer* in Rummel, ABGB³ § 1300 rc 7 with further references.
14. The prevailing opinion (compare *Koziol*, Haftpflichtrecht II² 185; *Karner* in KBB³ § 1300 rc 4) requires that intent to cause damage exists.
15. *Schacherreiter* in Kletečka/Schauer (eds.), ABGB-ON 1.01 § 1300 rc 9.
16. *Reischauer* in Rummel (ed.), ABGB³ § 1299 rc 12; *Koziol*, Haftpflichtrecht II² 185; *Karner* in KBB³ § 1300 rc 4.
17. *Schacherreiter* in Kletečka /Schauer (eds.), ABGB-ON 1.01 § 1301 f rc 6 ff; *Karner* in KBB³ § 1302 rc 14.
18. *Karner* in KBB³ § 1306a rc 4.
19. *Harrer*, Schadenersatzrecht 42 f. with further references.
20. For further information see *Karner* in KBB³ § 1310 rc 5 ff.

§ 1312: Liability for Acting without Authority

If the efforts made by a person acting without authority in an emergency are unsuccessful, he will usually not be held liable.[21]

§ 1318: Occupiers' Liability

An occupier will be held liable according to § 1318 if 'someone is damaged by the falling of a dangerously suspended or placed object or by the throwing or pouring out of a flat'. According to the correct view[22] the occupier will not be held liable for dangerously suspended or placed objects if he can provide proof that due care was taken. Fault in the narrow sense is not required.

Regarding the acts of throwing and pouring out the occupier is also responsible for conduct of third parties. Today, the analogous use of § 1318 is especially significant when referring to water damage of a building. Thus according to case law a property owner will be liable due to the 'hazardous storage'[23] of water if the lower situated rooms are damaged by liquids originating out of his property. This can be for example a defective tap or possibly also a defective dish washer.[24]

§ 1319: Building Possessor's Liability or Liability for a Construction

If the collapse of a building or a detachment of parts of the building is due to the defective state of the building, the possessor will be liable for the damage caused thereby, except if he can prove that he took the necessary care in the securing of the building.[25] The same applies for other constructions – for instance barrier systems and analogously for rotten trees.[26]

§ 1319a: Liability of the Custodian of a Public Road

The custodian of a public road will be liable for the defective state of a public road or a public way if he or his people intentionally or through gross negligence have caused the defectiveness. The 'people liability' ('*Leutehaftung*') stated in § 1319a is on the one hand more extensive than the vicarious liability mentioned in § 1315 and therein lies a liability increase. On the other hand, this liability assumes gross negligence. The measures which have to be taken by the custodian of a public road have to be in accordance with the principle of reasonableness: This has to be determined by the judicial authority in each individual case.[27]

§ 1320: Liability of the Keeper of the Animal

§ 1320 sentence 1 regulates the damage caused by an animal where a person incited or irritated the animal or neglected to keep it well guarded. § 1320 sentence 2 makes

21. *Harrer* in Schwimann (ed.), ABGB³ § 1312 rc 1.
22. Compare *Reischauer* in Rummel (ed.), ABGB³ § 1318 rc 2; *Danzl* in KBB³, § 1319 rc 4.
23. For further information see *Reischauer* in Rummel (ed.), ABGB³ § 1318 rc 10.
24. Ibid.
25. *Danzl* in KBB³ § 1319 rc 4.
26. *Reischauer* in Rummel (ed.), ABGB³ § 1319 rc 11.
27. *Harrer*, Schadenersatzrecht 52 ff. with further references.

provision for the liability of the keeper of the animal.[28] The keeper of an animal carries the burden of proof for taking the necessary care, i.e., 'solely based on the objectively required care'. If he cannot prove proper safe-keeping and supervision, he will be liable for his unlawful conduct.[29]

§§ 1325 f: Personal Injury Liability

In a personal injury case the wrongdoer has to pay the medical costs, the loss of earnings and the compensation for pain and suffering of the wronged party.

§ 1327: Liability for Wrongful Death

§1327 makes provision for the indirectly harmed party (surviving dependants) to claim compensation (in particular loss of maintenance).[30]

§ 1328: Liability for Violation of the Right to Sexual Self-Determination

The aim of § 1328 is to ensure that victims of sexual abuse receive 'reasonable' compensation. Children, women and men are covered by the gender-neutral formulation. The right to sexual self-determination is protected. The positive damage as well as the loss of profit has to be compensated. Furthermore, victims are entitled to the compensation of immaterial damage.[31]

§ 1328a: Liability for Unauthorised Invasion of Privacy

A wrongdoer is liable if he unlawfully and intentionally violates the privacy of the wronged party. The claim for damages encloses pecuniary damages and if there is a substantial breach then also non-pecuniary damages.[32] If special provisions regulating the invasion of the privacy exist (e.g., media law) then these regulations apply.

§ 1329: Liability for Deprivation of Liberty

In § 1329 the cases of forcible kidnapping, imprisonment by a private person and intentional illegal arrest by act of state are regulated. The greatest practical relevance has the case of an intentional illegal arrest. According to § 1329 full compensation has to be paid.

§ 1330: Liability for Insult and Defamation in Relation to Credit-Worthiness and Business Reputation

§ 1330 paragraph 1 regulates the protection against insults. The right to honour is an absolutely protected right and is a personality right as referred to in § 16. § 1330 paragraph 2 regulates defamation in relation to credit-worthiness and business reputation (damage to the person's reputation). According to paragraph 2 someone is liable, if he spreads false facts and thereby unlawfully affects the economic reputation of a

28. For further information see *Reischauer* in Rummel (ed.), ABGB$^3$ § 1320.
29. *Reischauer* in Rummel (ed.), ABGB$^3$ § 1320 20 f.
30. For further information see *Hinteregger* in Kletečka/Schauer (eds.), ABGB-ON 1.01 § 1327 rc 2 ff.
31. *Hinteregger* in Kletečka/Schauer (eds.), ABGB-ON 1.01 § 1328 rc 1 ff.
32. *Hinteregger* in Kletečka/Schauer (eds.), ABGB-ON 1.00 § 1328a rc 2 ff.

person.[33] If a justification is given, a claim for a suffered insult will not exist (e.g., § 6 paragraph 2 n 4 *Mediengesetz* (Media Act): There is no claim for damages for a suffered insult if 'it concerns a true reproduction of the statement of a third person and the public has had a prevailing interest according to the knowledge of the cited statement.')[34]

These special provisions can only be used as a sole basis of a claim if they direct something different from the general conditions of liability as can be seen in §§ 1318, 1319. If only the nature or the extent of the compensation (the legal consequence!) is regulated in detail or differently, the claim is founded in the general provisions of §§ 1293 ff. read with the relevant special provision; e.g., in §§ 1293 ff. read with § 1325 in case of personal injury.[35] Beside these independent substitutory provisions there are still many references in the ABGB to the general compensation rules (§§ 46, 866, 874, 920, 921, 932, 1079, etc.). Generally in respect to references one always has to evaluate carefully whether the reference was in whole, conditional – or based on a legal consequence.[36]

Beside these statutory special liability regulations the case-law of the Austrian courts expands the liability *praetor legem* or sometimes even *contra legem* in particular to non-pecuniary damages; in my opinion, this goes too far.[37]

If – as in many instances – no special provisions come into consideration, the general rules of fault liability apply. Due to its great importance in practice a detailed scheme is offered below, in which the above-mentioned basic elements (damage/loss, unlawfulness, causation and fault) are discussed in detail. There are also possible defences of an opposing party (such as contractual exclusion of liability, joint fault and prescription) taken into account.

Similar to cumulative conditions ('and') does one need to proceed with alternative elements of a tort. Only one 'or' linked element needs to be present in order to trigger a duty to compensate.

Caution should be exercised when adopting (real) alternative conditions of liability: Thus it does not apply that for the fault requirement either slight or gross negligence has to be present. In the case of slight negligence only the positive damage has to be compensated. However, with gross negligence also the loss of profit needs to be compensated (§§ 1331 ff.).The legal consequences are different so that – certainly not always – a clear decision has to be taken. The question can only stay open if there is only positive damage. A real alternative relation exists between gross negligence and intention. However, even here something else can apply: According to § 1331 the qualified intention also requires the compensation of the value of the special preference (*'Affektionsinteresse'*).

33. *Reischauer* in Rummel (ed.), ABGB$^3$ § 1330 rc 6e.
34. For further information on the justification see *Reischauer* in Rummel (ed.), ABGB$^3$ § 1330 rc 7a ff.
35. For § 1325 and § 1327 compare *Reischauer* in Rummel (ed.), ABGB$^3$.
36. Compare *Larenz/Canaris*, Methodenlehre der Rechtswissenschaft$^4$ (2008) 81 f.
37. For further information see *Kisslinger*, Dogmatik des Schmerzengeldrechts in Kerschner (ed.), Schmerzengeld – Kommentar und Judikatur (2013) 8 ff.

*Figure 6.2 Scheme for Fault Liability*

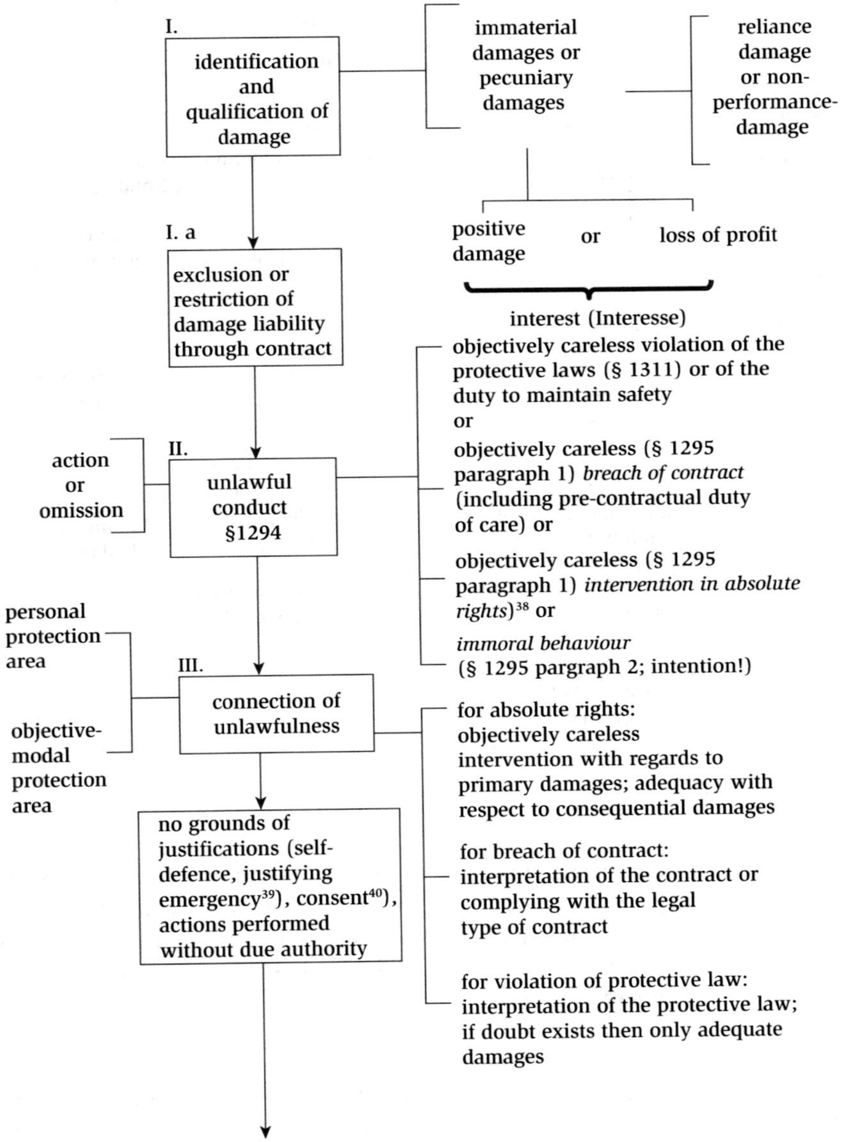


38. In some cases an intervention in (mere) property may be unlawful; more information see below.
39. Note § 1306a, also in terms of which a person who acts in case of emergency can be liable.
40. For further information see *Resch*, Die Einwilligung des Geschädigten (1997).

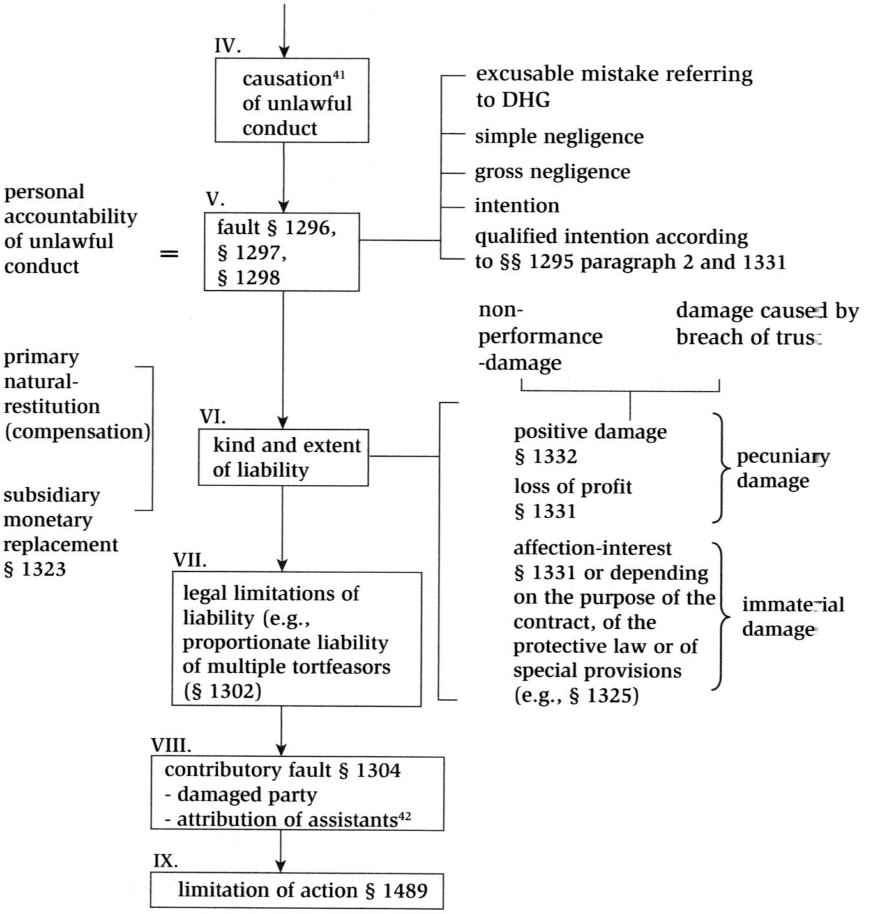


In addition to this scheme some problem areas have to be addressed, which in practice continuously lead to great difficulties. They concern the liability due to violation of the protective law, breach of the legal duties to maintain safety, breach of contract, contract with protective effect in favour of third parties, vicarious liability and the liability for mere pecuniary damage.

---

41. Often adequacy is also examined within the scope of the causation; but because someone can also be liable for inadequate damage and although the protective purpose of the violated provision determines this, adequacy properly needs to be examined in light of the connection of unlawfulness; in relation to adequacy and purpose of the provision *P. Bydlinski*; Schadenersatzrechtliche Überlegungen anlässlich eines Verkehrsunfalls, ZVR 1984, 197 ff.; *Karollus*, Schutzgesetzverletzung 381; compare also OGH 7 Ob 60/68v, ecolex 1998, 765.
42. See *Dullinger*, Mitverschulden von Gehilfen, JBl 1990, 20 ff. and 91 ff., *Kletečka*, Mitverschulden durch Gehilfenverhalten (1991); *F. Bydlinski*, Gehilfenmitverschulden beim Arbeitgeber und betriebliche Hierarchie, FS Tomandl (1998) 45 ff; rightly restrictive OGH 4.3.2013, 8 Ob 9/13a referring to *Sagerer*.

## §6.02 LIABILITY DUE TO THE VIOLATION OF PROTECTIVE LAW

If statutory behavioural provisions (e.g., *Straßenverkehrsordnung* (StVO; Road Traffic Act), authorisation obligations in terms of *Gewerbeordnung* (GewO; Trade Regulation Act) or Wasserrechtsgesetz (WRG; Water Act)) are violated a number of legal liability features are represented by judicature and doctrine.[43] The injured party is favoured here in that he only has to prove, first, that the wrongdoer has caused the damage by his (whole) conduct ('natural' causation) and second, has (objectively) violated a protective law .

Due to a lack of an objective and subjective breach of the obligation to exercise care a wrongdoer has to exonerate himself (§§ 1298, 1297). He also carries the burden of proof with regard to the defence of lawful alternative behaviour (*'Rechtmäßiges Alternativverhalten'*). If he cannot prove with the utmost probability that the damage would have been the same (at most to a lesser extent) when acting lawfully, he will be liable according to judicature and parts of the doctrine. An increase of risk (without proving the causation of the breach of duty) leads to the attribution of damage.[44] There are considerable doubts in the shift of the burden of proof in § 1298 as well in – at least a general – risk-increase liability (liability due to merely possible causation in non-excludable increase in risk!).[45] Only with regard to the defence of the lawful alternative behaviour as a justification will one agree with the case law.

## §6.03 LEGAL DUTIES TO MAINTAIN SAFETY

For long time does judicature acknowledge unwritten rules of conduct, the so-called legal duties to maintain safety (*'Verkehrssicherungspflichten'*), which require an active behaviour. It concerns special tort-based duties. Judicature has developed an extensive catalogue of 'case groups' of legal duties to maintain safety. The point of departure for the recognition of legal duties to maintain safety was the liability for public traffic area. Today's jurisprudence by far no longer limits this to streets and ways anymore.[46]

A person, who creates danger, is obliged to avert such cause of danger. He has to make sure by all means, that no one gets harmed.[47]

It depends on the individual case to what extent the legal duties to maintain safety exist. The OGH emphasises, that these must not be over-stressed. The criterion is that the measure must be reasonable.[48]

---

43. Compare comprehensively *Karollus*, Funktion und Dogmatik der Schutzgesetzverletzung (1992); OGH ZVR 1997/412.
44. For the risk-increase theory adopted by criminal law see *Karollus*, Schutzgesetzverletzung 399 ff.; *Rebhahn*, Staatshaftung wegen mangelnder Gefahrenabwehr (1997) 630 ff., who wants to differentiate with respect to the purpose of the provision; from case law OGH 2 Ob 83/95, JUS extra OGH-Z 2058; 2 Ob 41/94, ÖAMTC-LSK 1997/1 = ZVR 1997/105.
45. Compare *Koziol*, Haftpflichtrecht[3] I rc 8/66 f., 16/39.
46. *Harrer*, Schadenersatzrecht 21 with further references.
47. Compare *Karner* in KBB[3] § 1294 rc 6.
48. *Kodek* in Kletečka/Schauer (eds.), ABGB-ON 1.01 § 1294 rc 41.

## §6.04 LIABILITY DUE TO BREACH OF CONTRACT

Liability for a breach of contract (*ex contractu*) usually takes precedence over tortious liability. Therefore, the principally dispositive liability rules can (observe § 6 *Konsumentenschutzgesetz* (KSchG); § 879) be contractually modified (exclusion of liability = contractually agreed exemption of liability; limitation of liability;[49] guarantee). If a contract contains no special liability provisions, the liability *ex contractu* from special arrangements independently provides the wronged party with very significant advantages. First, the breaching party will generally be liable depending on the purpose of the contract or the contract interests for mere pecuniary loss[50] as well as for primary damage. At least with the contractual obligations which require the debtor to perform, the shift of the *burden of proof* applies *in terms of* § *1298*. The injured contracting party only has to prove that the damage has originated from the breach of contract (failure to perform[51]). The breaching party can exonerate itself with the fact that (a) the fulfilment of the contract would also not have been possible for an objectively reasonable debtor[52] or that (b) he could not prevent the damage although he was complying with all the care possible to him (fault in the narrow sense; § 1297). Furthermore, the strict vicarious liability in terms of § 1313a applies for breach of contract.

All these 'privileges' (liability for mere pecuniary damage; shift of the burden of proof in terms of § 1298; vicarious liability in terms of § 1313a are principally also applicable in the pre-contractual phase (*culpa in contrahendo*).

Finally, a contract can also provide for protective duties in favour of third parties (contract with protective effect in favour of third parties).[53]

The standard of care in § 1299 involves the knowledge and skills an expert has to have in his special field. An expert (specialist) according to § 1299 cannot exonerate himself due to a lack of subjective experience and knowledge. Depending on the circumstances, where knowledge and skills are not the main factor (e.g., reduced consciousness), a discharge of liability is possible.[54]

Only in the contractual and pre-contractual area a differentiation between damage resulting from non-fulfilment and damage resulting from reliance on a

---

49. Compare point I.a of the scheme.
50. Compare below to the connection of unlawfulness in case of breach of contract; see OGH 1 Ob 587/84, JBl 1986, 98, 101 and 103 with analyses *Koziol*.
51. See *Reischauer*, Der Entlastungsbeweis des Schuldners (§ 1298 ABGB) (1975), passim; *same one*, Neuere Rechtsprechung und Lehre zu § 1298 ABGB, JBl 1998, 473 ff. and 560 ff.; *Jabornegg*, Zurückbehaltungsrecht und Einrede des nicht erfüllten Vertrages (1982) 81 fn 93; *Spielbüchler*, Arbeitsrecht I[4] (1998) 208; *Kerschner*, Dienstnehmerhaftpflichtgesetz[2] (2004) § 2 rc 24; OGH 8 Ob 700/89, JBl 1990, 723. In this case the following have strongly adopted this doctrine *F. Bydlinski*, Zur Haftung der Dienstleistungsberufe in Österreich und nach dem EG-Richtlinienvorschlag, JBl 1992, 341 ff. (348) and *Welser*, Schadenersatz statt Gewährleistung (1994) 63 ff.
52. Referring to the also in Austria dominating '*Verhaltensunrechtslehre*' a harmful act is only unlawful, if it was objectively contrary to the duty of care; compare thereto the scheme above. § 1298 also requires a shifting of the burden of proof; see *Reischauer*, Entlastungsbeweis 116 ff.; as well as *Koziol*, Haftpflichtrecht[3] I rc 16/28.
53. For further information see below.
54. *Reischauer* in Rummel (ed.), ABGB[3] § 1299 rc 1 ff.

declaration becomes significant. Someone who fails to meet an effectively created contractual obligation has to compensate the creditors for the damage caused by the failure to fulfil the obligation (non-fulfilment damage or 'positive contract interest'). If someone has acted in reliance on the validity of the contract but a valid contract never came into existence then the wrongdoer, who intentionally created the false trust in the contract, has to compensate the wronged party for the damage caused by the breach of trust ('negative contract interest'; e.g., liability *falsus procurator* according to § 1019[55]); *culpa in contrahendo* (§§ 874, 878).

The distinction between damage resulting from reliance on declaration and non-fulfilment damage is often confused with that between positive damage and loss of profit. These questions strictly need to be separated from each other: Whether only the positive damage or also the loss of profit has to be compensated, depends in civil law solely on the degree of fault (§ 1331[56]). This separation is valid in general, hence, both in the tortious area as well as for liability due to breach of (pre-) contractual obligations. Someone who has acted slightly negligent is only obliged within the scope of the liability for breach of trust to compensate the positive damage.

## §6.05 CONTRACT WITH PROTECTIVE EFFECT IN FAVOUR OF THIRD PARTIES

A contract – as mentioned above – can establish protective duties in favour of third parties. Presently, this inclusion of third parties in the protective purpose of a contract has acquired great practical importance (e.g., violation of protective duties and duties of care towards third parties). Dogmatically this institute can only be established in accordance with the (supplementary) *interpretation of contract*: It determines the involvement of third parties in the contractual structure (principally, no third party involvement in for example an employment contract), the assessment of unlawful conduct (duty of care) directed at the third parties and the extent of the obligation to compensate. In order for the third party to fall within the scope of the protection there has to be according to settled case law a special proximity to the contractual performance. This proximity is generally present according to case law if the contact of the third party with the main performance was foreseeable at the time of concluding the contract and (a) an advantage through transfer of the main performance by the contracting party was recognisable or (b) the contracting party has a visible personal

55. For further information see *Perner* in Kletečka/Schauer (eds.), ABGB-ON (2010) to § 1019 with further references.
56. This structured damage concept should be abandoned in a possible compensation reform according to the prevailing view; compare thereto the suggestions for a reform in Griss/Kathrein/Koziol (eds.), Entwurf eines neuen österreichischen Schadenersatzrechts (2006) and in Reischauer/Spielbüchler/Welser (eds.), Reform des Schadenersatzrechts Band III – Vorschläge eines Arbeitskreises (2008) 29; in company law the loss of profit also needs to be compensated in terms of § 349 UGB; compare *Kerschner* in Jabornegg/Artmann (eds.), Kommentar zum UGB Bd I$^2$ to § 349.

interest in the main performance or (c) the contracting party has a legal duty of care towards the third party.[57]

According to the prevailing view, the third party who is covered by the protective purpose of the contract benefits from both the shift of the burden of proof in § 1298 and the wide vicarious liability of § 1313a. Depending on the purpose of the protective duties pure economic loss should also be compensated under certain circumstances.[58]

## §6.06 VICARIOUS LIABILITY

Standard cases in practice are those where the defendants have not acted in a harming way but are responsible for the acts of the assistants. Such situations occur very frequently in a division of labour economy. The assistant's accountability for his tortious conduct has to be determined. Special questions arise with regard to juristic persons, because in addition to the vicarious liability (§§ 1313a, in 1315) they are absolutely liable for their organs and certain executive employees (§ 337; 'representative's liability'[59]).

*Figure 6.3*

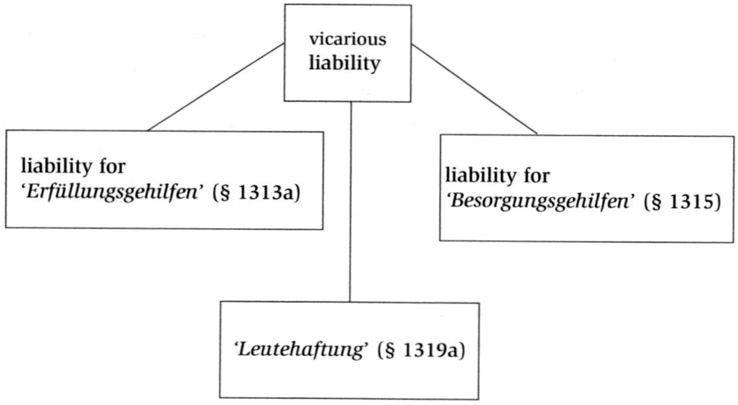


It will be far more advantageous for an injured party to rely on § 1313a because in this case the assistant's fault principally leads to the liability of the principal.

57. *Karner* in KBB³ § 1295 rc 19 with further references.
58. Compare *Koziol*, Grundfragen des Schadenersatzrechts (2010) rc 4/13 with further references: If pure pecuniary damage is always compensated in these cases, then a danger of a strong expansion of liability would be given.
59. For a natural person something similar must apply; see also *Reischauer* in Rummel (ed.), ABGB³ § 1315 rc 26 with further references.

## §6.07 REQUIREMENTS FOR LIABILITY OF THE *'ERFÜLLUNGSGEHILFEN'*

(1) *Special obligation* between *the injured party and the principal*. Such a special obligation exists especially not only where there are contractual duties, but also in the pre-contractual area and where there are contractual protective duties in favour of third parties. Statutory special obligations (such as the statutory obligation between finder and owner; fulfilment of an already existing compensation or enrichment claim) are also considered.

(2) At least (objectively careless) damage by the assistant *with the fulfilment* of the special obligation (not only occasionally, in the course of the fulfilment).

*Figure 6.4*

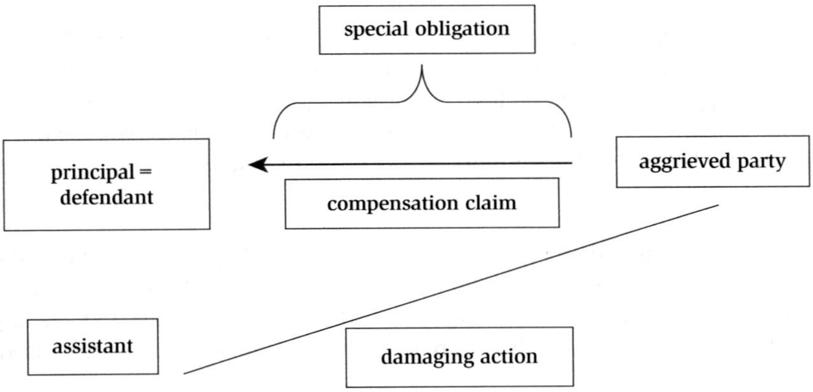


Outside of special obligations, essentially, in the tortious area, a principal currently is liable for his '*Besorgungsgehilfen*' only under the strict requirements of § 1315 which are hardly fulfilled.[60] A '*Besorgungsgehilfe*' must either be (habitually) *incompetent* or *dangerous*. Moreover, the principal must be aware of the dangerous characteristics of the assistant, which according to the general rules on the burden of proof has to be proved by the harmed party. In exceptional circumstances a vicarious liability exceeding the vicarious liability of § 1315 can be set out in the tortious area. (Compare § 19 paragraph 2 EKHG (Railway and Motor Vehicle Liability Act) that states a 'people liability' ('*Leutehaftung*')).[61]

60. For the legal-political proposal of an extended '*Besorgungsgehilfenhaftung*' compare Reischauer/Spielbüchler/Welser (eds.), Reform des Schadenersatzrechts Band III – Vorschläge eines Arbeitskreises (2008) 45 ff.
61. For further examples see *Reischauer* in Rummel (ed.), ABGB[3] § 1313 rc 2 and 3.

If the principal is liable to a third party, then he has a claim against his assistant (§ 1313). If the assistant is an employee of the principal, then the limitations of liability as set out in § 2 *Dienstnehmerhaftpflichtgesetz* (DHG; Employee Liability Act) need to be considered.[62]

## §6.08 VICARIOUS LIABILITY OF THE JURISTIC PERSON

First, a juristic person (e.g., association, company, territorial authority) is liable for the damage caused by its statutory organs, as far as they act in their capacity as an organ. This corresponds to a natural person's liability due to own fault. As in the case of a natural person, § 1313a or 1315 are applicable for unlawful conduct of an assistant. According to the prevailing view[63] a juristic person is liable beyond the tortious area of § 1315 for 'executive employees' ('representatives') with independent competences, which is based on an analogy to § 337 ('*Machthaber*').

## §6.09 LIABILITY FOR PURE PECUNIARY LOSS

Often the liability for pure pecuniary loss must be determined in practice. This occurs when there is a reduction of the assets without the violation of an absolutely protected legal right (e.g., right to property, lien, physical integrity, etc.). Someone misses out on a business opportunity or profit; liabilities or expenses occur. It is known that the assets as such do not fall within the absolute legally protected rights.

Example:

Excavation works cause damage to the neighbouring building. The tenant of a shop in this building suffers a loss due to the necessary repair work (pure pecuniary loss). Different scenario: As a result of the collapsed cellar the stored goods of the tenant are damaged. He loses the profit of the sale of the goods (pecuniary loss due to consequential loss).

The following overview shows in which circumstances a compensation for pecuniary loss needs to be considered:

62. See *Kerschner*, Dienstnehmerhaftpflichtgesetz[2] § 4 DHG rc 21 ff; *Oberhofer* in Schwimann (ed.), ABGB[3] § 4 DHG especially rc 4.
63. Compare *Koziol*, Haftpflichtrecht[2] II 376 ff with further references; but also compare *F. Bydlinski*, Die Verantwortung juristischer Personen in der Gesellschaft, in Götz/Seifert (eds.), Verantwortung in Wirtschaft und Gesellschaft (2000) 21 ff. and *Apathy*, Deliktshaftung und Gesellschaft bürgerlichen Rechts, in FS Krejci (2001) I 427 ff.

**compensation for pure pecuniary loss**

1. *for breach of contract* if a connection of unlawfulness is present
2. *for breach of a remedial statute* if the protective purpose also concerns property
3. *violation of moral principles*
4. *for tortious obligations* for the protection of mere pecuniary property (e.g. § 875 read with § 874[64])
5. *for prior damage*[65] or *consequential damage* when endangering or violating an absolute right within the scope of adequacy

## §6.10 LIABILITY OF PUBLIC AUTHORITIES AND EXECUTIVE ORGANS[66]

The cases where the '*Organwalter*' of the administration or the judiciary acting in his capacity as an organ causes harm to a private person are rising and are gaining more importance.[67] In such cases the special liability laws on public liability and liability for executive organs need to be determined. No complete system can be offered here. Only the basics can be pointed out.

The *Amtshaftungsgesetz* (AHG; Liability of Public Bodies Act) is only applicable if an organ has caused harm in the execution of the laws, thus when exercising sovereign rights. If the act occurs within the scope of the private sector administration, the liability rules of the ABGB are applicable. In this context numerous demarcation problems exist.[68]

64. Applicable *Reischauer* in Rummel (ed.), ABGB[3] § 1294 rc 16; *Karollus*, Schutzgesetzverletzung 49 ff. The general facts of § 1295 paragraph 1 also includes such duties for the protection of the property.
65. Compare *Kerschner*, RdU 1998, 147.
66. State liability for breach of the Community law in the EU (in particular due to lack of implementation of EU directives) compare e.g., *Rebhahn*, Staatshaftung wegen mangelnder Gefahrenabwehr (1997) 64 ff.; *Schermaier*, Der Gemeinschaftsrechtliche Staatshaftungsanspruch (1999); *Schwarzenegger*, Staatshaftung (2001); recently *Wagner*, note to EuGH 14.3.2013, C-420-11, *Jutta Leth versus the Republic of Austria, the country Lower Austria*, RdU 2013, 120 ff.
67. Compare for example, OGH JBl 1992, 253.
68. Compare e.g., *Schragel*, Kommentar zum Amtshaftungsgesetz[3] (2003) § 1 rc 72 ff.

If the AHG is applicable, then according to the recent legal position the liability of both the legal entity for which the organ acted and the legal entity to which the organ is organisationally assigned to are considered (§ 1 paragraph 3 AHG). The organ who acted unlawfully cannot be personally held liable to compensate the damaged party. If a legal entity is liable, recourse against the organ administrator (*'Organwalter'*) is possible under certain circumstances (§§ 3 ff. AHG).

The *Organhaftpflichtgesetz* (OrgHG; Public Officers Liability Act) applies if an organ administrator has damaged the legal entity even though acting in accordance with the laws (even if only slight negligence); for possible mitigation of damages see the reference in § 3 OrgHG of § 2 DHG (Employee Liability Act).

## §6.11 OUTLOOK

For some time work is being done towards a reform of the Austrian tort law. A draft of a working group[69] (the so-called*'Arbeitsgruppe'*) wants a comprehensive reform at the top and the various parts (*'Haupt und Glieder'*) according to a flexible system (key disadvantage: greatest legal uncertainty). Alternatively to that, another working group[70] (the so-called *'Arbeitskreis'*) only wants to amend certain areas, such as the vicarious liability and the strict liability. The systematic attempts, on the one hand a flexible system (draft of the *'Arbeitsgruppe'*) and on the other hand principally solid facts of the matter (draft of the *'Arbeitskreis'*) are hardly compatible with each other.[71]

## SELECTED BIBLIOGRAPHY

Walter Wilburg, Die Elemente des Schadensrechts (1941).
*Koziol,* Umfassende Gefährdungshaftung durch Analogie? FS Wilburg (1975) 173 ff.
*Reischauer,* Der Entlastungsbeweis des Schuldners (§ 1298 ABGB) (1975).
Schilcher, Theorie der sozialen Schadensverteilung (1977).
*Jabornegg,* Zurückbehaltungsrecht und Einrede des nicht erfüllten Vertrages (1982).
*Koziol,* Österreichisches Haftpflichtrecht II2 (1984).
*Dullinger,* Mitverschulden von Gehilfen, JBl 1990, 20.
*Kletečka,* Mitverschulden durch Gehilfenverhalten (1991).
*Karollus,* Funktion und Dogmatik der Haftung aus Schutzgesetzverletzung (1992).
*Welser,* Schadenersatz statt Gewährleistung (1994).
Koziol, Österreichisches Haftpflichtrecht I3 (1997).
*Rebhahn,* Staatshaftung wegen mangelnder Gefahrenabwehr (1997).
*Resch,* Die Einwilligung des Geschädigten (1997).
*Wagner,* Die Betriebsanlage im zivilen Nachbarrecht (1997).

69. See Griss/Kathrein/Koziol (eds.), Entwurf eines neuen österreichischen Schadenersatzrechts (2006).
70. Compare Reischauer/Spielbüchler/Welser (eds.), Reform des Schadenersatzrechts II: Vorschläge eines Arbeitskreises (2007).
71. A fundamental discussion with reform efforts can be found at *Reischauer* in Rummel (ed.), ABGB[3] ahead of §§ 1293 ff rc 1 ff. (2007).

*Harrer,* Schadenersatzrecht (1999).
*Schragel,* Kommentar zum Amtshaftungsgesetz[3] (2003).
*Kerschner,* Dienstnehmerhaftpflichtgesetz[2] (2004).
*Griss/Kathrein/Koziol* (eds.), Entwurf eines neuen österreichischen Schadenersatzrechts (2006).
*Reischauer/Spielbüchler/Welser* (eds.), Reform des Schadenersatzrechts III: Vorschläge eines Arbeitskreises (2008).
*Apathy/Riedler,* Bürgerliches Recht III, Schuldrecht Besonderer Teil[4] (2010).
*Koziol,* Grundfragen des Schadenersatzrechts (2010).
*Riedler,* Zivilrecht IV Schuldrecht Besonderer Teil - Gesetzliche Schuldverhältnisse[3] (2010).
*Hinteregger/Kerschner* (eds.), Kommentar zum Bundes-Umwelthaftungsgesetz (2011).
*Kerschner* (ed.), Schmerzengeld - Kommentar und Judikatur (2013).
*Danzl/Gutiérrez-Lobos/Müller,* Das Schmerzengeld in medizinischer und juristischer Sicht[10] (2014).
*Koziol/Apathy/Koch,* Österreichisches Haftpflichtrecht III[3] (2014).
*Khakzadeh-Leiler/Schmid/Weber* (eds.), Interessenabwägung und Abwägungsentscheidungen (2014).
*Perner/Spitzer/Kodek,* Bürgerliches Recht[4] (2014).

CHAPTER 7

# Law of Property

*Bernhard A. Koch & Kristin Nemeth**

## §7.01 INTRODUCTION

### [A] Terminology and Sources

From the viewpoint of the core codification of private law in Austria, the General Civil Code (*Allgemeines Bürgerliches Gesetzbuch,* ABGB), it is not easy to draw a clear picture of Austrian property law. To begin with, the wording as it stands, dating back to 1811, speaks of 'the law relating to things' in the heading of the second (of three) parts of the ABGB. This is misleading insofar as this part deals with both rights in rem in the modern meaning ('*Von den dinglichen Sachenrechten*', as the first subdivision of that part is entitled, §§ 309-858 ABGB) as well as with the law of obligations in the second subdivision, entitled '*Von den persönlichen Sachenrechten*' (literally meaning 'Of personal rights in things', §§ 858-1341 ABGB). This is due to the very wide definition of 'things' in § 285 ABGB, embracing 'everything that is distinct from the person and serves the use of humans'. This definition is, however, not even used consistently throughout the ABGB itself, but is rather meant to define assets in a very broad sense, including obligations and other rights as well.

Apart from this problem of categorisation, one should note from the outset that the rules on property law contained in the ABGB are incomplete, as important concepts such as retention of title (*Eigentumsvorbehalt*) and transfer of ownership for security reasons (*Sicherungsübereignung*) are not codified at all.[1] Outside of the ABGB, important rules governing property law are contained in special statutes such as the

* Institut für Zivilrecht, Leopold-Franzens-Universität Innsbruck.
1. See *infra* §7.06[A].

*Baurechtsgesetz* 1912 (Law on Construction Rights, BauRG)[2] or the *Wohnungseigentumsgesetz* 2002 (Law on Apartment Ownership 2002, WEG).[3]

In the following we will use the term 'rights in rem' (*dingliche Rechte*) to address those variations of object-related rights that are deemed to be universally enforceable under Austrian property law, in theory against the world at large. There is only a closed list of such rights, as will be explained below.[4] The most important type is of course ownership (*Eigentum*) as the most powerful right in rem.

As far as the object of such rights is concerned, we will use the term 'thing' (*Sache*) failing better alternatives. The wide definition of 'thing' contained in § 285 ABGB mentioned earlier comprises tangibles as well as intangibles (§ 292 ABGB), movables as well as immovables (§ 293 ABGB). Animals are expressly excluded from the definition of 'things' by § 285a ABGB, however, all property law rules apply nonetheless in the absence of (very few) special provisions.

Accessories (appurtenances, *Zubehör*, §§ 294 ff. ABGB)[5] normally share the fate of the thing they belong to or are dedicated to as long as they are not detached from it.

According to the principle of *superficies solo cedit*[6] (§§ 295 ff. ABGB) plants, but also constructions and accessories thereto share the legal fate of the land on which they grow or stand. This is different in the case of a so-called *Superädifikat* (§§ 297, 435 ABGB): Such a construction is – at least in theory – not supposed to remain on the land forever[7] and for that reason is not perceived as an integral part of that land. It can therefore have an owner different from the owner of the land. Rights related to a *Superädifikat* are thus not registered in the land register, but in a special collection of deeds.[8] A similar legal creation is the *Baurecht* (construction right) governed by the already mentioned *Baurechtsgesetz* (BauRG): A land owner can grant a right in rem to build on his land to another for a minimum of ten up to a maximum of 100 years.[9] The construction right itself is legally defined as immovable, once exercised, the structure erected is perceived as an accessory to that right (§ 6 BauRG).

### [B] Land Register (*Grundbuch*)

Before dealing with property law in general and the law relating to immovables in particular, it is important to take note of the Austrian land registry system. Starting at

2. See *infra* at fn. 9.
3. See *infra* §7.04[A][4].
4. See *infra* §7.02[B].
5. The ABGB uses the term *Zugehör* (note the letter G instead of B) as the generic term for accessories (*Zubehör*) and components (*Bestandteile*) combined.
6. Whatever is connected to land belongs thereto. A literal translation would be rather 'what is on the surface yields to the land'.
7. Typically, this would at least be claimed in the contract between the land owner and the developer, whereas in practice the construction may be as massive as a shopping centre.
8. Note, however, that the creation of a *Superädifikat* does not depend on the formal deposit of the deed which is necessary for a transfer of the right, though.
9. Once the designated period is expired, the construction becomes part of the land on which it was built and therefore belongs from then on to the land owner.

the end of the nineteenth century, land in Austria was systematically registered. Initially contained in actual books, which brought about the terminology that is still being used today (starting with the term *Grundbuch* or 'book of land' for the register and *Blatt* or 'sheet' for the various parts of each entry), the system was converted into an electronic database already in the 1980s, with several updates and amendments ever since, in the meantime allowing online access for everyone,[10] albeit not free from costs. The system is still administered by the district courts for land in their respective area of jurisdiction, even though the database is of course nationwide. Applications are nowadays also filed electronically, even though it is still possible to address the court in person.

Every single lot of land in Austria is registered. While all land is also filed with the database of the surveyor's office (*Bundeseich- und Vermessungsamt*), which attributes numbers to each parcel according to geographic borderlines (*Grundstücksnummern*), the land register entries are legal units (*Einlagen*, numbered by the so-called *Einlagezahl*) and may therefore contain more than one such geographic lot, even if not adjacent. The two systems are connected, however, so that it is possible to look up the actual location of what is included in one *Einlage* of the land register in the *Digitale Katastralmappe* (digital cadastre)[11] of the surveyor's office.

With very few exceptions, all transactions relating to land have to be done via the land register, which is attributed 'public trust' (*öffentlicher Glaube*): Whatever is in the register is presumed to be rightful and correct, what is missing is presumed not to exist. Entries are ranked according to strict priority (*Prioritätsgrundsatz*) and cannot be made without the consent of the person(s) registered as current holder(s) of the relevant right(s), which is granted in a so-called *Aufsandungserklärung* (permission to make changes)[12] in order to allow any addition to or modification (including deletion) of current entries.

The land register is divided into various parts, the so-called *Hauptbuch* (main book) containing the actual entries, the directory of deleted entries, certain indices and the collection of deeds (*Urkundensammlung*), which contains copies or originals of all documents that necessarily support an application for entry into the land register. While the latter was also converted into a digital system in 2006, deeds supporting earlier entries still have to be accessed in the district court where the entry was filed. This may often be necessary in order to determine the exact scope of rights such as servitudes that can be tailored to the needs of the parties, which for practical reasons cannot be fully reflected in the land register entry itself.

10. A sample extract of the digital land register can be seen at <https://www.help.gv.at/Portal.Node/hlpd/public/content/60/Seite.600400.html>.
11. The DKM of the Tyrol can be accessed, for example, at <https://portal.tirol.gv.at/mapAccelWeb/ClientServlet?CMD=Init&TYPE=-1&PRODUCTID=15>.
12. While the actual contract serving as the title for an entry (such as a sales contract) need not be in writing, registration therefore requires a certain formality: The *Aufsandungserklärung* has to be in writing and must be certified, e.g., by a notary.

## §7.02 IMPORTANT PRINCIPLES OF AUSTRIAN PROPERTY LAW

### [A] Absolute Rights (*Absolute Rechte*)

Rights in rem are absolute, i.e., can be enforced against everybody.[13] The holder of a right in rem has direct and immediate power over the object it concerns and can exclude everybody else from using it or interfering with it as far as his right goes. The most far-reaching absolute right is ownership, which is only limited by competing rights of the same or higher rank.[14] This becomes particularly clear in enforcement and insolvency proceedings where the holder of a right in rem to an object of the debtor can isolate it from debtor's remaining assets subjected to such proceedings.[15]

### [B] Numerus Clausus (*Typenbeschränkung, Typenzwang*)

As opposed to e.g., French law Austrian property law offers only a limited range of rights in rem to choose from. They are all statutorily defined.

The following rights in rem are provided for by the Austrian Civil Code: ownership (*Eigentum*),[16] pledge (*Pfandrecht*),[17] servitude (*Dienstbarkeit*)[18] and realty charge (*Reallast*).[19] Other rights in rem are defined and governed by separate acts, such as the afore-mentioned right to erect a building on the land of another (*Baurecht*),[20] mining rights (*Bergwerksberechtigung*)[21] and a special kind of co-ownership of apartments (*Wohnungseigentum*).[22]

The contents of these rights in rem are generally not subject to party autonomy either. This principle is, however, not exercised as rigorously in the law of servitudes, which allows parties to freely tailor such rights according to their needs.

---

13. In the law of obligations, however, a right can only be enforced against the obligor (cf. § 307 ABGB).
14. This is obvious in the case of two adjacent pieces of land: each owner has the right to use his lot only insofar as such use does not impede the enjoyment of the neighbouring land (see *infra* §7.04[D][2]). While the owner of a knife in general has the right to use that knife in any way he wants, he thereby must not hurt or endanger somebody else, as the fundamental right to physical integrity ranks of course higher than the right in rem. There may be further limitations imposed by public law in the general interest. Needless to say, the owner can also limit his own right e.g., by transferring the right to use his property, either contractually with e.g., a lease contract or by creating a limited right in rem such as a servitude (see infra §7.05).
15. In insolvency proceedings, the owner has an *Aussonderungsrecht* according to § 44 *Insolvenzordnung* (IO, Law on Insolvency), the holder of a security right in rem has an *Absonderungsrecht* (§ 48 IO; cf. *infra* fn. 94). In enforcement proceedings, beneficiaries of rights in rem will bring an *Exszindierungsklage* according to § 37 Law on Enforcement (*Exekutionsordnung*, EO) opposing the execution of a judgment with respect to the attached property.
16. §§ 353 ff. ABGB; *infra* §7.04.
17. §§ 447 ff. ABGB; *infra* §7.06.
18. §§ 472 ff. ABGB; *infra* §7.04[D][2].
19. § 530 ABGB; *infra* §7.05[B][3].
20. See *supra* §7.01[A] (at fn. 9).
21. §§ 22 ff., 40 *Mineralrohstoffgesetz* (Mineral Resources Act) 1999.
22. See *infra* §7.04[A][4].

The reason behind this rather strict concept is legal certainty, as these limited possibilities clearly define the object when rights in rem are transferred, which favours their marketability.

The concept of *Typenzwang* is also reflected in international property law as the relevant Austrian conflicts rule (§ 31 IPRG) is understood not to allow the parties to choose the applicable law in regard to rights in rem.

### [C] Principle of Speciality (*Spezialität*)

Rights in rem can only exist in relation to a concrete thing or object. It is not possible to target all assets of a company or an individual in one single act. Neither can a generic product be transferred before it is clearly identified in relation to the obligation to be performed. Austrian property law therefore does not recognise a floating charge, as a pledge can only relate to a specified object.[23]

The principle is, however, overridden by the concept of symbolic transfer (§ 427 ABGB): If a warehouse full of items is to be transferred, one need not necessarily hand over each item piece by piece, giving away the keys to the warehouse instead may already be sufficient, but only if the transferee thereby acquires immediate and exclusive power over the enclosed contents.[24]

### [D] Principle of Causality (*Kausalitätsprinzip*)

In § 380 ABGB Austrian law sets forth the Roman principle of *titulus* and *modus*. Every right in rem is based on a title, i.e., it needs a cause recognised by law. This might be a contract, a court order or judgment or a specific statutory provision (*Titel, causa*).[25] In order for the right in rem to come into existence or to be transferred, in addition to the title the object of the right in rem needs to be transferred to the beneficiary in a suitable manner (*Modus*), which is now commonly perceived to be a twofold step: First the parties concerned have to agree that the right in rem shall actually move from one to the other (*dingliches Verfügungsgeschäft*) – which can of course also take place together with the title contract, if applicable – and second the transfer has to be exercised physically in one of the modes of transfer set out in the relevant statutory provisions. None of the requirements alone but only their interplay suffices to create or to transfer a right in rem.[26]

Another principle that needs to be explained in this regard is the – again Roman – principle that in general nobody can transfer more rights than he actually has (*nemo plus iuris ad alium transferre potest quam ipse habet*).[27] An exception exists in regard to the concept of bona fide acquisition.[28]

23. See also *infra* at fn. 101.
24. See also *infra* §7.03[D].
25. In the case of original acquisition of ownership the cause would be the law itself.
26. See §7.03[D] below regarding modes of transfer.
27. § 442 ABGB.
28. See *infra* §7.04[B][3].

### [E] Publicity (*Publizität*)

The principle of publicity further promotes legal certainty the Austrian rules of property law strive for. Especially in the law of security rights this principle is regarded as being essential. The Austrian approach requires the existence as well as the transfer of rights in rem to be visible for the public so that such rights can be honoured. In the law of movables publicity is effectuated by possession, whereas the law of immovables largely relies on registration.[29]

## §7.03 POSSESSION (*BESITZ*)

Even though it triggers legal consequences, possession is deemed to be a mere fact and not a right, though not even the terminology of the ABGB strictly adheres to this distinction.[30] Unlike ownership, which is a statutorily defined all-encompassing absolute right, possession is a more flexible concept and can be qualified in various ways.[31] The rules protecting possession focus on preserving the status quo peacefully; the better qualified possession is, the more protection is granted.[32]

### [A] Holder (*Inhaber*) versus Possessor (*Besitzer*)

A holder (*Inhaber*) is the mere (physical) keeper of a thing, whereas the possessor (*Besitzer*) in addition also has the intention to keep it (*Besitzwille, animus rem sibi habendi*), though irrespective of a right to possess. Therefore, also a thief is deemed a possessor.

### [B] Qualifications of Possession

Lawful possession (*rechtmäßiger Besitz*) means that the possessor has a valid title for possession (§ 316 ABGB); a thief is therefore an unlawful possessor. Someone is referred to as a bona fide possessor (*redlicher Besitzer*, § 326 ABGB) if he believes and for justifiable reasons may believe that he is the lawful possessor.[33] This concept is particularly important in cases where ownership is transferred by someone other than the actual owner. Authenticity of possession (*echter Besitz*, § 345 ABGB) is given if it

29. See *supra* §7.01[B] on the land register system.
30. § 308 ABGB lists possession expressly as one of the 'rights in rem', as does the heading of §§ 309 ff. ABGB, which contain the rules governing possession.
31. See *infra* §7.03[B].
32. This becomes particularly obvious with the *actio Publiciana*; see *infra* §7.03[F][2].
33. *Redlichkeit* is presumed (§ 328 ABGB), so it is for the opponent to prove that the possessor was not in good faith.

was obtained without the exercise of coercion, deceit or by *precarium*.[34] If all three qualifications are given, one speaks of 'legal possession' (*rechtlicher Besitz*).[35]

### [C] Types of Possession

One cannot only possess tangibles (whether movable or immovable), which is called *Sachbesitz*, but also intangibles, i.e., rights (referred to as *Rechtsbesitz*). A tenant is therefore regarded a possessor with standing to sue for protection – while he does not possess the apartment itself (since he does not perceive it as his own, so the *animus* is missing for *Sachbesitz*), he still possesses the right granted by the lease to live there, which as such is being protected. The landlord remains *Sachbesitzer*, even though the factual use of the apartment is exercised by the tenant on his behalf.

Not all rights, however, give rise to *Rechtsbesitz*, only those which allow continuing exercise (*dauernde Rechtsausübung*) of an object such as in the case of the aforementioned tenant, a borrower of a thing or a holder of a servitude. Parties to a sales contract, for example, are not regarded possessors of their rights to receive the price or the good as these rights cease by a single act of performance.

A further distinction can be made between sole possession (*Alleinbesitz*) and joint possession (*Mitbesitz*).

### [D] Modes of Obtaining Possession

Austrian law adheres to the Roman principle of acquiring possession *animo et corpore*. Thus the possessor to be must have the intention to acquire possession and actually gain custody. According to § 314 ABGB possession can be obtained originally (*unmittelbar, originär*) if the thing is in nobody's custody[36] or derivatively (*mittelbar, derivativ*) from a former possessor.

Generally, obtaining possession requires that the thing moves from hand to hand (§ 426 ABGB); however, this need not be taken literally, as it is sufficient that the new possessor gains actual and exclusive power over the thing. Further modes of transfer include symbolic transfer (§ 427 ABGB) and transfer by declaration (§ 428 ABGB). Symbolic transfer is only permissible if a transfer from hand to hand is physically impossible or at least uneconomical;[37] instead keys or papers evidencing the factual control may be handed over. A transfer by declaration, however, is normally sufficient and only regarded problematic when it comes to security rights.[38] It can take place in three forms, namely in cases where the thing is already in the custody of the future possessor (*traditio brevi manu*), in cases where the earlier possessor shall keep the

34. A form of loan for use, however, with no obligation of the lender who can request the thing back at any time.
35. This is *inter alia* required for acquiring a right by prescription (§ 1460 ABGB), which is why this qualified possession is also referred to as *Ersitzungsbesitz*.
36. For a bona fide acquisition see §7.04[B][3] below.
37. *Untunlichkeit*, which is seen rather strictly in doctrine and case law.
38. See §7.06[B][1] below.

thing as a mere holder (*constitutum possessorium*)[39] or in cases where the thing is in custody of a third party who shall from then on hold it for the possessor to be (*Besitzanweisung*).

### [E] Loss of Possession

The possession of a thing ends with its destruction or loss, by relinquishment (*Dereliktion*), or if somebody else obtains possession.

Possession relating to rights ends once the possessor waives the right, discontinues to exercise it or is hindered to exercise it by another and fails to contradict.

### [F] Protection of Possession

#### *[1] Summary Proceedings* (Besitzstörungsverfahren)

Austrian law allows the exercise of moderate self-help in cases where the state cannot grant adequate relief in due time (§§ 19, 344 ABGB). Apart from this very limited possibility to protect possession on one's own, the law provides for a special summary proceeding in order to reinstate the *status quo ante* quickly once possession was interfered with by another (§§ 454 ff. ZPO[40]). This fast-track procedure only focuses on who was in peaceful possession of the object in dispute before the interference,[41] irrespective of the right to hold it.[42] A complaint (*Besitzstörungsklage*) has to be brought within thirty days from the interference.[43] The complaint can be filed against a third person but also, for example, against a joint possessor who disregards the agreement of usage.[44] The complainant fails if the opponent acted with the possessor's consent or was authorised by a public authority.

#### *[2]* Actio Publiciana

Qualified possession may also be protected by the *actio Publiciana*. While the relevant provision (§ 372 ABGB) is under the heading 'ownership action based on the legally presumed ownership of the claimant', ownership as such is not necessarily at stake.[45]

39. Which is the problematic form in the law of securities as it contradicts the principle of publicity, see *infra* §7.06[B][1]0.
40. Code of Civil Procedure (*Zivilprozessordnung*).
41. The only aspect of concern is therefore the authenticity of possession (see *supra* §7.03[B]) within the last thirty days before the claim was filed.
42. The proceedings therefore end by court order instead of judgment.
43. In case of repeated disturbance the first event counts.
44. The case may also be filed between a *Sachbesitzer* and a *Rechtsbesitzer* (such as between a landlord and his tenant), if the one interferes with the factual position of the other (again irrespective of the rights granted by the lease, which have to be subject to a regular civil procedure). The tenant may therefore successfully file a claim against the landlord who without the tenant's consent entered the apartment.
45. For an owner who seeks return of his property, the *rei vindicatio* would be the first choice of action, but that requires full proof of ownership. See *infra* §7.04[D].

Instead, this action serves to protect the interests of a 'legal possessor' (*rechtlicher Besitzer*)[46] who was deprived of the object and now seeks its return. The claimant succeeds against anyone else whose possession is not equally well qualified, so the court needs to balance the two competing positions. In case of equal qualifications, the current holder of the object in dispute (i.e., the defendant) succeeds (§ 374 ABGB).

## §7.04 OWNERSHIP (*EIGENTUM*)

### [A] Types of Ownership

#### *[1] Ownership Defined*

The concept of ownership in Austrian property law always refers to the full right; i.e., the right to use a tangible thing and to exclude everybody else from the usage thereof (§ 354 ABGB). Rights can by definition not be subject to ownership but only give rise to the position of an obligee.[47]

The full right may be restricted by statute, e.g., in line with the preservation of buildings of historic interest, or by party autonomy, as the owner can of course consent to any use by (or abstention of use for the benefit of[48]) another.[49] These restrictive rights can result in relative or absolute rights; a lease contract which normally only unfolds legal consequences for the parties involved can also have an effect for third parties if registered in the *Grundbuch*.

#### *[2] Co-ownership* (Miteigentum)

Co-owners of a thing own a certain share (but not a physical part) of the property (*schlichtes Miteigentum*, §§ 825 ff. ABGB). They have the full power over their respective share, they can therefore dispose of it and exclude everybody else from it (§ 829 ABGB). Moreover, subject to a (tacit or explicit) agreement of all co-owners on how to share the use (*Benützungsvereinbarung*), they are entitled to full use of the whole thing. Unless otherwise agreed, profits made from and expenses incurred for the property are divided according to the respective quotas of the co-owners. The administration of the property is equally shared by all co-owners. While ordinary administrative measures require a single majority decision (calculated per quota, not

46. See *supra* §7.03[B] at fn. 35.
47. Being subject to the law of obligations (§§ 859 ff. ABGB); the only exception in this respect is the assignment for security, which is normally dealt with in property law because of its affinity to the law of securities in general.
48. Cf. *infra* §7.05.
49. Another such restriction may be a contractual prohibition of encumbering a thing and/or of transferring ownership (so-called *Belastungs- und Veräußerungsverbot*). It can be held against third parties only if it concerns immovables, if it is registered in the land register, and if the parties to the agreement were spouses, registered partners, parents and their children or the latters' spouses (§ 364c ABGB).

per capita), more important measures, such as major changes to the property, require unanimity.[50]

### *[3] Joint Ownership* (Gesamthandeigentum)

Unlike co-owners, joint owners cannot dispose of their shares without the consent of others. While the ABGB itself does not provide for joint ownership, the property of a commercial partnership is understood to be jointly held by all partners.

### *[4] Apartment Ownership* (Wohnungseigentum)

Co-ownership of apartment buildings was introduced in the 1970s due to socio-economic changes and has always been subject to a separate act; currently it is the *Wohnungseigentumsgesetz 2002* (Law on Apartment Ownership 2002, WEG). Despite a misleading nomenclature, apartment owners do not actually own the apartment as such or any other physical part of the building or of one of its floors. Instead, they own a certain share (the so-called *Mindestanteil*) in the land on which the house is built; unlike other (mere) co-ownership of land, however, the right to use a specific (set of) room(s)[51] is inseparably tied to that share. One such share can be jointly[52] owned by two, but not more individuals (§§ 5 paragraph 1, 13 WEG 2002). All co-owners of an apartment building together form a legal entity (*Wohnungseigentümergemeinschaft*, §§ 18 et seqq. WEG), though with limited legal capacity.

## [B] Modes of Acquiring Ownership

Ownership is either acquired derivatively from a former owner (*derivativer Eigentumserwerb*) or directly (originally, *originärer Eigentumserwerb*), e.g., by occupation bona fide acquisition or by acquisitive prescription.[53]

### *[1] Derivative Acquisition* (Derivativer Eigentumserwerb)

Derivative acquisition basically entails three prerequisites: a valid title, the right of the person transferring ownership to do so (§ 442 ABGB), and one of the modes of transfer stipulated by §§ 426 ff. ABGB as described earlier.[54] For immovables, the proper *Modus* is registration (§ 431 ABGB).

50. §§ 834 et seq. ABGB provide for a procedure in case such unanimity cannot be achieved.
51. These rooms need not necessarily form an apartment for residential purposes, also business or office spaces can be subject to apartment property within the meaning of the WEG 2002
52. Cf. *supra* §7.04[A][3].
53. Other types of original acquisition of ownership include the finding of a thing (subject to restrictions aiming at identifying the person who had lost it, §§ 388 ff. ABGB) or accretion (§§ 404 et seqq. ABGB).
54. *Supra* §7.03[D].

The title has to be suitable to transfer ownership: It is normally a contract, such as a sales contract, a loan, or a donation concluded with the – if applicable – necessary formalities; also a testamentary disposition is a possible title. Ownership cannot pass if the title is void. In some cases (such as mistake or duress) ownership can be lost retrospectively if the title is successfully challenged; this leads to an abolition *ex tunc*, which also has an effect on the right in rem.

### *[2]* ***Occupation*** **(Zueignung)**

Things which are owned by nobody, either because they were abandoned (*derelinquiert*) or have never had an owner, can be acquired by occupation (*Zueignung* or *Okkupation*, § 381 ABGB). Occupation is a form of original acquisition, with the law itself being the title and seizure the *Modus*. Despite the wording of § 382 ABGB occupation is not only open to Austrian citizens but to everybody. It can, however, be restricted by law in certain cases: hunting and fishing e.g., require a licence, the same counts for mineral resources unless they are *bergfrei*, i.e., can be taken by everyone.[55]

### *[3]* ***Bona Fide Acquisition*** **(Gutglaubenserwerb)**

Bona fide acquisition is also regarded a form of original acquisition. It follows a strict regime of prerequisites depending on whether the object is movable or immovable.

Bona fide acquisition of movables is regulated by § 367 ABGB as the central norm.[56] It is constructed as an exception to the principle *nemo plus iuris ad alium transferre potest quam ipse habet*[57] and tries to carefully weigh the interests of the previous and the new owner. It requires a valid title designed for transferring ownership such as a sales contract or a barter agreement; a donation is no valid title in this respect since § 367 ABGB requires a synallagmatic relationship. The central prerequisite is good faith on the side of the acquirer who believes for justified reasons that the person transferring property is the lawful owner.[58] Here the law favours the acquirer, as the existence of good faith is subject to a legal presumption (§ 328 ABGB).[59] Section 367 ABGB moreover only acknowledges bona fide acquisition in one of the following three cases: either it takes place in a public auction, or in the course of the normal business activities of the person transferring property, or if the latter is somebody who the original owner had voluntarily put in custody of the object concerned, thereby becoming a so-called person of trust (*Vertrauensmann*). A thief is therefore no person of trust as the stolen item was not voluntarily handed over to him;

55. See the Mineral Resources Act (*supra* fn. 21).
56. Note that Austrian law also knows a bona fide acquisition of a pledge which largely follows this pattern in § 456 ABGB (infra §7.06[B][1]).
57. See *supra* at fn. 27.
58. In some circumstances also belief in the right to transfer ownership is sufficient, but this is the exception.
59. See *supra* fn. 33.

a bona fide acquisition thereof could, however, take place if it was sold in a shop selling such goods (i.e., in line with its ordinary business).

Based on § 367 ABGB the new owner acquires full property and is also protected from then onwards. He is not exposed to claims based on unjustified enrichment by his predecessor. The latter needs to turn to the transferring person for compensation.

Due to its clear wording § 367 ABGB is inapplicable to immovables. In line with the afore-mentioned principles of registration a bona fide acquisition of land may be based on a wrong entry in the land register; for example if after the entry of a new owner his title is successfully challenged, in which case that person will still be listed as the owner until the entry is deleted. As pointed out before the land register enjoys public trust; good faith can only be questioned if the person relying on the *Grundbuch* should have been aware of the falsity of the entry. An important tool in this respect is the so-called annotation of a dispute (*Streitanmerkung*, § 61 GBG) which signals that an entry in the register is being challenged and thereby prevents good faith acquisitions.

### *[4] Acquisitive Prescription* (Ersitzung)

Acquisitive prescription does not lead to an immediate change of ownership but requires a certain time of continuous[60] qualified possession. In the case of a movable thing, the possessor must have obtained it on the basis of a valid title and *nec vi, nec clam, nec precario,*[61] and he must believe to be the legitimate owner over a period of three years in good faith (*eigentliche Ersitzung*, § 1466 ABGB).[62] If his title is invalid or missing altogether,[63] then the required period of possession is thirty years (*uneigentliche Ersitzung*, § 1477 ABGB). The latter period applies to the acquisitive prescription of immovables, irrespective of whether the possessor had a valid title (§§ 1468, 1477 ABGB). If acquisitive prescription is claimed against a legal person (including the state) the three years period doubles to six years, and the thirty years period extends to forty years (§ 1472 ABGB).[64]

## [C] Loss of Ownership

Corresponding to the aforementioned modes of acquiring ownership, it necessarily ceases if it is passed on to somebody else or in cases of original acquisition.

60. The continuity has to correspond to the right acquired, so it need not be understood too strictly. Cf. *infra* fn. 86 for the corresponding case of acquiring servitudes by way of prescription.
61. See *supra* §7.03[B] (at fn. 35).
62. If the owner who is about to lose his right due to acquisitive prescription is absent for more than a year, a special rule may apply (§ 1475 ABGB).
63. This is the only aspect of qualified possession that may be lacking (e.g., if someone believes the object he found and intends to keep had no owner). Good faith and authenticity of possession are indispensable requirements, however.
64. It does not matter if the thing to be acquired is passed on to another person while the prescription period is still running as long as the same qualifications apply to the new possessor; he acquires ownership as soon as the remainder of the time has lapsed (§ 1493 ABGB).

Moreover, § 365 ABGB provides for the possibility of expropriation by the state in exchange for adequate compensation if the public good so demands. Constitutional law enacted afterwards requires a statutory authorisation of expropriations. Even though it no longer mentions an indemnity, almost all such statutes foresee some form of compensation. The *Eisenbahn-Enteignungsentschädigungsgesetz* (Law on the compensation for expropriation for the benefit of railways) may serve as an example (and is in fact used as the default model of expropriation in the absence of other specific rules): It authorises the temporary or permanent expropriation in the public interest for the construction or expansion of railways or its facilities, which also includes the creation of servitudes or of a duty to tolerate e.g., construction on one's property. Compensation is calculated on the basis of the current market value, costs incurred may also be recovered (e.g., for legal assistance in the administrative procedure leading to the expropriation order).[65]

## [D] Protection of Ownership

### *[1]* ***Rei vindicatio*** **(Eigentumsklage, § 366 ABGB)**

In order to recover the property from another, the owner can file the *Eigentumsklage*, though subject to proof of his ownership.[66] The owner will obviously not succeed against defendants who legitimately hold the property, e.g., due to a contractual right of use, but also if there are statutory justifications (such as legitimate seizure by the authorities).

The action does not only aim at restoring the property to its owner, but extends to returning the so-called fruits (*Früchte*) of the thing produced in the interim as well. This includes natural fruits such as crops or the young of an animal as well as so-called civil fruits (*Zivilfrüchte*) such as the proceeds of granting use to third parties (e.g., rent). If, however, the defendant held the thing in good faith, he need not return any fruits already separated.

The defendant also has to compensate the owner for the use of his property. Conversely, he can recover certain expenses incurred.[67]

### *[2]* ***Neighbourhood Claims*** **(Nachbarschaftsklagen, §§ *364 ff.* ABGB)**

In §§ 364 ff. ABGB Austrian law sets forth the concept of neighbourhood law providing for rather unique special rights and remedies.[68] In cases where a nuisance, such as

65. Full costs (within reasonable limit) can only be recovered if the expropriation fails, otherwise the amount recoverable for costs is capped at EUR 7,500.
66. Alternatively, he may choose to pursue the *actio Publiciana* (*supra* §7.03[F][2]), which only focuses on legal possession.
67. Necessary expenses which benefit the owner will always be reimbursed, other useful expenses only if the defendant was a bona fide possessor.
68. The causes of action resemble tort claims in other legal systems, such as the common law torts of trespass or nuisance. However, the neighbourhood claims provided by the ABGB do not

water, smoke, gas, heat, odour, noise or vibration[69] significantly disturbs the usage of a neighbouring piece of land in a way which exceeds what can be typically expected in such an area, the owner of the disturbed piece of land has a special remedy to reduce the disturbance to a 'normal' amount (§ 364 paragraph 2 ABGB) and to enjoin any exceeding use of the neighbouring property. Direct emissions (such as pipes leading to the neighbouring land) can always be enjoined irrespective of what is common local usage.

While the point of reference is the so-called 'neighbourhood', the two pieces of land concerned need not necessarily share a border, it is enough that they are located close enough to allow the interference from the one land get to the other.

Not only the owner of the disturbed piece of land may file such an action, but also *Rechtsbesitzer,*[70] i.e., tenants or others who have a right to use the land. The defendant is the owner of the land from where the disturbance originates, but also anyone who uses this land for his own interest.

In cases in which the source of disturbance is an officially authorised installation the sole remedy granted is a pecuniary indemnity, but not an injunction (§ 364a ABGB).

#### *[3] Other Actions against Disturbances of Ownership* (Eigentumsfreiheitsklage, § *523* ABGB)

While the *actio negatoria* foreseen by § 523 ABGB[71] in its core only aims at negating the existence of a servitude, it is commonly understood to be the legal basis for all claims of the owner to enjoin disturbances regarding his property, irrespective of whether the interferer claims to do so as the beneficiary of a servitude or not. One might argue that the definition of ownership in § 354 ABGB (stressing the right 'to exclude everyone else') already provides for such a cause of action.

## §7.05 SERVITUDES

### [A] Principles and Definitions

According to the definition in § 472 ABGB servitudes (*Servituten* or *Dienstbarkeiten*) are rights in rem to benefit from the property of another who either has to tolerate some use of his property (affirmative servitude, *bejahende Servitut*) or to abstain from a certain use (negative servitude, *verneinende Servitut*). The servient piece of property (*dienende Sache*) is typically, but not necessarily a piece of or interest in land. The

primarily aim at damages, but rather at enjoining the interference (even though they may also include duties to reinstate the status quo ante in the form of indemnities).

69. Nowadays also in cases of deprivation of light and air, e.g., by high-growing plants, see § 364 para. 3 ABGB.
70. See *supra* §7.03[C].
71. See *infra* §7.05[E].

addressee of these rights is the respective current owner of the servitude's object, so a transfer of ownership has no impact on the existence of the servitude.

As a principle, servitudes cannot oblige the owner of the servient property to actively do something (§ 482 ABGB); his role is primarily passive. Consequently, it is generally the beneficiary who is in charge of making the servient property ready for use and for maintaining whatever is needed for such purpose. If it is a right of way (*Wegerecht*), for example, the beneficiary has to pay – if necessary – for the construction of the road and for its maintenance. However, if the owner of the land that it crosses also uses the road, costs and efforts will be split accordingly if not mutually decided otherwise (§ 483 ABGB).

The rights granted by servitudes must not be expanded by the beneficiary, quite the opposite: The rights of the owner of the servient property have to be respected as much as is compatible with the exercise of the right granted (§ 484 ABGB). If a right of way was granted in order to connect the beneficiary's land with the public road system, for example, and if the beneficiary subsequently converts his originally private home into a business site, an ensuing significant increase of traffic is not covered by the original servitude, which envisaged an occasional passage of family members and guests, but not a frequent back and forth of customers.

### [B] Types of Servitudes

The ABGB distinguishes between real servitudes (easements, *Grunddienstbarkeiten*[72]) and personal servitudes (*persönliche Dienstbarkeiten* or *Personalservituten*, § 473 ABGB). The former variant is a right attached to a piece of land as the dominant estate (*herrschendes Grundstück*), so that the beneficiary is not a named individual but rather the current owner of that estate, and it typically grants some benefit with respect to another piece of land (servient estate, *dienendes Grundstück*). Personal servitudes are granted to an individual person and typically terminate with his death.[73]

For both types of servitudes, the ABGB gives several examples with specific provisions for each. This catalogue is, however, not exclusive, not even in regard to the classification as either real or personal servitude. It is therefore possible to create a right which the ABGB classifies as a real servitude in the form of a personal servitude and vice versa.[74] This effectively opens up the strict catalogue of rights in rem[75] to a rather flexible system (though somewhat in disguise): It is therefore possible to retain full ownership of a piece of property while effectively passing on every imaginable right to make use of it to others.[76] If the right of usage is limited in time, this may also come very

72. Other (synonym) German terms with Latin roots are *Realservituten* or *Prädialservituten*.
73. It may be passed on to the first legal heir (or even to subsequent heirs) if expressly so agreed when the right was created (§ 529 ABGB).
74. This is expressly granted by § 479 ABGB only for real servitudes, but is commonly understood to work both ways.
75. See *supra* §7.02[B].
76. This also works the other way around, of course: Parents who would like to regulate asset succession in advance may, for example, convey full property of the house and land where they live to their children while retaining a life-long right of residence (see *infra* §7.05[B][2]), which

close to the notion of a temporary ownership (which Austrian law does not recognise as such).

### *[1]* ***Real Servitudes*** **(Grunddienstbarkeiten)**

The number of provisions of the ABGB devoted to real servitudes and their detail (§§ 475-477, 487-502 ABGB) correspond to the needs of the time when the Code was enacted. Many of the specific servitudes provided for may have been relevant at the beginning of the nineteenth century in a predominantly rural society, but from today's perspective, it seems rather odd, for example, to specify the exact types of livestock which may be brought onto a servient pasture for grazing (§ 499 ABGB).[77]

The historical nineteenth century necessity also explains why the catalogue of real servitudes is further subdivided by § 474 ABGB into field servitudes (*Felddservituten,*[78] listed in § 477 ABGB) and building servitudes (*Hausservituten,*[79] enumerated in §§ 476-476 ABGB). The previously mentioned right of pasturage (*Weiderecht*) belongs to the former subgroup. The same applies for the presumably most frequent variants from today's perspective, the rights of way (§§ 492-495 ABGB). The latter subgroup includes – among many – e.g., the right to let rainwater run-off to a neighbouring piece of land (§§ 489-491 ABGB).[80]

### *[2]* ***Personal Servitudes*** **(Personalservituten)**

§ 478 ABGB lists three different kinds of personal servitudes: usufruct (*Fruchtgenuß*[81]), usage (*Gebrauchsrecht*) and the right of residence (*Wohnungsrecht*). Although some special provisions are devoted to the latter (§§ 521-522 ABGB), it is actually just a special variant of either one of the two former kinds. § 521 ABGB itself defines it as the right to use a certain part of a building for residential purposes either for one's own interest exclusively (usage) or without such restriction (usufruct).

#### *[a]* *Usage* (Gebrauchsrecht, §§ *504-508 ABGB)*

Usage is the right to use a thing of another under preservation of its substance for the beneficiary's own personal use (§§ 504, 507 ABGB). This implies that the object of a

– if in the form of a usufruct – barely reduces the effective rights of the parents. If combined with a *Veräußerungs- und Belastungsverbot* in their favour (*supra* fn. 49), their interests remain protected even though they are no longer owners of the home they inhabit.

77. It is any type of draught animal, cattle, sheep, but not pigs or poultry, and goats are excluded as well in woods. The provisions on pasture (§§ 498-503 ABGB) are mostly obsolete anyhow due to more recent special legislation.
78. Alternative terms include *Felddienstbarkeiten* or *Rustikalservituten*.
79. Alternative terms include *Gebäudedienstbarkeiten* or *Urbanalservituten*.
80. Oddly enough, the Austrian Supreme Court (OGH) refuses to apply these provisions to roof snowslides by analogy, despite the frequency of that phenomenon in Austria's winters.
81. Other synonym German terms are *Fruchtnießung* or *Nießbrauch*; the Latin-derived *Ususfruktus* (note the different spelling) is also often used.

right of usage can only be a thing that cannot be consumed.[82] The right cannot be transferred onto a third party, not even by a temporary contractual arrangement such as a lease. Unless otherwise agreed, the needs of the beneficiary at the time of creating the right of usage determine its extent; therefore a subsequent increase of his needs does not justify a more extensive usage (§ 506 ABGB).

#### *[b]* *Usufruct* (Fruchtgenuß, *§§ 509-519 ABGB)*

The beneficiary of a usufruct (*Fruchtnießer* or *Usufruktuar*) has the right to use the object of another with the sole limitation that its substance must not be affected (§ 509 ABGB). Usufruct is therefore an expanded right of usage, granting the beneficiary in addition to personal usage for example the right to collect all fruits and other gains as well as to pass the use on to third parties (e.g., by renting it out). The difference between a *Fruchtnießer* and the owner of the servient object can therefore be reduced to the mere fact that only the latter may dispose of his right. Ultimately, however, it is as always the title of the right that determines its extent, so it may be more limited, e.g., to a certain part of the object or in other ways.

### *[3]* ***Excursus: Realty Charge*** **(Reallasten)**

The mirror image of servitudes are realty charges (*Reallasten*), which are treated similarly even though they aim at the exact opposite: Unlike servitudes, realty charges oblige the current owner of a piece of land to actively do something for the benefit of another (the beneficiary), who may be a named individual (personal realty charge, *Personalreallast*) or the current owner of the dominant estate (real realty charge, *Prädialreallast*). This may include singular or periodical payments or services (such as assistance in certain activities).

## [C] Modes of Acquiring Servitudes

### *[1]* ***Title***

Like all rights in rem, servitudes can only be acquired on the basis of an appropriate title (§ 480 ABGB) coupled with a suitable *Modus* (§ 481 ABGB).[83] The most common titles for servitudes are contracts (either exclusively entered into for creating a servitude or combined with other dealings[84]). Further possible titles include wills, court rulings or decrees of administrative bodies. The law itself may provide for a title, as is the case with prescription, but also by way of certain specific statutory provisions (so-called *Legalservituten*).

82. Note, however, that Austrian law knows a phenomenon inherited from Roman law which is called *usufructus irregularis* (§ 540 ABGB).
83. See already *supra* §7.02[D].
84. Cf. the example *supra* in fn. 76.

### *[2] Modus*

In the case of movable objects, the *Modus* is effectuated by the exercise of the beneficiary's use. In the case of land, servitudes generally must be registered in the *Grundbuch* in order to come into existence, in the form of an entry on the servient estate. It is also made visible as an entitlement on the dominant estate.

Due to the flexible nature of servitudes coupled with technical constraints, the electronic land register only shows the nature of the servitude, whereas the full complexity of its details must be further researched in the collection of deeds linked to the land register, where the original documents evidencing the title can be found.[85]

### *[3] The Special Case of Prescription*

Servitudes can be acquired by way of prescription, particularly rights of way. If, for example, someone in good faith crosses the land of another regularly[86] during a term of thirty years or longer[87] in the erroneous but justified belief that he is entitled to do so, and the owner fails to object, the prevention of such use in the future may be time-barred. This construction even works in favour of an entire community such as a municipality, which can over time acquire a right of way for the general public if several of its members (including guests and visitors) repeatedly exercise it in good faith.[88]

The beneficiary can then claim to have the servitude registered in the land register, even though this formal step no longer contributes to the creation of the right, as it already exists 'outside the books' (*außerbücherlich*, without corresponding entry in the land register). This is one of the rare exceptions of the principle that no right in land can exist unless registered.

This may work the other way round as well, though – if the beneficiary of a servitude fails to exercise it over the same period, it ceases to exist (and the owner can have an existing entry cleared from the register). The loss of the servitude by way of prescription may happen much faster if the owner actively contests the right's existence – in that case, the beneficiary loses the servitude already after three years of failing to pursue (and exercise) his right (§ 1488 ABGB).

---

85. See also *supra* §7.01[B] at the end. In the case of a right of way, the entitlement to cross the land as such will be shown in the register itself, but the exact path (which will typically be agreed upon upfront) as well as further details of the right can only be identified when looking at the original deed.
86. The regularity depends upon the kind of right to be acquired – in case of a right of way, the aspiring beneficiary of a servitude need not cross the servient land without any interruption, of course, but only in a frequency that corresponds to adequate (and evident) use of such a right.
87. The period may be extended to forty years under certain conditions (§ 1472 ABGB).
88. This is not only true for walking paths, but also extends to ski slopes in the winter used for tourism as long as it is for the potential benefit of the community rather than of individual use. The good faith of those passing through need not be based on the belief that it is a right of the municipality as long as they believe in the legitimacy of crossing the land of another in general.

#### *[4] The Special Case of Ways of Necessity* (Notwege)

If there is no other reasonable way to reach the public road system from an otherwise inaccessible piece of land, its owner may ask the court to grant a so-called way of necessity (*Notweg*) over the land of another, who will be awarded a certain pecuniary compensation in exchange. This is regulated by a separate statute (*Notwegegesetz*).

### [D] Loss of Servitudes

Apart from the case of prescription as just described servitudes may end by way of renunciation, or if the right granted turns permanently and completely useless for the beneficiary, or if a continuation of the right becomes intolerable for the servient estate.

Due to the nature of the right, personal servitudes typically end at the latest with the death of the beneficiary (unless otherwise defined *ab initio*).

### [E] Protection of Servitudes

Section 523 ABGB foresees two causes of action for servitudes: The beneficiary of a servitude is granted a so-called *actio confessoria* (*Servitutenklage*) against all who challenge his right (typically the current owner of the servient estate).[89] The mirror image is the *actio negatoria* (*Eigentumsfreiheitsklage*) raised by the owner of a certain property against everyone who claims to be a beneficiary of a servitude regarding that property. The latter is also used more generally against all interferences with the use of one's property, even if the interferer does not claim to be the beneficiary of a servitude.[90] The action typically aims at an injunction.[91]

## §7.06 SECURITY RIGHTS IN PROPERTY

### [A] Types of Security Rights

In order to secure an obligation, the creditor has several options to choose from under Austrian property law,[92] not all of which are expressly addressed by the General Civil Code.

The classic security right in rem is the pledge (*Pfandrecht*, §§ 456 et seqq. ABGB), which grants the creditor the right to satisfy the debt[93] by realising the asset in pledge, conditional upon the debtor's default. This security interest is even honoured if the owner of the pledge is insolvent, which makes it particularly interesting for the

89. This would be the appropriate action filed, for example, by someone who has acquired a servitude by way of prescription against the owner of the property concerned.
90. See already *supra* §7.04[D][3].
91. It may also be asking for mere declaratory relief or restitution in case of past interferences.
92. Needless to say, there are other options such as a third person guaranteeing performance.
93. The security extends beyond the nominal value of the outstanding debt itself to interest and costs of pursuing the right.

creditor.[94] If the object offered as a pledge is movable, the creditor has to gain and retain custody of it (possessory pledge, *Faustpfand* or *Handpfand*). If it is a security interest in land instead (mortgage, *Grundpfand* or *Hypothek*), it must be entered into the land register in order to come into existence. The pledge need not be offered by the debtor himself, also a third party may serve as the pledgor (*Pfandbesteller*).[95]

The General Civil Code further provides for rights of retention (*Zurückbehaltungsrechte*), for example if someone holds the property of another and either has made expenditures for it (such as repairs) or has suffered any harm through it while in his custody (§ 471 ABGB).

Outside the wording of the ABGB, but firmly embedded in practice Austrian law knows other important security options such as the transfer of ownership for security reasons (*Sicherungsübereignung*), whereby the creditor becomes the full legal owner of the object serving as security but is under a fiduciary duty to transfer ownership back once the debt is paid off.[96] While no registration of that security right is necessary as in other jurisdictions, chattel has to be handed over to the creditor physically and cannot remain with the debtor for reasons of publicity.

Regarding sales contracts practice offers a further unwritten security option for the seller, namely retention of title (*Eigentumsvorbehalt*), which allows the buyer to take possession of the sold good before completing payment while the seller continues to be its owner. For the latter this bears the obvious risk that a third party purchases the object in good faith[97] from the buyer and thereby acquires full unencumbered ownership. Austrian law, however, provides for several options to preserve the seller's security interest despite allowing the buyer to pass on (or process) the object of purchase, e.g., by having the rights out of such further sales contracts assigned to him in advance so that he is at least secured by receiving a new creditor position.

## [B] Possessory Pledges in Particular

### *[1] Acquiring Possessory Pledges*

All assets tangible or intangible may serve as a pledge as long as they are realisable, i.e., can be assessed in money (§ 448 ABGB).[98] Tangible objects have to exist in order to be charged, whereas it suffices for obligations and other intangible assets to be determinable while not yet in existence (such as future obligations of the debtor's customers).

---

94. In case of insolvency, the pledgee can prevent the realization of the object pledged by a so-called *Absonderungsrecht* (a claim to isolate the object from the insolvency estate for preferential satisfaction of the secured creditor: §§ 11, 48 *Insolvenzordnung*); see already *supra* fn. 15.
95. In such case, the debtor is also referred to as the *Hauptschuldner* or *Personalschuldner* (main or personal debtor), whereas the pledgor is the *Realschuldner*.
96. If the security interest is in an obligation, the assignment is fiduciary correspondingly (*Sicherungszession*).
97. Good faith is commonly understood to be missing if someone buys an object from another where it is (or should be) known in the trade that the supplier of the seller will typically only provide the goods by retaining title.
98. Even pledges themselves may serve as security (*Afterpfand*, §§ 454 f. ABGB).

As with all rights in rem, pledges require a valid title such as a contract (*Pfandbestellungsvertrag*)[99] coupled with a suitable *Modus* (which is misleadingly called *Pfandvertrag* by § 1368 ABGB).[100]

For reasons of publicity, the only valid *Modus* for movable objects is to physically hand them over to the creditor or a third party on behalf of the latter (§ 451 paragraph 1 ABGB), which means that the so-called *Besitzkonstitut* (where the object would remain with the person providing security) does not suffice as a mode of transfer.[101] Due to this *Faustpfandprinzip* (principle of possessory pledge), the security interest lapses once the object returns to the pledgor (§ 467 ABGB). Also, it is impossible to provide a security right in bulk items as such or in the debtor's assets as a whole (specialty principle or *Spezialitätsgrundsatz*),[102] so floating charges are no option under Austrian law.

The pledgor needs to be the owner of the object or at least authorised by the latter to provide it as security. However, under conditions corresponding to the ones providing for a bona fide acquisition of ownership, a creditor may in good faith acquire a security interest in an object of which the pledgee cannot actually dispose (§ 456 ABGB).

#### *[2] Relationship between Creditor and Pledgor*

In order for a pledge to exist, it is essential that it is linked to an existing debt that is being secured (accessoriness, *Akzessorietätsprinzip*, §§ 449, 469 ABGB). As soon as the debt is paid off, the creditor consequently loses the right to keep the pledge.

Unless otherwise agreed, the pledgee must not use the object pledged but maintain it safe like a custodian (§ 459 ABGB) and return it as soon as the underlying debt is fully satisfied.

If it turns out that the object can no longer serve the security interest of the creditor, e.g., if it is damaged or if it was misvalued from the start, the creditor can ask for a substitute or additional security instead (§ 458 ABGB).

Since it is a right in rem, the pledgee creditor can prevent all (even just possibly) harmful impact on the object pledged (*Devastationsklage*) and reclaim it if taken by some third party (*Pfandklage*).

If an object serves as a security for more than one creditor, the relationship amongst them is governed by the principle of priority – in case the debtor defaults and the pledge will have to be realised, the proceeds thereof will first serve to satisfy the

---

99. If the pledge is created by contract, one also speaks of *Verpfändung*, whereas it is a *Pfändung* if the title is a court order instead. Pledges may also arise from statutory provisions such as § 1101 ABGB, which grants the landlord a statutory pledge on furniture and other movables of his tenants in order to secure the rent.
100. A register of security interests in certain movable objects such as vehicles was under discussion in Austria a few years ago but does not seem to be pursued by the legislator at present. There is, however, a register for ships and certain mining rights.
101. However, in case of bulky items which cannot easily be moved physically, symbolic forms of transfer are valid (§ 452 ABGB),see *supra* §7.03[D] on § 427 ABGB.
102. See already *supra* §7.02[C]. But note that, for example, the contents of a warehouse can be pledged (by way of symbolic transfer, see fn. 101) as long as they are specified and itemized.

(chronologically[103]) first pledgee creditor in full, the remainder will then be used to pay off the debts vis-à-vis the second creditor and so forth.

### *[3] Realising Possessory Pledges*

Generally, once the debtor has defaulted on his debt, the creditor needs to obtain a judicial decision confirming the existence of the (remainder of the) debt (serving as the *Exekutionstitel*) by suing the debtor on the basis of the latter's obligation (*Schuldklage*). On that basis, the laws of enforcement (*Exekutionsrecht*) allow the creditor to realise all assets of the debtor in order to satisfy what he owes to the creditor. The latter will typically (but not necessarily) choose the assets pledged for realisation at that stage.

If the pledgor was another person than the debtor, the creditor first has to file a so-called *Pfandrechtsklage* against the pledgor.[104] The judgment then serves as the *Exekutionstitel* only for realising the assets pledged.

Either way, the latter may be realised by way of an auction or by other options the *Exekutionsordnung* provides (such as compulsory administration). Proceeds from the enforcement proceedings that exceed the unpaid debt (the so-called *hyperocha*) will go to the debtor (§ 464 ABGB).

Since a few years, the creditor may also realise security rights in movable objects by extrajudicial (private) sale (§§ 466a ff. ABGB) unless otherwise agreed. He cannot do so before one month has lapsed after the debt has become due[105] and he has informed the debtor of his intention to sell the object(s) pledged out of court. If there is a market price for the objects, they may be sold directly to a third party, otherwise only by way of an auction (§ 466b ABGB).

## [C] Mortgages in Particular

To the extent applicable, the principles of the law governing possessory pledges apply accordingly to mortgages. However, due to the special nature of the security asset and the additional options the land register provides, there are some specialties with respect to security interests in land.

The principle of priority is of special importance with respect to mortgages as it is much more likely in practice that land is used to secure more than one debt as compared to chattel. The first creditor that applies for registration of his security interest is entered at the strongest position (with the rank lowest by number having top priority). Only after his debt is fully satisfied will the second-ranking creditor have a chance to also collect on his mortgage (and so forth) in case the land is materialised.

103. The order will be determined by the timing of the physical transfer of the pledge, irrespective of when the pledgor promised to offer it.
104. A third party pledgor may prevent the realization of the pledge by paying the debtor's dues, thereby acquiring the creditor's rights against the latter by way of statutory assignment.
105. Perishable things can be sold earlier (even before the debt has become due if at least a massive loss of their value is to be feared, in which case the proceeds replace the pledge: § 460a ABGB).

A rank in the land register may be reserved by the land owner who intends to use it as a security for a loan, for example. The next available rank can be blocked by a so-called *Anmerkung der Rangordnung* (annotation of priority, §§ 53 et seqq. GBG), which secures the priority for up to one year.

If an existing mortgage is ready for extinction, the land owner can preserve that rank by a so-called *Rangvorbehalt* (reservation of priority, § 58 GBG) and have a new mortgage entered with that priority rank within three years.[106]

Furthermore can the land owner have a conditional mortgage entered in the rank of an already existing mortgage in case the latter will be extinguished within one year (so-called *bedingte Pfandrechtseintragung,* § 59 GBG), which is useful if the debtor finds a lender with better conditions than his current creditor.

The specialty principle is somewhat less strictly applied with respect to mortgages inasmuch as it is possible to enter a so-called *Höchstbetragshypothek* (maximum amount mortgage, § 14 paragraph 2 GBG) into the land register, which is a mortgage with a pre-defined monetary value, but without a direct link to a specific secured debt, it only needs to be pre-determined. The beneficiary of that type of mortgage can instead use it to secure multiple debts up to the nominal (maximum) value of the mortgage, and – more importantly – can do so repeatedly. Still, the security interest as such is only valid to the extent there are outstanding debts at the time of realisation.

## SELECTED BIBLIOGRAPHY

M. Binder, *Sachenrecht. Theorie und systematisch aufbereitete OGH-Fälle,* Vienna 2003.

W. Faber, *National Report on the Transfer of Movables in Austria,* in W. Faber and B. Lurger (eds.), *National Reports on the Transfer of Movables in Europe,* Volume I. Austria, Estonia, Italy, Slovenia, Munich 2008, 12-218.

G. Iro, *Bürgerliches Recht IV. Sachenrecht,* 5th ed., Vienna 2013.

A. Riedler, *Zivilrecht V. Sachenrecht,* in A. Riedler (ed.), *Studienkonzept Zivilrecht I-VIII,* 3rd ed., Vienna 2010.

106. As long as the mortgage is not deleted from the register, the land owner can do so even without such reservation (as long as creditors with lower priority have agreed thereto upfront, § 469a ABGB). This bears the risk, however, that the former creditor transfers the (in fact no longer existing) security interest to a bona fide third party who may trust in the existence of the mortgage as evidenced by the land register.

CHAPTER 8

# Family Law

*Astrid Deixler-Hübner & Sebastian Reiter*

## §8.01 INTRODUCTION

From a structural point of view Austrian Family Law composes of matrimonial law, the law on registered partnerships (legally recognised same-sex relationships) and the law of parents and child (*Kindschaftsrecht*).

Since the 1970s family law has been evolving along the lines of society constantly. As a consequence several reforms brought about a paradigm shift from the patriarchal model of family towards a model of family based on partnership which rests on the equality of man and woman. As of now, not all family law is incorporated into the ABGB. Several acts of legislation contain statutes pertaining to family law. Non-marital cohabitation (*nichteheliche Lebensgemeinschaft*) is not explicitly regulated, although it features as a legal term in various statutes.

Important acts of reform legislation are the Federal Law, Amending Provisions on Legal Capacity and Capacity to Marry of 1973 (*BG, mit dem Bestimmungen über die Geschäftsfähigkeit und die Ehemündigkeit geändert werden, BGBl 1973/108*), the Federal Law, on Reform of the Personal Legal Effects of Marriage of 1978 (*BG über die Neuordnung der persönlichen Rechtswirkungen der Ehe*, BGBl 1975/412), The Federal Law on Changes of the Spouse's Intestate Share, Matrimonial Property and the Law of Divorce of 1978 (*BG über Änderung des Ehegattenerbrechts, des Ehegüterrechts und des Ehescheidungsrechts, BGBl 1978/280)*, the Federal Law for Protection Against Violence in Families of 1996 as amended by the 2nd Law for Protection Against Violence of 2009 (*BG zum Schutz vor Gewalt in der Familie*, BGBl 1996/759 idF *2. Gewaltschutzgesetz*, BGBl I 2009/40). Most recent legislation are the Act Amending Family Law of 2009 (*Familienrechts-Änderungsgesetz 2009*, BGBl 2009/75) and the Act Amending the Law of Parents and Child and the Law of Names of 2013 (*Kindschafts- und Namensrechts-Änderungsgesetz 2013*, BGBl I 2013/15), the Act Amending the Law of Adoption of 2013 (*Adoptionsrechts-Änderungsgesetz 2013*, BGBl I 2013/179) and the Act Amending the Law on Reproductive Medicine (*FortpflanzungsmedizinrechtsÄnderungsgesetz 2015*, BGBl I 2015/35). In recent years family law has been in constant flux towards equal rights for same-sex couples.

## §8.02 THE SOURCES OF FAMILY LAW

The sources of family law are scattered among several acts of legislation. Primary law of the European Union can exert influence on Austrian family law. Constitutional law contains various cornerstones for family law. Several federal law statutes contain civil law regulation for families. However, procedural laws as well as social security legislation are often closely linked with private family law. Therefore, if of general importance, they will be listed as well.

### [A] Constitutional Law

On a constitutional basis the right to equality (of man and woman) is proclaimed in Article 7 section 1 of the Federal Constitutional Law (B-VG, *Bundes-Verfassungsgesetz*) Furthermore, the federal state, the provinces and the communes avow themselves to factual equal treatment of men and women (Article 7 section 2 B-VG). The European Convention on Human Rights (ECHR)) has been incorporated into Austria's constitution. As a consequence, the right to respect for private life and family life, as guaranteed by Article 8 ECHR and the right to marriage, as guaranteed by Article 12 ECHR, are recognised as constitutional rights.[1] The same is true for Article 2 Protocol 1 to the ECHR so that the state is obligated to respect the right of parents to ensure such education and teaching in conformity with their own religious and philosophical convictions. Article 5 Protocol 7 ECHR guarantees equality between spouses and *vis-à-vis* children. In addition constitutional recognition has been given to the Convention on the Elimination of all Forms of Discrimination against Women including Reservations (BGBl 1982/443). Equality of man and woman and respect for personal rights of children are a consequence of these constitutional paradigms as is equality of legitimate and illegitimate children (a distinction now no longer part of Austrian family law).

### [B] Family Law Statutes

Many aspects of family law are incorporated into the ABGB. The first part (*Erster Teil*) includes provisions on family law in its main sections (*Hauptstücke*) two to five (§§ 44-235). The second main section (*Zweites Hauptstück*) consisting of §§ 44-100 is titled 'of Matrimonial Law'. The third main section (§§ 137-203) holds provisions on 'Rights between Parents and Children'. The fourth section (§§204-230) is concerned with child custody of third persons and the fifth main section (§§ 231-235) governs child support.

1. For further information see Christoph Grabenwarter's section on Constitutional Law in this book.

The ABGB contains further family law legislation in the 28th main section of its second part (§§ 1217-1266) concerning mainly matrimonial property and testamentary contracts between spouses.

The Law on Marriage (EheG, *Ehegesetz*) lays down the rules for the validity of the act of marriage and provides reasons for the end of marriage as well as its consequences. It is complemented by the First Executive Regulation on Marriage Law (1. DVEheG, *Erste Durchführungsverordnung zum EheG*) which has the character of a law. The Law on Registered Partnership (EPG, *Gesetz über die Eingetragene Partnerschaft*) is in many parts a copy of the text of the EheG although it deviates from the EheG in some aspects.

The recently modernised Act on Civil Status (PStG, *Personenstandsgesetz*) is concerned with the registration of civil statuses like birth, marriage, registered partnership and death in the Central Register of Civil Status (*Zentrales Personenstandsregister*). The competent civil servant is the Registrar (*Standesbeamter*) at any Office for Registration of Personal Status (*Personenstandsbehörde*). These offices are run by the local municipality. The Registrar issues birth certificates (*Geburtsurkunden*), marriage certificates (*Heiratsurkunden*), certificates of registered partnership (*Partnerschaftsurkunde*) and death certificates (*Sterbeurkunden*). In conjunction with the EheG and the EPG the PStG regulates the tasks of the Registrar during the marriage ceremony and the registration of partnership.

Medically assisted reproduction is governed by a Law on Reproductive Medicine (FMedG, *Fortpflanzungsmedizingesetz*).

Rules on the religious upbringing of children are provided by the Law on Religious Upbringing of Children (*Bundesgesetz über die religiöse Kindererziehung*).

The Hague Convention on The Civil Aspects of International Child Abduction and the European Convention on the Legal Status of Children Born out of Wedlock have been implemented by federal law and apply as such.

Procedural aspects of matters of marriage (*Eheangelegenheiten*), divorce and paternity are included into the second sections of the Law on Non-Contentious Proceedings (AußStrG, *Außerstreitgesetz*); however some lawsuits are assigned to the procedural rules of the Code of Civil Procedure (ZPO, *Zivilprozessordnung*). The execution of maintenance claims and interim injunctions against (domestic) violence are governed by the Code of Execution (EO, *Exekutionsordnung*).

The new Federal Law on Assistance for Children and Young Persons 2013 (B-KJHG 2013, *Bundes-Kinder- und Jugendhilfegesetz 2013*) establishes principles, aims and tasks of assistance for children and young persons. The federal state is the Authority for Assistance for Children and Young Persons (*Kinder- und Jugendhilfeträger*). As such, it is not only committed by the B-KJHG 2013 to tasks like service for parents-to-be, young families, assistance in foster parenting, and in adoption but also detection of danger for children. The federal states (*Länder*) are competent to legislate the details in matters of assistance for children and young persons.

The Law for the Protection of Maintenance (*Unterhaltsschutzgesetz*), the Law for Advance in Maintenance Payments (UVG, *Unterhaltsvorschussgesetz*) and the Law on Enforcement of Maintenance Abroad (*Auslandsunterhaltsgesetz*) ensure the payment of maintenance.

Matters of social security law pertaining to family are fragmented. Important legislation is included in the General Social Security Law (ASVG, *Allgemeines Sozialversicherungsgesetz*), the Commercial Social Security Law (GSVG, *Gewerbliches Sozialversicherungsgesetz*) and the Law on Health Insurance and Accident Insurance for Civil Servants (B-KUVG, *Beamten-Kranken- und Unfallversicherungsgesetz*).

The state offers Family Assistance Payments (*Familienbeihilfe*) for parents according to the Law on Balancing Financial Burdens of Families (*Familienlastenausgleichsgesetz*).

## §8.03 MATRIMONIAL LAW

Matrimonial law refers to rules for engagement, marriage (Eheschließung), matrimonial rights and duties, including matrimonial property law, termination of marriage and its consequences. Austrian legislation acknowledges only civil marriage. The Law on Registered Partnership offers legal recognition exclusively for same-sex partnerships.

### [A] Engagement

Engagement is the promise of two persons to marry, which cannot be enforced, but withdrawn from at any time. However, the person who culpably withdraws without reason owes compensation for non-psychological damages the other person suffered because of his/her trust in the promise.

### [B] Marriage

Marriage is programmatically described as a contract between two persons of different gender who declare their lawful wish to live in inseparable community, to raise children and to support each other mutually (§ 44 ABGB). Two basic requirements for marriage are that the person has reached the age of consent (18) (§ 1 EheG) and the person's legal capacity (§ 2 EheG). Minors or persons whose legal capacity is impaired for other reasons need the consent of their legal representative (§ 3(1) EheG). Over 16-year-old persons can be declared to be of capacity to consent in marriage (§ 1(2) EheG). A valid marriage requires that the fiancés declare personally in the presence of each other and in the presence of a Registrar that they want to marry (§ 17 EheG). The promise must be given unconditionally (§ 17(2) EheG).

A marriage ceremony that is not performed by a Registrar or is absent the fiancés consensual declaration of their wish to marry does not result in marriage, doctrine speaks of non-marriage (*Nichtehe*).

All other marriages have legal effects, however under some circumstances marriages can be declared void *ab initio* (*Nichtigerklärung*) or be annulled (*Aufhebbarkeit*).

Marriages can be declared void *ab initio* if the ceremony suffered from a severe lack of form according to § 17 EheG, if one spouse lacks the capacity to marry (*Geschäftsunfähigkeit*) (§ 23 EheG), if the marriage has the sole purpose of facilitating citizenship for a spouse (§ 23 EheG), in cases of bigamy (§ 24 EheG), if one spouse is part of a registered partnership and in cases of incest (§ 25 EheG). In general each spouse and the federal prosecutor (*Staatsanwalt*) may sue for nullity (§ 28 EheG). Some of these defects can be remedied if the spouses do in fact live married life.

Annulment of marriage is regulated by §§ 33-39 and 44 EheG. As a rule, a spouse can sue for annulment of marriage in cases where his/her freedom of the will was (severely) impaired. However, annulment is no longer common in practice because divorce is relatively easy to obtain and with regard to maintenance, property and children the consequences of annulment are the same as the consequences of divorce.

## [C] Matrimonial Rights and Duties

### *[1] In General*

Paragraphs 89-100 ABGB provide rules for married life. § 89 ABGB proclaims gender equality with regard to personal rights and obligations of spouses in relation to each other. Marriage evokes duties of comprehensive conjugal community (*umfassende eheliche Lebensgemeinschaft*), notably living in the same household, fidelity, respectful conduct and mutual support (§ 90(1) ABGB). These duties of one spouse correspond to rights of the other and vice-versa. The duty of mutual support is the principle of marriage life. Matrimonial rights and duties are legal specifications of this principle.

§ 91(1) ABGB encourages spouses to conjointly arrange their conjugal community with the intention of fair balance of their contributions and in consideration of each other and the well-being of their children, in particular with regard to homemaking, gainful occupation, mutual support and child custody. § 91(2) ABGB allows for a spouse to depart from such an arrangement for important reasons which weigh heavier than the others or the children's interests.

According to the optional rule of § 90(2) ABGB a spouse is obliged to contribute reasonable amounts of work to the other's vocational means of income (*Mitwirkung im Erwerb*) according to their personal circumstances. Spouses may reach a differing agreement. The contributing spouse is entitled to reasonable remuneration (§ 98 ABGB).

### *[2] Name*

Recent legislation has liberalised the choice of names available to spouses according to §§ 93-93c ABGB. For a family name the spouses may freely choose among (parts) of their prior names (*Meier(/-Jones), Smith*), or opt for a compound name. If the spouses opt for a compound name, they have to put their prior names in the same order. A hyphen connects the compound name (*Meier-Jones*). If a spouse has a prior compound name (*Meier-Jones*), the new compound name may include only one part of the prior compound name (*Meier-Smith* or *Smith-Jones*). The spouse (*Meier*) whose prior name is not chosen for a non-compound family name (*Smith*) is entitled to keep his/her former (non-compound) name in front or behind the family name, connected by a hyphen (*Smith-Meier* or *Meier-Smith*). Family names may be altered according to a spouse's gender, if this is consistent with the spouse's origin or the tradition of the language the name belongs to. If the spouses do not choose a common family name they keep their prior names. If one spouse's prior name changes (e.g., because of adoption), both spouses may choose a new family name according to the rules explained above.

If the marriage ends because of death, nullification or divorce the family name does not change. However, each (part of a) prior family name may be utilised by the former spouses henceforth. The family name may only be chosen once per occasion for change according to §§ 93 ff ABGB. The spouses declare their intent to change names before the Registrar in the form of public deed which can be issued by a notary (*Notar*) or the Registrar (*öffentliche Urkunde*) or in the form of a publicly authenticated document (*öffentlich beglaubigte Urkunde*) which can be authenticated by court, a notary, a Registrar or by a consular agency.

### *[3] Maintenance*

The rules on maintenance prescribe that both spouses shall contribute in order to provide for their reasonable needs according to their lifestyle (§ 94(1) ABGB). In conjunction with § 95 ABGB spouses are free to organise their marriage as they wish. If both spouses are gainfully employed, both have to contribute to housekeeping. If only one spouse works, the other contributes to the spouses' reasonable needs by means of housekeeping. § 94(2) ABGB creates rights to payment of maintenance for the spouse who manages the household but is not gainfully employed, furthermore for the spouse who used to keep house, if the spouses no longer live in the same household and finally for the spouse who is gainfully employed but earns less or who is incapable to contribute to the spouses' reasonable needs. Even though spouses can organise their lifestyle as they wish, within this arrangement they are obligated to contribute what they are capable of according to their abilities. This is expressed by the principle of true effort (*Anspannungsgrundsatz*). In general, maintenance has to be provided by payments, unless the spouses agree otherwise, or such a payment request of the spouse who keeps house is inequitable. The rates of maintenance payments are determined in discretionary manner case by case. However, case law has developed certain guidelines: Spouses who are not gainfully employed are entitled to 33% of the other spouse's income. Spouses who are earning, but less than their spouse, are entitled to 40% of their combined income. Maintenance payments are lowered at a rate of 4% per child. Maintenance contracts are possible. They are subject to the *clausula rebus sic stantibus*.

The spouse who receives no income but is in charge of the household represents the other spouse in legal transactions of everyday life which are linked to the household and appropriate to the spouse's lifestyle (§ 96 ABGB). This rule of representation is called 'power of the key' (*Schlüsselgewalt*).

### *[4] Marital Home*

As a rule, marriage includes an obligation to live in the same home. Nonetheless, § 92(1) ABGB allows a spouse to call for a relocation of the marital home, if he has justifiable reasons, unless the other spouse has equally important reasons not to relocate. Notwithstanding § 91(1), according to § 92(2) ABGB a spouse may take separate residence if it is justified for important personal reasons or for as long as there is a threat of physical violence. Spouses may appeal to court to decide in non-contentious proceeding if their (planned) activities are lawful according to § 92(1) or (2) ABGB.

During marriage § 97 ABGB protects a spouse's need for accommodation in residences of which the other spouse is entitled to dispose. § 97 ABGB protects one spouse *vis-à-vis* the other regardless of the legal nature of his right to dispose of the other's home.

## [D] Matrimonial Property

The ABGB contains statutes on matrimonial property in its 28th main section (§§ 1217-1266), offering both a statutory matrimonial property regime and contractual matrimonial property regimes.

The statutory matrimonial property regime is separation of property (§ 1237 ABGB). Marriage does not alter the status of property previously owned by the spouses. During marriage each spouse owns solely those assets which she or he acquires. The strict separation of property as devised by the statutory matrimonial property regime applies only until the termination of the marriage, upon which property is to be allocated among the former spouses notwithstanding former ownership.

Paragraphs 1233 ff ABGB typecast the matrimonial property regime of community of property. Spouses may opt for this regime by concluding a marriage contract (*Ehevertrag*) in the form of a notarial deed (*Notariatsakt*). Furthermore, they are free to contractually organise the matrimonial regime as fit to their needs within the general boundaries of contract law. Note however that as a rule these marriage contracts do not determine the consequences of divorce for matrimonial assets.

## [E] Divorce

Marriage can only be dissolved by a decision of the court (§ 49 EheG). The competent court is the district court (*Bezirksgericht*). Austrian divorce law recognises the principle of fault and other reasons, most importantly irreparable disruption (*unheilbare Zerrüttung*), as grounds for divorce. Different grounds for divorce have different consequences for maintenance obligations and in social security law. Most notably, the spouse[2] who is divorced without fault enjoys a better position than the spouse who is

2. Where the EheG postulates rules for the divorcés the text speaks of 'spouses'. We will use this terminology here accordingly.

guilty of causing the divorce. However, the consequences with regard to the name of the spouses and the distribution of assets are regulated independently of the grounds for divorce and thus apply to all divorces equally. In general, divorce suits are a matter of contentious jurisdiction according to the rules of the ZPO. However, in the case of divorce by consent non-contentious jurisdiction applies.

### *[1] Divorce for Fault (§ 49 EheG)*

Austrian law recognises the principle of fault in § 49 EheG. The question of fault is relevant for maintenance obligations, the costs of litigation, and has special consequences for marriage contracts.

A spouse may file for divorce, if the other spouse has committed severe marital misconduct (*schwere Eheverfehlung*) or acted dishonourably or immorally and in doing so has disrupted the marriage so severely that a restoration of a partnership that conforms with the nature of marriage cannot be expected. Adultery, physical violence and inflicting severe emotional suffering are particular examples of severe marital misconduct according to § 49 EheG. Furthermore, grave violations of matrimonial duties are considered as severe marital misconduct. They must have been the (objectively adequate) cause of a severe disruption of marriage, in order to constitute sufficient grounds for divorce. Furthermore, the violation of marital duties must have been culpable. A disruption of marriage has occurred, when the mental, emotional or physical community of spouses has broken down. However, it suffices as a breakdown of marriage, if one spouse has lost his or her wish to live in matrimonial partnership.

Spouses who themselves are guilty of severe marital misconduct may not file for divorce, if, considering the type of their misconduct, such a suit is morally (*sittlich*) unjustified in the light of a true appreciation of the nature of marriage. In order to determine whether such a divorce suit is morally justified or not, one has to consider in particular, if there is a connection between the misconduct on the part of the spouse who wants to file for divorce and the misconduct and guilt on the part of the other spouse (§ 49 EheG). The right to divorce is forfeited, if a spouse has forgiven the misconduct or did not consider the misconduct as disrupting the marriage (§ 56 EheG). The right to divorce expires, if the spouse does not file a divorce suit within six months of gaining knowledge of the grounds for divorce (§ 57 EheG). For as long as spouses do not live in a common household this period is suspended. However, the spouse who is at fault for severe marital misconduct can trigger this time limit by calling upon the other spouse to resume living in a common household and re-establish marital conjugal community or to file for divorce within six months. After a period of ten years severe marital misconducts cannot serve as grounds for divorce any more, whether the other spouse had knowledge of these actions or not (§ 57(2) EheG). The judge pronounces the fault of the defendant (*Beklagter*) in her divorce-judgment (§ 60(1) EheG). The defendant may file a counter claim, if he wishes to be divorced from the plaintiff (*Kläger*) for his fault at the irreparable disruption of the marriage. If the defendant does not wish to be divorced, nonetheless he can petition that the plaintiff's fault is to be pronounced. In summary, the judge may pronounce that one spouse is exclusively at fault, one spouse is predominantly at fault or that both spouses are equally at fault.

### *[2] Divorce on the Grounds of Illness*

In cases of mental defects, mental illness or infectious or revolting diseases §§ 50-52 EheG allow for a spouse to file for divorce, if a remedy of the ground for divorce cannot be expected. According to the hardship clause (*Härteklausel*) of § 54 EheG marriage may not be divorced, if the divorce suit is unethical. In general, this is presumed, if the dissolution of marriage would burden the other spouse extraordinarily in light of the facts, especially the duration of the marriage, the age of the spouses or the cause of a disease. The defendant may petition for the plaintiff to be found at fault (§ 61(2) EheG).

### *[3] Divorce for Irreparable Disruption of Marriage and Dissolution of Domestic Community*

According to § 55(1) EheG spouses may sue for divorce three years after domestic community (*häusliche Gemeinschaft*) has been dissolved on grounds of severe and irreparable disruption of marriage. Case law interprets domestic community as a combination of community in a conjugal home (*Wohnungsgemeinschaft*), of economic community (*Wirtschaftsgemeinschaft*) and of sexual relationship (*Geschlechtsgemeinschaft*). The defendant may oppose such a divorce suit pursuant to § 55(2) EheG if the spouse who has sued for divorce had culpably caused the disruption of marriage alone or predominantly and if the divorce would burden the defendant more gravely than the dismissal of the suit would burden the plaintiff.

Paragraph 55(3) EheG allows suing for divorce, if the domestic community has been dissolved for six years or longer. In this case the rules of § 55(2) EheG do not apply.

In any case the defendant may petition that the court pronounces the plaintiff (predominantly) at fault for causing the disruption of marriage (§ 61(3) EheG).

### *[4] Divorce by Mutual Consent*

Spouses may petition for divorce, if their conjugal community has been dissolved for at least half a year, both spouses concede that their conjugal relation has been irreparably disrupted and the spouses mutually agree about wanting a divorce (§ 55a(1) EheG). § 55a(2) requires that the spouses sign a written agreement in court that settles the consequences of divorce (*Schuldenfolgenvereinbarung*) pertaining to care and custody over children, the right to personal contact with children and the obligation to maintenance *vis-à-vis* children, as well as the consequences with regard to maintenance and statutory rights regarding property *vis-à-vis* each other.

### [F] Legal Consequences of Divorce

The most important consequences and issues of divorce are maintenance, child custody and distribution of matrimonial property as well as matters of social security. For consequences with regard to the name of the divorcés see above.

#### *[1] Maintenance*

The right to maintenance according to § 94 ABGB expires with the divorce. In principle the spouses are expected to pursue reasonable gainful employment in order to provide for their needs. They are free to settle post-divorce maintenance (§ 80 EheG). If the spouses do not reach an agreement §§ 66 ff EheG provide a post-divorce maintenance regime that is graduated according to fault and the needs of the spouses. If there is a claim to post-divorce maintenance, in general it is to be fulfilled by monthly payment (§ 70(1) EheG). Instead of a monthly payment, the spouse who is entitled to maintenance may demand a one-time compensation if there is an important reason and the demand does not burden the other spouse inequitably. The execution of maintenance claims is facilitated by §§ 291a ff EO. Maintenance claims become time-barred in three years (§ 1480 ABGB).

Section 66 EheG regulates maintenance obligations of the spouse who was (predominantly) at fault. In principle, every spouse is responsible for his own maintenance. However, the spouse who was (predominantly) at fault owes adequate maintenance insofar as the other spouse's income from assets and reasonable gainful employment does not suffice. The amount of the maintenance rates is determined according to the principles of § 94 ABGB (adequate maintenance, principle of true effort). They are lessened according to equity, if taking all other obligations into account, the spouse who was (predominantly) at fault would endanger his own maintenance, if he paid full maintenance (§ 67(1) EheG). In such cases the spouse who requires maintenance must turn to his relatives before he can demand maintenance from the other spouse (§ 71(1) EheG). No maintenance is due in cases of § 67(1) EheG, as long as the spouse who is entitled to maintenance can cover his/her maintenance needs from the stem of his assets (*aus dem Stamm seines Vermögens*).

Spouses who are equally responsible for causing the divorce are not entitled to maintenance payments in general. Yet § 68 EheG allows the spouse who cannot supply maintenance for himself a right to maintenance according to equity *vis-à-vis* the other. This right to maintenance is limited to covering some basic needs and may be limited to a certain period of time.

§ 68a EheG stipulates rights to maintenance independently of who is at fault for causing the divorce.

Pursuant to § 68a(1) EheG a spouse who is occupied with the care and upbringing of the spouses' child may claim a right to maintenance, as far as, taking the well-being of the child into account, it is not reasonable for the spouse to provide for himself. Until the child has turned five, the unreasonableness is presumed but may be disproved. As a rule the maintenance claim is limited and ceases three years after the fifth birthday of the youngest child in care.

Paragraph 68a(2) EheG provides a claim to maintenance for spouses who cannot reasonably provide their own maintenance. The conditions for this claim are that the spouses had agreed for the spouse to take care of the household and to care for the children of the spouses or to care for other family members and as a result of this the spouse cannot be reasonably expected to (fully) provide for his own maintenance because he lacks opportunities for gainful employment for example because of insufficient education, the duration of marital life, his age or his health. If this is the case, the other spouse owes maintenance according to the spouse's needs (*Lebensbedarf*). Maintenance rates according to the spouse's needs (§ 68a(2) EheG) are lower than the adequate maintenance of § 66 EheG, therefore case law determines them at an amount between 15%-33% of the other spouses income. The court limits these maintenance claims to three years if it can be expected that the spouse will be capable of providing for himself after this time.

Both maintenance claims according to § 68a(1) and according to § 68a(2) EheG are contingent on the equity clause of § 68a(3) EheG. These maintenance claims can be reduced to zero, insofar as granting them was inequitable because the spouse in need had either committed an especially severe marital misconduct (*besonders schwerwiegende Eheverfehlung*) or had caused his need for maintenance payments in a grossly negligent manner. Furthermore, the principles of § 67(1) EheG apply to cases of § 68a(1) and (2) EheG.

If the divorce was based upon §§ 50-52 EheG (divorce on the grounds of illness) and the judgment proclaims the spouse who sued for divorce guilty (§ 61(2) EheG), the other spouse has a claim to adequate maintenance as under the rules of §§ 66, 67 EheG (§ 69(1) EheG).

If in cases of §§ 50-52 EheG no spouse is pronounced at fault for causing the divorce the maintenance payments may be imposed according to equity on the spouse who sued for divorce (§ 69(3) EheG). Depending on the circumstances judges may vary the amount of maintenance between necessary maintenance and adequate maintenance. As long as the spouse in need can cover his maintenance needs from the stem of his assets, there is no claim to maintenance after § 69(3) EheG.

If the divorce is based upon the irreparable disruption of marriage (§ 55 EheG) and the court pronounces the spouse who sued for divorce to be at fault, this spouse owes maintenance as if the marriage was not divorced (§ 94 ABGB). This claim to maintenance is aimed at protecting the housekeeping spouse from the effects of divorce after long years of marriage. Therefore it includes the payment of premium for voluntary health insurance coverage. Maintenance obligations *vis-à-vis* a new spouse are not considered, unless it is equitable under the circumstances.

Paragraph 69a EheG provides for cases of divorce by mutual agreement. If there is no legally effective agreement about the consequences of divorce there is a claim to equitable maintenance payments according to § 69a(2) EheG.

Paragraph 69b EheG declares § 68a EheG to be applicable for cases of divorce after §§ 50-52 and 55 EheG and to be applicable if there is divorce by mutual agreement but no valid agreement about the consequences of divorce.

Spouses who are entitled to maintenance, but whose actions of moral fault (e.g., drug addiction or compulsive gambling) have caused their need for maintenance may demand only maintenance for necessities of life (*notdürftiger Unterhalt*) (§ 73(1) EheG). Spouses whose deliberate or grossly negligent actions increase their need for maintenance have no claim to increased payments (§ 73(2) EheG). Spouses forfeit their claim to maintenance, if they are guilty of very severe misconduct against the other, or if they lead a dishonourable or immoral life against the other's will (§ 74 EheG). If a spouse marries again or becomes part of a registered partnership, he loses his claim to maintenance *vis-à-vis* his former spouse (§ 75 EheG). Whether a claim to maintenance is suspended for as long as the spouse who has a claim to maintenance lives in non-marital cohabitation is a matter of controversy. Case law suspends the claim to maintenance. Newer doctrine is critical of this practice and proposes to consider if actual contributions by the new partner provide for maintenance-relevant needs, when determining whether the former spouse owes maintenance payments. The claim to maintenance is extinguished by the death of the entitled spouse (§ 77 EheG). When the spouse who is obligated to pay maintenance dies, the obligation passes on to the estate as a debt of the estate (*Nachlassverbindlichkeit*) and is then passed on to the heirs when the estate is devolved to the heir (*Einantwortung*) (§ 78(1) EheG). The restrictions of § 67 EheG do not apply to the heir. However, considering the heir's circumstances and the earning potential of the estate, the claim to maintenance is reduced according to equity (§ 78(2) EheG). Also, all public or private supplies that the spouse receives (widow's pension, life insurance) are taken into account. As an exception, maintenance obligations that are grounded in § 68 EheG expire, when the spouse who is obligated dies (§ 78(3) EheG).

### *[2] Social Security Law*

In general the end of marriage puts an end to a spouse's insurance coverage in social security that is dependent on the insurance coverage of the spouse who is gainfully employed (§ 123 ASVG, § 83 GSVG). However, divorcés may insure themselves voluntarily (§ 16 ASVG, § 8 GSVG). According to § 258(4) ASVG and § 136(4) GSVG a divorcé has a claim to a widow(er)'s pension, if the deceased was obligated at the time of his death to pay maintenance on the basis of a judgment, a judicial settlement (*gerichtlicher Vergleich*), or a contractual agreement that was concluded before the dissolution of the marriage, or if the deceased has paid maintenance up to his death constantly over a period of at least a year after the divorce of a marriage that had lasted for at least ten years.

### *[3] Division of Matrimonial Assets*

Within a year after the divorce, the decision to declare the marriage void or the annulment of the marriage the spouses may petition in non-contentious litigation for an equitable division of their assets (§§ 85, 95 EheG) or they may freely agree upon a division of assets. The right to petition for division of matrimonial assets expires within a year of the divorce (§ 95 EheG).

The statutory rule is that after the dissolution of marriage matrimonial utility assets (*eheliches Gebrauchsvermögen*) and matrimonial savings (*eheliche Ersparnisse*) shall be divided between the spouses according to equity (§§ 81 ff EheG).

The legal position of the spouses concerning their property does not predetermine the outcome of the division of assets. The aim of the division of assets is not to punish or to reward spouses according to their actions prior to the dissolution of the marriage, but to equitably divide assets according to the contributions of the spouses to building these assets and their respective needs.

Marital utility assets comprise movable and immovable objects (*körperliche Sachen*), which for the time of conjugal community served the purpose to be used by both spouses including household items and the matrimonial home (§ 81(2) EheG). Matrimonial savings are financial assets of any kind which the spouses have acquired during their conjugal community and are usually designated to be realised (§ 81(3) EheG). After § 81(1) EheG debts which are closely linked to matrimonial savings and marital utility assets must be accounted for. Objects that are neither marital utility assets nor matrimonial savings are not subject to division. Furthermore, § 82 EheG exempts certain objects from the division between the spouses: objects which one spouse has brought into the marriage, has acquired because of a testamentary disposition or which have been a present to one spouse by a third party; objects which serve the personal use of one spouse alone or which serve the occupation of a spouse; objects that are part of a company or the company itself and company shares, unless they are pure investments (*bloße Wertanlagen*) which serve no operational or entrepreneurial purpose. The latter exceptions are justified from an economic point of view because they protect companies and jobs. However, § 82(2) EheG provides a counter-exception. If a spouse depends on the marital home to secure his basic living needs or if a child of the spouses has an interest to continue living in the matrimonial home that is worthy of consideration, the matrimonial home is included into the division of assets. The same counter-exception applies to household items, which are essential to securing one spouse's basic living needs.

Paragraph 91 EheG protects spouses from disadvantageous transfers of assets by the other spouse. If a spouse diminishes matrimonial utility assets or matrimonial savings without the (implicit) consent of the other spouse in a manner that conflicts with the spouses' lifestyle during their conjugal community, the value by which the assets were diminished is included into the division of assets, if the transfer occurred two years before the spouse sued for divorce or, two years before the spouses ended their conjugal community, if this happened before the divorce suit (§ 91(1) EheG). § 91(2) EheG protects from transfers of assets into companies, because companies are shielded from the division of assets. In principle, if matrimonial assets are used for or transferred to a company their value is included into the matrimonial assets to be divided. In the process it must be considered which advantages were generated and if the marital assets that were used were created by the company's earnings. Most importantly, the company must not be endangered by the division of matrimonial assets.

Matrimonial assets are divided according to principles of equity, such as the extent of the respective spouse's contribution to the acquisition of assets, the well-being of the spouses' children and the spouses' debts which are related to matrimonial living expenses (§ 83(1) EheG). According to § 83(2) EheG providing maintenance, contribution of work to the other's vocational means of income (if not compensated for otherwise), housekeeping, care and education of the spouses' children and every other kind of conjugal support count as a contribution to the acquisition of assets. Other principles are that the division of assets shall ensure that the spouses' future areas of life interfere as little as possible (§ 84 EheG) and that the financial consequences of the division of assets should allow the spouses to carry on with their lives (*Grundsatz des Wohlbestehenkönnens*) (developed by case law). As mentioned above, fault is in general no determinant for the division of assets; however, if one spouse was at fault for ending the marriage, case law allows the other spouse a right to request certain parts of the spouses' assets.

The court divides matrimonial assets by allocating objects to the spouses. The court disposes of wide-ranging possibilities in order to achieve an equitable result, it may, for example, transfer property of matrimonial utility assets or matrimonial savings from one spouse to the other. With regard to the marital home the court may grant one spouse a right to tenancy *vis-à-vis* the spouse who owns the marital home. If an equitable division is otherwise impossible, § 94 EheG allows to determine a compensation payment.

If the spouses wish to arrange the division of assets mutually they may do so by concluding division agreements (*Aufteilungsvereinbarungen*). They can be freely concluded in the context of proceedings to end the marriage (§ 97(5) EheG). Beforehand concluded division agreements, so-called pre-(nuptial) agreements (*Vorausvereinbarungen*), are subject to the rules of § 97 EheG, including formal requirements. Agreements on the division of matrimonial savings or the marital home require the form of a notarial deed. Agreements on the division of matrimonial utility assets require the signature of both parties. Pre-(nuptial) agreements that do not meet the required form are invalid; nonetheless, the judge may take their arrangements into account when deciding about the division of assets. With regard to the marital home spouses may (beforehand) agree to include it into the assets to be divided upon the dissolution of marriage ('opt-in'-agreement). In contrast, they may agree that the court may not transfer property of the marital home in any case (§ 87(1) EheG). § 97(2), (3) and (4) EheG allow the judge discretion to deviate from division agreements concluded without the context of proceedings to end the marriage under certain conditions in order to prevent grave injustice.

### *[4] Loans*

The division of matrimonial assets includes debts which are connected to matrimonial savings and matrimonial utility assets as well as debts connected to the spouses' lifestyle. §§ 55a and 97 EheG allow spouses to settle an internal obligation to repay debts. Pursuant to § 92 EheG the court may establish such an internal obligation as well.

Furthermore, § 98(1) EheG allows for an allocation of the spouses' common debts with effect *vis-à-vis* third party creditors. Each spouse may petition the court to pronounce that the spouse who is internally obligated to repay the debt becomes the primary debtor, whereas the other spouse becomes a guarantor for cases of stoppage of payment (*Ausfallsbürge*). According to § 98(2) EheG the guarantor is not required to repay debt, unless the primary debtor does not pay within adequate time although the creditor has successfully petitioned for a title for judicial execution, has thereafter arranged for execution of movable property, income and real estate and has realised securities for the debt.

### [G] Registered Partnership

Most rules for registered partnerships are identical to the rules pertaining to marriage, especially with regard to pecuniary aspects. § 43 EheG pronounces several acts of legislation pertaining to marriage applicable to registered partnerships. Instead of a duty to fidelity there is a duty to comprehensive life-partnership and a relationship based on trust (§ 8(2) EheG). Registered partnership requires that the persons involved are of age (18) (§ 4(2) EPG). A civil servant of the regional administrative authorities (*Bezirksverwaltungsbehörden*) records the establishment of a registered partnership. The attendance of both future partners and their signatures are required (25(1) PStG). The registered partnership is recorded in the Central Register of Civil Status (§ 27, § 35 PStG). Registered partners keep their name (§ 7 EPG), however they may change their name according to administrative rules of the Law on the Changing of Names (*Namensänderungsgesetz*). The EPG concentrates the terms and rules for 'divorce' and 'annulation' in the term 'dissolution', thus registered partnership ends by dissolution or by declaration that it is void. § 15(3) EPG deviates from § 55(3) EheG insofar as three years without domestic community suffice for the dissolution of a registered partnership in any case. The privileged claim to maintenance according to § 69(2) EheG was not adopted for registered partners. The EPG contains no rules pertaining to the law of parents and child.

### [H] Non-marital Cohabitation

Non-marital cohabitation is not specifically regulated by civil law. The rules for marriage do not apply to non-marital cohabitation. There is no general legal definition of non-marital cohabitation although it features in some specific acts of legislation that apply the same rules to non-married partners and to spouses. Case law understands non-marital cohabitation as a relationship similar to marriage that is meant to last for a certain period of time and includes a common home, economic community and sexual relationship although not all criteria need to be satisfied. Partners of non-marital cohabitation are called *Lebensgefährten*. The rules for division of matrimonial assets (§§ 81 ff EheG) do not apply to non-marital cohabitation; therefore the assets of non-married partners are divided pursuant to general rules of civil law with regard to separation of property and unjust enrichment.

## §8.04 LAW OF PARENTS AND CHILD (*KINDSCHAFTSRECHT*)

The legal relation between parents and children has undergone constant change since the 1970s. The rights and duties of father and mother are now the same (§ 137(1) ABGB). Different rules applying to father and mother need justification. Hence, today different rules apply only with regard to the question of parentage. The child is no longer perceived as an object of the parents' rights or state supervision, but a subject of law with claims of his/her own. In recent years the jurisdiction of the Constitutional Court and the European Court of Justice has stimulated reform culminating in the Act Amending Law of Parents and Child and the Law on Names of 2013 which brought about extensive change and a restructuring of the law of parents and child. Notably an Assistance for Family Court (*Familiengerichtshilfe*) was established by §§ 106a-106c AußStrG. Social workers and psychologists support the judge in gathering information and try to facilitate an amicable agreement in matters of custody and personal contact.

### [A] The Child's Well-Being (*Kindeswohl*)

The KindNamRÄG 2013 includes a new § 138 ABGB: In all matters that concern the minor child, especially custody and personal contacts, the child's well-being must be considered as the leading principle; the child's well-being must be ensured in the best possible way. Paragraph 138 ABGB contains a list of various non-exclusive criteria for the child's well-being, for example: adequate provision with basic needs like nourishment, medical and sanitary care, housing and careful parenting; valuation and acceptance, care and security of the physical and emotional integrity of the child; encouraging of skills and faculties of the child; consideration of the child's opinion; reliable contact to both parents and other important persons; the prevention of conflicts of loyalty and feelings of guilt of the child; the lifestyle of the child and the parents.

### [B] Parentage

Parentage is the legal category that activates legal relations with the child as governed by law of parents and child. Austrian law recognises different grounds for parentage: natural birth, marriage to the mother, acknowledgement of paternity, adoption and establishment by court decision. The law no longer recognises the distinction of legitimate and illegitimate children.

#### *[1] Motherhood*

The woman who gives birth to a child is the mother (§ 143 ABGB). Egg donation and surrogacy are forbidden (§ 3(1) and (3) FMedG). The rule of § 143 ABGB applies strictly in cases of egg donation or surrogacy, if they are performed – illegally in Austria or legally abroad. The woman who gives birth to a child is the mother, not the person who is the immediate female genetic ancestor of the child.

### *[2] Paternity*

Paternity is a legal status that can be awarded because of marriage to the mother, acknowledgement of paternity, or a judicial decree (§ 144(1) ABGB). The general rule is that the person who has been married to the mother at the time of birth is the father. Unmarried fathers must acknowledge their child in the form of a public deed or publicly authenticated document. Paragraphs 140-154 ABGB establish very detailed rules regarding paternity. Both the child and the father may petition the court to determine paternity (§ 148 ABGB). If paternity is purported or contested, it is a matter of non-contentious proceedings. According to § 82(2) AußStrG the parties of proceedings in matters of paternity are the child, the person who wishes to (re-)establish or resolve paternity and the mother of the child. § 85 AußStrG arranges for obligations to co-operate in establishing proof of paternity.

### *[3] Medically Assisted Reproduction*

Medically assisted reproduction has been allowed since the introduction of the FMedG in 1992. Since 2015 pre-implantation diagnostics are allowed, but only in tightly restricted circumstances, for example, if the genetic disposition of one parent significantly increases the risk that the child is born with a severe hereditary disease (§ 2b). As a reaction to a recent decision by the Constitutional Court,[3] most recent legislation has opened all legally allowed forms of medically assisted reproduction for same-sex partners – since surrogacy motherhood is not allowed, male same-sex partners are de facto precluded from medically assisted reproduction. Persons who are married, who are registered partners or who live in non-married partnership may use medically assisted reproduction as a last resort, if it is impossible or unreasonable to conceive a child (§ 2 FMedG). The law allows artificial insemination, in-vitro-fertilisation and gamete intrafallopian transfer (§ 3 FMedG). If donated sperm was used for insemination, the person who has agreed to this form of medically assisted reproduction in the form of a notarial deed (the partner or husband of the mother) is the legal father of the child (§ 148(3) ABGB). Paternity of the sperm donor cannot be established (§ 148(4) ABGB).

### *[4] Adoption*

Adoption establishes a legal relation of parent and child by contract. Adoption brings about the same legal effects between the adopter and his descendants and the adopted

3. Constitutional Court, 10 Dec. 2013, G16/2013, G44/2013.

child and his minor children as those brought about by natural birth (§ 197 ABGB). If spouses adopt a child, most legal rights between the adopted child and the natural parents expire (§ 197(2)). However, the child and his/her natural parents remain related. The natural parents owe maintenance subsidiarily. The mutual right of succession remains, but the law of succession ranks the adoptive parents before the natural parents (199 ABGB). The new § 197(4) ABGB liberalises 'stepchild-adoption': a spouse, a registered partner or a hetero- or homosexual non-married/non-registered partner (*Lebensgefährte*) can adopt his/her partner's child. Then the child's legal relation to the other natural parent expires according to § 197(2) ABGB. The ban on joint-adoption and successive adoption by registered partners (§ 8(4) EPG) was declared unconstitutional by the Constitutional Court effective 1 January 2016.[4]

Adoption is established by a written contract between the adopter and the adopted. The contract must be authorised by court in order to come into effect (§ 192(1) ABGB). If the adoptive person is a minor, the legal representative concludes the adoption contract for the adoptive child (§ 192(2) ABGB). As a rule adoption can only be established between two persons. In contrast spouses must adopt an adoptive person together. However, there are several exceptions to this rule (§ 191(2) ABGB). The adopter must be a person *sui juris* who is of at least 25 years of age (§ 193(1) ABGB). Recently the Constitutional Court declared the rule that the adoptive child must be at least 16 years younger (§ 193(2) ABGB) unconstitutional.[5] The court may authorise an adoption of a minor only, if it is in the child's best interest and a relationship like it is common between natural parents and their children already exists or shall be established (§193(1) ABGB). If the adoptive person is of age the adoption may only be authorised, if the adopter and the adoptive child have established a relationship equal to one between natural parent and child and have been living in the same household for five years or have mutually supported one another in similarly close community (§ 194(1) ABGB). Authorisation is not possible, if the adoption endangers prevailing interests of a natural child like a claim to maintenance (§ 194(2) ABGB). According to § 195(1) ABGB the court may only authorise the adoption if the following persons consent to the adoption: the parents of an adoptive child who is a minor, the spouse or the registered partner of the adopter, the spouse or registered partner of the adoptive child and the adoptive child, if it is a minor but older than 14 years old. § 195(2) ABGB establishes exceptions from § 195(1) ABGB. According to § 195(3) ABGB the court may substitute the agreement of other persons but the child, if there are no reasonable grounds not to agree to the adoption. Several persons have a right to be heard in court: the at least five years old minor child to be adopted, unless it has already been living with the adopter; the parents of a person to be adopted who is of age; foster parents or the director of an orphanage, the Authority for Assistance for Children and Young Persons (§ 196(1) ABGB) and the children of the adopter.

Paragraph 88 AußStrG allows for a form of secret adoption that is called *Inkognitoadoption*. Thereby all parties agree to make the court's approval dependent on several persons whose consent is required or who have a right to be heard to forfeit

4. Constitutional Court, 11 Dec. 2014, G 119-120/2014-12.
5. Constutional Court, 11 Dec. 2014, G18/2014. The decision takes effect on 1 Jan. 2016.

their right to information on the name and place of residence of the adopter and to forfeit their right to notification of the court's approval.

With regard to the adoption of foreign children, several special rules apply. Austria has adopted the Hague Adoption Convention 25 May 1993 and the European Convention on the Adoption of Children. In facultative non-contentious proceedings the parties may petition the court to decide on the validity of a foreign adoption, or a foreign resolution of an adoption (§§ 91a-91d AußStrG).

Adoption must be revoked with retroactive effect (*ex tunc*) for serious reasons (§ 200 ABGB) concerning compliance with requirements of valid adoption. Adoption is annulled with *ex nunc* effect for reasons that concern the best interest and well-being of the child and if the adopter and the adopted child mutually petition for annulment.

### [C] Name

The person who is entrusted with care and education of the child has the right to name the child. The name is declared before a Registrar in the form of a public deed or publicly authenticated document (§ 157(3) iVm § 93c ABGB). Persons who have a right to name the child must make an effort to consent about the name. The declaration of one person that the other person consents to the name or that consent cannot be achieved with reasonable means suffices (§ 156(1) ABGB). If no consent is possible, or different names are declared, the parents may petition the court to decide (§ 181 ABGB). Since 2013 the child's name may be almost any combination of the parents' names; restrictions depend on whether the parents have one common family name or not. No child's name may consist of more than two names.

### [D] Custody and Care (*Obsorge*)

Custody comprehends care and education, managing of assets and representing the minor child (§ 158(1) ABGB). Custody is not only a right, but also a responsibility. Care of the minor child includes ensuring the child's physical well-being and health; parenting, especially the development of the child's physical, mental, emotional and moral abilities; promoting the dispositions, capabilities and potentials of the child and education in school and vocational training (§ 160(1) ABGB). The degree of care and education depends on the lifestyle of the parents (§ 160(2) ABGB). The person who is entrusted with custody is the legal representative of the child (§ 167 ABGB). The representative can act and conclude contracts in the child's name. Sole agency is the principle of legal representation of a minor (§ 167(1) ABGB). Paragraph 167(2) ABGB lists matters that require joint representation of parents who are entrusted with custody like changing the child's name, changing the child's citizenship or religious affiliation, entrusting a third person with caring for the child or acknowledgements of paternity for the child. Legal representation that concerns important financial matters which are not part of prudent regular managing of assets (*ordentlicher Wirtschaftsbetrieb*) requires the consent of both parents who are entrusted with custody and the courts approval (§ 167(3) ABGB). Such matters include for example the sale of real estate, important matters with regard to companies or taking legal action. According to § 162 ABGB parents manage their child's assets with the diligence of prudent parents. Money is to be invested in compliance with the rules on the investment of ward's money (*Mündelgeld*) in §§ 215-224 ABGB. Custody includes a right to determine the residence of the child. Children have to follow their parents' orders. In turn parents have to consider the child's age, development and personality (§ 161 ABGB). § 137(2) prohibits using physical violence and inflicting physical or mental pain for parenting. Medical treatments require the consent of the child, if he is able to understand and to assess the situation; the law presumes this for children who are at least 14 years old (§ 173(1) ABGB). If the child cannot consent, the person who is entrusted with care and education must consent to the medical treatment. In cases of emergency the child may be treated without obtaining consent first (§ 173(3) ABGB). Custody of a child ends when the child comes of age (§ 183 ABGB). All persons who are entrusted with the custody of a child, or have other rights and obligations *vis-à-vis* the child (maintenance, right to personal contact), must refrain from everything that may compromise the relation between the child and other such persons or that may impede their tasks (principle of good conduct, *Wohlverhaltensgebot* § 159 ABGB). The court must ensure the well-being of the child by taking appropriate measures, like ordering obligatory visitations of family council, mediation or violence prevention training (§ 107 AußStrG).

If the parents are married, both are entrusted with custody (§ 177(1) ABGB). They exercise custody consensually. If they cannot agree on an important issue each parent may petition a decision in court.

If the parents are not married, the mother is entrusted with custody. The parents may decide personally before a Registrar that both parents shall be entrusted with custody. Each spouse may revoke his decision within eight weeks (§ 177(2) ABGB). If both parents are entrusted with custody but do not live in the same household, they must declare where the child lives primarily (§ 177(4) ABGB). Both married and unmarried parents may settle custody by agreement (§ 177(3) ABGB). The parent who is not entrusted with custody may petition the court to grant him full custody or to establish shared custody (§ 180(1) [2] ABGB). Then the court must provide a provisional arrangement and decide on the question of custody after a period of provisional parental responsibility (six months) (§ 180(2) ABGB). Thereby unmarried fathers may be entrusted with the custody of the child without the mother's consent, if this is in the child's best interest. In the case of divorce or separation of the parents normally both remain entrusted with custody (§ 179(1) ABGB). The parents may reach a different agreement in court (§ 179(1) ABGB). If both (separated) parents are entrusted with custody, they must decide in court in whose household the child will live primarily (§ 179(2) ABGB). If they cannot reach an agreement the court must provide a provisional arrangement, if this is in the child's best interest (§ 180(1) [1] ABGB) and decide about custody after six months (§ 180(2) ABGB). If both parents are (partly) incapable of custody (e.g., if both parents are mentally disabled), the court decides that grandparents or foster parents shall be entrusted with custody. Foster parents are defined as persons who (partly) take care of and raise a minor child who have a relation to the child that comes close to that between biological parents and their children or with whom such a relation shall be established (§ 194 ABGB). Foster parents may petition the court to be entrusted with custody (§ 185 ABGB). If neither capable grandparents nor foster parents are available, other persons will be entrusted with custody, primarily relatives or if not possible, other persons who are close to the child (§§ 204-206 ABGB). The Authority for Assistance for Children and Young Persons is entrusted with custody, if a minor child is found whose parents are unknown (§ 207(1) ABGB) and will be entrusted with custody, if no other suitable person is available (§ 209 ABGB).

The Authority for Assistance for Children and Young Persons has to petition in court for orders to protect the child's well-being with regard to custody. In the case of imminent danger the Authority can take the necessary measures in matters of care and education with provisional effect until the court has decided. The Agency petitions for such a decision within eight days. To the extent of the measures taken the Agency is provisionally entrusted with custody (§ 211(1) ABGB).

If there is a clash of interest between the child and his legal representatives in a certain matter, the Authority for Assistance for Children and Young Persons is appointed as curator, if the clash of interests puts the child's interests at risk and the court cannot protect them sufficiently (§ 271 ABGB).

Each parent must cultivate a personal relation that includes personal contact to his child (186 ABGB). Correspondingly parent and child have a right to regular contact according to the needs of the child. Paragraph 186 f ABGB are especially important for parents who do not live in a household with the child. The parents shall arrange contact with the child mutually, but court may restrict or facilitate contact, if no agreement can be reached (§ 187(1) ABGB, § 110 AußStrG). According to § 111 AußStrG the court may arrange that suitable third parties supervise the visit of a parent, if this is requested by a parent or the child and in the child's best interest. The Assistance of Family Court may be given the task of a mediator in proceedings regarding the regulation or execution of the right of personal contact (§ 106b AußStrG).

According to § 188 ABGB grandparents and grandchildren have a right to personal contact, insofar it does not disturb the family life of the parents.

The parent who is not entrusted with custody has a right to be informed of important matters regarding the child in time by the person who is entrusted with custody, especially of intended measures that would require joint representation if both parents were entrusted with custody (§ 189(1) [1] ABGB). Furthermore, the parent has a right to voice his opinion on the matter. Also the parent may represent the child in matters of everyday life and to care for the child and raise it, as fit under the circumstances, if the child stays with the parent regularly (§ 189(1) [2] ABGB).

### [E] Maintenance

#### *[1] The Children's Right to Maintenance*

Children have a right to maintenance against their parents who must contribute to providing for the child's adequate needs in the light of the parents' lifestyle and the specific dispositions of the child. The parents share their obligation to maintenance depending on their abilities (§ 231(1) ABGB). The principle of true effort applies. The parent who keeps the household in which he cares for the child, contributes maintenance in this way (§ 231(2) ABGB). The grandparents owe maintenance subsidiarily (§ 232 ABGB). The child's right to maintenance is reduced insofar the child is able to cover his needs from his own income. If the child marries the claim to maintenance against the spouse precedes the claim against the parents. If the child lives in non-married partnership factual maintenance contributions by the partner reduce the child's claim *vis-à-vis* the parents. The parent who does not live in a household with the child owes maintenance payments. The rate of the maintenance payments depends on the needs of the child and the capacities of the parents. The determination base is the parents' income. Case law has developed percentages as guidelines: Children have a claim to 16% of their parents' income, when they are under 6 years old, to 18% when they are between six and ten, to 20%, when they are ten to fifteen and to 22% when they are over 15 years old. For every child under 10 years this percentage is lowered by 1%, for every child over 10 years the percentage is lowered by 2%. Maintenance obligations *vis-à-vis* a spouse reduce this percentage by 0%-3%. If the parents' income is very high case law draws a luxury-threshold at two and a half times the regular need of a child according to the analysis of the Central Statistics Agency (*Statistisches Zentralamt*).

The UVG facilitates federal advances for children's statutory maintenance, in order to protect them from difficulties with defaulting debtors of maintenance. The advance can be paid to minor Austrian Citizens and minor stateless children, who reside mainly in Austria, if the debtor has not paid maintenance despite a title for execution and the execution appears futile.

### *[2] The Parents' Right to Maintenance*

The child owes the parents and grandparents maintenance, if they cannot provide for themselves (§ 234 ABGB). The child is required not endanger his own needs by paying maintenance and does not owe maintenance if the parents or grandparents violated their own maintenance obligations *vis-à-vis* the child grossly.

## [F] Endowment (*Ausstattung*)

Parents must provide their children endowment, when they marry for the first time (§§ 1220-1223 ABGB). This endowment is grounded in the parents' statutory duty to supply for the child and shall help the child start-up a family. Case law awards 25%-30% of the parents' yearly net-income. There is no claim to endowment, if the child married without the knowledge of his parents or against their expressive will that is based on justified disapproval of the marriage.

### [G] Protection against Violence

The Code of Execution (EO) allow interim injunctions against domestic violence in §§ 382b, 382c and 382d EO. The court can order a person whose actions are a threat to the other person to leave the family home immediately. § 382e EO allows interim injunctions as a means of general protection from violence. The court can issue interim injunctions against stalking according to § 382g EO.

## SELECTED BIBLIOGRAPHY

Monika Hinteregger, *Familienrecht* (6th ed. 2013).
Ferdinand Kerschner, *Bürgerliches Recht. Band V: Familienrecht* (5th ed. 2013).
Astrid Deixler-Hübner, *Scheidung, Ehe und Lebensgemeinschaft* (11th ed. 2013).
Astrid Deixler-Hübner, *Der Ehevertrag* (3rd ed. 2013).
Kletečka, Andreas/Koziol, Helmut/Welser, Rudolf, *Bürgerliches Recht. Band I* (14th ed. 2014).

CHAPTER 9

# Law of Succession

*Constanze Fischer-Czermak & Katharina Windisch*[*]

## §9.01 GENERAL ASPECTS OF THE AUSTRIAN LAW OF SUCCESSION

### [A] Sources of Law

The Austrian law of succession is mainly laid out in §§ 531-824 of the Austrian General Civil Code (ABGB, *Allgemeines Bürgerliches Gesetzbuch*). Individual provisions can also be found in parts of ABGB which are assigned to family law, as well as §§ 197 and 199 concerning intestate succession in case of adoption or §§ 1248-1254 concerning joint wills and contract of inheritance. Procedural provisions are contained in §§ 143-185 of the Alternative Dispute Resolution Code (AußStrG, *Außerstreitgesetz*). Further provisions of law of succession can be found in some other statutes, for example the Marriage Act (EheG, *Ehegesetz*),[1] the Condominium Act (WEG, *Wohnungseigentumsgesetz*)[2] or the Rent Act (MRG, *Mietrechtsgesetz*),[3] and there are specific laws concerning the succession to agricultural property (*Anerbengesetz, Höferecht*).

### [B] Fundamental Terms and Principles

In Austrian law a single term is used for the law of succession in an objective and in a subjective sense: *Erbrecht* can be used as the law of succession as well as the right to inherit.

* Univ.-Prof. Dr Constanze Fischer-Czermak is University Professor at University of Vienna Faculty of Law, Department of Civil Law, Vienna, Austria; Mag. Katharina Windisch is University Assistant at University of Vienna Faculty of Law, Department of Civil Law, Vienna, Austria.

1. §§ 77 et seq. EheG.
2. § 14 WEG.
3. § 14 MRG.

The inheritance or estate (*Nachlass*) is the amount of money, property and other assets which a deceased person leaves behind. The decedent or testator (*Erblasser*) is the person whose property passes to another person after his death. The heir (*Erbe*) is the person who receives the inheritance after the decedent's death and who follows the decedent in all his rights by way of universal succession (*Gesamtrechtsnachfolge*). The transfer of title is acquired by a decision of the probate court (*Einantwortung*). Between the time of death and this court order, the inheritance is a legal entity and it is considered as in abeyance. It is called 'dormant inheritance' (*ruhender Nachlass*) and includes all heritable rights and duties. The decedent may also determine someone by a legacy or a bequest (*Legat, Vermächtnis*). The legatee (*Legatar, Vermächtnisnehmer*) receives a special asset of the inheritance by way of singular succession (*Einzelrechtsnachfolge*). Only the universal successors are called 'heirs'.

The Austrian law of succession connects the principle of testamentary freedom (*Testierfreiheit*) with the principle of succession of the next of kin (*Familienerbfolge*). Testamentary freedom allows the testator to determine the fate of his property after his death by testamentary disposition and to appoint his heirs. If the testator dies intestate, the spouse (or registered life partner) and the relatives become statutory heirs by a system of succession per stirpes. Testamentary freedom is limited by the statutory compulsory portion (*Pflichtteil*): If the testator has not appointed his spouse (or registered life partner) or his next relatives by testamentary dispositions, they have a personal money claim against the heir.

## [C] Estate

As a general rule, all rights and duties of financial value are heritable. These rights are for example rights in rem (*dingliche Rechte*), possession (*Besitz*), claims arising from contract or tort, debts or the copyright (*Urheberrecht*).

Rights which are related to the person of the decedent himself cannot be part of the estate (§ 531 ABGB). Thus personal rights, such as the power to exercise a profession or rights of the family amongst others do not count among the estate. It is possible to inherit a company, except the company is personally connected with the decedent, like a law office.

A mandate (*Auftrag* oder *Vollmacht*) expires at the time of death of the principal (*Aufgraggeber*) or the agent (*Auftragnehmer*), unless there are deviating agreements (§ 1022 ABGB). As opposed to this, a general commercial power of representation (*Prokura*) and the power of attorney (*Prozessvollmacht*) remain valid even after the principal's death. Maintenance claims are not heritable, though, legal maintenance claims of the decedent's children and of the spouse pass to the heirs and they are liable up to the amount of the value of the inheritance (§§ 233 and 796 ABGB). Moreover, claims for damages are heritable actively and passively. Social insurance benefits are heritable, if the decedent had a monetary claim against the social insurance and unless these claims devolve automatically upon the decedent's relatives due to specific provisions.

Furthermore, life insurance contracts as third-party beneficiary contracts are not part of the inheritance. The beneficiary does not have to participate in the probate procedure (*Verlassenschaftsverfahren*) and he may bring his claim directly against the life insurance.

## §9.02 THE RIGHT TO INHERIT

According to § 533 ABGB the right to inherit can be based on a contract of inheritance, on a will or on a statute. These forms of the right to inherit can exist in parallel, so testamentary succession together with intestate succession, when the testator did not dispose of the whole estate. One heir receives the same share in the inheritance only because of one title, but can inherit one share by way of intestate and another by testate succession. The contract of inheritance is the strongest title, followed by the will and the statute. Nevertheless, the de facto most common title for devolution is the statute, followed by a testament, and the contract of inheritance is rarely applied.

The heir must be alive at the time of the decedent's death (*Erbfall*) and has to have the 'legal capacity to inherit' (*Erbfähigkeit*) and the 'qualification to inherit' (*Erbwürdigkeit*). All persons with legal capacity also have the capacity to inherit. Even a child already conceived but not yet born is entitled to inherit on the condition of a subsequent live birth (§ 22 ABGB). The heir is not qualified to inherit in the event of special misconducts, like a crime having been committed against the decedent or if the obligations resulting between parents and children have been grossly neglected against the deceased. Furthermore, a person who manipulates the decedent's testamentary freedom is not qualified to inherit (§§ 540-542 ABGB).

Moreover, the heir can renounce an inheritance. The renunciation of future inheritance (§ 551 ABGB, *Erbverzicht*) is a contract between a person who will be entitled to be an heir in the future and the testator during the testator's life time. This contract has to be concluded before a notary or before court. While the absence of 'the qualification to inherit' has no effect on the descendants, in case of doubt a renunciation of inheritance excludes them from succession. A renunciation of inheritance increases the testator's freedom, because it normally includes the waiver of the compulsory portion, and is often linked to a compensation paid in satisfaction of the beneficiary's right of inheritance (*Abfindung*). It is also possible to renounce only the statutory compulsory portion, though this does not mean a renunciation of the right to inherit by intestate succession. If a person renounces the statutory compulsory portion and the testator does not draw up a will or the will is void, this person is nevertheless entitled to inherit his share in the intestate succession.

The right to inherit itself is heritable (§ 537 ABGB, *Transmission*): According to § 537 ABGB the heir's heir inherits if the heir is alive at the time of the decedent's death but deceases before the transfer of title by probate court order (*Einantwortung*).

## §9.03 INTESTATE SUCCESSION

Intestate succession (§§ 727-759 ABGB) is subsidiary and is only relevant if there is no contract of inheritance, no will or no testamentary disposition concerning the whole estate. Moreover, intestate succession applies if there is no valid last will or if the appointed heir does not receive the inheritance, for example because he predeceased. Statutory heirs (*gesetzliche Erben*) may be the spouse (or the registered life partner), relatives and adoptees.

### [A] System of Succession per Stirpes

If there is no surviving spouse (or registered partner), the whole estate passes to the decedent's relatives under system of succession per stirpes (*Parentelensystem*). The right to succeed depends on parentage according to the rules of family law (§§ 143-153 ABGB). Since a reform of family law and law of succession in 2004,[4] the right to succeed does not depend on determination of parentage during the decedent's life. This was the last step to eliminate differences in law of succession between illegitimate and legitimate children.

Under the system of succession per stirpes the decedent's family is split into different stirpes. At the top of each stirp is an ancestor or a pair of ancestors whose descendants also count to the stirp. *Stirp or class one* are the lineal descendants of the decedent himself, regardless of whether they are born in wedlock or not. So to the first class of heirs belong the children, the grandchildren and the great-grandchildren without limitation. If all decedent's sons and daughters (first degree of relationship) are alive and have legal capacity to inherit, they inherit in equal shares.

*Class two* consists of the parents of the decedent and their descendants. *Class three* are the grandparents of the decedent and their descendants. *Class four* are the great-grandparents of the decedent, however their descendants are not part of the class (*Erbrechtsgrenze*). Each parent receives half of the inheritance, each grandparent a quarter and each great-grandparent an eighth. A relative from a higher class does not become an heir if there is a surviving member of a lower class: for example the existence of children (first class) prevents the parents (second class) from inheriting.

According to 'the system of representation' (*Repräsentation*) descendants of a predeceased relative take the place of this deceased person in the class. Together they inherit the share of the predeceased relative and it has to be split between his surviving descendants. If, for example, the decedent is survived by a daughter whereas his son has predeceased him and left two children, the daughter inherits half of the estate and the son's part goes to the grandchildren, who inherit in equal shares (each ¼ of the estate). Only if a predeceased child does not leave descendants behind the siblings inherit its share.

Pursuant to § 541 ABGB 'representation' also occurs if the determined heir is disqualified to inherit (*erbunwürdig*). In case of doubt descendants cannot 'represent'

4. *Familien- und Erbrechtsänderungsgesetz 2004.*

their ancestor, if he has renounced his inheritance.[5] However, it is a controversial point if the renunciation of an estate prevents 'representation'.

Subsidiary to the 'system of representation', a share accrues to another heir if one heir has no descendants. First the accretion (*Anwachsung*)[6] occurs between a pair of ancestors in one class, for example the share of the mother passes to the father or the share of the maternal grandmother accrues to the maternal grandfather. If a pair of ancestors (e.g., the maternal grandparents) is also predeceased, these shares accrue to the other ancestors of the same class, for example the maternal grandparents' shares accrue to the paternal grandparents.

Due to the fact that a member of a lower class excludes the members of higher classes from inheriting combined with 'the system of representation', the right to inherit does not necessarily depend on the nearest relationship to the decedent and the next of kin do not always receive the inheritance. For example grandchildren (first class) will exclude the decedent's parents (second class), and nephews (second class) will exclude the decedent's grandparents (third class).

### [B] Adoption

The provisions concerning adoption are laid out in §§ 191 et seqq. ABGB. An adoptee has the equal right to inherit as relatives. However, in the family related through adoption the right to succeed only exists in the first and the second class, because adoption creates no relationship between ancestors of adoptive parents and the adoptee. The right to inherit of the biological relatives persists, though in the second class they are entitled to inherit only subsequently. The adoptee can inherit from his biological relatives as well as his adoptive parents and their descendants.

### [C] The Spouse's Share

The spouse's share depends on whether the decedent has descendants or not and whether he has surviving ancestors. If the heirs are from the first class the spouse inherits one-third of the estate; if the inheritance passes to the second or a higher class, the spouse inherits two-third.

Some of the rules of the system of succession per stirpes are modified if the deceased left behind a spouse: the second class is shortened and the shares of nephews and nieces pass to the spouse. Moreover, in the third class there is no 'representation'; for example if the only surviving relatives are the grandparent's descendants, the spouse inherits the entire inheritance. Furthermore, if the relatives of the fourth class would inherit, the spouse receives the whole succession.

Apart from this, the surviving spouse has the right to continue to live in the marital home and to inherit the personal chattel of the marital household (§ 758 ABGB,

5. See §9.02.
6. The term 'accretion' (*Anwachsung*) is used both in the intestate and in the testate succession, though, it has to be distinguished between them. 'Accretion' in the testate succession, see §9.04[C].

*gesetzliches Vorausvermächtnis des Ehegatten*). The spouse has no claim to it in the case of disinheritance (*Enterbung*). There are different opinions, if the residential right (*Wohnrecht*) of the spouse is terminated by remarriage or not.

Pursuant to § 796 ABGB the spouse is entitled to maintenance from the inheritance as in a valid marriage, but he loses this claim in the case of remarriage. Nevertheless, all perceived things have to be included in the calculation in addition to statutory compulsory portions and the creditors of the inheritance (*Nachlassgläubiger*) must first be satisfied. This right is also limited by the value of the inheritance.

If the marriage is annulled or divorced, the former spouse receives no intestate share, unless there are deviating agreements. According to § 759 paragraph 2 ABGB there is also no intestate succession if there are ongoing divorce proceedings and the reasons for a divorce are given by the surviving spouse.

There are special rules for tenancy and housing ownership, which are particularly important for the spouse or the registered life partner. Section 14 of the Rent Act (MRG, *Mietrechtsgesetz*) offers the possibility to enter into the lease after the death of the main tenant. According to § 14 paragraph 2 MRG some people are automatically included in the lease if they do not announce within fourteen days after the death of the main tenant to the landlord that they do not want to continue the tenancy. Admission is open to the spouse or, for example, the life partner, relatives in direct line, adopted children and siblings, if those persons have an urgent housing need and have already been living with the tenant in the same household in the apartment. The life partner is entitled only when he has lived at least three years with the tenant in the same household or founded the household together with the decedent. Section 14 Condominium Act (WEG, *Wohnungseigentumsgesetz*) specifies that the surviving co-proprietor incurs the share of the deceased by rights, unless he waived them within a period decided by the probate court. In the case of a release, the residential property is to be auctioned by the court. If the co-proprietor acquires the decedent's co-ownership share, he normally must pay a market related price of this share to the heirs. The co-proprietor benefits if he is a mandatory heir and if he has an urgent requirement of accommodation: In this case, he does not have to pay anything to the heirs or, if there are other persons who have a right to a statutory compulsory portion or if the estate is heavily indebted, he has to pay a reduced price.

### [D] The Registered Life Partner's Share

According to § 537a ABGB registered life partners have the same rights as a spouse and all provisions of the law of succession concerning the spouse apply to the registered life partner.

### [E] The State's Right to Succeed to Heirless Property

The state has a right to succeed to the inheritance (escheat) if no one else is entitled to inherit because the decedent has not made testamentary dispositions and there are no statutory heirs (§ 760 ABGB, *Heimfallsrecht, Kaduzität*). In this case, an inventory has to be made and it has to be announced in a public notice that the heirs may enforce their claim within six months. After this time, if no one has claimed the inheritance, the state automatically becomes the universal successor of the decedent. The state does not need to declare the acceptance of the inheritance (*Erbantrittserklärung*) and no order of the probate court is required for the transfer of title.

## §9.04 TESTATE SUCCESSION

### [A] General

The testator's capacity (*Testierfähigkeit*) is required to make testamentary dispositions. A person is testable at the age of 18. Before the age of 14 no valid testamentary dispositions can be made, and between the ages of 14 and 18 a will must be made before a notary or before a court and the testator's capacity is tested by notary or by court (§ 569 ABGB). Adults who are under guardianship (*Sachwalterschaft*) can make testamentary dispositions in all forms provided by the statute, unless it is stated in the order placing the person under guardianship that testamentary dispositions must be made before a notary or before a court. In this case, the court or the notary has to declare in the records that the testator has the necessary ability to reason and that he is considered unaffected (§ 568 ABGB). Persons suffering from a mental disorder, feeble-minded people and those who are not in the possession of their full mental faculties on any other reasons cannot make testamentary dispositions. The testator must know that he is drawing up a testamentary disposition and he must be aware of the content of this disposition (*animus testandi, Testierabsicht*). In the absence of this awareness, the dispositions are not valid. Furthermore, there must not be other absences of intent (§ 565 ABGB, *Fehlen von Willensmängeln*).

Austrian law offers different forms to make transactions mortis causa (*Rechtsgeschäfte von Todes wegen*). A testator can determine an heir by will (§ 553 ABGB, *Testament*); this is a unilateral transaction and it does not require acceptance. He may make a will together with his spouse or registered life partner (joint will, *gemeinschaftliches Testament*) or he may conclude a contract of inheritance with his spouse (or registered life partner). The formal requirements always have to be fulfilled. The testator must determine the heirs personally and he must not appoint a third person to determine his heirs (§ 564 ABGB). However, the testator may allow that the heir is determined on the basis of certain objective criteria.

The possibility to make testamentary dispositions does not limit the free disposition *inter vivos*. Austrian law guarantees testamentary freedom (*Testierfreiheit*),[7] which means the testator can decide whether he wants to make testamentary dispositions or not and to determine their specific content. Moreover, all the provisions for the case of one's death can be modified and are revocable. The right to revoke a will is inalienable and every disposition which violates the testator's freedom is void (§ 716 ABGB).

7. See §9.01[B].

However, the testamentary freedom is limited by general civil law: according to § 878 ABGB only things which might be possible can be part of a testamentary disposition (*Möglichkeit einer Verfügung*). Pursuant to § 879 ABGB it is not allowed to make provisions which are against the law or in contrary to public policy (*Erlaubtheit einer Verfügung*).

In summary, the requirements for valid testamentary dispositions are the testator's capacity, the consciousness of making a testamentary disposition and the absence of other failures of intent. If one of these requirements is not fulfilled, the testamentary disposition may be contested (*Anfechtung*).[8] Moreover, the formal requirements have to be observed and the possibility and permissibility of the content are needed.

## [B] The Will

### [1] *Forms of Will* (Testamentsformen)

A will is a testamentary disposition in which the testator determines someone as heir. If the provisions for the case of the testator's death contain only other dispositions, it is called codicil (§ 553 ABGB). Nevertheless, a codicil also has to be drawn up in one of the forms of will.

The appointment as heir may be for the whole inheritance or for a certain quota. If it is unclear whether the testator intended to draw up a will or a codicil, the testator's intent must be determined by interpretation.[9] In case of doubt, the testamentary disposition is considered as a will, unless it is proved that the testator did not want to appoint an heir.

The formal requirements of wills are constraining law and are very strict, since the adherence of these requirements serves as a warning for the testator and as evidence. The testator may choose between different forms of will. On the one hand there are 'private wills' (*private Testamente*), to which the holographic will (*eigenhändiges / holographes Testament*) belongs and the will written by another party (*fremdhändiges / allographes Testament*). On the other hand there are 'public wills' (*öffentliche Testamente*), to which the wills executed before a court (*gerichtliches Testament*) belong and the wills executed before a civil law notary (*notarielles Testament*). A will drawn up in emergency situations has to fulfil only reduced formal requirements (*Nottestament*).

#### *[a] Private Wills*

*The holographic will* (§ 578 ABGB) has to be handwritten by the testator and signed at the end of the text. The testator has to sign with his name, though his first name or his cognomen also fulfils the formal requirements if the testator is identifiable. A will written on a computer and signed by the testator or a will handwritten by another

8. See §9.04[B][6].
9. See §9.04[B][5].

person and signed by the testator does not correspond to the formal requirements. If a testator adds some further dispositions or modifies his holographic will afterwards, he has to sign it again. The location and the date are not needed for the validity, but it is advisable to add them.

*The will written by another party* (§§ 579-581 ABGB) consists of a transcript of the last will of the testator, of the signature of the testator and the signature of three witnesses. The witnesses have to add a note that they sign in their capacity as witnesses (*Zeugenzusatz*). The testator has to declare before all witnesses, whereby two of them have to be present at the same time, that the content of the will corresponds to his last will (*nuncupatio, Bekräftigung*). But the witnesses do not have to know the content of the will.

#### *[b] Public Wills*

The testator can make a will both *in writing and verbally before a court*, which has to consist of a judge and two other witnesses or a second member of the court (§§ 587-590 ABGB). The testator may render his written will personally to the court and must declare that the document is his will. It can be written by a third person, but must be signed by the testator himself. The court has to log the receipt. The testator also may declare his intent verbally before the court. The court has to record the will and to give the testator a written confirmation that the will is deposited with the court.

The testator also can make a will both *verbally and in writing before a civil law notary* (§§ 70 et seqq. *Notariatsordnung*). Two notaries or one notary and two witnesses have to record the last will of the testator. The provisions of the will before a court (§§ 587-590 ABGB) apply to the will before a notary.

#### *[c] Wills in Emergency Situations* (Nottestament)

In a situation of imminent danger, where there is a risk of dying or losing the testator's capacity, the formal requirements for drawing up a will are reduced. If the testator has no possibility to make one of the above-mentioned forms of a will, a valid will can be made both verbally and in writing in the presence of two witnesses (§ 597 ABGB). The witnesses have to confirm the verbal will afterwards, otherwise it is void. The imminent danger must be objectively reasonable and the will becomes invalid after three months if the testator is still alive and the emergency situation no longer exists. This form of a will is also available to persons from the age of 14 and adults who are under guardianship. Even if the requirements are reduced, the will in emergency situations has the same power as the other forms of will and it can override testamentary dispositions made earlier.

### ***[2] The Joint Will* (gemeinschaftliches Testament)**

Pursuant to § 583 ABGB it is not provided by the statute that a will can be drawn up by more than one testator. An exception to this rule is laid out in § 1248 ABGB, which allows a joint will between spouses or registered life partners. The joint will can also be drawn up by engaged couples and it is valid on condition they marry afterwards. As opposed to the contract of inheritance the joint will is not a contract but a testamentary disposition. If the spouses (or registered life partners) appoint each other as heirs, the joint will is called a 'reciprocal will' (*gegenseitiges Testament*). The spouses (or registered life partner) are also free to determine a third person as heir; the joint will is then called a 'mutual will' (*gemeinsames Testament*).

It is possible to determine that the dispositions in a joint will bear reference to the validity of the dispositions of the other spouse. If the dispositions are mutually contingent, it is called an 'interdependent will' (*wechselbezügliches Testament*). However, in case of doubt, it cannot be presumed that testamentary dispositions refer to those of the partner. The joint will may contain all dispositions that are allowed in other forms of a will: the spouses (or registered life partners) can determine someone as their heir, they can determine a person to receive some parts of their inheritance by legacy and they can draw up testamentary burdens. Furthermore, every spouse may revoke his dispositions without restrictions (§§ 713 et seqq. ABGB).

Theoretically a joint will can be made in all forms mentioned above. The difficulty is that both testators have to observe the formal requirements of a will. Therefore a will written only by one of the spouses would not correspond to the statutory requirements of a holographic will. Thus to make a joint will in this form, both of the testators have to write the full text by hand and sign it.

Although the joint will is reserved for spouses (or registered life partners), it is not invalid in the event of the dissolution of the marriage, unless the interpretation results in something else. Furthermore, if a joint will is invalid because of reasons in the sphere of one of the testators, for example one of the spouses has no testator's capacity, the joint will may be reinterpreted as a 'single will' (*Einzeltestament*).

#### *[3] Witnesses*

Some forms of wills need to be made before witnesses. Pursuant to § 591 ABGB persons under the age of 18 and persons with disabilities who do not have the capacity to give evidence of the testator's last will are incapable of being witnesses. Moreover a person who does not speak the language of the testator cannot witness.

Section 594 ABGB declares some groups of persons as biased: the beneficiary, his spouse (or registered life partner), his parents, his children, his siblings and people in the same degree related by marriage. This section also applies to the family related through adoption. Furthermore, the person who wrote the will in the case of a will written by another party, salaried cohabitants and the executor of the estate cannot be witnesses because of bias.

#### *[4] Revocation*

The testator may always revoke his testamentary dispositions and this right of revocation is inalienable (§ 716 ABGB). To revoke a previous testamentary disposition, the testator has to have the testator's capacity (*Testierfähigkeit*).[10] The testator may declare the revocation expressively (§ 719 ABGB, *ausdrücklicher Widerruf*) or by implication (§ 721 ABGB, *stillschweigender Widerruf*). To revoke a testamentary disposition expressively, the testator has to fulfil the formal requirements of one of the forms of will, however, it is not necessary to use the same form as the previous testamentary disposition. A revocation can also be made by destroying the written document (§ 717 ABGB) or by writing a new will (§ 713 ABGB).

### *[5] Interpretation*

Even if a testamentary disposition is not clear from its terms alone, the disposition is not automatically void. The true intention of the testator has to be ascertained by way of interpretation. According to § 655 ABGB, the wording of the text has to be interpreted in the subjective word usage of the testator. For example if it is known that the testator was used to call his car 'my road bike', a testamentary bequest concerning his 'road bike' is interpreted as a bequest concerning his car. However, to fulfil the formal requirements the interpretation only can follow the testator's hypothetical intention if the text of the will gives any indication to the testator's mind (*Andeutungstheorie*). In case of doubt, a testamentary disposition has to be interpreted in a way which does not lead to invalidity of the disposition (*favor testamenti*). Furthermore, a disposition has to be interpreted rather that only a part of it is valid than the whole disposition is void (*Teilungültigkeit statt Gesamtungültigkeit*). If the meaning of a testamentary disposition is not clear even if these rules of interpretation have been applied, the disposition is invalid. If the meaning of an appointment of an heir cannot be found by interpretation, the heirs are determined by intestate succession.

### *[6] Contestation of a Will*

A will or a codicil may be contested (*Anfechtung*) if the formal requirements are not fulfilled, if the testator's capacity is not given or in the case of absences of intent (*Willensmängeln*). Furthermore a child who is not bequeathed by the decedent because the latter had no knowledge of the child's existence, the mandatory heir may contest the will and he may demand more than his compulsory portion (§§ 777 et seq. ABGB).

The will may be contested within three years of the testator's death (§ 1487 ABGB). Entitled to litigate is every person who would benefit from the invalidity of the testamentary disposition, for example that person would receive a part of the inheritance as a legal heir or would be relieved of a burden (*Anfechtungsberechtigter*). The contestation has to be directed against the beneficiaries of the testamentary disposition (*Anfechtungsgegener*).

---

10. See §9.04[A].

### [C] Accretion

The share of a testamentary heir may rise if another heir determined by the testator does not obtain his share (§§ 560 et seqq. ABGB, *Anwachsung*). The reason why the impeded heir does not receive the inheritance is indifferent (e.g., he predeceased, has no qualification to inherit[11] or has renounced the inheritance). It is required for the accretion that there is no appointment of substitute heirs[12] and that there are no persons who inherited the right to inherit (*Transmissare*). In addition, it does not come to accretion if the testator has appointed his heirs with a certain quota. In this case, the statutory heirs receive the share of the impeded person (§ 562 ABGB).

### [D] Testamentary Bequests

According to § 535 ABGB, the testator may leave a certain person a bequest or legacy by testamentary disposition (*Legat*). A bequest is the grant of a pecuniary advantage like a special asset or a group of assets, a certain amount of money or some rights. The person receives the bequest by way of singular succession and he is not called an heir, but he is a legatee (*Legatar*). It is also possible to determine more than one legatee concerning one article, and they participate in the bequest in equal parts or certain quotas (*Mitvermächtnisnehmer*). A testamentary bequest may be arranged in a will in addition to an appointment of an heir, but also alone in a codicil.

Everything which is tradable can be bequeathed. The testator must be the owner of the article bequeathed, though he may determine that the heir has to procure the object and to surrender it to the beneficiary (§ 662 ABGB, *Verschaffensvermächtnis*). If the testamentary bequest consists of an amount of money, the heir is obliged to pay that amount to the legatee, regardless whether there are sufficient funds in the inheritance or not. The same applies to other fungible goods, if the testator did not dispose something else (§ 658 ABGB).

The bequest must be drawn up in one of the forms of a will or in a contract of inheritance. As opposed to the testamentary bequest, there are also bequests provided by law, for example the surviving spouse's entitlement to personal chattels (§ 758 ABGB, *Voraus des Ehegatten*).[13] The legatee acquires no property right; he merely has a personal claim against the heir. The acquisition of ownership occurs through the surrender of the articles bequeathed. Obligors of the bequest are the heirs in the rate of their proportional right to the inheritance. Upon the death of the testator, the legatee's right to receive the bequest arises (§ 684 ABGB, *Anfallstag, dies legati cedens*), except the legacy is left into subject to a condition precedent. If the testator does not determine something else, the bequest can be demanded one year after the testator's death (§ 685 ABGB, *Zahlungstag, dies legati veniens*). Some legacies as things which belong to the decedent's estate or charitable bequests have to be fulfilled immediately (§ 685 ABGB). The legatee has an action against the heir to receive the bequest (*Vermächtnisklage,*

11. See §9.02.
12. See §9.04[F].
13. See §9.03[C].

*Legatsklage*) and he may apply for separation of the inheritance from the heir's property if there is the danger that the creditors of the heir demand the bequest (*Nachlassseparation*).

The claim of the legatee is secondary to the testator's debts (*Erblasserschulden*), the liabilities that are connected with the death of the testator (*Erbgangsschulden*, for example the fees of the funeral) and the statutory forced share. The bequest can be reduced if these demands are not met by the inheritance (§ 692 ABGB, § 783 ABGB).

Sometimes testators do not clearly define whether they intend to bequest a person or to appoint an heir, especially if they use the term 'inherit' (*erben*) to determine that a person should receive a special asset of the inheritance. In this case, the intention of the testator has to be determined by way of interpretation.

If neither the heirs determined by the testator nor the statutory heirs get the inheritance, because they do not want to become heirs or because they are not able to inherit, the legatees follow the decedent in his legal position like heirs determined by will in proportion to the value of their bequests (§ 726 ABGB, *außerordenliches Erbrecht der Legatare*).

### [E] Testamentary Burdens, Conditions and Time Limitations

It may be in the interests of the testator to link a testamentary disposition to a condition or a time limitation. Moreover, he may determine by a testamentary burden. Section 695 ABGB describes these dispositions as 'right of the testator to restrict his last will' (*Einschränkungen des letzten Willens*).

#### *[1] Testamentary Burdens*

Testamentary burdens oblige the recipient of a testamentary benefit to certain behaviour (§§ 709 et seqq. ABGB, *Auflage*). A testamentary burden may be connected with an appointment as heir as well as with a testamentary bequest. It has to fulfil the requirements of one of the forms of will.

A testamentary burden may be in the interest of the testator himself or in the interest of a third person. For example, the testator may burden the heir to open a museum in memoriam of the testator or to look after the testator's mother. If the burden cannot be accomplished exactly, it has to be fulfilled approximately. If it is not even possible to realise the burden roughly, the recipient receives his share or his bequest anyway, if he has no fault unless the testator had determined otherwise.

As opposed to a testamentary bequest, the testamentary burden is not enforceable by the beneficiary of the burden. However, the executor of the estate (*Testamentsvollstrecker*) or another heir, who is not encumbered with the charge, has the right to sue for the fulfilment of the burden. The benefits granted in connection with the testamentary burden will be lost if the testamentary burden is not realised although it would be possible to realise it.

### *[2] Conditions and Time Limitations*

Concerning conditions and time limitations in testamentary dispositions, the same provisions as those of dispositions *inter vivos* are applied. A condition is an uncertain, future event on which the entrance or non-arrival of legal consequences depend. If the consequences are a loss of rights, it is called a resolutive condition (*auflösende Bedingung / Resolutivbedingung*). In the case of an acquisition of rights, it is called a suspensive condition (*aufschiebende Bedingung / Suspensivbedingung*).

A time limitation concerns an event which will certainly arrive, though it is not necessary that the time of the event is fixed. It has to be distinguished between a start date (*Anfangstermin*) and a finish date (*Endtermin*).

In the case of a suspensive condition or a time limitation with a start date, the inheritance passes to the heir at the entrance of the condition or the time limitation. In the case of a resolutive condition or a time limitation with a finish date, the heir ceases to be heir at the entrance of the condition or the time limitation.

## [F] Substitution

Austrian law offers legal instruments which allow the testator to determine the legal fate of the inheritance also beyond his direct successors. The testator may appoint one or more persons to receive the inheritance if the designated heir does not obtain it (substitute heir, §§ 604 et seqq. ABGB, *gemeine Substitution / Ersatzerbschaft*). The testator may also determine to whom the inheritance passes after the preliminary designated heir has received the inheritance (subsequent heir, §§ 608 et seqq. ABGB, *fideikomissarische Substitution / Nacherbschaft*). If the testator did not determine a substitution, the inheritance first passes to his heirs, who become owner of the estate, and it then passes to their statutory or testamentary heirs.

If the meaning of a substitution is not clear on its own, the content of the disposition has to be found by interpretation. According to § 614 ABGB a substitution has to be interpreted in the way which least affects the heir's power of disposition.

The testator may also provide one of the forms of substitution concerning testamentary bequests and the provisions of substitution apply to such dispositions (§ 652 ABGB).

### *[1] Substitute Heirs*

A substitute heir takes the legal position of the heir preliminary designated, if this person does not become owner of the inheritance, for example because he predeceased, because of disqualification to inherit or a renunciation of inheritance. The testator may appoint as many substitute heirs as he wishes and he has to provide in which order they are entitled to inherit (§ 604 ABGB). The substitute heir is burdened with all liabilities of the heir preliminary designated, unless the testator has determined otherwise or unless the burdens are connected with the individual of the heir preliminary designated (§ 606 ABGB).

The appointment as substitute heir expires if the preliminary designated heir obtains the inheritance (§ 615 ABGB).

### [2] Subsequent Heirs

As opposed to a substitute heir, the subsequent heir inherits after the preliminary heir has obtained the inheritance. This form of substitution includes impliedly the appointment as substitute heir, which means that a person entitled as subsequent heir also becomes heir if the person first appointed by the testator does not obtain the inheritance.

The testator may oblige his heirs to pass the inheritance to another person after the heir's death or at a date or an event provided by the testator (§ 608 ABGB). The estate first falls to the preliminary heir (*Vorerbe*), who becomes owner of the estate and who is allowed to use it. His legal position is similar to that of a usufructuary (§§ 613 and 511 ABGB, *Fruchtnießer*), which means that the use of the inheritance is allowed, but he has to save the material (§ 509 ABGB). Upon the time of the event determined by the testator, the preliminary heir is no longer owner of the estate and the subsequent heir (*Nacherbe*) gets in the legal position of the preliminary heir concerning the testator's estate. However, the subsequent heir is not the legal successor of the preliminary heir; he is the legal successor of the testator. The accrual of the inheritance occurs in the case of a suspensive condition at the entrance of the condition, whereas a time limitation does not delay the accrual of the inheritance and enables to bequeath the right to succeed when the subsequent heir survives the decedent (§§ 703 and 705 ABGB).

The appointment of a subsequent heir only concerns the estate of the testator and the heirs cannot be obliged to pass their estate to someone determined by the testator. Moreover, the statutory compulsory portion has to be free from any restrictions. Therefore, an appointment of subsequent heirs which constrains the statutory compulsory portion is invalid.

Pursuant to § 612 ABGB the testator may provide an infinite number of subsequent heirs if they are coeval with the testator or at least conceived during the lifetime of the testator (§ 611 ABGB). If the testator wants to appoint a subsequent heir who is not coeval with him, he is bound to certain restrictions: if the substitution concerns money or goods, he is restricted to the appointment of two subsequent heirs, and if it concerns immovable property, he may appoint only one subsequent heir (§ 612 ABGB).

It is similar to an appointment of a subsequent heir if the heir is appointed on a suspensive condition (or time limitation with a start date): As long as it is not fulfilled, the inheritance passes to the statutory heirs by intestate succession and after the entrance of the condition or the start date the inheritance passes to the heir determined by the testator. It is called 'constructive substitution of subsequent heirs' (*konstruktive Nacherbschaft*) and the provisions of the substitution apply: the statutory heirs are the preliminary heirs and the heir determined by the testator is the subsequent heir. In the opposite case of a resolutive condition (or time limitation with a finish date) the heir appointed by the testator becomes a preliminary heir and at the entrance of the condition or at the defined moment the inheritance passes to the testator's statutory heirs.

If the testator imposes the prohibition that his heirs must not make a will concerning his inheritance, it is a form of an appointment of subsequent heirs, because in this case the testator determines that the statutory heirs of his heirs follow them in their legal position concerning the inheritance of the testator. However, the prohibition of selling the inheritance of the testator does not include the prohibition to testate (§ 610 ABGB).

The appointment as subsequent heir expires if none of the designated subsequent heirs is alive or if the event provided by the testator cannot be realised anymore (§ 615 ABGB).

### [G] The Contract of Inheritance (*Erbvertrag*)

The contract of inheritance is a bilateral transaction between spouses or registered life partners. Fiancées may also draw up a contract of inheritance on condition of marriage (§§ 1249 et seqq. ABGB).

Due to the fact that the contract of inheritance contains both aspects of a contract between spouses regulating conveyance of property and aspects of a testamentary disposition, the requirements of both have to be fulfilled: the contract of inheritance has to be drawn up before a notary and in the presence of another notary or two witnesses (§ 1 NotAktsG, *Notariatsaktgesetz*, § 1249 ABGB). In consequence of the character of a testamentary disposition, agency is not allowed (§ 564 ABGB). The spouses may determine each other as heirs or one of them may make unilateral dispositions which benefit the other. It is also possible to appoint a third person as beneficiary in the contract of inheritance, however, according to the prevailing view this disposition is revocable. The contract of inheritance restricts testamentary freedom, but it does not limit testator's dispositions *inter vivos* (§ 1252 ABGB). Moreover, according to § 1253 ABGB, the spouses must leave a quarter of their inheritances to their free testamentary disposition ('free quarter', *freies Viertel*) and so the limitation of the testator's freedom does not concern the inheritance in its entirety. This 'free quarter' must not be burdened with any liabilities or claims of statutory compulsory portions. But all forms of will or a joint will[14] can be used additionally to a contract of inheritance to determine the spouse (or registered life partner) as universal successor concerning this quarter. If the testator did not make any dispositions concerning his 'free quarter', the intestate succession determines the heirs of this part of the inheritance.

The contract of inheritance is the strongest title to inherit: the dispositions of the contract of inheritance have priority even if it is in conflict with a will. The contract of inheritance is not revocable, but the spouses can modify or cancel it mutually before a notary. Section 1266 ABGB provides that the contract of inheritance expires in the case

14. See §9.04[B][1] and [2].

of a divorce or an annulment of the marriage, unless the parties agreed otherwise. However the innocent party in a divorce can assert his rights arising from the contract of inheritance.

## §9.05 STATUTORY COMPULSORY PORTION

### [A] General

The statutory compulsory portion guarantees close relatives and the spouse (or registered life partner) the participation in the inheritance with a certain quota if the testator has determined his heirs by testate succession. The statutory compulsory portion limits the decedent's testamentary freedom, because he has to leave behind a certain part of his inheritance to the persons entitled to a compulsory portion (mandatory heirs, *Pflichtteilsberechtigte*). Pursuant to § 774 ABGB the testator can determine the statutory compulsory portion in the form of a quota or in the form of a testamentary bequest. However, the statutory compulsory potion must not be burdened with any restrictions or any liabilities. The right to receive a statutory compulsory portion is no right to inherit and the persons entitled to a statutory compulsory portion do not become heirs, but they have a personal pecuniary claim against the heirs provided the testator does not bequeath them the compulsory portion (§ 775 ABGB, *Pflichtteilsanspruch*). A mandatory heir who has only received a part of his statutory compulsory portion has the right to a supplement to the compulsory portion (§ 775 ABGB, *Pflichtteilsergänzungsanspruch*). The claim to the statutory compulsory portion occurs at the time of death of the decedent and this right is heritable and assignable. Moreover, the right to the statutory compulsory portion is pawnable and distrainable.

According to §§ 762 et seqq. ABGB the testators' descendants, and in the absence of children, his parents, his grandparents and great-grandparents, and the spouse (or registered life partner) have a right to the statutory compulsory portion (*pflichtteilsberechtigte Personen*). The adoptive parents and the adoptees also have the right to a statutory compulsory portion. Collateral relatives, for example siblings, do not have a right to a reserved portion.

The testator's descendants and his spouse (or registered life partner) have the right to receive half of their share of the intestate succession as compulsory portion (§ 765 ABGB), and the testator's antecedents receive a third of their share of the intestate succession (§ 766 ABGB). However, these persons are only entitled to a reserved portion in theory (*abstrakt pflichtteilsberechtigt*); their de facto right to the statutory compulsory portion depends on whether they would receive a share in the intestate succession (§ 763 ABGB, *konkret pflichtteilsberechtigt*). For example, if the decedent appoints a friend as universal heir by will and in the decedent's family there are a surviving grandfather and a surviving brother. The brother is not even entitled to a statutory compulsory portion in theory, because he is a collateral relative of the decedent. The grandfather is entitled to a statutory compulsory portion in theory, but since he would not receive a share in the intestate succession (because the brother in the second class would inherit and not the grandfather in the third class), he de facto also does not get a statutory compulsory portion.

The amount of the statutory compulsory portion is calculated on the basis of an appraisal of the assets and liabilities of the decedent. The liabilities of the testator (*Erblasserschulden*) and the liabilities which are connected with the death of the testator (*Erbgangsschulden)* have to be subtracted from the assets, but testamentary bequests and testamentary burdens count to the calculation basis of the statutory compulsory portions (§§ 784 et seqq. ABGB).

All things which the mandatory heir has received through bequests or other testamentary dispositions have to be included in the calculation of the statutory compulsory portion (§ 787 ABGB). Moreover, also advancements of the compulsory portion received before the deceased's death are brought into account (§§ 788, 789 *Anrechnung von Vorempfängen und Vorschüssen*). Due to this, the testator's freedom is raised and it shall bring equality between the mandatory heirs. The testator may determine by last will that advancements should not be deducted from one's statutory compulsory share. This disposition must not be to the detriment of the other mandatory heirs, but it can be to the detriment of the heirs. Nevertheless, the recipient of an advancement is not obliged to surrender the property to the mandatory heirs if the amount of the inheritance is not sufficient to the claims to statutory forced shares.

Donations *inter vivos* from the decedent can raise the de facto amount of the statutory forced share (§ 785 ABGB, *Pflichtteilserhöhung wegen Schenkungen*) and due to this some mandatory heirs receive an 'additional statutory compulsory portion' (*Schenkungspflichtteil*). Persons who can demand the imputation of donations are the testator's children and his spouse (or registered life partner) if they are entitled to a reserved portion. This provision serves as protection of those mandatory heirs. Donations towards mandatory heirs have to be imputed without a time limit. Donations to other persons are only reflected in the calculation within two years before the testator's death. The imputation of the donations is placed to the debit of the heir and the heir is liable up to the value of the inheritance. Moreover, if the inheritance is not sufficient to offset the claims, the recipient of the donation can be obliged to give the donation or an equal amount of money to the mandatory heirs (§ 951 ABGB, *Herausgabepflicht des Beschenkten*). The mandatory heirs have to impute the donations they received in the calculation of their 'additional statutory compulsory portion' (§ 787 paragraph 2 ABGB). For example there is an inheritance in the amount of EUR 200,000.00 and the decedent determines his friend F as universal heir. The decedent has two children, A and B, and they are entitled to a reserved portion. Child A received EUR 100,000.00 as a donation *inter vivos*. The statutory compulsory portion of each child is 50,000.00, which corresponds to a quarter of the inheritance (half of the share in the intestate succession). Child A has to impute the donation and it receives only the statutory compulsory portion in the amount of EUR 50,000.00. Child B, who did not receive the donation, gets an 'additional compulsory portion' in the amount of EUR 25,000.00 (a quarter of the donation) and he gets EUR 75,000.00 in total.

Austrian law provides a number of provisions to protect the rights of the mandatory heirs: the persons entitled to compulsory portions are party in the probate procedure. They also have the right to participate in the appraisal of the assets and the liabilities (§ 784 ABGB) and to demand the raising of an inventory (§ 804 ABGB). According to § 812 ABGB the mandatory heir can apply for separation of the inheritance from the heir's property if there is the danger that the creditors of the heir demand the reserved portion (*Nachlassabsonderung*).

The mandatory heir can institute legal proceedings to receive his statutory compulsory portion. The right to the reserved portion must be enforced before a court within three years (§ 1487 ABGB) after the transmission of the testamentary disposition in the probate procedure. Until the transfer of title by an order of the probate court (*Einantwortung*), the mandatory heir has to sue the inheritance as a legal entity, and after the probate court's order he has to litigate against the heirs.

### [B] Withdrawal of the Statutory Compulsory Portion

The heir may withdraw the statutory compulsory portion by last will (disinheritance, *Enterbung*). The reasons which may lead to disinheritance are exhaustively enumerated in §§ 768 et seqq. ABGB: A descendant can be disinherited if he had not helped the testator in contingency, if he is sentenced to more than twenty years imprisonment because of an intentionally committed crime or if his way of life was immoral. A spouse can be disinherited for the same reasons and, moreover, if she had grossly violated her matrimonial obligation to stand by her husband. Even if these are the only reasons statutorily regulated, these reasons are interpreted exhaustively (§ 771 ABGB). Furthermore, the decedent may withdraw the statutory compulsory portion because of all reasons which impede the 'qualification to inherit' (*Erbunwürdigkeitsgründe*).[15]

If a mandatory heir was disinherited although none of the reasons of disinheritance were given, he has the right to his statutory compulsory portion.

The testator may disinherit expressively or tacitly (*ausdrücklich oder stillschweigend*). Therefore, the implied disinheritance can be made by disregard in the testamentary disposition. However, the heir has to prove that one of the reasons of disinheritance is given. The burden of proof also lies on the heirs in the case of expressed disinheritance.

The testator may revoke the withdrawal of the statutory compulsory portion both expressively or tacitly, although the legal text presumes that only an expressed revocation is valid (§ 772 ABGB). The testator can revoke the withdrawal of the statutory compulsory portion in the form of one of the forms of will (expressed revocation). The testator impliedly revokes the disinheritance if he bequeaths something of his inheritance to the disinherited person or if he revokes the testamentary disposition that includes the disinheritance.

The disinheritance has no consequences on the descendants of the disinherited person. If there is no appointment of heirs, the descendants of the disinherited person receive the share which the disinherited person would have received in the intestate succession (§ 541 ABGB). If it comes to the testate succession, the descendants receive the statutory compulsory portion of the disinherited person (§ 780 ABGB).

15. See §9.02.

### [C] Reduction of the Statutory Compulsory Portion

The testator may reduce the statutory compulsory portion of ascendants and descendants by half if there was no close relationship between the testator and a mandatory heir (§ 773a ABGB, *Minderung des Pflichtteils*). A close relation in the meaning of this provision is a typical relation between relatives in the respective degree of kinship. The testator does not have the right to reduce the statutory compulsory portion if he refused to have personal contact with the person entitled to a compulsory portion.

The reduction has to be determined by the last will, but it does not have to be stated expressively. The statutory compulsory portion can also be reduced if this intention of the testator is found by interpretation, for example, if the testator disregards a mandatory heir. The burden of proof lies on the heirs and they have to prove that the reduction of the statutory compulsory portion corresponds to the intention of the testator and that there was no close relationship between the testator and the mandatory heir.

The reduction of a statutory compulsory portion of one mandatory heir does not lead to an increase of the reserved portions of other mandatory heirs (§ 767 paragraph 2 ABGB). The descendants of a predeceased person whose statutory forced share would have been reduced are allowed to demand only the reduced statutory compulsory portion (§ 779 paragraph 2 ABGB).

## §9.06 LEGAL STATUS OF THE HEIRS

### [A] Community of Co-Heirs

If more than one person is entitled to inherit, either by intestate or by testate succession or by both forms of succession, they are presumed to be one legal person concerning their right to inherit until the transfer of title by probate court order (§ 550 ABGB, *communio incidens*). Afterwards the heirs are co-proprietors of the estate (*Miteigentümer*) and the provisions for co-ownership apply. Each co-proprietor is owner of a quota of the estate as a whole according to his share determined by testate or intestate succession and not of specific assets of the inheritance. The position of creditors depends on the type of debt claim. If the debt claim is divisible, each co-proprietor may claim pursuant his quota, but if the demand cannot be divided, the heirs may enforce only jointly (*Gesamthandgläubigerschaft*).

The community of co-heirs may be dissolved either by partition and each of the heirs gets one part (*Realteilung*) or the inheritance may be vended and the amount realised is split into different parts (*Zivilteilung*). But the partition gets real effect not until the transfer of title by probate court order. The testator may prescribe the form of distribution by last will, or, in the absence of that, the heirs may draw up an agreement concerning the partition (*Erbteilungsübereinkommen*). Even if the testator made a binding prescription concerning the partition, the heirs may depart from that by mutual agreement. If one of the heirs is a minor (under the age of 18), these agreements have to be authorised by the guardianship court.

Moreover, each heir has the right to demand the partition before court, but the court can interdict it if the distribution would be to the detriment of the other co-heirs (§ 830 ABGB, *Erbteilungsklage*). The testator may also provide by last will that an heir or a third person has the right to acquire the inheritance or a certain thing from the inheritance for a certain amount of money (*Aufgriffsrecht*).

### [B] The Heir's Liability for the Debts of the Estate

Until the transfer of title by probate court order the estate as a legal person is the debtor of all liabilities the deceased person left behind.[16] Afterwards the co-proprietors are liable for those debts. If all heirs declare the acceptance of the inheritance unconditionally, they are jointly and severally liable for the debts of the inheritance without any restrictions (§ 820 ABGB, *solidarische Haftung*). This liability also concerns their personal means. The joint and several liability means that a creditor may litigate against one co-proprietor for the full amount of the debts and this co-owner has recourse against the others in the rate of their proportional rights to the inheritance.

In the case that at least one of the heirs declares the acceptance of the inheritance conditionally, an inventory has to be raised. If the debts are divisible, the heirs are liable only in the rate of their proportional right to the inheritance and only up to the amount of each share of the inherited assets. If the liabilities are indivisible, the heirs are jointly and severally liable, though only up to the amount of the inheritance (§ 821 ABGB).

## §9.07 PROCEEDINGS BEFORE THE PROBATE COURT

The form of the proceedings before the probate court is an alternative dispute resolution (*Außerstreitverfahren*) and the procedural provisions are laid out in §§ 143-185 of the Alternative Dispute Resolution Act (AußStrG, *Außerstreitgesetz*). After the time of death of a person, preliminary proceedings (*Vorverfahren*) are initiated ex officio: the office for registration of personal status (*Standesamt*) transmits the death certificate (*Sterbeurkunde*) to the probate court and a notary is commissioned by the court (*Gerichtskommissär*) to review if the deceased has made testamentary dispositions and if there are statutory heirs (*Todesfallaufnahme*).

After that, the 'general proceedings' (*Verlassenschaftsabhandlung*) serve to clear up who has the rights to succeed: the heirs declare the acceptance of the inheritance (*Erbantrittserklärungen*) and if there are contradictory declarations of acceptance, the probate court has to state the right to inherit of certain persons if the notary who is commissioned by the court reached no agreement (§§ 160 et seqq. AußStrG). The proceedings are concluded and the transfer of title is acquired by the entry of final judgment of a court order (§ 797 ABGB, *Einantwortungsbeschluss*). Through this court order the heir becomes the universal successor of the deceased. However, no court order is needed if the inheritance is of a very low value or if the inheritance is

16. See §9.01[B].

over-indebted. If there are no heirs, the proceedings are also concluded without this court order and the state has the right to succeed to the inheritance (*Heimfallsrecht*).[17]

The declaration of acceptance of the inheritance is a unilateral, irrevocable declaration before the notary commissioned by court. The heir may declare unconditionally or conditionally; the difference between these two forms of declaration is in the consequences concerning liability. An heir who declares unconditionally is liable for the debts of the inheritance, for example the liabilities of the deceased and the testamentary bequests, and he has to pay them if there are no sufficient funds in the inheritance (§ 801 ABGB, *unbedingte Erbantrittserklärung*). In the case of a conditional declaration of acceptance of the inheritance an inventory has to be raised and the heir is only liable up to the amount of the value of the inheritance (§ 802 ABGB, *bedingte Erbantrittserklärung, pro viribus-Haftung*).

Instead of a declaration of acceptance of the inheritance, the heir may renounce his right to inherit (§ 805 ABGB, *Erbsentschlagung*). As opposed to the renunciation of inheritance,[18] the renouncement can be made only after the time of death of the decedent. The declaration of renouncement of the inheritance has to be expressive and is irrevocable.

After the devolution of the estate by the entry of final judgment of the court order, a person who asserts a stronger title to succeed than the legal successor of the decedent may bring a legal action against the heirs (§ 823 ABGB, *Erbschaftsklage*). The successful complainant becomes the universal successor of the deceased and he retrospectively gets the status of an heir which has conditionally declared the acceptance of inheritance. This legal action can be taken within thirty years after the time of the decedent's death (§ 1478 ABGB). If the action is against testamentary dispositions, the right to litigate prescribes after three years (§ 1487 ABGB).

Section 824 ABGB provides for a bona fide right protection. A purchaser may acquire in good faith from an unlawful heir, if the vendor received the title by probate court order. Therefore the probate court order affects the presumption to be the true heir (*Erwerb vom Scheinerben*).

## §9.08 INTER VIVOS DONATIVE PROMISES FOR THE EVENT OF THE DONOR'S DEATH

Pursuant to § 956 ABGB a donation without payment which shall take effect only after the donor's death is seen as a bequest if the formal requirements of a bequest are fulfilled.[19] The same outcome could be reached through a donation with suspensive effect and with the donator's right to withdraw. However, by way of this donation, the formal requirements of the law of succession would be circumvented. Therefore § 956 ABGB states some criteria which prevent this circumvention: the donee has to accept the donation and the donor has to relinquish expressively the right of withdrawal. Furthermore, the donation has to be made in form of a notary act (*Notariatsakt*).

17. See §9.03[E].
18. See §9.02.
19. See §9.04[C].

After the death of the donor, the donation does not pass to the donee on its own, except if the donated article is already in ward of the donee. The donee has a right against the inheritance to transference of title.

## §9.09 PREVIEW ON LAW REFORM OF LAW OF SUCCESSION

A comprehensive reform of Austrian Law of Succession is in planning. However, on completion of this chapter no official draft bill has been published. By this planned law reform the numbering of paragraphs will change partly, which could not be worked into the manuscript.

The reform intends among other things to strengthen the statutory right of intestate succession of the spouse (or registered life partner), who shall inherit the entire inheritance, if the only existing statutory heirs are the grandparents of the decedent. The statutory compulsory portion of the parents shall be removed and the minimum age for witnesses of a will shall be reduced to the age of 14. Moreover, the appointment of a special guardian (Sachwalter) shall not restrict a mentally ill or mentally disabled person to any type of form of will. Furthermore, free gifts of the decedent shall be taken into account under a uniform system and there shall no more be a distinction between donations on the one hand and advancements on the other hand.

## SELECTED BIBLIOGRAPHY

### Textbooks

Bernhard Eccher, *Bürgerliches Recht VI, Erbrecht* (5th ed. 2014).
Helmut Koziol & Rudolf Welser, *Grundriss des bürgerlichen Rechts II* (13th ed. 2007).
Wolfgang Zankl, *Erbrecht* (7th ed. 2008).

### Handbooks

Susanne Ferrari & Gundula Likar-Peer (eds), *Erbrecht* (2007).
Michael Gruber, Susanne Kalss, Katharina Müller & Martin Schauer (eds.), *Erbrecht und Vermögensnachfolge* (2010).

CHAPTER 10

# Company Law

*Susanne Kalss*

## §10.01 COMPANY LAW: GENERAL REMARKS

### [A] Historical Introduction

Company law is the law of associations under private law, founded by one or more persons to follow common goals. Company law serves the purpose to realise the interests of several people and seek compromise between individual interests. Company law provides a standardisation of the legal relationships between the members of a company and their legal relationship to the company, as well as the legal status towards creditors and other third parties.

Austrian company law is closely related to German company law due to their historical connection. Thus, the General Commercial Code of 1861 constitutes the common basis for company law, namely the law on partnerships as well as the law on stock exchange. In 1938 significant German acts regarding company law, were introduced, namely the German Commercial Code of 1897 and the German Stock Company Act of 1937. The development of Austrian company law was historically orientated towards Germany but is now gaining greater sovereignty.

Within the last two decades company law has especially been influenced by European harmonisation. The biggest contribution of the European Union to Austrian company law is the enforcement of modern standards in the law on accounting and auditing. The European Union has also had a major impact on Austrian law in the field of publicly traded stock companies. Furthermore, without the European development the mobility of companies across borders would be far more restricted.

### [B] Important Legislation

Austrian company law is ruled by a widespread number of different acts. The Austrian Civil Code (*Allgemeines Bürgerliches Gesetzbuch, ABGB*) governs the initial form of all partnerships, namely the partnership under civil law (*Gesellschaft nach bügerlichem Recht*). Two further types of partnerships, namely the general partnership (*Offene Gesellschaft – OG*) and the limited partnership (*Kommanditgesellschaft – KG*) are governed by the Commercial Code (*Unternehmensgesetzbuch*), which also includes legislation on the so-called silent partnership (*Stille Gesellschaft*), which is a mixture of partnership and qualified credit accommodation. Corporations, namely stock companies (*Aktiengesellschaften*) and the limited liability company (*GmbH*) have their own laws according to each type of corporation: the Stock Company Act (*Aktiengesetz, AktG*) and the Law on Limited Liability Companies (*Gesetz über Gesellschaften mit beschränkter Haftung, GmbHG*). Cooperatives are regulated by the Cooperatives Act (*Genossenschaftsgesetz*) and the Act on Mergers of Cooperatives (*Genossenschaftsverschmelzungsgesetz*). In addition to these major legal acts for companies, there are a growing number of smaller more specific laws, regulating only very particular procedures or situations for all or individual types of companies. Thus, Austrian legislation provides a Division Act (*Spaltungsgesetz*), a Transformation Act (*Umwandlungsgesetz*), a Merger Act (*Verschmelzungsgsetz*), an EU-merger Act (*EU-Verschmelzungsgesetz*), which deals with cross border mergers within the EU, the Act on the Squeeze-Out of Shareholders (*Gesellschafterausschlussgesetz*) and the Law on Takeovers (*Übernahmegesetz*). The merger rules themselves, however, are to a large extent set out in the Stock Exchange Act (*Börsegesetz*) and to a smaller extent in the law on the limited liability company. Further specific legislation for emergency situations include the Company Reorganisation Act (*Unternehmensreorganisationsgesetz, URG*) and the Equity Subordination Act (*Eigenkapitalersatzgesetz, EKEG*). Beyond that, the Company Register Act (*Firmenbuchgesetz, FBG*) constitutes an important part of company law.

In addition to this national diversity of singular laws, for some types of organisations there are also European provisions. Accordingly, the European Economic Interest Grouping (EEIG), the Societas Europaea and the European Cooperative Society are ruled by provisions under EU law, which again were complemented by specific Austrian legislation. Thus, the people working with Austrian company law are facing a diverse picture of different legal sources, which often have to be applied together.

### [C] Numerus Clausus in Company Law

Austrian company law provides a *numerus clausus* of legally recognised types of companies.

The valid types of partnerships are:

- the partnership under civil law (*Gesellschaft bürgerlichen Rechts, GesbR*);
- the general partnership (*Offene Gesellschaft, OG*);
- the limited partnership (*Kommanditgesellschaft, KG*);

- the silent partnership (*Stille Gesellschaft*);
- the European Economic Interest Grouping.

The valid types of corporations are:

- the stock company (*Aktiengesellschaft, AG*);
- the Societas Europaea (SE);
- the limited liability company (*Gesellschaft mit beschränkter Haftung, GmbH*);
- the registered cooperative society (*eingetragene Genossenschaft*).

Moreover, the association law and especially the private foundation law are of great importance in social as well as in economic life. Their range of application exceeds the field of company law. Even though the number of recognised company types is restricted by the *numerus clausus*, company law does actually allows for much freedom of contract design. It is also possible to combine different types of companies. The most popular form is the *GmbH & Co KG*, where a limited liability company (*GmbH*) is the single general partner of a limited partnership (*KG*).

### [D] Practical Significance

According to statistics of the company register of 2012 currently there are about 18,000 general partnerships, 42,900 limited partnerships, 1,760 stock companies, 127,200 limited liability companies and 29 SE. The most numerous type of corporation registered is the limited liability company, the reason being a comparatively greater freedom of contract design, the simple foundation process and the limitation of capital investment and liability of the partners. Out of the 1,760 stock companies as well as the 29 SE only 80 to 100 are publicly listed among which only few declare to comply with the corporate governance code. The higher number of limited partnerships compared to general partnerships may be explained mainly by the differences in liability of the partners (partly limited/unlimited). Partnerships under civil law are not entered into the company register. However, it may be assumed that the partnership under civil law is the most common type of company due to its broad range of application (consortium, working group, syndicate agreement, loose cooperation).

### [E] Mandatory Provisions

In order to protect certain interest groups, e.g., minority share-holders and third-party creditors, some mandatory standards are set out in company law. A particularly high number of mandatory provisions is set out in the field of stock companies because of their strong orientation towards new third-party investors. For all other types of company the mandatory provisions focus only on the protection of creditors and to some extent to protection of minority partners.

For publicly oriented stock companies the Stock Exchange Act and the Law on Capital Markets provide additional rules. Oftentimes the provisions interlink. There are standardised duties of capital market orientated companies, which include disclosure and special procedural duties. Furthermore, the antitrust and competition law (merger-control) are of great importance for company law.

Since company law is part of civil law general principles of civil law apply, insofar as they are suited to company law. Mandatory rules in labour law influence both management contracts and the composition of supervisory boards. In recent years, it has become evident that criminal law connects with company law in order to mitigate principle-agent conflicts and to provide additional third-party creditor protection.

### [F] Classification of Company Law

Traditionally company law is divided into the law on partnerships and the law on corporations. Corporations include the stock company, the limited liability company and cooperative societies. Partnerships include the general partnerships and the limited partnership, which are recorded in the company register and feature legal personality. In contrast the partnership under civil law and the silent partnership are not recorded in the company register and feature no legal personality. Corporations are characterised by the fact that they operate as a legal personality, the limited liability of their shareholders, the generally free transferability of shares and the possibility of third party management. Stock companies and limited liability companies may be founded by one or more persons. Typically the interests of the shareholders can be more disassociated from the interests of the corporation compared with partnerships.

While only some partnerships feature legal personality, in all partnerships the personal liability of at least one partner is not limited by the capital investment that constitutes his contribution and share-quota. In general, the principle of self-governance applies, i.e., all partners also fulfil management and representative functions. Partnerships must always be founded by at least two persons – all partnerships cease to exist, when the next to last partner exits.

From a functional perspective company law should be doctrinally organised not by the conceptual distinction corporation – partnership, but according to their field of application. This functional approach bisects the categories of partnerships and corporations according to their different goals. The stock company and the limited partnership are types of organisation designed to allow the collection of capital from partners and shareholders respectively in order to use it for a specific purpose. The general partnership and the limited liability company, whereas, form the types of organisation attractive to entrepreneurs, who are personally dedicated to the company. A functional approach therefore allows to classifications within company law along the public – non-public distinction.

In publicly oriented stock companies and limited partnerships, the management lies in the hand of a small number of people. The shareholders and limited partners do not fulfil the role of entrepreneurs with power of control; their primary purpose is to allocate money. The control over the assets of a stock company lies in the hands of the managing board and in the limited partnership in the hands of the general partners.

In general, partnerships and the limited liability companies, however, the more entrepreneurship-friendly character of the organisational structure of the company favours partners and respectively shareholders who personally want to engage in business activities. In the general partnership as well as in the limited liability company, partners/shareholders usually hold management positions. A functional analysis of the respective legal models allows revealing and understanding the differences in regulation.

### [G] The Company Register

Under Austrian law, a company (corporation or partnership) is recognised as featuring legal personality only after it has been registered in the company register. As the name suggests, the company register is the central register for companies. The company register said to fulfil three important functions.

It serves documentation and certification purposes as all companies have to be recorded and registered. The relevant data is stored and protected. As a reflexion of its generally public accessibility the company register is vested with public trust and therefore its publicity and information function forms a backbone of Austrian company law. All entries into the company register are publicly accessible according to § 9 of the Austrian Commercial Code (*Unternehmensgesetzbuch, UGB*) and § 33 of the Company Register Act (*Firmebuchgesetz, FBG*) and may be easily called up through the Internet. For about ten years all documents that are relevant for the entries have been scanned and are therefore electronically available. Lastly, the company register fulfils a control function when registering all foundations of companies and any amendments to their founding documents and controlling the lawfulness of the registration of these documents.

The company register is run as singularly organised database and it is maintained and operated by the courts in the first instance (*Landesgerichte*).

### [H] Participation of Employees

In Austria, the participation of employees in the bodies of a company focuses on the supervisory board. Thus, only companies with a supervisory board or who have established a body fulfilling the same function are subject to employee participation. The ratio between shareholder representatives and employee representatives is 2:1, i.e., for two shareholder representatives one employees representative is allowed to join the supervisory board. Only a person who is an employee of the company and member of the company's work council may be elected into the supervisory board. As a result, employee participation is strongly tied to the company. In groups of companies the participation is designed in a way that the employee representatives are preferably members of the supervisory board of the group's parent company. Only if the parent company is merely a holding company, without any strategic influence, the employees hold no rights of participation at the level of the holding company but participate one level below, where the actual management and control of the other companies are performed.

## §10.02 TYPES OF ORGANISATION

### [A] The Partnership under Civil Law

The partnership under civil law has been regulated in the Austrian Civil Code (*ABGB*, §§ 1175 et seq.) for about 200 years. In December 2014, it has undergone a significant modernisation. The rules on the partnership under civil law apply to all of company law, unless there are provisions that are more specific and as long as the application of these rules is consistent with the principle of the respective type of corporate organisation. For example, the newly passed § 1186(2) ABGB states the general principle that all partners receive equal treatment in equal circumstances. It applies to all of company law. The partnership under civil law is not listed in the company register and has no legal personality. It does not bear any rights and duties itself. It is characterised by the mutual cooperation of at least two persons in order to pursue a common goal, whenever no other organisational structure was chosen. The partnership under civil law may regulate only the relation among the partners (*Innengesellschaft*) or allow representation of the partners towards the public (*Außengesellschaft*). An organisational structure is said to be a consequence of a partnership under civil law, but no condition for the foundation of such partnership. With few exceptions the partners can design their partnership agreement freely. There are no formal requirements for the conclusion of the contract.

Following the principle of self-governance under partnership law, all partners are in general appointed to fulfil management functions. However, the partnership agreement may state different rules (e.g., one-partner management) and even third-party management can be allowed for. Decision making follows the majority rule, which depends on the capital contribution. If a partner contributes services but no capital, and the partnership agreement does treat the service as a capital contribution, the voting rights are allotted per capita.

The external representation falls to the managing partners.

They can legally represent all partners in matters relating to the partnership, unless the partnership agreement provide otherwise. Business-orientated and non-business-orientated partnerships that are made up of business-orientated members are subject to a third party protection rule stating that a partners' lack of representative power cannot be held against third parties who contracted with the partner in good faith.

The assets dedicated to the partnership are jointly owned by the partners but they are dedicated to a specific purpose. Thus, internally, the right of disposal of the individual partner over the assets is restricted.

Every partner can demand financial reports from the managing partner(s). The profit distribution depends on the equity interests. A loss is to be divided among the partners according to the ratio of their capital contributions.

While the exit of a partner and the entry of a new partner require a change of the partnership agreement, the substitution of one resigning partner for another entering partner requires the agreement of all remaining partners. Detailed rules govern third-party protection in the case of a change in the partnership structure.

The partnership under civil law is dissolved, if the partnership agreement expires, if the partners agree on the dissolution, in case of bankruptcy of a partner, if a partner resigns, or if a partner dies and by court decision. Should the last partner resign, the partnership dissolves and the assets of the partnership are transferred on to the last remaining partner via universal succession in exchange for a compensation of the resigning partner.

### [B] General Partnership (*OG*)

A general partnership is a partnership, which can establish legal relations in pursuit of a common purpose under its own name. The assets of the partnership are held in joint-ownership and all partners bear unlimited liability towards company creditors. The general partnership has legal capacity. It may actually have any legal purpose. Therefore, it does not necessarily need to conduct a business. Besides economic and entrepreneurial activities, the general partnership may engage in non-commercial and other activities, for instance in the management of assets. According to § 105 of the Austrian Commercial Code there must be at least two partners. Due to the unlimited liability, the general partnership complies with the model of the business and entrepreneur partnership. Typically, the partners also hold the management positions. The general partnership is founded on basis of a contract and comes into existence upon registration into the company register. As a legal entity it can be entered into the land register as a proprietor. It can enter into contracts and has the capacity in its own name to sue and be sued.

With exception to the rudimentary facts (type of company, company name, partners, representation), which are recorded in the company register, the documents of a general partnership are not public. An annual statement of accounts is to be produced a year after the turnover has topped EUR 700,000 in two subsequent years. The annual accounts however, do not have to be published. If the turnover lies below the mark, a statement on incomes and expenses or a similar statement of account must be produced.

Even though the *OG* has legal capacity, it does not necessarily need to have any company assets. The company assets are to be separated from the other assets of the partners. As the law does not require any assets, there is no obligation for a minimum amount of capital for the company. Creditor protection is guaranteed by the joint liability of partners. The company's liability is not restricted to the company assets. Rather private assets provide an additional liability fund. The unlimited and unrestricted personal liability of all partners is a legal consequence of the foundation of a general partnership.

If the partners make a contribution, each partner receives a capital share according to § 109 of the Austrian Commercial Code. The capital share reflects the participation of the partners in form of a specific fixed amount or a ratio of participation. Basically, the capital share remains steady and unchanged. It determines the share partners' quota of the company's assets. It serves as basis for the assessment of the profit share, for the liquidation share and the severance pay for when a partner leaves the partnership, and forms the basis for the voting right. Frequently, partnership agreements deviate from the default rules on these issues.

As a partnership, the general partnership is subject to the principle of self-governance. The organisational rules are optional and may be designed for the specific needs of the company. A distinction is to be made between the management, namely the inner management, and the external representation. The law governing general partnerships provides the principle of single management, i.e., every single partner is authorised to make decisions in matters of ordinary business. The other partners have to accept it or – in the case that they do not agree with the measure – they may object to the measure. In that case the measure must not be executed. Extraordinary business dealings require a decision of all partners, and thus, are a matter of joint management. Amendments of the contract require unanimity, unless otherwise provided for in the partner agreement. Fiduciary duties prevent the abuse of majority rights against minority partners. This means that in decision making, whilst respecting the principle of equal treatment and the principle of proportionality, the interests and the legal position of the minority is to be considered and the measures in question must serve the interest of the partnership.

In exercising their rights in the context of management and extraordinary transactions, the partners have the duty of loyalty towards the company, but also towards the other partners. A distinction is to be made between the duties of loyalty by virtue of membership towards the company and the other partners, and the duties of loyalty based on the legal positions of the management, which is significantly higher. The duty of loyalty is a principle of company law, which is acknowledged in all types of companies. The intensity of the duty of mutual consideration and the duty to include company members in decision-making is determined according to the specific design of the partnership and actual circumstances.

The principle of equal treatment applies to general partnerships.

The law governing general partnerships sets out the principle of single representation (§ 125, section 1). That is, every partner is in the position to represent the partnership by himself and may acquire rights and originate obligations for the partnership. The representation is, therefore, basically a general power of agency, which is determined by law, but may be restricted insofar as the partners agree on a joint representation. This means that a partner may only represent the company together with another partner. Managerial and representative powers may be withdrawn only for important reason. However, managers may step aside from these powers voluntarily.

The liability of the company may not be restricted by contract. Creditors can target assets directly from the liability fund or from one of the partners. In case partners have to repay liabilities of the company, they have the right of recourse against the partnership.

The partners must make and approve annual accounts or other financial statements. All partners are appointed to approve the annual accounts. After approval of the annual accounts, the partners are entitled to a share of the profits, which is based on the value of the contributions of each member or otherwise regulated by contract. All profits may be withdrawn in full, even after the end of the fiscal year. They must only be left to the partnership if necessary to prevent the infliction of obviously threatening damage to the partnership.

Basically, the shares in a general partnership may only be transferred with the approval of the other partners. It is subject to the legal right of assent, which may, however, be waived. Every partner has the right to resign from the partnership. The resignation leads to the dissolution of the company. However, it may also just lead to the retirement of the partner if provided for by the partnership agreement. The other partners may also expel a partner if there is substantial reason. In any situation, in the case of withdrawal as well as in the case of expulsion, the partner is entitled to appropriate severance pay.

The death of a partner leads to the dissolution of the partnership. However, the partnership agreement may take precaution against this by providing a succession provision in order to avoid this consequence. Such a provision may in advance appoint heirs or other successors as partners or determine that the heirs are not allowed to join the partnership against the wish of the other partners or without severance pay. As a potential heir has no right to a future inheritance, the articles of association may deny the heir the otherwise due compensation.

### [C] Limited Partnership (*KG*)

The limited partnership is designed as a partnership with two classes of partners. There is a general partner who – like a partner in a general partnership – bears unlimited and unrestricted personal liability for the company's obligations, and there are limited partners (*Kommanditisten*). The limited partners are liable for the obligations of the partnership up to a fixed amount that is publicised in the company register. They are investors with a limited capital investment. Thus, the management of the partnership is vested in the personally unlimitedly liable general partners. As provided by law, the limited partners do not take part in management activities. This concept reflects the combination of entrepreneurial activities with unlimited liability and the limited capital investment with limited risk. Thus, it becomes clear that this type of company is suited to raising external funds.

Like the general partnership, the limited partnership only comes into existence after it has been recorded in the company register. It is based on a written, oral or even only tacitly concluded contract. It may follow any legal purpose. Thus, it is not necessarily oriented towards economic and entrepreneurial activities. Only basic information on the company is recorded in the company register. As in the general partnership, the accounting documents do not need to be published. The law provides disclosure requirements only for the *GmbH & Co KG*, which is oftentimes treated like a corporation.

One reason why the limited partnership is very popular in practice is the limited liability of the capital investor; another is the possible combination with the limited liability company in the form of the *GmbH & Co KG* because it allows combining the contractual freedom of a partnership with a closed corporation. In the partnership under civil law or the general partnership the personal liability serves as major capital fund (*Haftungsfonds*) and forms the fundamental basis of creditor protection. This means creditor protection is provided by the assets of the partnership as well as the additional liability fund of the partners within the framework of the joint liability. Creditor protection in the limited partnership, in contrast, is more complex. Yet the assets of the partnership and the assets of the general partners are unlimitedly liable for the obligations of the partnership. The limited partners, whereas, make only limited contributions. Their liability is restricted to the amount of liability which is recorded in the company register. If the contribution is paid, there is no further liability. There is no minimum to the amount of liability of the limited partners, nor is there a minimum of capital for the partnership determined by law. It is legally permitted that the contribution is refunded to the limited partner by the company, but as a legal consequence the limited partner's liability comes into effect. The liability also comes into effect in case the capital contribution of the limited partner has been used up by losses and the following earned profits are not being retained but are distributed to the limited partner and are not used to cover the losses suffered in the meantime.

The management of the partnership is vested in its general partners. Because of their unlimited liability including private assets, they should also conduct the partnership's business. The limited partners are usually excluded from management. But this only holds true for ordinary management. All extraordinary business dealings need the approval of the limited partners, according to § 164 of the Austrian Commercial Code. It is contractually permissible to grant management powers for ordinary dealings to a limited partner. He may also receive special rights to approve certain management decisions. The partnership is externally represented by its general partners. A limited partner may be nominated as a general agent (procurator, *Prokurist*) in order to represent the company without limitations.

As limited partners are usually not included in the management, they have the right of information and control, according to § 166 of the Austrian Commercial Code. Former managing general partners also have a reporting obligation towards the limited partners.

Like a general partnership, a limited partnership must produce annual accounts or other financial statements. The annual accounts must be approved by the partners. This creates an entitlement to profits. General partners are entitled to a liability bonus, as appropriate compensation for their risk of unlimited liability. The other partners receive shares of the residual profits according to their capital contributions. A limited partner is not entitled to distribution of profits if he, contrary to the contractual agreement, did not make his contribution or in case the contribution serves to cover the losses. The limited partner is only entitled to extract profits from the limited partnership.

The limited partner's share may be transferred to another person. However, the limited partner may also withdraw from the partnership by resignation leading either to the dissolution of the partnership or the cancellation of his limited share and entitling him to severance pay. According to § 177 of the Austrian Commercial Code, the death of a limited partner does not lead to the dissolution of the company. The heirs of the deceased partner will then enter the company.

### [D] *GmbH & Co KG*

The *GmbH & Co KG* is a special form of the limited partnership. The position of the general partner is not held by a person, but by a limited liability company (*GmbH*). The position could also be held by a public company or an association or any other legal entity. The main purpose of the use of the limited liability company as general partner is to de facto limit the liability of personally liable partner. In addition, in the past, tax considerations also used to incentivise the foundation of *GmbH & Co KGs*.

In this constellation with the limited liability company being the sole personally liable partner of the limited partnership, the similarity to a corporation becomes very obvious. Therefore, at various points legislature treats a capitalistic *GmbH & Co KG* the same way as a corporation, especially with regard to the publication of the annual accounts, the design of reorganisation and the declaration of crisis or insolvency of the company, since the capital cover of a *GmbH & Co KG* is the same as that of a private limited company. The private limited company does not only fulfil the liability function in the *GmbH & Co KG,* it also bears the responsibility for management and representation of the limited partnership. This means that those who hold management positions in the limited liability company also hold them in the *GmbH & Co KG.*

Since the creditor protection system of the limited partnership with the joint liability of general partner and limited partnership does not work for the *GmbH & Co KG* (because the limited liability company itself has only limited liability), there is a danger to creditor protection. The Austrian case law has balanced this deficit by applying the provisions on the financial constitution of the limited liability company (§ 82 of the law on the limited liability company, *GmbHG*), especially the provisions on the maintenance of company capital, to the limited partnership. As a *GmbH & Co KG* is similarly designed to a corporation, the law provides – and this is unique for a partnership – that a *GmbH & Co KG* which is employing more than 300 employees in both of its companies, has to set up a supervisory board, where employees have representative rights, meaning they are represented with one employee representative for every two capital representatives.

### [E] Limited Liability Company

The limited liability company is the most common type of company in Austria as recorded in the company register. The limited liability company is the type of corporation which is tailored to the specific needs of a small number of partners who cooperate with each other and usually know each other very well. It is the type of company for entrepreneurs.

The limited liability company is characterised by high freedom of design and default regulations. What is significant here is the strong position of the partners. Normally, one or a number of the partners hold the managing positions. Mandatory rules are mostly related to the protection of creditors and to some extent to minority partners. The articles of association are usually designed for the long term and they are often complicated contracts which frequently turn out to be incomplete because at the conclusion of the contract future developments and economic consequences cannot be foreseen.

Since creditor protection and the capitalisation are limited to the company's assets, the law provides stricter provisions on the foundation, financial packaging and the maintenance of capital than it does for partnerships.

The company is established by the articles of association. A limited liability company may be founded by one or more persons. The articles of association require in any case a notarial deed. The limited liability company comes into existence when it is recorded in the company register. Apart from the important information concerning company name, number of shareholders and share capital which all have to be entered into the company register, the articles of association also have to be recorded in the collection of documents in the company register. Therefore they are publicly available and accessible. Creditor protection is concentrated on the assets of the company. Thus, the law on the limited liability company provides a fixed minimum capital of the company and requires a permanent maintenance of the assets contributed to the company. Furthermore, the shareholders have subsidiary responsibility to raise and maintain the capital.

A newly founded limited liability company (*gründungsprivilegierte GmbH*) has a share capital of at least EUR 10,000 and at least EUR 5,000 are payable in cash at the formation of the company. After ten years, the newly founded limited liability company must reach a share capital of at least EUR 35,000 that is the general capital requirement for limited liability companies. If the company is founded with a share capital of EUR 35,000, each shareholder must deposit at least one quarter of his initial cash contribution. In the case that no cash contributions but contributions in kind are made, they must be at the company's free disposal immediately. The shareholders are not only liable for raising their own shares, but also for the other shareholders and in the case of an illegitimate return of capital to shareholders, they are liable at least as far as the share capital is affected.

The raising of the capital is complemented by the principle of capital maintenance. Under § 82 of the law on the limited liability company (*GmbHG*), any payments of the company to the shareholders which lead to a reduction of company assets are prohibited. Only the distribution of profits is legitimate. The contract of association or a shareholders' resolution design specific rules for the distribution of capital. Any legal transaction in accordance with the arm's-length principle is also permissible by law; that is, a transaction where the shareholders must provide a service or good which is equivalent to the payment of the company. The purpose of the maintenance of capital assets is not only the protection of creditors but also of minority partners because the value of the company and thus of every share, decreases with every unfavourable transaction at the expense of the company. The provisions on the raising and maintenance of capital are mandatory and may not be amended by the shareholders.

In case assets are returned to a shareholder in violation of the prohibition of hidden distribution of share capital, the transaction is null and void. The shareholders must refund the payment to the company. Managers who participate in measures that infringe the prohibition of returning contributions, are liable towards the company.

The shareholders are liable for their own shares and the shares of the other shareholders only towards the company, but not towards third party creditors.

The company's share capital may only be reduced in compliance with a creditor protection proceeding. The creditors must be informed about the reduction of the share capital in advance and may require guarantees. Only after a period of three months it is permissible to pay out partners and thereby reduce the capital.

The organisation of the limited liability company is dominated by the shareholders. The authority and power of decision making on basic questions and also on other important measures of management is concentrated with the shareholders. A limited liability company must feature a managing director and a meeting of shareholders (*Generalversammlung*). The latter appoints the managing director. A supervisory board is generally optional except for larger or more capital intensive companies. The limited liability company is a corporation, and, thus, the principle of third party management applies. This means that the management of the company is not connected to the membership in the company by law, but requires a special act of appointment. If a shareholder shall resume the position of managing director, he may also be appointed through the articles of association.

The managing director controls and represents the company. However, his position may be strongly restricted because he is subjected to the instructions of the shareholders' meeting in all matters. In addition, a number of measures require the approval of the shareholders' meeting by law. Further, the managing director has to submit to the shareholders' meeting all important and risky business matters as well as such dealings which, in his opinion, would not find the approval of the shareholders. Only the shareholders' meeting and not the individual shareholder has the right to issue instructions.

The shareholders' meeting decides, for example, on the approval of the annual accounts and investments that exceed 20% of the share capital. The voting rights in the shareholders' meeting are based on the shares. However, it could be organised differently with multiple voting rights, veto rights and special rights to approve certain decisions. The shareholders' meeting also decides on amendments of the company's articles of association, increases of share capital and all other far-reaching management measures.

Next to the two mentioned bodies, a limited liability company must install a supervisory board if the share capital is higher than EUR 70,000 and the number of shareholders exceeds 50, if the number of employees is more than 300 on average, or if the limited liability company controls other companies that require a supervisory board. Employee representatives make up one third of the company's supervisory board. They are, however, not remunerated.

The main purpose of the supervisory board of a limited liability company is the supervision of the management. It may also have additional rights of direction.

Every limited liability company has to produce annual accounts regardless of its size and activities. This is the responsibility of the managing directors. The annual accounts have to be approved by the shareholders' meeting and must be audited by an external auditor if the profits exceed a certain limit. The annual accounts always have to be published.

The profit is distributed according to the share ratio. A disproportionate distribution requires a special provision under the articles of association or a decision of the shareholders' meeting.

In general, the shares are freely transferable; however, this may also be subjected to the approval of the company (managing directors, shareholders' meeting or individual shareholders). It is also legitimate to install acquisition, pre-emption, or join-acquisition rights in the articles of association. It is illegitimate to leave the company with a claim for severance pay at any random time.

The share capital of a limited liability company may be increased by means of a capital increase. It is also permissible to demerge, merge or transform the limited liability company into a different company. This is also possible with universal succession.

## [F] Stock Company (*AG*)

The stock company is designed as an institution to accumulate capital and, thus, its organisational structure is geared towards a publicly oriented corporation. Therefore, the provisions for the stock company are mostly mandatory, leaving neither the financial constitution nor the organisational structure at the disposal of the shareholders. In reality, though, this legal model fails to meet the practical needs. Only few companies come close to the model. It is far more often the case that stock companies are in the hands of a few people, who are also actively engaging in the company's business and that they are not just established as an institution to accumulate capital.

Like a limited liability company, a stock company may be established by one or more persons. The articles of association require a notarial deed. The stock company comes into existence upon registration in the company register. The statutes must again be recorded in the collection of documents in the company register. The minimum share capital amounts to EUR 70,000. At the issue of registered shares, at least one quarter of the contribution must be paid in cash, at the issue of bearer shares the whole contribution must be paid in full (contribution plus agio).

Increasingly, the law makes a distinction between companies that are publicly listed and those that are not listed. Thus, the organisational structure of the supervisory board and the preparations of the shareholders' meeting are far more complex in listed companies than in unlisted companies. Moreover, listed companies have to follow the accounting principles of IAS (International Accounting Standards) and not the accounting standards of the Austrian Commercial Code and are bound by additional information and procedural duties imposed by capital market laws. Whereas, it is much easier for listed companies to repurchase and sell own shares. Recently, jurisdiction has granted unlisted companies a significantly higher freedom of design related to the transfer of shares in comparison to listed companies because of the difference in protection needs. Listed companies may issue registered shares and bearer shares. As with limited liability companies the principle of capital maintenance applies. This means that the shareholders must not receive any funds apart from the approved profits recorded in the balance sheet with exception of dealings at arm's length that justify the payment to the shareholder.

The organisation of the stock company follows a three-level structure. Next to the meeting of the owners, that is the shareholders' meeting, and the board of directors, a supervisory board must be established. According to the legal model, the significant position of power and control in stock companies – in deviation from the model of the limited liability company – is concentrated with the board of directors, the executive body of the company. The board acts independently from instructions and must only submit certain measures to the supervisory board for approval. The supervisory board has to appoint and remove the board of directors. However, the board of directors may only with good cause be removed before expiration of term. The board of directors represents and controls the company. Its responsibilities reach from financing and day-to-day business to strategic work and management and supervision of the company. The shareholders' meeting decides on all extraordinary transactions such as capital increase, merger and other major dealings. It appoints and removes the supervisory board. However, it is not involved in any other management issues by law. As opposed to the shareholders' meeting of the limited liability company, it may not take business decisions on its own.

The supervisory board is the third body of the corporate governance structure of the stock company. It appoints and removes the board of directors and provides supervision. However, usually its effectiveness very much depends on the cooperation with the board of directors although its obligations and rights have been strongly expanded during the past years. In its role as the body supervising the leadership it has become increasingly a complementary body to the board of directors. In any case, there is a two-level administration structure; the board of directors and the supervisory board are organisationally separated.

A stock company has different options to increase its share capital, namely either through ordinary capital increase, contingent capital increase or through authorised capital. In case of capital increase through authorised capital, the final decision on the capital increase is delegated by the shareholders' meeting to the board of directors together with the supervisory board. Corporations may be merged and demerged and also transformed. Transformation with universal succession is possible for stock companies too.

The Societas Europaea basically follows the Austrian legal model with a few minor differences.

### [G] Cooperative Society

Cooperative societies play an important role in Austrian economic life – in the agricultural as well as the commercial sector, and especially in the area of the credit industry. Cooperative societies are associations with legal personality and an unlimited number of members. They mainly serve the support of their members' acquisitions and economic activities.

Under the Austrian law on cooperatives there are cooperatives with unlimited liability and cooperatives where liability is limited by shares or limited to a fixed amount.

Every member must at least subscribe one share, but may also subscribe more. Members may leave the cooperative either by transfer of the corporative share or by resignation against a severance pay. Despite the general openness, the cooperative contract may establish a minimum or maximum number of members as well as certain requirements for membership.

In cooperative societies with limited liability each member must – in addition to the liability of his share – undertake liability for an amount equivalent to the value of his share. Only in case of credit cooperatives, this additional liability may be eliminated.

Basically, cooperatives are organised on a two-level basis with the meeting of the members and the board of directors. Under certain circumstances, a supervisory board has to be established. In order to avoid mass meetings, the meeting of the members may establish a meeting of delegates. Due to this design, there is a risk that certain officers gain too much influence in relation to individual cooperative members. Therefore, in cooperatives a strong emphasis is to be made on balanced corporate governance.

## §10.03 GROUP OF COMPANIES

Naturally, the Austrian economy is familiar with groups of companies. The Stock Exchange Act and the law governing the limited liability company also include definitions of a group of companies. However, there is no codification of group law. Rather, the law governing groups of companies has to be derived from general company law. A group of companies exists when legally independent companies are combined under common leadership. A group of companies also exists when a legally independent company is under the influence of another company. However, thereby it is not necessary that this influence is actually exercised.

Whereas group management of limited liability companies is easy due to the right of direction, it is more difficult with stock companies as the board of directors of the subsidiary is not subjected to the instructions of the shareholder who is the parent company. However, the board of directors has the right to follow instructions. Nonetheless, they cannot be directly enforced. The board of directors has to decide whether the measures instructed by the parent company are also in the interest of the subsidiary. The board of directors of the parent company, however, is obliged to affect the subsidiary to the best interest of its company, in order to properly control and supervise the group.

## §10.04 CLOSING REMARKS

Austrian company law has been subjected to a high number of amendments during the past years. In many cases, however, these have brought along minor changes which oftentimes have been formed with regard to specific cases, and, thus, have impaired the clarity and consistency of company law in general. But, basically, the legal provisions serve as necessary and adequate infrastructure for Austrian companies.

## SELECTED BIBLIOGRAPHY


### General Literature

Jabornegg/Artmann, *Kommentar zum UGB*[2] (2012).
Kalss/Nowotny/Schauer, *Österreichisches Gesellschaftsrecht* (2008).
Kalss/Probst, *Familienunternehmen* (2013).
Kalss/Schauer/Winner, *Allgemeines Unternehmensrecht*[2] (2014).
Krejci, *Unternehmensrecht*[6] (2013).
Nowotny/Fida, *Kapitalgesellschaftsrecht, Umgründungsrecht, Übernahmerecht*[2] (2013).
Ratka/Rauter/Völkl, *Unternehmens- und Gesellschaftsrecht* (2011).
Straube, *Kommentar zum UGB*[4] (loose-leaf, since 2009).
Torggler, *Kommentar zum UGB* (2013).

### Literature on Limited Liability Companies

Koppensteiner/Rüffler, *GmbHG*[3] (2007).
Straube, *Wiener Kommentar zum GmbHG* (since 2008 loose-leaf).
Nowotny in Kalss/Nowotny/Schauer, *Österreichisches Gesellschaftsrecht* (2008), marginal no. Chapter 4.

### Literature on Cooperative Societies

Dellinger, *Kommentar zum Genossenschaftsgesetz* (2005).
Kalss/Nowotny/Schauer, *Österreichisches Gesellschaftsrecht* (2008) pp 1189 et seq.
Keinert, *Österreichisches Genossenschaftsrecht* (1988).

### Literature on Stock Companies

Doralt/Nowotny/Kalss, *Kommentar zum Aktiengesetz*[2] (2012).
Jabornegg/Strasser, *Kommentar zum Aktiengesetz*[5] (2011).

CHAPTER 11

# Introduction into Austrian Labour Law

*Franz Marhold**

## §11.01 INTRODUCTION: SOURCES OF LAW

The main sources of Austrian labour law are European law, international treaties – particularly the European Convention on Human Rights, which is directly applicable in Austria – numerous federal laws and ministerial orders. In addition, collective regulations through collective agreements and works council agreements play an important role when determining employment relationships. In Austrian labour law there is no comprehensive statute – like one singular codex – regulating all aspects of employment issues. Thus provisions are scattered in various statutes.

Diverse statutes regulate individual and collective labour law issues. The 'General Civil Code' ('*Allgemeines Bürgerliches Gesetzbuch*', in the following: ABGB) contains basic rules on the employment relationship. While the 'Labour Constitution Act' ('*Arbeitsverfassungsgesetz*', in the following: ArbVG) mainly regulates collective agreements, works councils and their agreements, it also serves as protection against dismissal.

Separate statutes regulate the employment relationship of different categories of employees. The most important are the 'White-Collar Employees Act' ('*Angestelltengesetz*', in the following: AngG) and the 'Trade Regulation Act' ('*Gewerbeordnung 1859*', in the following: GewO). Furthermore, the 'Act on the Adjustment of Employment Contract Law' ('*Arbeitsvertragsrechts-Anpassungsgesetz*', in the following: AVRAG) is worth mentioning, which particularly serves to implement European law into the Austrian system, and also regulates *inter alia* the transfer of undertakings. Certain aspects of employment law are regulated in themed statutes, like the 'Working Time

* With significant assistance of Dr Erika Kovacs, Assistant Professor, Institute for Austrian and European Labour Law and Social Security Law, WU Vienna University of Economics and Business.

Act' ('*Arbeitszeitgesetz*', in the following: AZG), the 'Holidays Act' ('*Urlaubsgesetz*'), 'Equal Treatment Act' ('*Gleichbehandlungsgesetz*'), 'Continued Payment of Remuneration Act' ('*Entgeltfortzahlungsgesetz*'), etc. The 'Employment of Foreigners Act' ('*Ausländerbeschäftigungsgesetz*') applies to topics regarding the employment of foreigners.

## §11.02 INDIVIDUAL LABOUR LAW

### [A] Employment Contract

The conclusion of an employment contract is not bound to certain formalities. It can be concluded in writing, orally or also by implication. The employer has the obligation to lay down significant rights and obligations of the employee in a record and hand it over to the employee immediately after the beginning of the employment relationship or conclusion of the employment contract (§ 2 AVRAG and § 6 paragraph 3 AngG). This document is the so-called 'note of service' ('*Dienstzettel*'), which, however, only has a declarative effect.

Employment protection regulation only fully applies to employees. Besides, there are other forms of performing dependent or quasi-dependent work. The law differentiates between the employment contract and contract for services ('*Werkvertrag*'). The latter is characterised by someone who promises a performance in exchange for remuneration without being personally dependent. (§ 1151 ABGB). Another way of performing work is the so-called 'free contract of service' ('*freier Dienstvertrag*'), where one person provides services without or with reduced personal dependency and restrictions regarding one's behaviour (typical for company doctors, veterinaries in meat inspection, journalists, etc.). This form of relationship is similar to the employment contract in the sense that it is concluded for a particular time – not for a specific (and successfully achieved) performance – and the performance is specified according to the type of activity. Only those labour law regulations, which are not based on the idea of protecting employees, apply to this relationship.

### [B] Categories of Employees

The term 'employee' does not have a uniform and consistent meaning in Austrian labour law. Different statutes contain various definitions. Whereas for example the executive staff ('*leitende Angestellte*') does not fall within the scope of the Working Time Act (§ 1 paragraph 2 point 8 AZG) and the Labour Constitution Act (§ 36 ArbVG), employment contract law applies to these persons (§ 1151 ABGB).

Austrian labour law has been coined by a traditional and somewhat archaic differentiation between blue-collar workers ('*Arbeiter*') and white-collar employees ('*Angestellte*'). Whereas both employment relationships are mostly regulated by the same statutes, the most significant differences still exist in the AngG and the GewO as well as the Continued Payment of Remuneration Act ('*Entgeltfortzahlungsgesetz*', EFZG). The former two statutes contain different terms of terminating employment contracts and obligations from the employment contract. There is a clear tendency to adjust the rules regarding blue-collar workers to the white-collar employees' level of protection. However, there are still significant differences between their situations. A good example is the distinction concerning the periods of notice. Whereas blue-collar workers have a statutory minimum period of notice of fourteen days from which the employment contract and the collective agreement can derogate in both directions, white-collar employees enjoy a minimum period of notice of six weeks in case of an employer's dismissal with notice.

The term white-collar employee ('*Angestellter*') is defined in the White-Collar Employees Act (§ 1 AngG). According to this rule, white-collar employees primarily carry out commercial services, higher non-commercial services or office work. This definition is to be understood in a historical context. All persons, who do not qualify as white-collar employees, are regarded as blue-collar workers.

### [C] Working Time

The Working Time Act ('*Arbeitszeitgesetz*', in the following: AZG) and the Rest Period Act ('*Arbeitsruhegesetz*', in the following: ARG) regulate working time respectively rest periods. Most of their provisions are cogent law. The parties in the employment contract shall agree on duration and division of working time, if they are not set by collective agreement. The employer can change the division of working time unilaterally only if (a) it is objectively justified with reasons lying in the kind of the work performed, (b) the employee is informed about the change two weeks before, (c) interests of the employee worth considering do not exclude the change and finally (d) there is no agreement between the parties about the division of working time (§ 19c paragraph 2 AZG).

The normal working time may not exceed the maximum of forty hours per week and eight hours per day (§ 3 AZG). Yet, there are many exceptions to this rule. Furthermore, many important collective agreements have reduced working time to thirty-eight hours per week for most industry sectors. Overtime exists, if the normal daily or weekly working time is exceeded (§ 6 AZG). The employer has to pay a premium of 50% for overtime work or provide compensatory time off even if s/he does not expressly orders overtime, but assigns an amount of work that it is not manageable within the normal working time. This also applies if the employer tolerates overtime or accepts the performance of the work (§ 10 AZG). The parties can agree in paying a fixed rate premium for overtime work or agree on an 'all-in clause'. However, this premium must not be lower than the hypothetical extra pay which an employee would have earned without this clause. It is only permitted to order overtime if there is an increased workload, for preparatory or closing work (§§ 7-8 AZG). Even if the one-sided assignment of working time is allowed, important interests of the employees – as for instance child care – can oppose to such action.

The maximum daily working time amounts to ten hours and the maximum weekly working time to fifty hours. In the reference period of seventeen weeks the average weekly working time must not exceed forty-eight hours. Certain exceptions exist for, e.g. shift work, the readiness to work, increased workload, preparatory and closing work, the public transport sector, pharmacies (§ 9 AZG) and hospitals to which a special Hospital Working Time Act (*'Krankenanstalten-Arbeitszeitgesetz'*, KA-AZG) applies.

Flexibility of working time is ensured by several rules. Collective agreements and works council agreements can set a normal daily working time of ten hours while respecting the forty hours normal weekly working time . The parties of the employment contract can consent to longer daily working times of nine hours if the average of forty hours per week is not exceeded. Bridge days –between bank holiday and the weekend – can be incorporated into the normal working time within a frame of thirteen weeks.

Flexible working time (*'Gleitzeit'*) can only be agreed upon if the employee can determine the beginning and end of the working time on its own (§ 4b AZG). The employer needs the works council's approval for the introduction of flexible working time schemes. If there is no works council in the undertaking, the employer and employee can agree on the flexible working time themselves.

Part-time work (*'Teilzeit'*) is a shorter weekly working time than the statutory or in collective agreements settled normal working time (§ 19d paragraph 1 AZG). If the part-time employee works more than the working time agreed but less than the normal working time (statutory 40 hours per week), it is not considered overtime but extra work (*'Mehrarbeit'*). The employer has to reimburse extra work with a 25% premium of the hourly wage (§ 19d paragraph 3a AZG). Pursuant to § 19d paragraph 3f AZG it is however permissible to differ from the overtime premium by means of collective agreement.

The daily rest period lasts eleven hours, which can be reduced to eight hours by a collective agreement. The weekly rest period shall last thirty-six hours, starting at the latest at 1 pm on Saturday and including Sunday (§ 3 ARG). Only if the employee's work schedule plans employment during weekends, it is allowed to replace the weekend rest period with one during the week (§ 4 ARG).

### [D] Remuneration

Wages are primarily determined in the employment contract negotiated between the employer and employee. If such an agreement on remuneration is missing, the employee is entitled to fair remuneration (§ 1152 ABGB, § 6 paragraph 1 AngG). Collective agreements are important in the determination of wages since they cover over 90% of employees in Austria.

Statutes regulate the remuneration of civil servants and public servants. There is no statutory minimum wage in Austria. The objective of the Wage and Social Dumping Combating Act (*'Lohn- und Sozialdumping-Bekämpfungsgesetz'*) is to guarantee posted employees a level of remuneration, which corresponds to the basic wage set forth in collective agreements for all employees employed in Austria – thus even for those, who have a foreign employer. In case of violation of this rule, the employer is fined for each underpaid employee (§ 7i paragraph 3 *'Arbeitsvertragsrechtsanpassungsgesetz'*, AVRAG).

There are several forms of performance-related remuneration like piece wage, commission work, premium, bonus, profit-sharing etc. Certain performance-related remuneration must not result in a wage drop below the minimum wage declared in the respective collective agreement.

The introduction and regulation of performance-related wage systems requires the approval of the works council if the collective agreement does not contain a regulation itself (§ 96 paragraph 1 point 4 ArbVG).

### [E] Remuneration without Work

The idea of social protection in labour law requires that the employee retain the right to remuneration even if s/he does not perform the work in certain circumstances. In case the obstacle to carry out work lies on the employer's side (in his sphere) and the employee was ready to perform, the employee maintains her/his right to remuneration (§ 1155 ABGB).

In certain cases, if the obstacle to perform the work lies in the person of the employee, the employer is obliged to continue to pay the remuneration. In practice, the most important case is the continuation of remuneration in the event of disease or accident (§ 8 paragraphs 1-2 AngG; regarding white-collar employees). To blue-collar workers a separate statute applies, namely the Continued Payment of Remuneration Act (*'Entgeltfortzahlungsgesetz'*, EFZG).

First the situation of white-collar employees will be reviewed: According to § 8 paragraph 1 AngG a white-collar employee maintains her/his right to remuneration, if s/he was prevented from performing work by a disease or accident and the situation was not deliberately or grossly negligently caused by her/him. It is essential that the employee is incapable of working, i.e. s/he is temporarily not able to perform the work or the performance would risk worsening her/his health condition. Consequently, the terms disease and accident are not uniformly understood, but depend on the kind of work owed. The white-collar employee is obliged to inform the employer immediately about her/his inability to work and to submit a medical certificate about the reasons and duration of the incapability to work on request of the employer. The employee has the right to full-continued remuneration for six weeks. This period increases correspondingly by two, four or six weeks, if the time of employment lasted at least five, fifteen of twenty-five years. Subsequently, the employee has the right to continued payment of the half of the amount of her/his regular remuneration for four further weeks. After that time, the employee can receive sick pay from her/his health insurance. In case of recurrence of a disease within half a year after returning to work, the employee is once more entitled to full continued remuneration for the general time periods mentioned above (§ 8 paragraph 1 AngG). The employee's claim amounts in the case of a recurred disease within half a year only to half the remuneration compared to the amounts of the initial case

The regulation of continued payment of remuneration for blue-collar employees is similar to that of white-collar employees but with some significant differences. If the temporal limit of six, eight, ten or twelve weeks of full-continued payment is exceeded (depending on the length of the employment relationship), s/he is entitled to four further weeks of half remuneration. One of the most important distinctions is that in case of recurrence of disease blue-collar employees are eligible to continued payment only until the periods mentioned above are exhausted (§ 2 paragraph 4 EFZG). In case the incapability was caused by work accident or occupational disease, the employee's entitlement to continued remuneration comes into existence once again.

### [F] Holiday

The Holidays Act ('*Urlaubsgesetz*', UrlG) uniformly regulates holidays for white-collar and blue-collar employees. The employee is entitled to thirty working days off, which increase to thirty-six working days after the completion of twenty-five years of employment (§ 2 UrlG). This requirement refers to the employment with one certain employer. Times of prior employments, studies or other specific occupations can be taken into account to a limited extent (§ 3 paragraphs 2-4 UrlG). The term 'working day' comprises all days with the exception of Sundays and bank holidays. In the first six months of an employment relationship, the employee is only entitled to consume the pro rata part of the annual holiday. For the sake of calculating holidays, the year starts with the day employment is taken up. The specific time of the holiday has to be agreed upon between employer and employee while taking into account the firms needs and the recreation purpose of the employee. If the employee applies for an at least twelve working days long holiday and the employer and employee cannot agree on it three months in advance, the works council is to involve in the negotiation. If even then they do not reach an agreement, the employee can take the holiday at the suggested date (§ 4 paragraph 4 EFZG). However, if the employer involves the court within a set timeframe and it declares the employee's leave unjust, this states a reason for a dismissal without notice.
This rule applies only in enterprises, where a works council is established, which is competent for that employee. A company holiday has to be agreed individually with all employees and cannot be regulated by collective agreement or works council agreement.

The holiday should be used within the holiday year, but if it is not consumed it will be added to the next year's holiday. The right to holiday expires by limitation two years after the end of the original holiday year. If the employee falls ill during the holiday and the disease lasts longer than three days, the days of the illness cannot be calculated as holiday, unless it was caused incidentally or by gross negligence (§ 5 paragraph 1 UrlG). During the holiday the employee receives her/his regular remuneration.

### [G] Severance Pay

Severance pay is regulated in the Act on the Occupational Severance Pay of Employees and Self-employed ('*Betriebliches Mitarbeiter- und Selbständigenvorsorgegesetz*'). The system of severance pay has been extended to self-employed persons in 2007. The so-called 'new severance pay' has to be applied to employment relationships established since 2003 and to those in which the employer and employee agreed to the application (§ 46 paragraph 1 BMSVG). The previous severance pay model still applies to employment relationships which commenced before 2003. Consequently, two parallel systems of severance pay exist. The regulations regarding white-collar and blue-collar workers have been basically aligned with minor differences.

According to the old severance pay provisions, the employee's entitlement to severance pay depends on the duration and the way of terminating the employment relationship. The right to severance pay accrues after at least three years of continuous employment regardless of one's working performance during this time. The amount of severance pay is staggered based on the duration of the employment relationship. The employee generally loses her/his entitlement to severance pay if the employment relationship is terminated by the employee giving notice, the employee's premature resignation without having a substantial reason or the employer's summary dismissal based on an employee's fault.

Aim of the introduction of the new severance pay was to abolish the rule that the entitlement arose only after three years of continuous employment in order to prevent the employer's motivation to terminate the employment relationship prior to lasting three years. Furthermore, the old system burdened particularly small employers and forced them to create provisions for this purpose. The personal scope of the regulation on new severance pay is wide (§§ 1-2 BMSVG). The new system introduced provident funds (*'Betriebliche Vorsorgekasse'*) with employers being obliged to contribute 1.53% of the employee's monthly salary (including all additional payment) into the fund. (§ 6 paragraph 1 BMSVG). The employee cannot encash the severance pay directly from the employer but only from the fund. The employer and the works council choose a particular fund together, which then applies uniformly to the whole undertaking and all employees. The novelty of the new system is the entitlement to severance pay independent from the kind of termination of the employment relationship. Not in all cases can the beneficiary demand the funds to be paid out to her/him, though (§ 14 BMSVG). The payment to the beneficiary can basically be required under the same circumstances as in the old system (after three years, under certain forms of termination). However, the difference between the new and old systems is: Whereby one would have lost its claim in the old system, the new system arranges that the funds remain invested until they can be taken out for when the criteria therefore are met.

## [H] Dismissal with Notice (*'Kündigung'*)

### *[1] General Rules*

Generally, Austrian labour law intends the freedom of dismissal. Notice is understood as a declaratory act, which has to be received by the other party and set the date for terminating the employment relationship in the future. The dismissal is not bound by formal requirements. However, dismissal is statutorily regulated and limited in several ways. The employer can unilaterally terminate indefinite employment contracts by dismissal with notice ('*Kündigung*') and without notice (summary dismissal) ('*Entlassung*').

The most significant regulations are set forth in the provisions regarding employee representation in the Labour Constitution Act. As a result, dismissal protection is not considered as an individual right of the employee but as part of the participation rights of the works council. Consequently, general dismissal protection applies only to undertakings, where a works council is or ought to be established. This is the case in undertakings, in which at least five employees are permanently employed. Thus, employees in small undertakings with less than five employees do not happen to have general dismissal protection.

In principle the employer is free to dismiss whomever he wants to with the restraint that the works council or the employee himself (if a works council ought to be installed) can contest the dismissal in court.

Certain types of employees, like members of the works council, pregnant women, women and men during maternity leave, disabled persons, persons performing military or civil service enjoy special dismissal protection.

Temporary employment contracts cannot be terminated by dismissal with notice. However, the parties of the contract can provide for the possibility of dismissal with notice. If an employment contract is concluded for a fixed period of more than five years, the employee can terminate after the period of five years with six months of notice (§§ 21 AngG, 1158 paragraph 3 ABGB).

### *[2] Notice Period*

Giving notice changes the type of employment relationship from one for an unlimited time to one for limited time. The notice periods differ for blue and white-collar workers. The extent of compensation in case of unfair (summary) dismissal is therefore also different. As a general rule, the notice period for blue-collar workers amounts to fourteen days, but deviation from this rule is allowed both in favour of and to the disadvantage of the worker (§ 77 GewO 1859). Most collective agreements contain in practice minimum standards for blue-collar workers, though.

On the contrary, the statutory notice period for white-collar employees is unilaterally compulsory. Thus, one cannot derogate to the disadvantage of employees. In the first two years the notice period amounts to six weeks and increases according to the duration of the employment relationship (§ 20 AngG). If white-collar employees work part-time (in case of 40 hours normal weekly working time less than 34.4 hours a month), instead of the above mentioned rules, the general rules of the General Civil Code (ABGB) apply. Another peculiarity of white-collar workers is that – if not agreed to the employee's advantage – employment relationships solely end at the end of calendar quarters. The parties can differ from that and set forth an option for dismissal on the fifteenth and the last day of the month. White-collar employees can terminate the relationship by giving notice one month prior to the end of the month. This period might be extended, but must not be longer than employer's corresponding period of time.

In case the employer sets an incorrect day as the end of the employment relationship, the relationship will nevertheless end prematurely at that date. The employee can then demand damages in order to be financially put in the position as if s/he had been given notice according to the rules.

### *[3] Contesting the Dismissal*

Prior to giving notice the employer is obliged to observe a preliminary procedure (*'Vorverfahren'*, § 105 paragraphs 1, 2 ArbVG). However, this does not apply in establishments with fewer than five people being regularly employed. The employer has to inform the works council about her/his intention of dismissing a certain person. The works council is given one week to respond to the employer's intent. If the employer fails to comply with this rule and gives notice before the expiration of the one-week period for consideration, the dismissal is legally void, i.e., it does not terminate the employment relationship.

The works council can approve the dismissal, can remain silent or can expressly disagree with the dismissal. If the works council agrees with the dismissal, the employee cannot contest the dismissal in court alleging social adversity (*'Sozialwidrigkeit'*), but only alleging proscribed reason(s) for the dismissal (*'verpöntes Motiv'*). If the works council remains silent and does comment on the planned dismissal, the employee can contest the dismissal within two weeks her/himself. However, the employee cannot invoke a social comparison with the colleagues alleging that other colleagues find themselves in better social circumstances than s/he would after the pending termination (*'Sozialvergleich'*). Therefore the decision of the works council significantly influences the possibilities of contesting the dismissal. Only if the works council expressly objects to the dismissal, the employee has all opportunities to contest. In this case the works council can lodge an appeal with the Labour and Social Court at request of the employee within one week after the notification that notice has been given.

Irrespective of the works council's conduct, the employee can contest the dismissal based on the assumption that it was based on a proscribed reason (*'verpöntes Motiv'*, § 105 paragraph 3 point 1 ArbVG). It is not allowed to dismiss the employee due to her/his membership or activity in a trade union, because of an earlier activity in the works council or any other representative organisation of employees. Moreover, dismissal is unlawful due to one performing military or civil service. The same applies if the dismissal neglected the prohibition of discrimination or the reason was a planned or consumed maternity leave (*'Karenzierung'*) or working time reduction due to childcare.

If the works council does not react or object to the planned dismissal, the employee can contest because of social adversity (*'Sozialwidrigkeit'*). Prerequisite is an employment duration of at least six months in the undertaking or in the group of undertakings. In order to prevail, the employee has to demonstrate that the dismissal adversely affects significant interests, which means that as a result the employee's situation fundamentally (and financially) worsens. Therefore, the entire social and financial situation of the employee comes into consideration, e.g., age, duration of employment in the company, asset, credits, income of the spouse, obligation to pay maintenance. Predictions regarding future reduction of income and probable length of unemployment can be important arguments. According to jurisprudence, an employee might accept an income reduction of around 10% in a new job, but no more than 20%. Presumable long unemployment also signals for social adversity of the dismissal.

However, even if employees find themselves in the above-mentioned circumstances, a dismissal is not socially adverse if it is justified by personal or enterprise-related reasons, which adversely influence the interests of the undertaking. Personal-related reasons can be associated either with the person of the employee, e.g., missing physical or mental skills to perform the work, or with the behaviour of the employee which violates her/his duty, e.g., refusal to work, underperformance, habitually coming late, etc. Enterprise-related reasons can be of different sorts, as for example a decline in orders or turnover, technical or structural restructuring, which lead to a reduction in workforce. The employer is given a great scope of discretion in this regard. Nevertheless, the employer is obliged to consider all possibilities to keep the employee in the undertaking – social obligation of organisation (*'soziale Gestaltungspflicht'*). Therefore, vocational retraining and dismissal with the option of altered conditions of employment (*'Änderungskündigung'*) shall be taken into consideration.

Last step of the examination of the dismissal is the so-called 'social comparison' (*'Sozialvergleich'*) if the reason of the dismissal is enterprise-related and the works council expressly objected. Employees with the same activity profile are compared, who might be interchangeable as they perform the same or a similar kind of work. The employee, who would be least affected by the dismissal, shall then be the one the employer dismisses. In order to assess the level the adverse effects the same criteria as for the social adversity test (e.g., age, seniority, obligation for child support, income of the spouse, credits, expected length of unemployment, expected decrease of income in the future employment) are used.

## [I] Dismissal without Notice

### *[1] General Rules*

Both, indefinite and temporary employment contracts can be subject to termination without notice. In case the employer terminates the relationship without notice, this is called *'Entlassung'*, whereas termination by the employee without notice is called *'Austritt'*. As a general principle, an important reason is necessary for a termination without notice. It has to be so severe that is objectively unacceptable for one party to stick with an ongoing employment relationship until expiry of the notice. Dismissal without notice is considered as the *ultima ratio* solution, where no other measure can be taken.

The declaration of (summary) termination without notice is not bound to formal requirements. It can happen orally, in writing and by conclusive behaviour. The employer has to evidently and without delay (*'Grundsatz der Unverzüglichkeit'*) express, that the employment relationship is to be instantly terminated. The reason does not need to be expressly specified, but has to substantive.

For white-collar employees the termination without notice is regulated in §§ 26-27 AngG, where possible reasons are exemplarily listed. By contrast, the regulation concerning blue-collar workers in §§ 82, 82a GewO 1859 contains a complete and concluding list of reasons for termination without notice.

In case of fair dismissal without notice based on the employee's behaviour, the employee has to compensate for the damages arisen. However, the employer has to compensate the employee for the damage caused if the employer dismisses her/him unjustly. The unfairly dismissed employee can contest the summary dismissal in court, and in case of successfully lodging a complaint the dismissal will be qualified void.

Certain groups of employees, like members of the works council, pregnant women, women and men during maternity leave, public employees and persons performing military or civil service, etc., enjoy special protection vis-à-vis dismissal without notice.

### *[2] White-Collar Employees*

The grounds that create a substantive reason for the employer to dismiss white-collar employees without notice are diverse. First, the violation of the duty if the employee receives unjustified benefits in service for her/his activities without the knowledge or the will of the employer. Also if s/he carries out an activity, which results in the employer's loss of trust (e.g., sideline, forgery of documents for one's own benefit, crime against the employer, intentional disclosure of business secrets, etc.). Second, if the employee finds her/himself unable to perform her/his activities in an appropriate way and this condition turns out to be permanent, e.g., due to an illness or loss of driving licence. Third, if the employee violates the prohibition of competition to employer. Fourth, if the employee fails to perform her/his duties or refuses to perform her/his work or ignores the instructions of the employer. Fifth, an unreasonably long absence from the workplace (e.g., imprisonment) can result in termination without notice if the absence is not caused by illness or accident. Finally, the employer can dismiss an employee without notice, if the employee is guilty of an act of violence, breaches morals or libels against the employer, her/his relatives or colleagues.

The employee can terminate the employment relationship without notice if s/he becomes unable to perform her/his duties or cannot perform them without the damaging her/his health or morals. Furthermore, if the employer violates significant obligations resulting from the employment relationship, particularly, if the employer reduces or deprives the employee of the employee. Refusing to provide the necessary protection of the life, health and moral of the employee in spite of her/his demand, states another reason. The employee can equivalently terminate the relationship without notice if the employer is guilty of an act of violence or breaches morals, or libels against the employee or her/his relatives.

### [3] *Blue-Collar Workers*

The grounds for blue-collar workers' dismissal without notice are in many cases similar to those of white-collar employees. The list of reasons is exhaustive and differences result particularly from the white-collar employees' increased duty of loyalty. Reasons for dismissal without notice are: deceiving the employer at conclusion of the employment contract; incapacity to perform one's work; chronic alcoholism in spite of repeatedly having been warned; certain crimes; disclosure of business secrets; additional occupation, which adversely affects the employer; failure to perform the duties of the employment relationship; insult, assault or dangerous threat; careless behaviour with fire and light; deterrent illness and self-imposed inability to perform work as well as prison term of over fourteen days.

To blue-collar worker, the relationship can end without notice in the following cases: if her/his health is endangered; in case of gross ill-treatment or breach of morals; attempt of the employer to incite the worker to immoral or illegal activity; breach of significant obligations of the employment relationship; non-payment of wages; insolvency of the employer. Some other special reasons are listed in various provisions.

Dismissal without notice terminates the employment relationship with immediate effect independently of the fact whether it was fair or unfair. If a dismissal without notice violates a special protection provision shielding an employee against dismissal, it is however considered void and does not terminate the employment relationship.

## [J] Transfer of Undertaking

The Council Directive 2001/23/EC on safeguarding employees' rights in the event of transfers of undertakings was implemented into the Austrian labour law by §§ 3-6 AVRAG. Since the regulation reflects the provisions of the Directive, only certain special features of the Austrian system will be mentioned.

The personal scope of the regulation is limited. Various groups of persons, as for instance those employed by the state government, working in agriculture and home workers, are excluded.

Employees do not have a general right to object to the undertaking's transfer. One can however object to the automatic transfer of her/his employment relationship if the transferee does not comply with the provisions and safeguards concerning termination and company pension commitments made in the collective agreement of the transferor (§§ 4-5 AVRAG).

Although there is no statutory prohibition of dismissals with notice in connection with the transfer of undertakings, jurisprudence developed counteracting legislation. If the working conditions of the employee worsen significantly due to the transfer and the application of another collective agreement or works council agreement, the employee has a preferential right to dismissal with notice. The dismissal then has the same effect as a dismissal effected by the employer (§ 3 paragraph 5 AVRAG).

## §11.03 COLLECTIVE LABOUR LAW

### [A] Social Partners

#### *[1] The Statutory Representation Organisations*

Individual and collective labour law are strongly interconnected in Austria. Various issues of the employment relationship are dominantly influenced by the social partners and their collective regulations, e.g., dismissal protection, protection against posting, data protection, etc.

The social partners representing the interests of employees and employers in Austria can be divided into two major groups, namely compulsory and the voluntary organisations.

The first group of organisations contains the compulsory representation organisations, the Chambers of Labour (*'Arbeiterkammern'*) and Economic Chambers (*'Wirtschaftskammern'*), which are also called statutory representation organisations. There are further chambers for doctors, notaries and pharmacists on the employers' side. The existence of compulsory representation organisations is a special feature of the Austrian labour law. They play a significant role in the representation of social interests. They are legal entities of public law regulated in separate statutes (*'Arbeiterkammergesetz'* and *'Wirtschaftskammergesetz'*). They have the authority to act independent of instructions.

Nearly all employees (both blue and white-collar) are compulsory members of the Chambers of Labours with the exception of managers, certain public servants, doctors, certain persons in the agriculture, etc. Membership in the Economic Chamber is acquired automatically with the acquisition of the entitlement to run an undertaking in certain fields (business license). Consequently, almost all persons performing dependent or independent forms of work are bound by a statutory representation organisation. Thus, chambers have a strong influence in policy-making. That is why Austria is ironically called a 'state of chambers' (*'Kammerstaat'*).

The chambers' scope of work contains delegating members to the Labour and Social Courts, advising their members in labour and social law issues, potentially representing them in court and assessing drafts of statutes in labour and social issues. The statutory representation organisations have the right to conclude collective agreements. However, voluntary organisations have legal priority over statutory organisations in this context.

#### *[2] The Voluntary Representation Organisations*

The second group of social partners' right of existence derives from the freedom of association; they are called coalitions (*'Koalitionen'*). The most powerful coalition on the employees' side is the Austrian Trade Union Federation (*'Österreichische Gewerkschaftsbund'*), which consists of seven trade unions with about 1.2 million members in

2014. This amounts to about 34% of the workforce. Besides, only a few other – historically grown –trade unions exist.

Contrary to the employees' side, an overarching organisation for the all industries is missing on employers' side. The employers usually acknowledge the activity of the Economic Chamber. In sectors, where compulsory and voluntary organisations coexist, usually the compulsory organisations conclude collective agreements. Practical exceptions to this rule only exist in the banking and credit sector as well as in the insurance, media and electricity sector. One of the most important voluntary organisations is the Federation of Austrian Industry (*'Vereinigung der Österreichischen Industrie'*), which represents the interests of the Austrian industry and comprises 4,200 companies as its members.

These coalitions are based on free membership and have also set their aim to regulate working conditions within their scope. They can conclude collective agreements, advise their members in labour and social law issues, represent them in court and assess drafts of statutes in labour and social issues.

### [B] Collective Agreements

#### *[1] Parties*

The right to conclude a collective agreement depends on certain conditions. Generally, only associations – not the single employers – are entitled to conclude collective agreements. By virtue of statute – *ex lege* – the right to conclude collective agreements is granted to the statutory representation organisations of the employees and the employers. Those are mainly the Economic Chamber and the Chambers of Labours of labour as well as certain other organisation like the Austrian Broadcasting Corporation (ORF), the Confederation of the Universities concerning the employees of the universities, etc. The ability to conclude collective agreements depends on the prerequisite that they are free of opponents in their decision-making process and within their bodies.

Furthermore, the Federal Conciliation Board, the competent authority of the ministry (*'Bundeseinigungsamt'*), can constitutively provide certain associations with the right to conclude collective agreements. This applies to voluntary organisations of employers, like the Austrian Trade Union Federation. Conditions to grant this right are the following: the organisation concerned has to comply with the negative and positive effects of the freedom of association. Hence, they have to be free from the opponents in its decision-making process and have the objective to regulate working conditions. Important criterion is that the organisation has to be socially significant (*'sozial mächtig'*), i.e., based on its membership and scope of activities should have a significant economic relevance (§ 4 paragraph 2 point 3 ArbVG).

Collective agreements concluded by a voluntary organisation have priority over collective agreements of statutory organisations. Once a voluntary organisation concludes a collective agreement, the statutory organisation loses its right to conclude agreements on behalf of the members of the voluntary organisation. This applies however only to the personal, professional and temporal scope of the collective agreement concluded by the voluntary organisation.

### *[2] Content and Legal Effect*

The parties of the collective agreement do not have the right to unlimited regulation. The Labour Constitution Act sets forth what can be subject to collective agreements (Article 2 paragraph 2 ArbVG). A collective agreement can regulate the contractual obligation between the parties of the agreement, e.g., the period of notice of the agreement, details of the implementation of the agreement, peace obligation, etc. Of great significance are the regulations of the normative part of the collective agreement. There the rights and obligations of the employees and the employers influencing the employment relationship are defined. Moreover, the agreement can set measures to prevent, remove, or alleviate the consequences of a transfer of undertaking, which is called social plan (‘*Sozialplan*’). In a collective agreement certain – very limited – works council issues can be regulated, namely the kind and scope of works council participation rights regarding the implementation of social plans and the humane design of the workplace. Furthermore, the parties may create a common institution – for instance a pension fund – and regulate the rights and obligations regarding this institution in the collective agreement. The law leaves the possibility open to solely regulate other issues based on the authorisation of statutes. Consequently, it is not permitted to deal with other issues than that.

The normative part of the collective agreement is itself – not only between the parties, but also to the employees and employers covered by its scope – legally binding. It is to be interpreted like a statute. Provisions of collective agreements are usually unilaterally compulsory.

### *[3] Scope*

Unless otherwise agreed, the collective agreement comes into effect the day of its announcement. Validity ends due to lapse of time, unilateral or mutual termination or concluding a new collective agreement. The law intends to prevent a situation without a collective agreement in force and therefore provides its ‘*continued validity*’ (‘*Nachwirkung*’). The collective agreement remains temporary applicable to those employment relationships, which it has already covered, until a new collective agreement becomes relevant. The ‘*continued validity*’ also ends regardless if the new agreement is more or less advantageous to employees.

The territorial scope of the collective agreements can cover Austria or certain regions only.

As far as the personal scope of the collective agreement is concerned, all members of the concluding parties and those employees and employers, who become members of the concluding parties later, fall within the scope of the collective agreement. Resignation from the concluding organisation does not automatically bring about an end of the collective agreement’s application. In this case the agreement remains applicable. Austrian law provides a special effect for those, who not members of any union. The 'outsider effect' (*'Außenseiterwirkung'*) states that a collective agreement applies in this case to employees if only her/his employer is covered by a collective agreement, i.e., if the employer is affiliated to any organisation, which concluded a collective agreement (§ 12 ArbVG). Consequently, the personal scope of the collective agreements predominantly depends on the employer's affiliation.

Based on the compulsory membership of the employers in the Economic Chamber, over 90% of the employment relationships are covered by a collective agreement.

### *[4] Collision of Collective Agreements*

If two or more collective agreements are potentially applicable to an employee, the question arises, which collective agreement applies. The principle of unity of collective agreements (*'Tarifeinheit'*, § 9 ArbVG) states that only one collective agreement applies to one employee. In undertakings different agreements potentially apply to different employees according to the employee's scope of work. In practice different collective agreements are relevant for blue-collar workers and white-collar employees. The general rule implies that – within the order of agreements – the newer and more specific collective agreement has priority. If an employer, who is subject to more than one collective agreement, disposes of more than one undertaking (or organisational respectively professional section within an undertaking), the collective agreement with the closer organisational and professional ties to the undertaking (or section) applies. If there is no structural or professional separation (mixed undertaking, *'Mischbetrieb'*), the agreement applies, which professional field is economically more important for the undertaking. This can be subject to regulation through works agreement. If neither of the fields is economically more significant for the undertaking, the collective agreement of the professional sector is applicable, which employs more employees in absolute terms in Austria.

However, if an employee works in different undertakings (or sections within an undertaking) with different applicable collective agreements, s/he is subject to the agreement, which corresponds to the employee's predominantly exercised occupation. If it cannot be established, the collective agreement with the higher level of personal coverage in Austria applies.

### *[5] Substitutes of the Collective Agreement*

The Austrian law knows three forms of substitution for collective agreements. The common feature of all three forms is that the Federal Conciliation Board (*'Bundeseinigungsamt'*) can determine certain working conditions generally applicable at the request of the competent association. These forms are legally relevant to those to whom a collective agreement does not otherwise apply. The first substitute is called 'charter' (*'Satzung'*). This legal instrument declares the normative part of a collective agreement to be generally applicable outside its original personal scope. Second, minimum wage scales (*'Mindestlohntarif'*) can only be applied if there is no employer's association with the capacity to conclude collective agreements and no relevant charter has set standards in this regard. The third substitute for collective agreements is the 'apprenticeship compensation' (*'Lehrlingsentschädigung'*), which sets schemes for financial compensation applicable to apprentices unless a collective agreement is in force.

### [C] Industrial Action

In practise, industrial actions do not play an important role in Austria as they are taken seldom if ever. Between 2005 and 2011 there were no strikes at all in Austria. Since then only few have taken strike action.

Austrian law does not specifically regulate any form of industrial action. The state neither prohibits nor protects industrial actions in its statues. The reluctance of the state reflects its 'neutrality' in this regard. The situation can be described by a freedom of industrial actions. Due to missing regulation, infrequency of actions and insufficient case law, there is a legal uncertainty.

However, Article 11 of the European Convention on Human Rights (ECHR) – which is self-executing in Austria – permits industrial action. In the process of time, the European Court of Human Rights has construed Article 11 of the ECHR in such way that it permits industrial actions in certain cases but leaves secondary industrial actions to the discretion of its Member States. As of 2007 industrial actions were prohibited in Luxemburg, the Netherlands, the UK and Austria.

The peace obligation (*'Friedenspflicht'*) in Austrian law states that during the validity of a collective agreement it is not allowed to go on strike against issues, which are covered by the agreement. Certain other limitations can be observed, e.g., wildcat or political strike. Also strikes, which cause huge damages, violate the morals, and endanger health and safety are not allowed.

Austrian provisions occasionally deal with strike, though. Hence, it is not allowed to place an unemployed person in an undertaking affected by strike. Meanwhile the unemployed person is not obliged to accept a job post in such an undertaking. Strikers do not to receive unemployment benefits. An undertaking affected by strike must not hire temporary workers to compensate for strikers.

The prevailing doctrine in Austria differentiates between the legitimacy of the industrial action from a collective labour law perspective and the individual legal consequences for the employee on the other hand. As a result, even the participation in a legal strike can have negative consequences for the employee. When considering the legitimacy of a strike, it has to be stated that in relation to the individual parties a strike does not suspend employment relationship obligations. Participation in a strike is not a justified reason for one's refusal of performance. A strike consequently results in a breach of contract and may entitle the employer to dismiss the employee without notice. Considering the court ruling of the ECHR opinions in Austrian literature voice against the permissibility of a summary dismissal in the latter case. Employees participating in a strike do not have the right to continued payment of remuneration.

### [D] Works Councils

#### *[1] Scope and Definition*

Austrian law has coined a special expression for the regulation of the participation rights of the workforce through the works councils, namely 'Constitution of the Undertaking' (*'Betriebsverfassung'*). This topic is dealt with in the second part of the 'Labour Constitution Act' (*'Arbeitsverfassungsgesetz'*, ArbVG). This regulation applies above all to undertakings, in which a works council has to be established. The term 'undertaking' (*'Betrieb'*) has the following statutory definition: a workplace, which constitutes an organisational unit, within which a natural or legal person or a community pursue the objective of realising certain results with technical and intangible means independently from a profit or non-profit orientation (§ 34 paragraph 1 ArbVG).

In order to differentiate between an undertaking and a part of an undertaking the following criteria should be taken into account: (a) independence of the workplace meaning the discretionary competence of the executives regarding those tasks, which have been assigned to the undertaking; (b) autonomous performance of a service or creation of a separate product; (c) finally the geographical distance between the workplaces plays also a – rather subsidiary – role. At request, the court declares whether a certain workplace is an undertaking or not. From a structural point of view the next higher organisational unit above the undertaking is the company (*'Unternehmen'*), followed by the group of companies (*'Konzern'*). At company and group of companies level representation bodies can be established too.

In every undertaking, in which at least five employees are permanently employed, a works council shall be constituted. Following this rule, small undertakings with less than five employees are basically excluded from most provisions regarding works councils.

The statute established a special notion of the employee in the context of the Labour Constitution Act. Employees, apprentices and home workers fall within its scope, whereas (executive) employees with significant influence on the management of the undertaking and persons, whose employment follows primarily a non-profit goal, are excluded from participation (§ 36 ArbVG).

#### *[2] Forms of Works Councils and Their Competences*

Depending on the structure of the company, various forms of representation bodies can be constituted. Primary condition for the establishment is the employment of at least five permanent employees in the undertaking. White-collar employees and blue-collar workers form representation bodies of their own if both groups reach the five employees threshold. They are then called 'group works council' (*'Gruppenbetriebsrat'*). The 'committee of the undertaking' (*'Betriebsausschuss'*) is the representative body where the group works councils of the white-collar employees and blue-collar workers interact. If one of the groups does not reach this threshold, or only white-collar or blue-collar employees work in the undertaking, then the 'common works council' (*'Gemeinsamer Betriebsrat'*) is to be constituted comprising all employees in the undertaking. If young or disabled employees reach the five employees threshold, they can form special works councils.

At company level the representation body of several undertakings is called 'central works council' (*'Zentralbetriebsrat'*). Precondition for establishing a 'central works council' is that works councils have been formed in at least two undertakings on subordinate levels. Likewise, at the group of the companies level, a separate works council can be formed.

The distribution of competences between the different works councils is as follows: the basic principle states that rights related to personal decisions should be exercised by the lowest possible level of representation. Only competences for decisions, which affect more undertakings or companies, should be passed on to the higher level. The right to conclude a works council agreement is granted to the committee of the undertaking, the common works council or the representation at company level. Section 113 ArbVG lists the competencies of the different representation bodies. The central works council may for instance conclude an agreement regarding the choice of a pension fund. Further competences are transferrable to the central works council and the group of companies' works council in coordination with lower works councils.

#### *[3] Election, Composition and Operation of the Works Council*

The members of the works councils are elected by personal, equal, direct and secret election. In order to be elected, the candidate must have been employed in the undertaking for at least six months with the exception of new and seasonal undertakings.

The number of the works council members depends on the quantity of employees in the undertaking or company. The works council has to meet at least once a month. Decisions are taken by simple majority of its members.

The statute provides various regulations to protect council members by prohibiting discrimination, forbidding limitations in exercising works council activity or preventing any disadvantage arising from the works council activity (§ 115 ArbVG). Moreover, works council members enjoy special protection against dismissal with and without notice (§120 ArbVG).

The works council is elected for a term of four years. The office can end prematurely if (a) the undertaking is permanently discontinued and ceases to be an undertaking in legal sense; (b) the undertaking becomes inoperative; (c) the assembly of the workforce decides to suspend the works council from office; (d) the works council resigns; (e) the election is declared for void; etc (§ 62 ArbVG).

#### *[4] The Rights of the Works Councils*

The works council disposes of strong participation rights. It represents the workforce towards the employer and outward.

The rights of the works council vary according to their intensity as well as the employer's level of autonomy in her/his decision-making. The works council is to be provided with information at respectively without its request. Other rights comprise the control of the employer's legal compliance with, e.g., employment protection, as well as consultation with the employer. It also raises objections to certain decisions and some decisions even need its approval. The works council's co-determination right is exercised along with the employer and takes place in equally and unequally represented commissions as for instance in the supervisory board of a public limited company.

Participation rights cover general, social, personal and economic matters. In relation to general matters – like protection of health and safety, support of women, compatibility of family and work, etc. – the works council has the right to be informed and consulted with. It can further control if the employer complies with the labour and social law regulations. Depending on the issues, the different participation rights differ. In social affairs, the works council has participation rights regarding in-firm training and company welfare institutions.

The works council has competences vis-à-vis the employer's human resource decisions as for instance in the recruiting process. The employer is obliged to inform the works council about the future demand of workforce, planned measures and action in this regard as well as the conclusion of new employment contracts (§ 98 and § 99 paragraph ArbVG). The employer has to contact the council when considering dismissing an employee with or without notice, imposing disciplinary actions, determining individual performance-related remuneration or allocating accommodations belonging to the undertaking. In these matters the works council has to be at least informed and in most cases a consultation process on the planned decision takes place. For a secondment or dislocation, which takes longer than thirteen weeks and brings about a deterioration of working conditions, the employer needs the prior permission of the works council (§ 101 ArbVG). Certain disciplinary actions have to be set forth in works agreement. The imposition of a sanction based on this catalogue then requires the approval of the works council (§ 102 ArbVG). The participation right of the works council in the process of dismissal with notice is particularly important. The condition for a valid dismissal with notice is that the employer informs the works council about the planned dismissal (§11.02 I.)

The works council also has participation rights regarding economic matters of the undertaking. The employer has to inform and at request consult regularly with the works council about the financial situation of the undertaking. Particular information obligation is laid upon the employer about the planned transfer of undertakings. The works council can agree on a social plan with the employer in order to mitigate the consequences of the transfer of an undertaking. It can force the employer to conclude a social plan if the undertaking employs at least twenty employees and the transfer brings about significant disadvantages for a substantial part of workforce.

The works council participates in the supervisory board. One-third of the members of the supervisory board are members of the works council. In undertakings with more than 200 employees the works council can raise an objection against a financial measure that would bring about crucial disadvantages for the employees. If the parties cannot find a solution to that objection, a common conciliation board has to decide on this issue.

### *[5] Works Agreements*

The works agreement is a written agreement between the competent works council and the employer. It can only be concluded in matters listed exclusively in the statute and must not violate superior law.

Works agreements can be divided into four groups based on the fact, whether the employer can decide on the respective issue alone or only together with the works council and whether the conclusion of an agreement is enforceable by the conciliation board or not. Thus, the employer needs the approval of the works council in several matters, i.e., the employer may not make a decision as long as the works council does not approve it. In other issues the employer is free to make decisions without the permission of the works council. In case that the parties cannot agree in certain issues, generally the conciliation board can decide and force on the issue, as last resort.

1. The employer has to agree with the works council on disciplinary sanctions, the use of detailed staff questionnaires, the application of control measures and systems, which affect the human dignity and finally the introduction of performance-related remuneration. In these issues the employer has to agree with the council because of the conciliation board's legal inability to make a decision (lacking enforceability). Binding conciliation is not possible in this case. (§ 96 ArbVG)

2. The employer has to come to a mutual decision with the works council on the electronic research, processing and transfer of personal related employee data as well as on the personnel assessment and evaluation systems. In case of disagreement, both parties can turn to the conciliation board. However, it is not possible to regulate the topics concerned otherwise than in works agreements. (§ 96a ArbVG)

3. General rules on the employees' conduct, the regulation of working time, social plans, the use of the undertaking's facilities, principles in employing temporary workers and other issues. In case of disagreement the conciliation board can decide in these matters. It is however necessary to regulate these topics in a works agreement. (§ 97 paragraph 1 point 1-6a ArbVG)

4. Regarding the other group of issues, e.g., health and safety, specific matters of remuneration and some particular questions regarding working time, etc., the conciliation board cannot intervene. Those are optional issues, which can normally be found in individual labour contracts. (§ 97 paragraph 1 point 7–26 ArbVG)

Finally, the normative elements of the works council agreement are directly legally binding on the undertaking's owner and the employees. Latter group can unilaterally refer to the agreement to its advantage. That means that in individual agreements it can be derogated from to the employee's favour.

## SELECTED BIBLIOGRAPHY

Brodil, Wolfgang/Risak, Martin E./Wolf, Christoph, *Arbeitsrecht in Grundzügen*, 8th edn., Vienna, 2013.

Drs, Monika, *Arbeits- und Sozialrecht*, 2nd edn, Vienna, 2012.

Floretta, Hans/Spielbüchler, Karl/Strasser, Rudolf, *Arbeitsrecht Band I. Individualarbeitsrecht*, 4th edn., Vienna, 1998.

Floretta, Hans/Spielbüchler, Karl/Strasser, Rudolf, *Arbeitsrecht Band II: Kollektives Arbeitsrecht*, 4. edn., Vienna, 2001.

Laimer, Hans Georg, *Employment Law*, 2nd edn., Graz, 2012.

Löschnigg, Günther, *Arbeitsrecht*, 12th edn., Vienna, 2014.

Marhold, Franz / Friedrich, Michael, *Österreichisches Arbeitsrecht*, 2nd edn., Vienna, 2012.

Risak, Martin E., Austria, In: Blanpain, Roger/Colucci, Michele, (ed.) *International Encyclopaedia for Labour Law and Industrial Relations*, National Monographs, Kluwer Law International BV, The Netherlands, 2010.

Windisch-Graetz, Michaela, *Arbeitsrecht II.*, Tomandl, Theodor/Schrammel, Walter (ed.), 8th edn., Vienna, 2013.

Kietaibl, Christoph, *Arbeitsrecht I.*, Tomandl, Theodor/Schrammel, Walter (ed.), 8th edn., Vienna, 2013.

CHAPTER 12

# Private International Law

*Brigitta Lurger*

## §12.01 INTRODUCTION

*Figure 12.1*

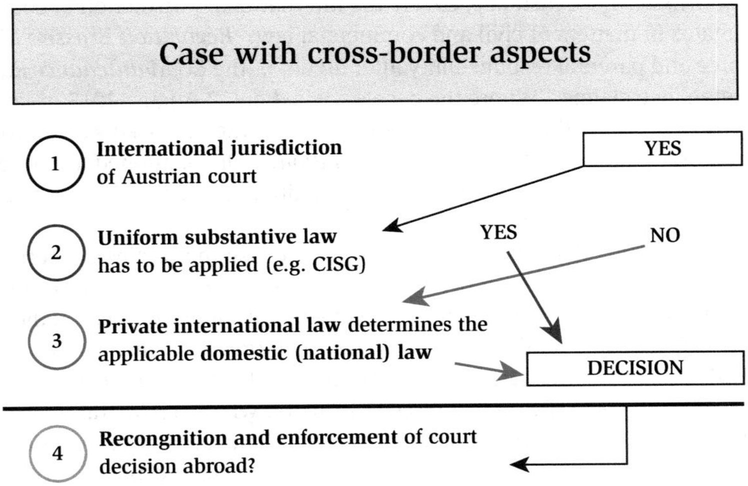


Cases of private law which have cross-border aspects raise four additional questions (in addition to questions of substantive law) that have to be answered by the parties involved or their respective lawyers and the judges in court:

(1) **Which court has international jurisdiction?** In what circumstances is it appropriate for a legal order to charge its juridical institutions (courts) with the adjudication of multistate or multinational controversies? (problem of international jurisdiction = 'internationale Zuständigkeit'). (2) and (3) **Which substantive law will the court apply?**

(2) the **uniform private law** in force in the states concerned – or in the absence of uniform substantive law

(3) the national (non-uniform) private law of a certain state which is selected by the **private international law** (= choice of law) rules of the forum (= 'Internationales Privatrecht').

The court bases its decision either on (2) the applicable uniform private law or (3) the applicable national private law. Both belong to the level of substantive (or 'material') law (= 'materielles Recht' or 'Sachrecht').

(4) **Will judgments be recognised and enforced abroad?**

If recognition and enforcement of the court decision is required in a country different from the forum country this will be made possible by legal rules of recognition an enforcement of foreign judgments. In what circumstances and to what extent should a legal order accord respect to foreign decisions rendered in a multistate or multinational controversy? (= 'Anerkennung und Vollstreckung').

*Ad (1) and (4)*: As far as EU Member States are concerned, the rules of their international jurisdiction in many fields of private law are found in EU regulations. *Regulation Brussels I*, for instance, covers the international jurisdiction of courts of the Member States in matters of civil and commercial law.[1] *Regulation Brussels IIbis* deals with divorce and parental responsibility after divorce,[2] the *EU Maintenance Regulation* with maintenance claims.[3] Where the deceased died on 17 August 2015 or later, court proceedings concerning the cross-border succession to the deceased's estate follow the jurisdiction rules of the *EU Succession Regulation*.[4] All mentioned EU Regulations provide also for a simplified procedure of recognition and enforcement of decisions rendered in other Member States.

Where these EU Regulations do not apply because the parties concerned or the judgment stem from a Non-Member State the *autonomous national rules* of international jurisdiction and recognition and enforcement have to be applied. In the Austrian legal system these are found in the '*Jurisdiktionsnorm*' (JN), in the '*Exekutionsordnung*' (EO) and the '*Außerstreitgesetz*' (AußStrG).[5] Foreign judgments of Non-EU-Member States are generally only enforced in Austria where a bilateral treaty ('*Staatsvertrag*') providing for the reciprocal duty to recognise and enforce exists (§ 79 EO). For some decisions concerning family law (adoption, parental responsibility, status of

1. Regulation No. 1215/2012, OJ L 351/1 (20 Dec. 2012) in force since 10 Jan. 2015. Old version: Regulation No. 44/2001, OJ L 12/1 (16 Jan. 2001).
2. Regulation No. 2201/2003, OJ L 338/1 (23 Dec. 2003).
3. Regulation No. 4/2009, OJ L 7/1 (10 Jan. 2009).
4. Regulation No. 650/2012, OJ L 201/107 (27 Jul. 2012).
5. Available online: http://www.ris.bka.gv.at/Bundesrecht/.

parenthood) provisions of the AußStrG lay down more lenient requirements (§§ 91a et seq.; §§ 112 et seq.). The JN contains provisions of international jurisdiction for some types of claims: see for instance § 108(3) JN for status of parenthood; § 113b JN for adoptions; § 76(2) and (3) JN and § 114a(4) JN for marriages and partnerships; § 99 JN contains the jurisdiction of location of property (‘*Vermögensgerichtsstand*’). § 27a JN provides that in all cases where the local jurisdiction of an Austrian court exists on the basis of the rules of local jurisdiction in the JN, the international jurisdiction of the Austrian court must also be confirmed.

*Ad (2) and (3)*: In the area of private law only a few sources of internationally uniform substantive law exist. One of the most comprehensive international sources is the CISG, the UNCITRAL Convention on the International Sale of Goods. It has been in force in Austria since 1989. Where no uniform substantive law exists the rules of *choice of law* or *private international law* (abbreviation: *PIL*) which are in force in Austria will point to the applicable national substantive private law rules.

In Austria the following sources of choice of law rules (= PIL) have to be applied.[6]

The central source of PIL rules in the autonomous Austrian law is the *IPRG* (Statute on Private International Law) of 1978.[7] Its conception is a comprehensive coverage of all areas of private law in its ‘special part’ in §§ 12-49 IPRG (including labour law, corporations, intellectual property). However, this conception has been dismantled over the years by numerous international treaties, EU regulations or TFEU provisions which have priority over the IPRG and have rendered large parts of the IPRG inapplicable (see § 53 IPRG). In particular the many EU regulations adopted during the last decade, in areas like contracts, torts, maintenance, succession, divorce and matrimonial property, have turned the IPRG into a subsidiary source of law that is only applicable where no EU regulation or international treaty exists. Examples of legal questions to which the IPRG still applies are: marriages and registered partnerships (divorce and matrimonial property excluded), the status of parenthood, some types of tort claims, corporations and partnerships, powers of representation created by voluntary unilateral act of represented party.

Where the IPRG is applicable, but does not contain a PIL rule for a particular question of substantive private law, this gap has to be filled by the court in accordance with the general principle of § 1(1) IPRG: The court has to apply the law of the country with the ‘strongest relation’ (‘*stärkste Beziehung*’) to the case. The ‘strongest relation’ is often determined by the analogous (if necessary modified) application of an IPRG rule dealing with a group of similar questions. *Example*: § 25 IPRG determines the applicable law for the question of fatherhood to a child born out of wedlock. The IPRG contains no PIL rule for the determination of motherhood (as needed in cases of surrogate motherhood). The rule of § 25 IPRG (personal statute of child) will be applied

6. The standard literature on Austrian private international law (PIL; in German: IPR) is the following (exclusively written in German): Lurger/Melcher, *Internationales Privatrecht* (2013); Verschraegen, *Internationales Privatrecht* (2012); Nademleinsky, *Internationales Scheidungsrecht* (2014); Nademleinsky/Neumayr, *Internationales Familienrecht* (2007); Verschraegen in Rummel, *ABGB-Kommentar* vol 2/6, 3rd edition (2004).
7. Internationales Privatrechts-Gesetz, BGBl 304/1978 (BGBl I 158/2013).

to the issue of motherhood by analogy as an adequate expression of the principle of strongest relation in § 1(1) IPRG in motherhood cases.

On the level of international sources of law, the *Conventions* of the Hague Conference of Private International Law (the Netherlands)[8] have a prominent role:

- Hague Convention on the International Recovery of Child Support and Other Forms of Family Maintenance (ratified by the EU on the basis of Article 81 TFEU)[9] (= HCMain) and Hague Protocol on the Applicable Law (= HPAMain) of 23 November 2007 in connection with EU Regulation No 4/2009 of 18 December 2008 (OJ 2009 L 7/1) Article 15: HPAMain is applicable to proceedings on or after 18 June 2011. [abbreviations: *HCMain* and *HPAMain*; in German: HUntÜ, HUP].
- Hague Adoption Convention 1993 (BGBl III 145/1999). [abbreviation: *HCAdop*].
- Hague Convention on Child Protection 1996 (BGBl III 2011/49) – in force since 1 April 2011. [abbreviation: *HCChildP*; in German: KSÜ].
- Hague Convention on International Child Abduction 1980 (BGBl 512/1988). [abbreviation: *HCChildA*; in German: HKÜ].
- Hague Convention on the International Protection of Adults 2000 (BGBl III 287/2013), applicable since 1 February 2014. [abbreviation: *HCAdultP*; in German: HESÜ].
- Hague Convention on Traffic Accidents 1971 (BGBl 387/1975). [abbreviation: *HCTAcc*; in German: HStVÜ].
- Hague Convention on the Form of Testamentary Dispositions 1961 (BGBl 295/1963). [abbreviation: *HCFTest*; in German: HTFÜ].

The influence of rules of *EU law* on Austrian PIL has been quite strong in the last decade. The following rules have to be taken into account:

(1) *EU Directives* (for instance on the basis of Article 114 TFEU): e.g., consumer contract directives, E-Commerce Directive, ECJ decisions like in *Ingmar* of 9 November 2000.[10]
(2) *EU primary law*: general prohibition of discrimination (Article 18 TFEU), Union citizenship (Article 21 TFEU), fundamental freedoms of TFEU.[11]
(3) *EU Regulations* according to Article 81 TFEU:

8. http://www.hcch.net/index_en.php?act=conventions.listing.
9. The Convention will enter into force between Austria and other contracting states that are not EU Member States on 1 Aug. 2014.
10. ECJ 9 Nov. 2000, C-381/98 – *Ingmar*, ECR 2000 I-9305.
11. As examples see the ECJ judgments concerning the freedom of establishment of corporations in ECJ 9 Mar. 1999, C-212/97- *Centros*; ECJ 30 Sep. 2003, C-167/01 – *Inspire Art*; ECJ 5 Nov. 2002, C-208/00 – *Überseering*; ECJ 13 Dec. 2005, C-411/03 – *SEVIC*; ECJ 16 Dec. 2008, C-210/06 – *Cartesio;* ECJ 12 Jul. 2012, C-378/10 – *VALE Epitesi*; and the ECJ decisions concerning family names in ECJ 2 Oct. 2003, C-148/02 – *Garcia Avello*; ECJ 14 Oct. 2008, C-353/06 – *Grunkin-Paul* and ECJ 22 Dec. 2012, C-208/09 – *Sayn-Wittgenstein.*

- Articles 4-15 *Insolvency Regulation* No. 1346/2000, OJ 2000 L 160/1. [abbreviation: *InsReg*].
- *Regulation Rome II* No. 864/2007 on the law applicable to non-contractual obligations (to be applied to events [giving rise to damage] on or after 11 January 2009), OJ 2007 L 199/40. [abbreviation: *Rome II*].
- *Regulation Rom I* No. 593/2008 on the law applicable to contractual obligations (to be applied to contracts concluded on or after 17 December 2009), OJ 2008 L 177/6 (OJ 2009 L 309/87). [abbreviation: *Rome I*].
- *Maintenance Regulation* No. 4/2009 (OJ 2009 L 7/1) Article 15 refers to Hague Protocol on the Applicable Law 2007 (to be applied since 18 June 2011). [abbreviations: *MainReg* and *HPAMain*; in German: UntVO, HUP].
- *Regulation Rome III* No. 1259/2010 implementing enhanced cooperation in the area of the law applicable to divorce and legal separation (in force since 21 June 2012 – in fourteen EU Member States), OJ 2010 L 343/10. [abbreviation: *Rome III*].
- *Succession Regulation* No. 650/2012 on jurisdiction, applicable law, recognition and enforcement of decisions and acceptance and enforcement of authentic instruments in matters of succession and on the creation of a European Certificate of Succession, OJ 2012 L 201/107 (OJ 2012 L 344/3): to be applied on cases of death on or after 17 August 2015. [abbreviation: *SuccReg*; in German: ErbVO].
- Two Commission *Proposals* on *matrimonial property* regimes[12] and the property relations of registered partners[13] (covering jurisdiction, applicable law, recognition and enforcement) are in the legislative procedure.

## §12.02 FAMILY LAW

Questions of *legal capacity* of natural and legal persons follow the PIL rule § 12 IPRG: The law of the '*personal statute*' ('*Personalstatut*') of the person has to be applied. The personal statue of *natural persons* is defined in § 9 IPRG: Personal statute means the nationality of a person. Persons with more than one nationality can only have one relevant personal statute for the purposes of PIL. Where one of the nationalities is the Austrian nationality, the person will be considered to have an Austrian personal statute (alone). The foreign non-Austrian nationalities will be neglected in that case.[14] Where the person has only foreign nationalities, the nationality to which he/she has the strongest relation has to be determined. Refugees according to the Geneva Convention have their personal statute in their domicile or place of habitual residence. The same applies to persons without any nationality.

12. COM (2011) 126 final.
13. COM (2011) 127 final.
14. This rule does however not apply in cases like the one decided by ECJ 2 Oct. 2003, C-148/02 – *Garcia Avello*.

The personal statute of a *legal person* (e.g., a corporation or partnership) is defined by § 10 IPRG: it is the factual place of its central administration (*'tatsächlicher Sitz der Hauptverwaltung'*). Thus, Austrian law follows the so-called 'principle of seat' or principle of place of central administration (*'Sitzprinzip'*) as opposed to the so-called 'principle of incorporation' (*'Gründungsprinzip'*). Under the incorporation principle the legal personality and capacity of a corporation or partnership would be determined in accordance with the law of its incorporation (= initial registration). Under autonomous Austrian law, the law of the country of foundation is irrelevant, the corporation has to meet the requirements of the law of its central administrative seat. However, this rule does not apply where its application would constitute an infringement of the *freedom of establishment* under *Articles 49 and 54 TFEU*. When this is the case is determined by ECJ decisions[15] which will be discussed in the last part of this chapter, which deals with the PIL of corporations.

The restriction of legal capacity of an adult and the appointment of a *guardian* are principally covered by § 15 IPRG,[16] which determines the law of the personal statute of the adult, i.e., her nationality, to be applicable. However, this rule does not apply within the scope of the Hague Convention on the International Protection of Adults 2000 (*HCAdultP)*,[17] i.e., when the adult has her habitual residence in a contracting state of the HCAdultP. The HCAdultP contains as its main point of reference the habitual residence of the adult, not her nationality (Articles 5, 13 HCAdulP). It also applies to powers of representation granted by the adult to be exercised only after restriction or loss of capacity of the grantor (Article 15 HCAdultP; in German: *'Vorsorgevollmacht'*).

The law applicable to legal issues concerning *names* of *natural persons* is determined by § 13 IPRG: the relevant point of reference is again the 'personal statute', i.e., the nationality of natural person. According to the ECJ judgments in *Garcia Avello*,[18] *Grunkin Paul*[19] and *Sayn-Wittgenstein*[20] made on the basis of *Articles 18 and 21 TFEU* the following modifications to this national rule apply in cases involving EU Member States: Where a person has a double nationality composed of the nationalities of two Member States, she must be enabled to choose the law of the nationality which shall be relevant to determine its family name (*Garcia Avello*). § 9 IPRG must be modified or interpreted narrowly to allow such a choice. Where the family name has been registered in the Member State of the (former) habitual residence of an EU citizen in accordance with the law of that Member State, other EU Member States must recognise this family name and may not apply their own PIL rules which would eventually lead to the application of a different law than that applied by the first registering Member State (*Grunkin Paul*). § 13 IPRG must not be applied in such cases.

15. ECJ 9 Mar. 1999, C-212/97- *Centros*; ECJ 30 Sep. 2003, C-167/01 – *Inspire Art*; ECJ 5 Nov. 2002, C-208/00 – *Überseering*; ECJ 13 Dec. 2005, C-411/03 – *SEVIC*; ECJ 16 Dec. 2008, C-210/06 – *Cartesio;* ECJ 12 Jul. 2012, C-378/10 – *VALE Epitesi.*
16. BGBl I 158/2013, in force since 1 Nov. 2013.
17. BGBl III 287/2013, in force since 1 Feb. 2014.
18. ECJ 2 Oct. 2003, C-148/02 – *Garcia Avello.*
19. ECJ 14 Oct. 2008, C-353/06 – *Grunkin-Paul.*
20. ECJ 22 Dec. 2012, C-208/09 – *Sayn-Wittgenstein.*

Instead the PIL rule of the registering state must be applied or the result of the registration must be directly recognised by Austrian authorities. Member States of reception (e.g., Austria) may depart from this rule (application of PIL of state of origin or recognition) if there are compelling reasons of public policy to do so and these goals are pursued in a proportional manner (*Sayn-Wittgenstein*).

With respect to the *name* of a *firm* or a *corporation*, opinions as to the applicable PIL rule differ.[21] Some want to apply the ordinary rule of § 13 IPRG: the personal statute according to § 10 IPRG is the law of the place of the central administration. The Austrian Supreme Court[22] applies the incorporation principle (= law of the country of initial registration) to corporations incorporated in another EU Member State, referring to the above cited line of decisions by the ECJ (Articles 49, 54 TFEU).[23] Another opinion applies the country of protection principle ('*Schutzlandprinzip*') of § 34 IPRG (intellectual property) to the protection of names of enterprises and corporations, because the question is similar to that of the protection of intellectual property rights:[24] The law of the country for which the protection is claimed applies.

*§ 49 IPRG* contains the PIL rule for *powers of representation* created by voluntary unilateral act or contract (not for powers of representation created *ex lege* or by act of a state authority). The law can be chosen unilaterally by the represented party. In the absence of a choice, the law of the country in which the representative shall become active applies. Cases of *ex lege* representation (e.g., of a child by its parents) and of powers of representation created by act of state authority (e.g., guardianship) are covered by specific PIL rules contained in: e.g., the HCAdultP, the HCChildP, § 15 IPRG and § 27 IPRG.

The formal validity of a *marriage* concluded in Austria can only be achieved by fulfilling the formal requirements of Austrian substantive law (§ 16[1] *IPRG*). However, a marriage concluded abroad is formally valid if it fulfils the formal requirements of the foreign country of conclusion *or* the formal requirements of the nationality or nationalities of both spouses (§ 16[2] IPRG). The substantive validity of a marriage has to be determined by the application of the personal statutes of both spouses (§ 17 IPRG). The validity must be affirmed by both national systems if the personal statutes of the spouses differ. The rights and duties of spouses during marriage (with the exception of matrimonial property regimes and maintenance claims) have to be determined in accordance with § 18 IPRG: if both spouses have the same personal statute, this law applies. In case of different personal statutes, the law of the common country of habitual residence or the former common country of habitual residence of both spouses has to be applied. Questions pertaining to the matrimonial property regime follow the law determined by the spouses by express agreement in accordance with § 19 IPRG. In the absence of such an agreement the law applicable in accordance with § 18 IPRG at the time of the conclusion of the marriage is relevant.

---

21. Lurger/Melcher, *Internationales Privatrecht* (2013) 2/19 with further references.
22. OGH 16 Mar. 2011, 6 Ob 67/10m (available at: http://www.ris.bka.gv.at/Jus/).
23. ECJ 9 Mar. 1999, C-212/97- *Centros*; ECJ 30 Sep. 2003, C-167/01 – *Inspire Art*; ECJ 5 Nov. 2002, C-208/00 – *Überseering*.
24. Lurger/Melcher, *Internationales Privatrecht* (2013) 2/19 with further references.

Issues of *divorce* and legal separation are dealt with in § 20 IPRG and in EU Regulation *Rome III* (see the introductory part of this chapter).[25] Rome III determines the applicable law for the divorce itself: The parties can choose the applicable law by agreement (law of common state of present or former habitual residence, law of nationality of one of the spouses, law of the competent forum) (Article 5 Rome III). In the absence of such agreement the law of the common state of present or former habitual residence of both spouses applies. Where there is no such common residence state, the law of the common nationality of the spouses applies. In the absence of common nationality the law of the forum applies (Article 8 Rome III). All legal consequences of separation (with the exception of maintenance claims) are covered by § 20 IPRG: The law applicable under § 18 IPRG at the time of the divorce (closing of court proceeding of 1st instance) is to be applied.

The respective rules for registered (homosexual) *partnerships* are to be found in §§ 27a-27d IPRG. They entered into force on 1 January 2010. The formal and substantive validity has to be determined exclusively in accordance with the law of the country of registration (country of registration principle; § 27a IPRG). The same law applies to issues of the property regime (§ 27c IPRG). In this area the partners may also choose the applicable law (see the parallel in § 19 IPRG for married couples) Other rights and duties of the registered partners (with the exception of maintenance claims) follow the rule of § 27b IPRG: the law of the present or former common state of habitual residence applies. In the absence of such state, the law of the common nationality of the partners applies. If no common nationality exists as well, Austrian law will apply. If the law of the common habitual residence and the law of the common nationality (if applicable) do not provide rules for registered partnerships, Austrian law will apply. A similar rules applies to divorce and separation (§ 27d IPRG).

The status of fatherhood or motherhood of a *child* is to be determined in accordance with § 21 or § 25 IPRG depending on whether the child was born in or out of wedlock. The parenthood of a child born in wedlock follows the rules of the law of the common personal statute (nationality) of the spouses (§ 21 IPRG). Where the nationality of the spouses differs (§ 21 IPRG) or the child is born out of wedlock (§ 25 IPRG) the status question of fatherhood (and by analogy also of motherhood) has to be determined in accordance with the law of the personal statute of the child. The Austrian nationality of the child has to be determined in particular in accordance with § 7 StbG (*'Staatsbürgerschafts-Gesetz'*, nationality statute). The child can acquire Austrian nationality from the person who is her 'legal mother' in accordance with Austrian substantive law (§ 143 ABGB – Austrian Civil Code) *or* from the person who is her 'legal father' in accordance with Austrian substantive law (§ 144(1) No. 1-3 ABGB) if this person has Austrian nationality.

The substantive validity and the termination of an *adoption* have to be determined in accordance with the law of the personal statutes of the adopting persons and the personal statute of the adopted child (§ 26[1] IPRG). Mere form requirements

25. Regulation No. 1259/2010 implementing enhanced cooperation in the area of the law applicable to divorce and legal separation (in force since 21 Jun. 2012 – in 14 EU Member States), OJ 2010 L 343/10.

follow the general rule of § 8 IPRG (the form of the place of execution of the adoption act suffices). The legal consequences of an adoption follow from the personal statute of the adopting person(s), and where these persons are married, from the 'personal statute' of the marriage as laid down in § 18 IPRG (§ 26[2] IPRG). The rules of the Hague Convention on Adoptions (*HCAdop*) have to be taken into account (see the introductory part of this chapter).[26] If an adoption took place abroad procedural and substantive recognitions have to be distinguished. If the adoption is based on a foreign court judgment or an act of a foreign public authority this judgment or act is subject to procedural recognition in Austria. Where the adoption decision or act stems from a contracting state of the HCAdop, it will be recognised under the conditions of the Convention (Article 23 HCAdop). Where the decision or act originated in a non-contracting state, the procedural recognition will follow the rules of §§ 91-91c *AußStrG* (see introductory part of chapter).[27] Where both tracks do not lead to a recognition of a foreign decision or public act in Austria, or where no such public act exists (adoption based only on a private contract), the validity of the adoption has to be determined on the basis of the substantive private law provisions designated by § 26 and § 8 IPRG.

The *parental responsibility* (for a child) follows the rules of the *HCChildP* (see introductory part of this chapter)[28] which entered into force in Austria on 1 April 2011. The international jurisdiction/competence for measures of protection lies with a court or other public authority in the country of habitual residence of the child (Article 5 HCChildP). These institutions apply their own substantive law (Article 15 HCChildP). For parental responsibility rights or duties arising *ex lege* (in the absence of any court or other public act) the law of the habitual residence of the child will apply as well. Where the child moves her habitual residence from one country to the other, parental responsibility rights/duties which existed under the old law, but do not exist under the law of the new country of habitual residence will not be extinguished but survive.

The law of *maintenance* obligations is covered by the *HPAMain* (see introductory part of this chapter),[29] the Hague Protocol on the law applicable to maintenance obligations, which forms part of the HCMain,[30] and has to be applied on the basis of Article 15 of the EU MainReg.[31] The MainReg and the HPAMain entered into force on 18 June 2011. The HPAMain applies to all maintenance obligations based on family relations, including registered partnerships and relationship by marriage. The parties may choose among a limited number of legal systems (Articles 7, 8 HPAMain: e.g., law of nationality or law of habitual residence of one of the parties). In the absence of a choice, the law of the habitual residence of the creditor applies (Article 3 HPAMain).

---

26. Hague Adoption Convention 1993 (BGBl III 145/1999).
27. Außerstreit-Gesetz, BGBl I 111/2003 (BGBl I 158/2013): http://www.ris.bka.gv.at/GeltendeFassung.wxe?Abfrage=Bundesnormen&Gesetzesnummer=20003047.
28. Hague Convention on Child Protection 1996 (BGBl III 2011/49) - in force since 1 Apr. 2011.
29. Hague Protocol on the Applicable Law of 23 Nov. 2007.
30. Hague Convention on the International Recovery of Child Support and Other Forms of Family Maintenance (ratified by the EU on 9 Apr. 2014 on the basis of Art. 81 TFEU), in force in Austria with respect to Non-EU-Member States since 1 Aug. 2914.
31. EU Regulation No. 4/2009 of 18 Dec. 2008 (OJ 2009 L 7/1).

For claims between children and parents and between spouses and former spouses some more specific rules apply (Articles 4-6 HPAMain).

## §12.03 SUCCESSION LAW

The PIL regime as well as the legal regime for international jurisdiction and recognition and enforcement in the area of succession law are marked by a big change: national rules will – to a large extent – be replaced by the rules of the EU Succession Regulation (SuccReg).[32] The *SuccReg* applies to cases of death on or after 17 August 2015. However, its rules will be applied to the validity of testamentary dispositions (including choice of law declarations) drafted on any earlier date, provided the deceased did not die earlier than 17 August 2015 (Article 83 SuccReg). The issue of formal validity of a testamentary disposition is covered by the *HCTest* (see in introductory part of this chapter),[33] which has been in force in Austria since the early 1960s and will stay applicable also after 17 August 2015 (Article 75 SuccReg).

The legal regime applicable to earlier cases is found in § 106 JN (international jurisdiction of Austrian courts) and §§ 28-30 IPRG. Austrian courts always have jurisdiction with respect to immovable property in Austria, they never have jurisdiction over immovable property abroad. Their jurisdiction over movable property located in and outside Austria depends on the strength of the connections of the deceased with Austria, namely on whether she had her last habitual residence in Austria and/or was Austrian national. According to § 28 IPRG the law of the personal statute (§ 9 IPRG) of the deceased at the time of his death applies. Where the deceased did not have Austrian but a foreign nationality, this reference includes the choice of law provisions of the foreign legal system and may ultimately lead to a reference back to Austrian law, when the foreign PIL rules for instance point to the habitual residence of the deceased in Austria (§ 5 IPRG). In this case the Austrian court will have to apply Austrian substantive law.

The new system under the *SuccReg* uses one central point of reference which is the habitual residence of the deceased at the time of her death. According to Article 4 SuccReg (general jurisdiction) the courts of the country of the last habitual residence of the deceased have international jurisdiction over the whole estate (including property located in Non-Member States and immovable [and movable] property abroad). 'Member States' in the sense of the SuccReg are all EU Member States with the exception of Denmark, Great Britain and Ireland.[34] The court of the country of habitual residence has to apply its own law (Article 21[1] SuccReg). The notion of 'habitual residence' is not defined in the text of the Regulation, but only in the preliminary deliberations points 23 and 24. Where the deceased had a manifestly closer connection

32. Regulation No. 650/2012 on jurisdiction, applicable law, recognition and enforcement of decisions and acceptance and enforcement of authentic instruments in matters of succession and on the creation of a European Certificate of Succession, OJ 2012 L 201/107 (OJ 2012 L 344/3).
33. Hague Convention on the Form of Testamentary Dispositions 1961 (BGBl 295/1963).
34. See preliminary deliberations points 82 and 83 SuccReg.

to a state other than the state of her habitual residence (e.g., the state of her nationality) the law of this state will have to be applied (Article 21[2] SuccReg).

The deceased can choose the law of her nationality (including nationalities of Non-Member States) at the time of choice or at the time of death in an express declaration made in the form of a testamentary disposition (Article 22 SuccReg). Where such choice was made, the courts of the country of nationality can be made competent by agreement of the parties of the procedure (Article 5 SuccReg) or by decision of the court in the country of habitual residence (Article 6 SuccReg), provided the chosen state is a Member State. The choice of the law of the nationality of a Non-Member State cannot serve as a basis of jurisdiction of that state under the Regulation. The courts of a Member State can have international jurisdiction even if the deceased has her habitual residence in a Non-Member State, when she had the nationality of that Member State or a former habitual residence in that Member State (less than five years ago) (Article 10 SuccReg).

Where the deceased had her habitual residence in a Non-Member State, the competent courts of a Member State in the sense of Article 10 SuccReg will have to apply the law of this Non-Member State (Articles 20 and 21[1] SuccReg). If the PIL rules of that Non-Member State of habitual residence provide the application of the law of a Member State, the law of that Member State will apply (Article 34 SuccReg). If the PIL rules of the Non-Member State provide the application of its own law, the substantive law of that state will have to be applied.

The law applicable to the admissibility and the substantive validity of testamentary dispositions and of agreements as to succession is prescribed by Articles 24-26 SuccReg. Mainly the law applicable to the succession at the time at which the disposition was made (as if the person had died on that day) is applicable. The formal validity of a written agreement as to succession is governed by the law designated in Article 27 SuccReg. The formal validity of unilateral testamentary disposition is governed by the law designated in Article 1 HCTest. Both provisions are more or less identical and contain alternative references to the formal requirements of the law of the state in which the disposition was made, of the state of the nationality of the testator, the state of domicile, the state of habitual residence of the testator (at the time the disposition was made or at the time of death) and to the state where immovable property is located (with respect to this immovable property). It is sufficient to meet the formal requirements of only one of these laws. The formal validity of oral dispositions is not governed by the Regulation (Article 1[2] f SuccReg).

The question of acquisition of rights in movable or immovable property registered in a Member State is not governed by the SuccReg (Article 1[2] l SuccReg). The state of registration may determine the requirements for registration and the legal effects (declaratory or constitutive) of registration (see preliminary deliberations point 19). Forms of transfer of property which are not succession transfers upon death are excluded from the scope of the Regulation: as for instance transfers relating to matrimonial property regimes, transfers governed by company law, by gifts, resulting from joint ownership with a right of survivorship, from pension plans, and insurance contracts (Article 1[2] d, g, h SuccReg).

The enforcement of decisions, authentic instruments and court settlements relating to succession rights in other Member States is facilitated by special provisions on the recognition and enforcement of court decisions (Articles 39-58 SuccReg) and on the acceptance and enforceability of authentic instruments and court settlements (Articles 59-62 SuccReg). In addition a 'European Certificate of Succession' is created. It is issued by the authorities of the Member State which has international jurisdiction and is effective in all other Member States (Article 69 SuccReg).

## §12.04 CONTRACTUAL OBLIGATIONS

The PIL of contracts is governed by Regulation No. 593/2008 on the law applicable to contractual obligations (= *Rome I*).[35] It has to be applied to contracts concluded on or after 17 December 2009. Contracts concluded between 1 December 1998 and 16 December 2009 are governed by the Convention on the law applicable to contractual obligations (Rome Convention; German abbreviation: EVÜ)[36] which is the predecessor of Rome I containing very similar PIL provisions. The general rules of Articles 3 and 4 Rome I only apply where no more specific rule for a particular type of contract exists. Such more specific rules are Article 5 Rome I for contracts of carriage, Article 6 Rome I for consumer contracts, Article 7 Rome I for insurance contracts, Article 8 Rome I for employment contracts and Article 14 Rome I for contracts of assignment of claims.

The general rule of Article 4 Rome I is superseded by a choice of the applicable law made by party agreement in accordance with *Article 3 Rome I*. The parties may choose the law of every country on earth, no relation of the contract to the law chosen is required. The agreement can be express or implied and does not have to meet any formal requirements. The substantive validity of the choice agreement is determined by the law chosen by the parties (Article 3[5] Rome I). The chosen law replaces the law otherwise applicable under Article 4 Rome I in its entirety (with the exception of internationally mandatory provisions of the forum, see Article 9 Rome I), unless all elements relevant to the situation at the time of choice are located in one country (Article 3[3] Rome I). Internationally mandatory provisions of EU law cannot be replaced by the chosen of law of a Non-Member State, where all elements relevant to the situation at the time of choice are located in the EU (Article 3[4] Rome I).

*Article 4(1) Rome I* contains PIL rules for specific types of contract: For sales contracts, service contracts, franchise contracts and distribution contracts the rule of characteristic performance applies, i.e., the law of the place of the habitual residence of party which has to render the performance which is characteristic for this particular type of contract applies.[37] The characteristic performance of a contract of sale is the delivery of goods, of a service contract the provision of the services, of a franchise contract the performance of the franchisee, of a distribution contract the performance of the distributor. Contracts relating to rights in rem in immovable property and to a

35. OJ 2008 L 177/6 (OJ 2009 L 309/87).
36. OJ 1980 L 266/1 and OJ 1998 L 27/34.
37. All references in Regulations Rome I and Rome II are references to the substantive law of a country, they do not extend to the PIL rules of a foreign country: Art. 20 Rome I, Art. 24 Rome II.

tenancy of immovable property are governed by the substantive law of the country where the land is located (Article 4[1] c Rome I). Contracts of sale of goods by auction are governed by the law of the country where the auction takes place (Article 4[1] g Rome I). Types of contract which are not mentioned by Article 4(1) Rome I follow the reference rule of Article 4(2) Rome I: which is the rule of characteristic performance as mentioned supra. Article 4(3) Rome I contains an exception clause: The law of Article 4(1) and (2) Rome I may not be applied where it is clear from all the circumstances that the contract is manifestly more closely connected with a different country. This exception clause has to be interpreted narrowly. The most classical case of its application is the sale of land located in a foreign country (for instance Spain) by a seller and a buyer with their habitual residence both in the same other country (for instance Austria). In this case Austrian contract law will be applied despite the rule of Article 4(1) c Rome I, on the basis of Article 4(3) Rome I.

*Consumer contracts* are subject to a special protective regime in favour of the weaker party. *Article 6 Rome I* applies to all contracts between a consumer and business with the exception of contracts on rights in rem and tenancy in immovable property, contracts of carriage, insurance contracts and some others (see Article 6[4] Rome I). The business must have exercised some professional activity in the country of habitual residence of the consumer or must have directed such activity to that country (for instance via an Internet offer or information) and the contract must 'fall within the scope of such activities' (Article 6[1] Rome I). If these requirements are met, the consumer is protected against a contractual choice of law clause which points to a law less favourable for the consumer than the law of her own country of habitual residence (Article 6[2] Rome I). Where the consumer contract contains no choice of law clause the law of the country of the consumer's habitual residence will apply.

*Article 5 Rome* distinguishes between *contracts of carriage* of goods and carriage of persons. Contracts for the carriage of goods are governed by similar rules as found in Articles 3 and 4 Rome I (Article 5[1] Rome I). Contracts for the carriage of persons are more favourable to the interests of the passenger than the general rules (Article 5[2] Rome I). Where the place of departure or the place of destination is situated in the country of the habitual residence of the passenger the law of this country applies. A choice of law by contract may only appoint the law of a country to which the contract has a relation as specified in Article 5(2) 2nd paragraph Rome I.

*Article 7 Rome I* grants a certain protection to insurance customers (implementation of EU insurance directives). *Article 8 Rome I* protects employees by limiting the validity of contractual choice of law clauses: The law chosen in the employment contract is only applicable if it is at least as favourable to the employee as the law designated by Article 8(2) Rome I: i.e., the law of the country in which or from which the employee habitually carries out his work in performance of the contract. According to *Article 14 Rome I* the relationship between the assignor and the assignee under a contractual assignment is governed by the law designated by Articles 3, 4, and 6 Rome I. However, the law governing the assigned right or claim shall be applied to the question of its assignability, to the relationship between the assignee and the debtor, the conditions under which the assignment may be invoked against the debtor and to the question whether the debtor's obligations have been discharged (Article 14[2]

Rome I). *Article 15 Rome I* applies to legal subrogation and designates the law which governs the third person's (= potential assignee's) duty to satisfy the creditor (= potential assignor).

*Article 9(1) Rome I* contains a definition of internationally mandatory provisions of the forum country which override the law designated to apply by the ordinary references in Articles 3-8, 14, 15 Rome I: such mandatory provisions serve to realise public policy goals pertaining to the political, social or economic organisation of the forum state. Examples are fundamental rights, the protection of tenants and regional planning and development policy.

Questions of formal validity of contractual obligations are examined separately: According to the general rule of *Article 11 Rome I* the contract has to comply with the formal requirements of the law applicable to the contract itself (according to Articles 3-9, 14 Rome I) *or* with the formal requirements of the country where it is concluded. Where the parties are located in two different countries at the time of conclusion, the formal requirements of only one of these countries will have to be met. An exception to the general rule applies with respect to consumer contracts in the sense of Article 6 Rome I: There the formal requirements of the law of the consumer's habitual residence will always have to be complied with (Article 11[4] Rome I). Alternative references to other countries do not exist. Contracts over immovable property shall be subject to the formal requirements of the country of location of this property if these requirements are mandatory in the sense of Article 9 Rome I (Article 11[5] Rome I).

## §12.05 NON-CONTRACTUAL OBLIGATIONS

The PIL of non-contractual obligations is governed by Regulation No. 864/2007 on the law applicable to non-contractual obligations (= *Rome II*).[38] It has to be applied to events giving rise to damage on or after 11 January 2009. For all events prior to that date the old rules of the IPRG, in particular old §§ 46, 47 and 48 IPRG,[39] will have to be applied. Rome II covers tort law (Articles 4-9), unjust enrichment (Article 10), benevolent intervention in another's affairs (= negotiorum gestio) (Article 11) and culpa in contrahendo (Article 12). Therefore, the definition of damage employed in Rome II must be a very wide one: 'damage', according to Article 2(1) Rome II, covers all consequences arising out of tort/delict, unjust enrichment, negotiorum gestio and culpa in contrahendo.

Rome II is not applied in two groups of cases: where an *exception* according to Article 1(2) Rome II exists (as for instance for non-contractual obligations arising out of nuclear damage, or arising out of violation of privacy or personality rights) or where an international treaty which has priority according to Articles 27, 28 Rome II has to be applied. In Austria the main treaty falling in this latter category is the HCTAcc (see introductory part of this chapter), the Hague Convention on Traffic Accidents.[40]

38. OJ 2007 L 199/40.
39. BGBl 304/1978, see § 50(4) IPRG.
40. BGBl 387/1975.

Claims arising out of nuclear damage are governed by § 23 AtomHG (statute on civil law liability for damages through radioactivity).[41] Claims arising out of the violation of *privacy* or *personality rights* (including defamation) are subject to § 48 IPRG. The parties may, without any restrictions, choose the applicable law by agreement (§§ 48[1], 11 IPRG). Where there is no such agreement, the law of the country in which the conduct which caused the damage occurred will have to be applied (§ 48[2] IPRG). This general rule does not apply when the parties have a 'stronger relation' to one and the same other state. In this case the law of this other state will apply. Cases of 'stronger relations' in that sense are the common country of habitual residence of both parties, or the place where the damage itself occurred where this place was easily foreseeable for the defendant.[42] One case of protection of a personality right, the right of name, is covered by § 13 Abs 2 IPRG: The law of the country where the act of violation occurred (= country for which the protection is asserted) applies (country of protection principle, 'Schutzlandprinzip'). This is the same rule as the PIL rule applied to violations of intellectual property rights according to § 34 IPRG and Article 8(1) Rome II.[43]

The *HCTAcc* applies to tort liability arising out of a *traffic accident* (this is an accident involving one or more vehicles; a bicycle being sufficient). Claims of contractual liability (for instance of a contract of carriage of persons) are covered by Rome I, not by the HCTAcc. According to the general rule of Article 3 HCTAcc the substantive tort law of the country in which the accident occurred will apply. The rule of exception is found in Article 4 HCTAcc: Where both vehicles involved in the accident are registered in the same other country the law of this country will apply. Non-registered vehicles, like bicycles, are judged by the country of habitual presence. Where a pedestrian is involved her habitual residence will be relevant. Where the law of a country other than the country of the accident is applicable according to Article 4 HCTAcc, the traffic rules of the country in which the accident occurred will apply nevertheless (Article 7 HCTAcc).

The general rules of Rome II for non-contractual liability are found in Articles 14 and 4. According to *Article 14 Rom II* the parties can choose the applicable law under two alternative conditions: Parties pursuing a commercial activity can make a choice of law agreement before or after the event giving rise to the damage occurred. Other parties can choose the applicable law only by an agreement made *after* the event giving rise to the damage occurred. In the absence of such an agreement the rules of objective reference in Articles 4-9 Rome II apply. The *general rule* of *Article 4 Rome II* only applies, where no specific rules for particular torts exist. Special rules are provided for product liability (Article 5 Rome II), unfair competition and anti-trust (Article 6), environmental liability (Article 7), violations of intellectual property rights (Article 8) and industrial action (Article 9). If the parties with respect to a non-contractual obligation arising out of a tort/delict have their habitual residence in the same country, the substantive law of this country will apply (Article 4[2] Rome II). If this is not the

41. Atomhaftungs-Gesetz 1999, BGBl I 170/1998 (BGBl I 33/2003).
42. Lurger/Melcher, *Internationales Privatrecht* (2013) 5/109 with further references.
43. Lurger/Melcher, *Internationales Privatrecht* (2013) 5/113 with further references.

case, the law of the country in which damage occurs (irrespective of the country in which the event giving rise to the damage occurred) has to be applied (Article 4[1] Rome II). The exception clause of Article 4(3) Rome II prescribes the application of the law of a different country to which the tort/delict is manifestly more closely connected than to the law of Article 4(1) or 4(2) Rome II, if this is clear from all the circumstances of a particular case. Example is a closely related contractual relationship that may exist between the parties.

*Product liability* claims are governed by *Article 5 Rome II*. The parties may choose the applicable law under Article 14 Rome II. In the absence of such a choice, the law governing the (sales) contract between the parties (producer and injured customer) will apply (Article 5[2] Rome II). Without a contract between the parties, the law of the country in which both parties have their habitual residence applies according to Article 5(1) 1st sentence Rome II (by reference to Article 4[2] Rome II). Where no such common state of habitual residence exists either, the law of the habitual residence of the person sustaining the damage is to be applied, provided the product was marketed in that country (Article 5[1] a Rome II). If it was not, the law of the country in which the product was acquired applies, provided the product was marketed in that country and the injured person was the acquirer (Article 5[1] b Rome II). If this is also not the case, the law of the country in which the damage occurred applies, provided the product was marketed in that country (Article 5[1] c Rome II). Where all these rules do not fit, the law of the country of habitual residence of the defendant will apply (Article 5[1] last sentence Rome II).

The law applicable to unfair *competition* and acts restricting free competition (*anti-trust*) under *Article 6 Rome II* may not be derogated from by a party agreement choosing the applicable law (Article 6[4] Rome II). As a general rule, the law of the country in which the acts of unfair competition or acts restricting competition show their effects has to be applied. Pursuant to *Article 7 Rome II*, in cases of *environmental damage* the injured party may choose between the law designated by Article 4(1) Rome II, i.e., the law of the country where the damage occurred (place of damage), and the law of the country in which the event giving rise to the damage occurred (place of action). Where infringements of *intellectual property* rights give rise to tort liability, the law of the country for which the protection is claimed has to be applied (*Article 8[1] Rome II*) (country of protection principle, *'Schutzlandprinzip'*). A derogation by party agreement pursuant to Article 14 Rome II is excluded (Article 8[3] Rome II).

Non-contractual obligations arising out of *unjust enrichment* are generally governed by the PIL rule of *Article 10 Rome II*. However, all claims to return performances rendered under a contract that was void or avoided or repealed later on (in Austrian law: *'Leistungskondiktionen'*) are qualified as contractual (Article 12 Rome I) and are therefore governed by the law of the contract according to Rome I. Thus, Article 10 Rome II applies only to claims that have no direct connection to a (void) contract, as for instance claims resulting from enrichment through use of a property or right that belongs to someone else. Where no law is chosen by the parties (Article 14 Rome II), there is no manifestly closer connection to another country (Article 10[1] [4] Rome II), and there is no common country of habitual residence of the parties (Article 10[2] Rome II), the law of the country in which the unjust enrichment took place has to be applied (Article 10[3] Rome II). A similar rule applies to negotiorum gestio in *Article 11 Rome II*. The country of enrichment is replaced by the country where the act of negotiorum gestio was performed.

*Article 12 Rome II* (*culpa in contrahendo*) governs non-contractual obligations arising out of dealings prior to the conclusion of a contract, regardless of whether the contract was actually concluded or not. Thus, unlike under Austrian substantive law, liability arising from the violation of pre-contractual duties of disclosure or fairness is qualified as non-contractual obligation under Rome II and Rome I. In the absence of a contractual stipulation of the applicable law in the sense of Article 14 Rome II, the law applicable to the contract that was concluded or was intended to be concluded by the parties applies (Article 12[1] Rome II). The law applicable to the (potential) contract is determined by Rome I. Where the applicable law to this contract cannot be determined, the law of the common country of residence of the parties applies or (in absence thereof) the law of the country where the damage occurred (Article 12[2] Rome II).

## §12.06 PROPERTY LAW

The PIL rules for questions of property law and of intellectual property law are mainly found in §§ 31-34 IPRG (see introductory part to this chapter). Only a few rules are inspired by EU legislation: namely the return of cultural objects according to the *Kulturgüterrückgabe-Gesetz*[44] (see § 20 KultRGG) is based on Directive 93/7/EC;[45] § 33a IPRG is an implementation of Directive 2002/47/EC;[46] the EU Insolvency Regulation[47] contains in its Articles 4-15 some rules of PIL.

The main rule, the lex rei sitae ('situs rule'), is expressed in § 31 IPRG: The acquisition and loss of rights in rem in tangible (movable and immovable) property including possession is governed by the law of the country in which the property is located at the time of completion of all facts and acts relevant for this acquisition or loss. According to § 5 IPRG references by foreign PIL rules of a different legal system have to be taken into account (renvoi, '*Gesamtverweisung*').

Where a movable is moved from one country to the other, this normally does not effect a change of rights in rem acquired (or lost) with respect to that movable, because the relevant facts on which the acquisition was based will normally be completed before the change of location occurs. *Example*: A person X acquires a painting at a public auction in Switzerland. None of the parties knows or ought to have known that the painting was stolen from its owner a long time ago. The next day, the potential acquirer takes the painting with her to Austria. According to Austrian law, stolen objects can be acquired by good faith buyers on public auctions, under Swiss law stolen objects are excluded from good faith acquisition. X did not acquire ownership in

44. BGBl 67/1998.
45. Directive on the return of cultural objects unlawfully removed from the territory of a Member State, OJ 1993 L 74/74.
46. Directive on financial collateral arrangements, OJ 2002 L 16/43.
47. Regulation No. 1346/2000, OJ 2000 L 160/1.

Switzerland, the transport to Austria occurred after completion and will not change this result. However, a different result is achieved for a security right over movables, which is acquired abroad before the goods are brought to Austria. Where the security right (for instance the German security ownership) does not comply with the strict Austrian publicity rules (§ 451 ABGB:[48] *'Faustpfandprinzip'*) the security right will be extinguished when the movables cross the Austrian border.[49]

Rights in rem in land or water *vehicles* which are registered are not judged by the law of the country in which the vehicle is located, because this would imply constant changes of the applicable law for vehicles moving frequently from one country to the next. Therefore the law of the country of registration applies (§ 33[1] IPRG). With respect to rights in rem in trains the law of the country in which the railway enterprise for which train is employed has its seat of central administration has to be applied (§ 33[1] IPRG).

According to § 33a IPRG the type, content and the acquisition of rights in rem in book entry securities collateral are governed by the law of the country in which the relevant account is maintained (Article 9 Directive 2002/47/EC). The location of the document in which the securities collateral is incorporated is irrelevant.

With respect to *immovable property* the law of the country of location is applied to all property law aspects (for instance requirements of transfer, numerus clausus of rights in rem) even where a different PIL rule governs (the reason of) the transfer: e.g., PIL rules for matrimonial property or for succession upon death (§ 32 IPRG).

Under Austrian substantive law *'rights'* are considered intangible property or 'things' (*'Sachen'*, see §§ 285, 292 ABGB). Intangibles are obviously not covered by the situs rule of § 31 IPRG and, provided they are not intellectual property, also not by the country of protection rule of § 34 IPRG. The in rem aspects of a transfer of such rights (as for instance publicity requirements) are governed by the law of the country of the 'strongest relation' to the case according to § 1(1) IPRG. The leading opinion refers to the 'location' ('situs') of the right, which is said to be the law which governs the right itself (statute of the right).[50]

*Intellectual property* rights in the sense of § 34 IPRG are copy rights and related rights, trade marks, patent rights, registered designs, and company identifiers. *Article 8 Rome II* contains a PIL rule for all tort claims, injunctive relief, claims for remedial action, claims for rendering profits, unjust enrichment and accounting based on an infringement of intellectual property rights. The rule of § 34 IPRG applies to the creation, the content and the extinction of intellectual property rights and refers to the law of the country for which the protection is claimed (i.e., the law of the country in which the act of infringement occurred). Thus, § 34 IPRG is an expression of the so-called country of protection principle (*'Schutzlandprinzip'*) and contains the same PIL rule as Article 8(1) Rome II for tort claims and related claims.

48. ABGB = Allgemeines Bürgerliches Gesetzbuch 1811 = Austrian Civil Code.
49. Lurger/Melcher, *Internationales Privatrecht* (2013) 6/10-12 with further references.
50. Lurger/Melcher, *Internationales Privatrecht* (2013) 6/16 with further references.

## §12.07 CORPORATIONS

All questions concerning the incorporation (= birth), organisation, operation, inner relations, employee participation, representation, etc, until the liquidation (= death) of a corporation or partnership are governed by the 'personal statute' (*'Personalstatut'*) of the corporation ('lex societatis', statute of the corporation). The statute of a corporation is defined by § 10 IPRG: It is the factual place of its central administration (*'tatsächlicher Sitz der Hauptverwaltung'*). Thus, Austrian law follows the so-called 'principle of seat' or principle of place of central administration (*'Sitzprinzip'*) as opposed to the so-called 'principle of incorporation' or 'principle of foundation' (*'Gründungsprinzip'*). Under the incorporation principle, the legal personality and capacity of a corporation as well as all other questions of the law corporations would be determined in accordance with the law of its foundation and initial registration. Under autonomous Austrian law the law of the country of incorporation is irrelevant, the corporation has to meet the requirements of the law of its central administrative seat.

However, this principle of seat, as laid down in § 10 IPRG, has been severely restricted with respect to the cross-border movements of corporations on the internal market of the EU by some landmark decisions of the ECJ. The decisions were rendered by the court when it was asked to interpret the *freedom of establishment of corporations* under *Articles 49 and 54 TFEU.* § 10 IPRG is still relevant for corporations founded in Non-EU-Member States which move to Austria or for Austrian corporations moving to a Non-Member State, because the fundamental freedoms of the TFEU do not apply in these cases. The reference of § 10 IPRG to a foreign law includes a reference to the PIL rules of the foreign legal system (§ 5 IPRG).[51]

In its famous decisions in *Centros*[52] and *Inspire Art*[53] the ECJ stated in view of the secondary freedom of establishment (the opening of branches of the mother corporation in other Member States) that the legal personality of the mother corporation has to be determined only on the basis of the law of the country in which the mother corporation was incorporated (registered, founded). The law of the Member State of reception (of establishment of the branch) may be only applied as a specific proportional exception which realises compelling public policy goals of this Member State. In *Überseering*[54] the court confirmed that the same rule applies to the primary freedom of establishment of corporations, i.e., the movement of the main administrative seat from one Member State to the other. In all of the above mentioned cases the exercise of the free movement of corporations was initially restricted by the Member States of reception by the application of their own substantive law. The corporations wanted to 'immigrate' to the state of reception. The ECJ required the state of reception to apply the law of the state of incorporation (origin) in order to determine the existence and legal personality of the company in question, instead of applying its own law. This

51. Lurger/Melcher, *Internationales Privatrecht* (2013) 7/11-17 with further references.
52. ECJ 9 Mar. 1999, C-212/97- *Centros.*
53. ECJ 30 Sep. 2003, C-167/01 – *Inspire Art.*
54. ECJ 5 Nov. 2002, C-208/00 – *Überseering.*

means that Austrian courts will have to refuse the application of § 10 IPRG in such cases of 'immigration' of corporations from other Member States to Austria and will have to apply the principle of incorporation instead.[55]

In *SEVIC*[56] the ECJ extended its line of decisions to the merger of two corporations (by dissolution and transfer of assets of one of corporations to the other) which may not be restricted by the national law of the Member State of reception. The ECJ decisions in *Daily Mail,*[57] *Cartesio*[58] and *VALE Epitesi*[59] dealt with cases of 'emigration' of corporations from a Member State that wanted to restrict this outbound movement. The court was obviously more lenient in these cases and acknowledged the right of the Member State of 'emigration' to determine the conditions of incorporation and existence of corporations under its own law. However, the two Member States of incorporation and reception must, according to the ECJ, enable the migrating corporation to transform into an equivalent corporation in the country of reception without liquidation and without loss of its legal personality.[60] In a recent decision the Austrian Supreme Court applied this ECJ rule to a partnership registered in Italy which wanted to move its seat to Austria.[61] As opposed to the above mentioned the decisions concerning the 'immigration' of corporations (*Centros, Inspire Art, Überseering*), the decisions in *SEVIC, Daily Mail, Cartesio* and *VALE Epitesi* have no direct impact on the applicability of § 10 IPRG. They rather require the Austrian judge and legislator to adapt Austrian substantive law to the end of making the identity preserving transformation of corporations, which intend to move their seat from one Member State to the other, possible.

55. Lurger/Melcher, *Internationales Privatrecht* (2013) 7/23-27 with further references.
56. ECJ 13 Dec. 2005, C-411/03 – *SEVIC.*
57. ECJ 27 Sep. 1988, case 81/87 – *Daily Mail.*
58. ECJ 16 Dec. 2008, C-210/06 – *Cartesio.*
59. ECJ 12 Jul. 2012, C-378/10 – *VALE Epitesi.*
60. Lurger/Melcher, *Internationales Privatrecht* (2013) 7/20-22, 7/28-33 with further references.
61. OGH 10 Apr. 2014, 6 Ob 224/13d: http://www.ris.bka.gv.at/Dokumente/Justiz/JJT_20140410_OGH0002_0060OB00224_13D0000_000/JJT_20140410_OGH0002_0060OB00224_13D0000_000.pdf.

CHAPTER 13

# Civil Procedure

*Paul Oberhammer*

## §13.01 SOURCES OF LAW

### [A] General

The Austrian law of civil procedure is mainly codified in a number of statutes which were enacted in 1895 and came into force in 1898: the *Jurisdiktionsnorm (JN)* (Statute on Jurisdiction),[1] the *Zivilprozessordnung (ZPO)* (Code of Civil Procedure)[2] and the *Exekutionsordnung (EO)* (Code of Enforcement)[3] and the respective introductory statutes.[4] Special codes provide for specific proceedings for labour law and social security disputes (*Arbeits- und Sozialgerichtsgesetz*) (Statute on Labour Law and Social Security Courts)[5] and non-adversarial proceedings (*Außerstreitgesetz*) (Statute on Non-Adversarial Proceedings).[6] The Statute on Non-Adversarial Proceedings is applicable in a broad variety of cases[7] such as family law and custody matters, succession law or proceedings relating to the land and commercial register and many others. The

1. *Reichsgesetzblatt* (Imperial Legal Gazette – RGBl) 1895/111.
2. RGBl 1895/113.
3. RGBl 1896/79; see for an English outline of Austrian enforcement law Oberhammer, *Austria*, in Andenas/Hess/Oberhammer (ed.), *Enforcement Agency Practice in Europe* (2005) pp. 105 et seq.
4. *Gesetz vom 1.8.1895, betreffend die Einführung des Gesetzes über die Ausübung der Gerichtsbarkeit und die Zuständigkeit der ordentlichen Gerichte in bürgerlichen Rechtssachen* (EGJN, RGBl 1895/110); *Gesetz vom 1.8.1895, betreffend die Einführung des Gesetzes über das gerichtliche Verfahren in bürgerlichen Rechtsstreitigkeiten* (EGZPO, RGBl 1895/112); *Gesetz vom 27.5.1896, betreffend die Einführung des Gesetzes über das Exekutions- und Sicherungsverfahren* (EGEO, RGBl 1896/78).
5. *Bundesgesetzblatt* (Federal Legal Gazette – BGBl 1985/104).
6. BGBl I 2003/111.
7. See for an overview on the relevant matters Fucik & Oberhammer, *Allgemeiner Teil eines neuen Außerstreitgesetzes und außerstreitige Materiegesetze*, in Rechberger (ed.), *Außerstreitreform in*

following outline will only deal with the ordinary proceedings governed by the Code of Civil Procedure (ZPO).

### [B] The Austrian Code of Civil Procedure

The Austrian Code of Civil Procedure of 1895 was the successor of the *Allgemeine Gerichtsordnung* (General Court Ordinance) of 1781. While the 1781 statute was based on concepts of civil procedure deriving from the Romano-Canonical tradition in the German speaking countries, the Code of Civil Procedure reflects a legislative development of civil procedure which took place all over Continental Europe, and in particular in the German speaking countries, in the nineteenth century.[8] In many respects, the Austrian code drew upon the example of the German *Reichszivilprozessordnung* of 1877 which, in turn, was influenced by a joint development which took place in both the Habsburg empire and what was subsequently the German Reich founded in 1871. In spite of many amendments, many details of civil procedure are identical or similar in Austria and Germany even today. However, the German Code was normally described as based on a more 'liberal' approach while the Austrian legislator was influenced by a more 'social' understanding of civil procedure. The main reason for this difference was the legal thought of *Franz Klein* who drafted large parts of the Austrian Code of Civil Procedure.[9] While initially the German Code heavily relied upon party initiative as the driving force of civil procedure, the position of the judge was (initially) much stronger under the Austrian Code. As a consequence of both subsequent amendments of the German Code and actual court practice in both countries, this historical difference has faded away almost entirely. Today, both systems provide for a comparatively strong position of the judge.

From a comparative perspective, one might say that the Codes of Civil Procedure of Germany, Austria and Switzerland form a 'Germanic' tradition of civil procedure which also influenced the legislators of a number of other European and even

*der Zielgeraden*, Veröffentlichungen des Ludwig-Boltzmann-Institutes für Rechtsvorsorge und Urkundenwesen XX (1999) pp. 91 et seq.; cf. Mayr & Fucik, *Verfahren außer Streitsachen* (2013) pp 43 et seq.

8. See for a general outline of this development Oberhammer & Domej, *Germany, Switzerland and Austria (CA. 1800-2005)*, in van Rhee (ed.), European Traditions in Civil Procedure (2005) pp 103 et seq.

9. See, e.g., Klein, *Pro futuro: Betrachtungen über Probleme der Civilproceßreform in Österreich* (1891); Klein, *Die neuen österreichischen Civilprocess-Gesetzesentwürfe*, 19 ZZP 1 (1894); Klein, *Vorlesungen über die Praxis des Civilprocesses* (1900); cf. Esser, *Die Überwindung des dogmatischen Schuldenkens im Prozeßwerk von Franz Klein*, in Festschrift zur Fünfzigjahrfeier der Österreichischen Zivilprozessordnung 1898-1948 (1948) p. 98; Kralik, *Die Verwirklichung der Ideen Franz Kleins in der Zivilprozessordnung von 1895*, in Hofmeister (ed.), Forschungsband Franz Klein (1988) p. 89; Oberhammer, *Richterliche Gewalt, gegenseitige Unterstützung und anwaltliche Vertretung im österreichischen Zivilprozeßrecht*, in: L'assistance dans la résolution des conflits, 4e partie: Europe médiéval et moderne, suite, Recueils de la Société Jean Bodin LXV (1998) p. 215; Oberhammer, *Die Aufgabenverteilung zwischen Gericht und Parteien – Überlegungen à propos 'Een nieuwe balans' aus Sicht des deutschen Rechtskreises*, in Ingelse (ed), Commentaren op fundamentele herbezinning (2004) pp 81 et seq.; Oberhammer & Domej, *Powers of the Judge – Germany, Austria, Switzerland*, in van Rhee (ed.), European Traditions in Civil Procedure (2005) pp 295 et seq.

non-European jurisdictions.[10] As a result of the historical development of civil procedure on the European continent, there are, however, also many similarities with those codes of civil procedure which were influenced by the French tradition.[11] As a whole, this continental European tradition is opposed to the tradition and the law of civil procedure in the Anglo-Saxon jurisdictions. Note, however, that in the last decades some aspects of civil procedure originating in particular from the U.S. tradition have been subject of discussions and to some extent also of law-making in these countries, such as, in particular, means of collective redress[12] or the improvement of the position of a claimant in the process of obtaining information at the outset of the proceedings.[13] Nevertheless, such influences remained quite limited and one might say that also the Austrian civil justice community is still convinced of what was once called the 'German Advantage in Civil Procedure'.[14]

Austria became a Member State of the European Union in 1995. As a consequence, Austria today is part of the European Area of Justice based on the European legislation enacted since then.[15] This outline will not address aspects resulting from European law as this relates to common features of civil procedure in all Member States of the European Union.

## §13.02 THE COURT SYSTEM

All Austrian courts of civil law – i.e., all courts where the Code of Civil Procedure is applicable – are federal courts. Therefore, there is only one court structure governed by federal law.

The lowest courts in this hierarchy are the *Bezirksgerichte* (district courts) which have jurisdiction to try cases up to an amount in dispute of EUR 15,000.[16] Moreover, the district courts have jurisdiction irrespective of the amount in dispute in cases such as family law or tenancy law matters.[17] Where the district courts have jurisdiction for the first-instance proceedings, the *Landesgerichte* (regional courts) serve as appellate courts. In matters where the amount in dispute exceeds EUR 15,000, these regional courts serve as first-instance courts for these proceedings. In this case, the *Oberlandesgerichte* (upper regional courts) decide on remedies against the decisions of the

10. See, e.g., Jelinek, *Einflüsse des österreichischen Zivilprozeßrechts auf andere Rechtsordnungen*, in Habscheid (ed.), Das deutsche Zivilprozessrecht und seine Ausstrahlung auf andere Rechtsordnungen (1991) pp 41 et seq.; van Rhee, *Der Einfluss des Zivilprozessmodells von Franz Klein in den Niederlanden*, in Bundesministerium für Justiz (ed.), Franz Klein Symposion (2005) p. 19; Ya Xin Wang, *The various roots of Civil Litigation in China and the influence of foreign laws in the global era*, 2 Civil Procedure Review 119 (2011).
11. See van Rhee, *Introduction*, in van Rhee (ed.), European Traditions in Civil Procedure (2005) pp 3 et seq.
12. See, e.g., Bruns, *Einheitlicher kollektiver Rechtsschutz in Europa?*, 125 ZZP 399 (2012); Domej, *Einheitlicher kollektiver Rechtsschutz in Europa?*, 125 ZZP 421 (2012).
13. See, e.g., Schlosser, *Die lange deutsche Reise in die prozessuale Moderne*, 46 JZ 599 (1991).
14. See Langbein, *The German Advantage in Civil Procedure*, 52 U. Chi. L. Rev. 823 (1985).
15. See Hess, *Europäisches Zivilprozessrecht* (2010) pp 29, 79 et seq.
16. See § 49 para. 1 JN.
17. See § 49 para. 2 JN.

regional courts. In any event, the Austrian Federal Supreme Court (*Oberster Gerichtshof*) in Vienna is the third and last instance.

Outside Vienna, commercial cases are tried by the district courts and regional courts, but by specific panels of judges which are called commercial courts. A similar solution applies for labour law and social security disputes where special panels of said regional courts serve as labour law and social security courts. In Vienna, however, the court structure is different as such matters are dealt with by separate courts, i.e., the *Bezirksgericht für Handelssachen Wien* (District Court for Commercial Cases), the *Handelsgericht* (Commercial Court) and the *Arbeits- und Sozialgericht* (Labour Law and Social Security Court) of Vienna.[18]

The great majority of cases are decided by professional judges only. First-instance proceedings are normally tried before single judges; in cases involving an amount in dispute higher than EUR 100,000, a party may apply for a panel of three judges (see § 7 a JN). This, however, does not happen often. All second and third instance proceedings, however, take place before panels of judges.[19]

Normally, young lawyers become trainees with the court after their university studies and are appointed as judges for an unlimited period of time (i.e., until their retirement) after a period of practical training with courts and law firms and the necessary exams.[20] Commercial court cases and labour law and social security cases are, however, decided by panels of judges which consist of both professional judges and part-time lay judges.

## §13.03 JURISDICTION

The jurisdiction of Austrian courts is mainly governed by the *Jurisdiktionsnorm* (JN – Statute on Jurisdiction) mentioned above.[21] Note, however, that the international jurisdiction of Austrian courts is not only governed by Austrian law, but also by European law; the applicability of the Austrian and European rules on international jurisdiction depend on the nature of the case and the domicile of the parties involved. As already mentioned above, the jurisdiction ratione materiae to try a case at the first-instance level is divided between the *Bezirksgerichte* (district courts) and the *Landesgerichte* (regional courts).[22]

The law of the *Jurisdiktionsnorm* is sometimes called a 'venue jungle' as it provides for a broad variety of venues (which does not necessary mean that Austrian law provides for long-arm jurisdiction).[23] Basically, there are the following types of

18. Cf. Rechberger, *Austria*, in Taelman (ed.), International Encyclopaedia for Civil Procedure (2011) para. 32 et seq.
19. Cf. Rechberger, *Austria*, in Taelman (ed.), International Encyclopaedia for Civil Procedure (2011) para. 39 et seq.
20. Rechberger, *Austria*, in Taelman (ed.), International Encyclopaedia for Civil Procedure (2011) para. 41.
21. See above §13.01[A].
22. See above §13.02.
23. See, e.g., Mayr, *Pro futuro – Betrachtungen über die Reform der österreichischen Zuständigkeitsordnung*, 133 JBl 492 (2011).

venues: The general place of jurisdiction is situated at the respondent's domicile (see §§ 65 et seq. JN) or – in the case of a company or other legal entity – at its place of business (see § 75 JN).[24] §§ 86a et seq. JN provide for a broad variety of venues of which claimants can avail themselves in addition to the general place of jurisdiction in specific situations.[25] Different from that, §§ 76 et seq. JN provide for exclusive venues, that is, cases where said venues apply exclusively and not in addition to the general place of jurisdiction. There are generally two types of exclusive venues under Austrian law, as in some cases the existence of an exclusive venue does not prevent the parties from entering into a jurisdiction agreement, while in other cases it does.[26] According to § 104 JN, parties who have entered into a jurisdiction agreement must be able to prove such agreement in writing.[27] Note, however, that, in particular, the admissibility of such jurisdiction agreements is limited in different respects in cases involving consumers[28] or labour law issues.[29]

## §13.04 FIRST-INSTANCE PROCEEDINGS

As a principle, a claimant initiates proceedings by submitting his or her statement of claim to the court. In cases before the district courts, the court then schedules a first hearing.[30] This first hearing ('preparatory hearing' according to § 258 ZPO) serves the purpose of deciding on procedural objections, hearing the parties' allegations and discussing the relevant legal and factual issues with them; moreover, the court may direct the parties to enter into settlement negotiations and may also already take evidence if this is practical at this stage of the proceedings.[31] In cases before the regional courts, the respondent is first ordered to submit a statement of defence within four weeks; if the respondent does so, the court has to schedule the first hearing mentioned above.[32]

Note, however, that in the majority of the cases the code provides for an alternative commencement of the proceedings: In proceedings on payment claims up to EUR 75,000, the claimant must first apply for an order for payment.[33] This application for the order for payment also serves the purpose of initiating the

24. Mayr in Rechberger (ed.), Kommentar zur ZPO (2014) § 65 JN para. 1.
25. Cf. Rechberger & Simotta, *Zivilprozessrecht* (2010) pp 122 et seq.
26. See, e.g., Kodek & Mayr, *Zivilprozessrecht* (2013) p. 124.
27. Mayr in Rechberger (ed.), *Kommentar zur ZPO* (2014) § 104 JN para. 9.
28. Cf. Kathrein in Koziol & Bydlinski & Bollenberger (eds.), *Kurzkommentar zum ABGB* (2014) § 14 KschG para. 1.
29. Cf. Neumayr in Neumayr & Reissner (eds.), *Zeller Kommentar zum Arbeitsrecht* (2011) § 9 ASGG para. 5.
30. See, e.g., Rechberger & Simotta, *Zivilprozessrecht* (2010) pp 378 et seq.
31. See Rechberger & Klicka, in Rechberger (ed.), *Kommentar zur ZPO* (2014) § 258 para. 1 et seq.
32. See Rechberger & Simotta, *Zivilprozessrecht* (2010) p. 379.
33. See for an outline of the development of this requirement Oberhammer, *Speeding Up Civil Litigation in Austria: Past and Present Instruments*, in van Rhee (ed.), The Law's Delay. (2004) pp. 228 et seq.

proceedings as a very brief statement of claim.[34] The claimant must avail himself of a specific form (*Mahnklage*); where the claimant is represented by counsel or a notary public or where the claimant is a bank or insurance company, the application must be made online via the electronic filing system of the Austrian federal judiciary.[35] Subsequently, the court issues an order for payment (*Zahlungsbefehl*). If the respondent does not object to such order within four weeks, the order becomes final, binding and enforceable. If the respondent, however, does object to the order, ordinary court proceedings are initiated ex officio.[36]

According to the initial intention of the legislator of the Code of Civil Procedure, the proceedings should have been conducted in one single hearing.[37] In practice, however, this only happens in rather simple cases today. In all other cases, evidence will be taken in two or more oral hearings within a couple of weeks or months. Nevertheless, the Austrian civil justice system is quite expedient by international comparison and the vast majority of cases take less than one year before the first-instance court.[38]

According to § 179 ZPO, the parties must submit their factual allegations and evidence as soon as possible.[39] Both this provision and court practice are, however, quite liberal with respect to late allegations and evidence. After the evidence has been taken, the parties will submit their statements of cost at the end of the last oral hearing and the court will close the oral hearing. In theory, the court may then render the judgment orally immediately after the close of the oral hearing. In practice, however, the court will almost always render the judgment at a later stage in writing.[40]

According to § 411 ZPO, the res judicata effect of a judgment is strictly limited to the decision on the prayers for relief submitted to the court by the claimant or in a counterclaim;[41] moreover, the decision on the counterclaim on the basis of a mere

34. Cf. G. Kodek in Fasching & Konecny (eds.), *Kommentar zu den Zivilprozessgesetzen* (2002) § 244 para. 23 et seq.
35. See § 89c para. 5 GOG (*Gerichtsorganisationsgesetz*, RGBl 1896/217 as amended by BGBl I 2012/26); cf. Rechberger, *Austria*, in Taelman (ed.), International Encyclopaedia for Civil Procedure (2011) para. 127.
36. Cf. Oberhammer & Domej, *Delay in Austrian Civil Procedure*, in van Rhee (ed.), Within a Reasonable Time: The History of Due and Undue Delay in Civil Litigation (2010) p. 267; Rechberger & Kodek, *Orders for Payment in the European Union* (2001) pp 89 et seq.
37. See Klein, *Pro futuro*, pp 5 et seq.; Oberhammer & Domej, *Delay in Austrian Civil Procedure*, in van Rhee (ed.), Within a Reasonable Time: The History of Due and Undue Delay in Civil Litigation (2010) pp 258, 267 with further references.
38. Oberhammer & Domej, *Delay in Austrian Civil Procedure*, in van Rhee (ed.), p. 256.
39. See, e.g., Rechberger & Simotta, *Zivilprozessrecht* (2010) p. 236; Schragel in Fasching & Konecny (eds.), *Kommentar zu den Zivilprozessgesetzen* (2002) § 179 para. 1; Oberhammer, *Prozessbeschleunigung als rechtspolitisches Gestaltungsanliegen*, in Bundesministerium für Justiz (ed.), Franz Klein Symposion (2005) p. 55; Oberhammer, *Speeding Up Civil Litigation in Austria: Past and Present Instruments*, in van Rhee (ed.), The Law's Delay. (2004) pp. 226 et seq; Oberhammer & Domej, *Delay in Austrian Civil Procedure*, in van Rhee (ed.), Within a Reasonable Time: The History of Due and Undue Delay in Civil Litigation (2010) pp 268 et seq.
40. Kodek & Mayr, *Zivilprozessrecht* (2013) p. 315.
41. Rechberger in Rechberger (ed.), *Kommentar zur ZPO* (2014) § 411 para. 6; cf. Oberhammer, *Objektive Grenzen der materiellen Rechtskraft: Bindung und Präklusion*, 122 JBl 205 (2000).

set-off defence has res judicata effect as well.[42] Consequently, the court's findings on preliminary issues of fact and law are not subject to the res judicata effect.[43]

## §13.05 THE FACT-FINDING PROCESS

According to § 226 of the Code of Civil Procedure, it is the claimant's burden to allege specific facts at the outset of the proceedings.[44] In particular, there is no pre-trial fact-finding process such as a discovery.[45] While, in principle, the party bearing the burden of proof has to assert the relevant facts and submit means of evidence, the court is under an obligation to actively become involved in the fact-finding process by asking questions and directing the parties towards alleging facts and presenting evidence and may even go so far as to order the taking of evidence ex officio.[46] In practice, however, such taking of evidence ex officio does not take place often. The court's duty to actively participate in the fact-finding process by asking questions and disclosing its preliminary legal findings, however, is of high practical relevance, as the court must not render a 'surprise decision' according to § 182a ZPO.[47] Consequently, a lack of court activity in the fact-finding process might qualify as a procedural error and might, therefore, result in a successful challenge of the first-instance judgment.[48]

All allegations must be made and all evidence must be taken in the course of the oral hearing (strict principle of orality[49]) before the judge who will actually render the final decision (principle of immediacy of the proceedings[50]). There are, however, certain exceptions to this principle which apply e.g., in cases where the judge changes in the course of proceedings in order to prevent procedural delay.[51]

The Code of Civil Procedure provides for the five 'classical' means of evidence, i.e., witness evidence, party interrogation, documents, expert evidence and inspection.[52] § 272 ZPO enshrines the principle of free evaluation of evidence. With the exception of the rules on public documents,[53] the Code of Civil Procedure does,

---

42. Fasching & Klicka in Fasching & Konecny (eds.), *Kommentar zu den Zivilprozessgesetzen* (2004) § 411 para. 58; Rechberger in Rechberger (ed.), *Kommentar zur ZPO* (2014) § 411 para. 13 with further references.
43. See, e.g., Rechberger in Rechberger (ed.), *Kommentar zur ZPO* (2014) § 411 para. 10.
44. See, e.g., Kodek & Mayr, *Zivilprozessrecht* (2013) pp 221, 280.
45. Rechberger, *Austria*, in Taelman (ed.), International Encyclopaedia for Civil Procedure (2011) para. 91.
46. Oberhammer & Domej, *Powers of the Judge – Germany, Austria, Switzerland*, in van Rhee (ed.), pp 300, 304.
47. Cf. Fucik in Rechberger (ed.), *Kommentar zur ZPO* (2014) § 182a para. 1; Oberhammer & Domej, *Powers of the Judge – Germany, Austria, Switzerland*, in van Rhee (ed.), p. 300.
48. See, e.g., E. Kodek in Rechberger (ed.), *Kommentar zur ZPO* (2014) § 496 para. 3.
49. See §§ 176 ZPO et seq. and § 414 para. 1 ZPO; cf. Kodek & Mayr, *Zivilprozessrecht* (2013) p. 63.
50. See, e.g., § 276 para. 1 ZPO and § 412 para. 1 ZPO; cf. Rechberger & Simotta, *Zivilprozessrecht* (2010) pp 232 et seq.
51. Cf. Kodek & Mayr, *Zivilprozessrecht* (2013) p. 64; Rechberger & Simotta, *Zivilprozessrecht* (2010) pp 232 et seq.; Rechberger, *Austria*, in Taelman (ed.), International Encyclopaedia for Civil Procedure (2011) para. 27.
52. See, e.g., Grill, *Civil Procedure*, p. 57; cf. Rechberger, *Austria*, in Taelman (ed.), International Encyclopaedia for Civil Procedure (2011) para. 170.
53. See, e.g., § 292 ZPO.

therefore, not establish binding rules of evidence determining under what circumstances a specific fact has been proven.[54] It follows that the judge has to take into account all results of the proceedings when establishing the facts of the case on the basis of his or her personal conviction.[55]

In the course of the examination of witnesses, parties or experts, the court will normally play a leading role while the parties or counsel will in most cases only ask follow-up questions.[56] In practically all cases, the judge drafts the minutes of the hearing himself by summarising the parties' allegations and the outcome of the examination of parties, witnesses and experts in a step-by-step process availing herself of a dictaphone.[57] This results in minutes which do not provide a verbatim record of the hearing, but are rather detailed in practice. In general, each party produces the documents on which it intends to rely in support of its case. If a party wants to rely on a document in the possession of the other party it can request the court to order the opposing party to produce said document.[58] However, according to § 303 paragraph 2 ZPO the party requesting the production of a document has to specify its content as precisely as possible and to point to the facts it intends to prove with the requested document. If a party does not comply with its obligation to produce a document, the court may draw adverse inferences from such behaviour in the course of the evaluation of the evidence; the court, however, has no other sanction against a party in such a situation.

## §13.06 REMEDIES

The Code of Civil Procedure provides for four types of ordinary remedies (save for specific remedies such as objections against an order for payment): The appeal (*Berufung*) is the remedy against first-instance judgments; the remedy against court orders other than a judgment is called recourse (*Rekurs*); the revision (*Revision*) is the remedy against the judgment of the Court of Appeal, while the revision recourse (*Revisionsrekurs*) is the remedy against a decision on a recourse against a court order.[59]

Austrian law provides for very lean appellate proceedings: Recourse proceedings are in writing in any event.[60] Different from that, a Court of Appeal and even the

54. See, e.g., Rechberger, *Austria*, in Taelman (ed.), International Encyclopaedia for Civil Procedure (2011) paras 160 and 174.
55. Cf. Mayr, *Law of Evidence in Austria*, in Civil Procedure in Europe Vol. 5 (2004) p. 63; Rechberger, *Austria*, in Taelman (ed.), International Encyclopaedia for Civil Procedure (2011) para. 160.
56. Rechberger, *Austria*, in Taelman (ed.), International Encyclopaedia for Civil Procedure (2011) para. 175.
57. See § 212a ZPO; cf. Kodek & Mayr, *Zivilprozessrecht* (2013) p. 192.
58. Cf. Grill, *Civil Procedure*, p. 65.
59. See, e.g., Kodek & Mayr, *Zivilprozessrecht* (2013) p. 342; Rechberger & Simotta, *Zivilprozessrecht* (2010) pp 551 et seq.; Rechberger, *Austria*, in Taelman (ed.), International Encyclopaedia for Civil Procedure (2011) paras 130 et seq.
60. Rechberger & Simotta, *Zivilprozessrecht* (2010) p. 602.

Austrian Supreme Court may order oral appellate or revision proceedings.[61] Oral appellate proceedings do not take place very often in practice, however, while oral revision proceedings practically never take place. The main reason for that is that Austrian law strictly prohibits new factual allegations and new evidence in appellate or recourse proceedings.[62] It is not the purpose of appellate proceedings to re-try the case at the appellate level, but only to examine the fact-finding process and the application of the law before the Court of First Instance. Moreover, a revision (and also a revision recourse) is limited to cases where the decision depends upon the solution of an issue of substantive law or of procedural law which is of 'considerable relevance' for the uniformity of the law, legal certainty or the development of the law according to § 502 ZPO. In addition, certain restrictions of remedies based on the value in dispute or the nature of the dispute apply.[63]

In addition, the Code of Civil Procedure provides two extraordinary remedies: First, the action for the annulment of a judgment (*Nichtigkeitsklage*) which may be raised if the proceedings are tainted by very serious irregularities.[64] Second, the action for re-opening of proceedings (*Wiederaufnahmsklage*) covering cases where the factual basis of the decision is seriously flawed,[65] e.g., cases where the decision is based on a forged document or where a party was unable to bring forward facts or evidence in the initial proceedings in spite of having used its best efforts to do so. Both actions are available against decisions that have already become res judicata.[66] However, the action for re-opening of proceedings can already be filed prior to that moment as the parties are prohibited from submitting new facts and evidence already at the appellate stage of the proceedings.[67]

## §13.07 SPECIAL PROCEEDINGS

The Austrian Code of Civil Procedure provides for a number of specific rules for certain types of proceedings which are of considerable practical relevance. In the following, only the most important types of proceedings will be mentioned. While the general

61. Cf. Kodek & Mayr, *Zivilprozessrecht* (2013) pp 362 and 371; Rechberger & Simotta, *Zivilprozessrecht* (2010) p. 580.
62. See, e.g., E. Kodek in Rechberger (ed.), *Kommentar zur ZPO* (2014) § 482 para. 1; Oberhammer & Domej, *Delay in Austrian Civil Procedure*, in van Rhee (ed.), p. 271; Rechberger, *Austria*, in Taelman (ed.), International Encyclopaedia for Civil Procedure (2011) para. 131.
63. § 502 ZPO also stipulates some exceptions to the value limit, especially in family law, tenancy law and labour law matters; cf. Rechberger & Simotta, *Zivilprozessrecht* (2010) pp 584 et seq.; Rechberger, *Austria*, in Taelman (ed.), International Encyclopaedia for Civil Procedure (2011) para. 140 et seq.
64. See § 529 para. 1 ZPO; cf. E. Kodek in Rechberger (ed.), *Kommentar zur ZPO* (2014) § 529 para. 4.
65. See § 530 para. 1 ZPO; cf. E. Kodek in Rechberger (ed.), *Kommentar zur ZPO* (2014) § 530 para. 1; Rechberger, *Austria*, in Taelman (ed.), International Encyclopaedia for Civil Procedure (2011) para. 146.
66. See, e.g., Frad & Schimka, *Austria*, in Grubbs (ed.), International Civil Procedure (2003) p. 68; Rechberger & Simotta, *Zivilprozessrecht* (2010) pp 621, 623 and 628.
67. Rechberger, *Austria*, in Taelman (ed.), International Encyclopaedia for Civil Procedure (2011) para. 146; Rechberger & Simotta, *Zivilprozessrecht* (2010) p. 628.

provisions on first-instance proceedings apply before the regional courts, i.e., in the larger cases, the Code provides for certain modifications of the proceedings before the district courts.[68] Nevertheless, the difference between such 'small claim proceedings' and the ordinary proceedings before the regional courts is rather limited by international comparison.[69] There are specific provisions for certain types of tenancy law proceedings, labour law and social security proceedings and state liability proceedings.[70] As already mentioned above, many important cases are tried according to the rules of the Statute on Non-Adversarial Proceedings ('Außerstreitgesetz');[71] this is especially true for most family law issues. The Code of Civil Procedure also contains the provisions on arbitration in both domestic and international cases at §§ 577 et seq. These provisions were drafted on the basis of the UNCITRAL Model Law on International Commercial Arbitration and enacted in 2006.[72] Since 2014, the Austrian Supreme Court has been competent as a first-instance court for matters relating to arbitration such as the challenge of the award, an arbitrator or the constitution of the arbitral tribunal.[73]

68. See, e.g., Kodek & Mayr, *Zivilprozessrecht* (2013) pp 332 et seq.
69. See, e.g., Uzelac, *Goals of Civil Justice and Civil Procedure in the Contemporary World – Global Developments – Towards Harmonization*, in Uzelac (ed.), Goals of Civil Justice and Civil Procedure in Contemporary Judicial Systems (2014) p. 22.
70. Cf. Kodek & Mayr, *Zivilprozessrecht* (2013) pp 394 et seq.; Rechberger & Simotta, *Zivilprozessrecht* (2010) pp 637 et seq.
71. See above §13.01[A].
72. See, e.g., Oberhammer, *Der Weg zum neuen österreichischen Schiedsverfahrensrecht*, German Arb. J. 57 (2006); Reiner, *The New Austrian Arbitration Act*, 24 J. Int'l Arb. 529 (2007).
73. Cf. Oberhammer & Koller, *Schiedsrecht im Wettbewerb der Rechtsordnungen – Zum österreichischen Schiedsrechts-Änderungsgesetz 2013*, 17 ZZPInt 75 (2012).

CHAPTER 14

# Criminal Law and Criminal Procedure

*Peter Lewisch*

## §14.01 GENERAL

Austrian Criminal Law is of a continental European character. As such it is based on statutory law, both with regard to its substantive and procedural provisions. Although judicial interpretation is of course important, it is not a primary source of law. In terms of procedure, judges are not only referees, but they may also actively search for 'material truth' (e.g., they may take the initiative to summon a witness for questioning).[1]

Criminal law has always played an important (though slightly declining) role in academic education. Its practice, however, has for many years been in the hands of a few specialised 'boutique-style' lawyers, rather separated from large business-oriented law firms. This picture has changed completely over the last decade. White-collar criminal law has become one of the legal fields experiencing significant growth, both with regard to doctrine and practice and it has regained importance on university curricula. As for the judiciary, the Austrian Supreme Court in civil and criminal matters has played an increasingly active role in interpreting criminal law and has developed the rights of the accused in several seminal rulings. Criminal trials in Austria are still

1. With regard to the literature, all textbooks and commentaries are in German. The easiest access to detailed questions may be found by means of the 'Vienna Commentary', 2nd edition (continuously edited), a printed and online commentary both on the Criminal Code, Höpfel/Ratz (ed), '*Wiener Kommentar zum StGB*' (WK-StGB) and the Criminal Procedure, Fuchs/Ratz (ed), '*Wiener Kommentar zur StPO*' (WK-StPO). See for the General Part in particular the textbooks by Fuchs, Strafrecht Allgemeiner Teil $I^8$ (2012) and Kienapfel/Höpfel/Kert, Grundriss des Strafrechts Allgemeiner Teil $I1^4$ (2012), for the Special Part the textbook by Fuchs/Reindl-Krauskopf, Strafrecht Besonderer Teil $I^4$ (2014), and for the procedure the textbooks by Bertel/Venier, Strafprozessrecht8 (2015) and Seiler, Strafprozessrecht14 (2015).

(for the most part) extremely swift by international comparison, even though the criminal procedure does not recognise 'plea bargains'.

The Austrian Criminal Code ('*Strafgesetzbuch*', in short 'StGB') was enacted in 1974, and the Austrian Procedural Code ('*Strafprozessordnung*', in short 'StPO') was re-enacted in 1975. Both have since been amended numerous times. As for the Procedural Code, Austria adopted, following lengthy debates, a reform of the preliminary (investigative) procedure in 2008, introducing a complete switch from a judge-controlled system ('*Untersuchungsrichter*' = 'magistrate') to a system dominated by a prosecutor, in which the prosecutor is the sole head – and 'manager' – of the proceedings, and judicial interference is reduced to the approval of certain acts and control of the legality of prosecutorial acts. In the years to come, the parts of the Procedural Code relating to main proceedings and appeals will be amended. Substantive criminal law is more static in the sense that, despite plentiful amendments, no fundamental changes have occurred. In light of the 40th anniversary of the Criminal Code in 2015, a major revision is in preparation and is due to enter into force by 2016. A draft amendment, which is still subject to further discussion, was published in February 2015. Possible changes, as of today, primarily concern technicalities and extensions of existing concepts rather than any reform of basic principles it is, however, likely that a number of more substantial changes (general introduction of gross negligence, restrictions on the concept of 'commission of crimes for commercial gain', streamlining of the provisions against 'infliction of physical injury') will be introduced.

It should be noted that Liechtenstein has copied, subject to certain variations, its criminal law from Austria. Liechtenstein's Criminal Code is practically identical to the Austrian Code. The Procedure follows the Austrian model with a few, however not unimportant differences (*inter alia*, still having the judge-controlled preliminary procedure, no lay participation in the first instance, and three instances).

## §14.02 BASIC PRINCIPLES OF SUBSTANTIVE CRIMINAL LAW

Austrian substantive criminal law is based on two core principles, namely:

- the 'Principle of Legality'; and
- the 'Principle of Culpability', holding that every criminal punishment requires some kind of – also personal – fault on the part of the wrongdoer.

### [A] Principle of Legality

With regard to substantive criminal law, the principle of legality, as enshrined in § 1 StGB, provides the traditional formula of '*nullum crimen, nulla poena sine lege*'. Whereas § 1 StGB is as such part of the Criminal Code (and, therefore, in the rank of ordinary laws), its main principles are also guaranteed at the constitutional level, namely by the Austrian Federal Constitution[2] and by Article 7 of the European Convention of Human Rights (in short, 'ECHR'). The principle of legality holds that:

- no conduct shall be deemed to be criminal unless it is specifically covered by the wording of a statutory crime (already in force at the time of the commission of the act);
- no harsher punishment may be imposed, as provided already at the time of the commission of the act;
- sanctions relating to criminal offences may not be applied retroactively;
- penal statutes shall be strictly construed; an offence may not be extended beyond the outmost boundaries of the language used to define the crime (no analogous application of a statutory offence to the detriment of the perpetrator = 'strafrechtliches Analogieverbot');
- customary (national) criminal law is precluded;
- criminal offences may not be of undue ambiguity: since this element of 'foreseeability' of the crime is directed towards the lawmaker (and not to the judiciary), it requires a parallel guarantee also at the constitutional level (Article 18 Federal Constitution, Article 7 ECHR).

Further to the aforementioned basic guarantees, § 62 StGB provides that repeal or amendment of the offence after the deed also apply to an act previously committed if these amendments are beneficial for the perpetrator.

Wrongful acts and justification: A criminal offence makes the behaviour described therein an unlawful act. Commission of the act, therefore, implies a criminal 'wrong'. This 'wrong' may, however, be overcompensated under certain conditions, say, based on consent or to avoid greater harm in case of an imminent danger ('justification'). There is no *numerus clausus* of reasons for justification under Austrian law. Justification may stem from all legal provisions (say, from an act of law enforcement, such as an arrest warrant) that explicitly or implicitly allow the commission of an act that would otherwise constitute an offence. The General Part of the Austrian Criminal Code only defines one single cause for justification, namely 'self defence' in § 3 (also covering the defence of another party). Whereas justification by 'necessity' is not explicitly provided for in the Code's General Part, it is generally acknowledged by doctrine and court practice, and even in the official explanations to the Criminal Code ('*Erläuternde Bemerkungen*'). Several specific reasons for justification can be found in the Criminal Code's Special Part in the context of the respective offences.

### [B] Principle of Culpability

The Principle of Culpability is twofold. First, culpability in the broad sense holds that each crime requires, with regard to all of its elements, personal fault (intent or

2. In particular, by Art. 18 of the Federal Constitution; see Grabenwarter, *Constitutional Law*, 2. f).

negligence), precluding all forms of strict (or vicarious) criminal liability. Second, culpability in the narrow sense means that a person can only be punished for his deeds if he is personally responsible for them. This personal responsibility requires that, in addition to objective fault, the perpetrator could have acted differently, namely avoided the wrong ('personal guilt'). The 'concept of guilt', as provided for in the Austrian Criminal Code, includes, however, objective benchmarks in the sense that each individual has to provide a certain degree/standard of legal values (*'Verbundenheit mit den rechtlich geschützten Werten'*).

*Fault:* Unless otherwise stated in the Criminal Code's Special Part (§ 7 subparagraph 1 StGB), all criminal offences require intent. Austrian criminal law does not include a *'mens rea'* concept, but strictly distinguishes between intent (defined as knowledge of the pertinent facts and their normative meaning and wilful action related thereto) on the one hand and questions of guilt in the narrow sense (encompassing, *inter alia*, questions of error in law) on the other hand. The least demanding form of intent is *'dolus eventualis'* (§ 5 subparagraph 1 StGB). A perpetrator acts *dolo eventuali* if he (i) perceives that his actions may bring about a certain criminal act and (ii) still, accepting the materialisation of that negative risk, performs the act anyway. Unless otherwise provided, intentional crimes only require *dolus eventualis* (§ 5 subparagraph 1 StGB). Some offences provide for explicit positive knowledge (*'Wissentlichkeit'*, as defined in § 5 subparagraph 3 StGB) of a certain fact, say, regarding the abuse of powers of representation in § 153 StGB (*'Untreue'*) and of state powers in § 302 StGB (*'Amtsmissbrauch'*) or of intentionality (*'Absichtlichkeit'*, as defined in § 5 subparagraph 2 StGB).

The Criminal Code defines negligence (§ 6 StGB), in line with the respective general concept, as the absence of due care (both in the sense of objective negligence and the perpetrator's individual ability to comply with the respective requirements). Austrian criminal law provides (for the most part) only one category of negligence, and not variations of it, such as recklessness, wilful ignorance or slightest negligence. The envisaged reform is, however, likely to introduce a general concept of 'gross negligence'.

*Guilt:* As for the requirement of 'guilt' in the narrow sense, criminal law does not positively require any proof of the perpetrator's ability to have acted differently, but defines criteria under which the perpetrator lacks this (presumed) ability. At the core of these guilt-related provisions are incapacity (§ 11 StGB), 'excusable necessity (§ 10 StGB) and excusable legal error (under the conditions defined in § 9 StGB). A person is not responsible for his acts if he lacks, based on a mental state defined in the law (e.g., a disease of the mind or a comparable mental disorder), the ability to either perceive the unlawfulness of the act or to act in accordance with the perceived legal commands (*'Zurechnungsunfähigkeit'* = 'incapacity', as defined in § 11 StGB). As for 'errors', failure to correctly perceive the facts of the case (and their normative meaning) always precludes the respective intent (so that a perpetrator cannot be punished for that intentional offence), while only excusable errors regarding the legal dimension of correctly perceived acts ('is this a prohibited act?') constitute lack of guilt (§ 9 StGB).

Under the rubric 'excusable necessity' (*'entschuldigender Notstand'*, as defined in § 10 StGB), previously referred to as 'irresistible compulsion', the law (§ 10 StGB) treats an offence as being excused if the perpetrator, in light of an imminent danger, commits an offence to prevent *lesser* harm which would otherwise occur (otherwise, if the perpetrator prevents greater harm, the act is already justified) if the proportion of the 'goods' at stake is not excessive and also if a reasonable person may not have acted differently (§ 10 StGB).

If the perpetrator lacks guilt (in the aforementioned sense), he is not personally responsible for his acts and may not be punished for them. Under certain requirements (in particular, the commission of an act that constitutes a fully specified crime with the sole exception of incapacity and, moreover, the likelihood that the perpetrator would commit other crimes with severe consequences, the Court may still, instead of issuing a guilty verdict, order that the perpetrator be restrained until such time as he no longer poses a risk to society at large (§ 21 subparagraph 1 StGB). In some other cases (§ 21 subparagraph 2, § 22 and § 23 StGB), the law provides for restraint because of dangerousness *in addition to* a criminal penalty within some maximum term prescribed by law.

There is a special 'Act on Juvenile Delinquency' (*'Jugendgerichtsgesetz'*), providing (i) that criminal responsibility commences at the age of 14 and (ii) for some special rules applicable to perpetrators who have committed an offence between the ages of 14 and 18 (and, in some respect, 21 years) with regard to both substantive and procedural criminal law.

### [C] Extensions of Criminal Responsibility

The scope of the offences, as defined under criminal law, is broader than it appears at first glance because the Criminal Code's General Part extends criminal responsibility in various dimensions (modality, time, and personal scope).

*Modality (Omissions):* Pursuant to § 2 StGB, all criminal offences that are defined in terms of action *and result* may also be committed by omission, provided that there is a legal (and not merely moral) duty to act. Such a duty may be derived from other legal provisions, contract, or the preceding 'creation of the peril'. This general rule is supplemented by criminal offences that are specifically defined in terms of failure to act (so called 'pure omissions'). Under these offences, e.g., everybody must assist a person in need of help to escape the danger of serious injury or death (§ 95 StGB).

*Attempts:* Under Austrian criminal law, all intentional crimes (without exception) may be attempted (§ 15 StGB) and are amenable to the same punishment as the completed offence; non-completion (only) being deemed a mitigating circumstance (§ 34 StGB). An attempt always requires the (full) intent to commit the crime and the commission of an act sufficiently proximate to the intended crime. This is the case if the perpetrator either is already executing (a part of) the deed (without having fully completed it) or has at least reached a situation immediately preceding the commission of the criminal act. Whether an act is 'immediately preceding' the commission of the crime has to be decided in light of the perpetrator's plan according to the criteria of immediate vicinity in time and place, the lack of further decisive preparatory acts and the will of the wrongdoer 'to do it now'. Voluntary abandonment of the deed relinquishes the perpetrator from respective criminal responsibility (§ 16 StGB). An impossible attempt is not deemed a criminal act (§ 15 paragraph 3 StGB).

*Parties to the crime:* Austrian criminal law has a simple rule with regard to the parties to a crime. Pursuant to § 12 StGB, the immediate perpetrator (i.e., the person performing at least part of the act: '*unmittelbarer Täter*'), any person soliciting the act ('*Bestimmungstäter*'), and any person encouraging or assisting the act ('*Täter durch sonstigen Tatbeitrag*') are equally criminally responsible for the crime 'as perpetrators', punishable with the same penalty. Whereas criminal responsibility for the immediate perpetrator commences at the time of his (own) attempt and for the person soliciting the act at the time of the attempt to influence someone else to commit the crime, even where this ultimately fails, encouragement/assistance is not punishable as such, but only upon the immediate perpetrator's commission of (at least) the respective attempt (§ 15 subparagraph 2 StGB). All parties have to act by themselves with the 'mens rea', as required under the respective offence. Still, criminal responsibility for an intentional crime as an accomplice only requires that the accomplice himself acts with required intent (and that the respective act furthers the commission of the deed by the immediate perpetrator), not necessarily that the immediate perpetrator himself acts intentionally.

The Criminal Code provides for a special offence against conspiracy (§ 277 StGB), and also various types of organisational crimes (§§ 278 et seq. StGB).

### [D] Punishment

The Criminal Code's principal ways of punishment are imprisonment and monetary fines; parole being, of course, possible (also for parts of the penalty) and widely used. The degree of the perpetrator's guilt provides the basis for his punishment (§ 32 subparagraph 1 StGB); the principle of proportionality applies. Unlike the laws of many other countries, Austrian criminal law does not allow for the compounding of penalties if the perpetrator repeatedly commits an offence or commits various separate offences;[3] instead, the overall sentence is restricted to the maximum sanction of the most severe single crime (§ 28 subparagraph 1 StGB).[4]

Under certain conditions, Austrian criminal law allows for confiscation (§ 20 StGB: '*Verfall*'); the provisions on 'disgorgement of gains' have been repealed.

3. The compounding of penalties may occur, however, if separate offences provide different mandatory sanctions (§ 28 subpara. 2 StGB), say a prison term in one offence and a monetary fine in the other offence – a very rare case though.
4. However, various offences against foreign property provide harsher penalties if the perpetrator acts with the purpose to derive or procure for himself a quasi-income from the commission of comparable acts in the future ('*Gewerbsmäßigkeit*' = 'commission of crimes for commercial gain'). The current reform is likely to bring a more restrictive version of this concept.

### [E] Punishment of Legal Persons

Austrian criminal law not only provides for the criminal responsibility of the individual perpetrator, but also allows for the punishment of legal persons ('Act on the Responsibility of Legal Entities' = '*Verbandsverantwortlichkeitsgesetz*', in short 'VbVG'). Such responsibility requires that the respective offence is committed in the sphere of the legal person (for the advantage of the legal person or under violation of pertinent duties) and attributable to it (§ 3 VbVG). Whereas a legal person cannot, by itself, commit a criminal act, such an act is criminally attributable to it (§§ 2 and 3 VbVG) if it has been committed either directly by someone within the company's inner circle (someone holding a position that allows him/her to substantially direct the legal person's management or a supervisory position) or by an agent[5] (defined as someone providing services for the legal person) provided in that case for the additional requirement of a negligent organisation, surveillance or control on the part of the legal person's management that has at least contributed to the act's commission. Sanctions are penalty-like monetary fines ('*Verbandsgeldbußen*' pursuant to §§ 4 and 5 VbVG). So far, there have been few cases of criminal responsibility only and hardly any convictions; recently, however, prosecutors have been more active in attempting to enforce the VbVG.

The whole concept of criminal attribution is, however, problematic from a constitutional standpoint: The criminal responsibility of the legal person allows a criminal penalty to be imposed in respect of an act that the punished (legal) person has not committed itself (but for which it is only held criminally accountable), departing from the basic requirement that punishment may only be based on the culprit's own action.[6] Whereas attribution is commonly acknowledged in civil law and tort law, it has – at least so far – not been accepted in criminal law. The Constitutional Court will have the ultimate word on this issue.

### [F] Criminal Jurisdiction

The Austrian Criminal Code also contains provisions (§§ 62 et seq. StGB) that define the scope of Austrian jurisdiction in the international context (referred to as 'international jurisdiction'). The basic principles are the following: If the *situs* of the crime is within Austrian territory (or on Austrian ships or aircrafts), Austrian criminal law applies, irrespective of the nationality of the actor. The *situs* of the crime covers both

5. In this case, the law does not require 'guilt' (in the sense of the individual ability to avoid the act) on the part of the perpetrator (agent). It is here that the VbVG suffers from a basic misconception: It assumes that the further requirement of negligence on the part of the management compensates for this 'lack of guilt'. If, however, an intentional offence is at stake, the lack of guilt with regard to an intentional crime cannot be compensated by negligence. § 3 VbVG allows, therefore, punishment of the legal person for an intentional crime, even without guilt for this intentional crime in the technical sense. It is probable that this concept will be held unconstitutional if challenged before the Constitutional Court.
6. This requirement is also a constitutional principle, see *Collection of Decisions of the Constitutional Court* 15.200/1998.

(i) the commission/omission of the wrongful act and/or (ii) its results in the sense of materialisation of harm. For crimes that penalise only a certain action (and do not also define its 'results'), only the first criterion applies; otherwise either criterion suffices to constitute Austrian jurisdiction. If, therefore, a murderer shoots someone abroad while actually located on Austrian territory (i.e., he/she fires the weapon in question across a border), Austrian jurisdiction may be derived from the *situs* of the act, and if the shot is fired from abroad into Austria, from the location of the effect. It suffices that an act is at least partly committed in Austria. As for crimes committed entirely abroad (with no cross-border materialisation of harm occurring in Austria), Austrian jurisdiction may apply based on well-established principles of international law (nationality, 'protective principle', 'universal jurisdiction'), even irrespective of concurrent criminal law provisions in the foreign state (§ 64 StGB). Otherwise (§ 65 StGB), criminal acts committed abroad require (i) that the act is also punishable at the *situs* of the crime and that (ii) the perpetrator is either an Austrian citizen or, if this is not the case, has at least been arrested in Austria without extradition being possible for reasons other than those stemming from the peculiarities of the deed. The criteria of Austrian criminal jurisdiction are objective prerequisites for the application of Austrian criminal law, but not part of the crime as such (and, therefore, not the object of intent, negligence or 'personal guilt').

## §14.03 AN OVERVIEW REGARDING THE CRIMINAL CODE'S SPECIAL PART

The Criminal Code's Special Part provides criminal offences that prohibit certain unwanted acts of sufficient gravity relating to aspects of 'general life'. Whereas some parts of these offences have become increasingly technical, one can still label many of these crimes as embodying '*mala per se*'. Criminal offences that relate to certain special activities (mostly covered by specifically tailored legal rules), such as reporting activities in companies, the trading of securities, banking, immigration, the carrying of arms, etc. are provided mostly in the respective special pieces of legislation (in the Austrian Banking Act, for instance). Following the above terminology, one may label these offences as '*mala prohibita*' because of their technical and regulatory nature. Whereas these statutory offences exist outside of the Criminal Code proper, the Code's General Part remains applicable to them.

Financial crimes are covered by a special piece of legislation, the 'Act on Financial Offences' ('*Finanzstrafgesetz*'). This Act defines certain acts that constitute (i) financial crimes if committed intentionally with regard to a relevant value ('harm') exceeding EUR 100,000.00 and (ii) administrative (penal) offences otherwise.[7]

The Criminal Code's Special Part consists of various sections, covering for instance crimes against the person ('*Leib und Leben*') and crimes relating to property.

7. The 'Act on Financial Offenses' covers, further to defining – both in the administrative and criminal context – the unlawful behaviour, the (overall) General Part and the entire administrative procedure. As for the criminal procedure, the Act basically refers to the Procedural Code, providing only specific deviations where required.

Systematically, these sections may be grouped together in two main parts, one containing the offences against the individual, the other the offences against the community.

The following brief outline is confined to a few selected offences.

*Crimes against the person:* The principal provision regarding the intentional killing of another person is the crime of 'murder' (§ 75 StGB).[8] This offence broadly covers all variants, such as premeditated or deliberate killings, killings under special ('atrocious') circumstances, with or without malice aforethought or motivation, and so-called 'mercy killings'. Whereas suicide as such is, of course, not a criminal offence, inducing or aiding another to commit suicide is (§ 78 StGB). It is also a crime to kill someone upon his explicit request (§ 77 StGB). § 76 StGB provides for a special ('privileged') offence for heat-of-passion murder ('Totschlag' = '*voluntary manslaughter*') requiring a loss of self-control in circumstances under which a reasonable person could also have come into such a state of mind. Whereas the perpetrator's reduced guilt justifies *his* special treatment, an accomplice assisting in 'cold blood' would be punishable by the crime of regular 'murder'. Another 'privileged' variant of murder on the basis of presumed 'reduced guilt' because of extraordinary circumstances is the intentional killing of a baby by the mother either during birth (from the time at which the woman goes into labour) or immediately afterwards (still under the influence of the birth-process), as provided in § 79 StGB.[9] As for the protection of the unborn child, the applicable criminal law provisions are found in the subsequent section: Whereas it is a criminal offence to perform an abortion (defined as the termination of a pregnancy) with (§ 96 StGB) or without (§ 98 StGB) the mother's consent, an abortion with the mother's consent is not punishable (§ 97 StGB) if performed by a physician either within the first three (calendar) months of pregnancy or even afterwards, until the woman goes into labour, provided there are grounds for doing so (mother is younger than 14 at the time of becoming pregnant, risk that the child will be born with severe deformities, danger to the health/life of the mother).[10]

The infliction of physical injury (or of an illness) is a criminal offence both when committed negligently (§ 88 StGB) or intentionally (§ 83 StGB).[11] There are two variants for an intentional injury: Either (§ 83 subparagraph 1 StGB) the perpetrator acts with the (immediate) intent to injure another (or to cause an illness) or (§ 83 subparagraph 2 StGB) the intentional part is confined to a mere 'mistreatment' provided that such mistreatment effectively leads to a (negligently caused) injury/illness. There is no special offence for 'assault' as such. An assault may qualify, under the respective conditions, as an attempted intentional injury or may, in the

8. The negligent killing of another is covered by § 80 StGB and if committed under extremely dangerous circumstances by § 81 StGB.
9. An accomplice to the act would again, because there is no reduced guilt on his part, be punishable pursuant to the crime of murder.
10. Whereas the Austrian Constitutional Court has held, in a highly problematic ruling (see Collection of Decisions of the Constitutional Court VfSlg 7.400/1974), the mentioned three-months-rule constitutional, the Court has so far not ruled on the (un-)constitutionality of the equally problematic third term abortions.
11. A separate offence (§ 87 StGB) covers the infliction of a severe injury/illness on purpose; this provision may undergo a slight change in the upcoming reform.

absence of such intent, not constitute a criminal offence altogether. Various 'qualifications' apply in the realm of intentional infliction of injury/illness; on the one hand, related to the gravity of the injury/illness (§ 84 subparagraph 1 and §§ 85, 86 StGB) and on the other hand based on the modality of the act (relating to certain 'aggravating circumstances'), as provided in § 84 subparagraph 2 StGB. The current reform is likely to bring a certain streamlining of these provisions. A special variant of intentional injury (§ 86 StGB) covers the case of the infliction of injury/illness (in both variants of § 83) ultimately leading to the (negligently caused) death of the victim.

*Crimes against property:* Under Austrian criminal law, property is not protected as such, but only with regard to certain (technically defined) types of offences, such as theft, embezzlement, and fraud, etc.[12] These offences cover a broad range of activities/fields including a large portion of what is commonly considered 'white collar crime'. Among the core provisions are the following:

*Theft:* Theft (§ 127 StGB) is defined as the wilful 'taking' (= breaking the possession of someone else and establishing own possession) of a certain item of value belonging to someone else, committed with the intent of undue enrichment Theft always requires a 'taking' (and appropriation) in the aforementioned sense; this provision is, therefore, not applicable if the item taken is either in no one's possession[13] or already, for whatever reason, in the perpetrator's possession (who simply decides to keep it in an illegal manner). In the latter cases, the act may qualify (if the item has been 'entrusted' to the perpetrator) as an 'embezzlement' or (if the perpetrator himself has brought the item in his possession without unlawful intent) as an offence called '*Unterschlagung*' ('unlawful keeping of an item with intent of undue enrichment' = § 134 subparagraph 2 StGB). The requirement of the item having a certain 'exchange value' implies that the object taken must already have a certain value in and of itself, such that the perpetrator, when appropriating the object, can possibly enrich himself. The taking of items that may (only) be used to obtain something of value later on, but do not represent this immediate value per se (such as documents, credit cards, smart cards,[14] etc.) does, therefore, not qualify as a crime against the property, but may constitute an offence of a different kind, namely 'suppression of documents' ('*Urkundenunterdrückung*', as provided in § 229 StGB) or 'suppression of non-cash means of payment' ('*Entfremdung unbarer Zahlungsmittel*', as provided in § 241e StGB). The subsequent usage of these items to obtain objects of wealth may constitute a crime against the property, namely, if used to deceive another person, the offence of 'fraud' (e.g., if someone takes another person's saving account passbook and, pretending to be its owner, requests the bank to pay out the balance) or, if used to directly break someone else's possession (e.g., by retrieving money out of a cash box by means of a

12. For most of the offences against property, the Code provides a schedule of harm-based thresholds ('*Wertqualifikationen*'); if the perpetrator exceeds these value-thresholds intentionally, higher penalties apply.
13. For this case, there is the separate offence of 'stealing by finding' ('*Fundunterschlagung*'), as provided in § 134 subpara. 1 StGB.
14. To the extent, however, that the smart card also provides an uploaded 'cash equivalent', the offence of theft is applicable.

banking card), the offence of 'theft'. Burglary is not a separate offence, but a special case of theft (a so-called 'qualification', provided in § 129 StGB).

*Embezzlement:* Embezzlement (*'Veruntreuung'*, as defined in § 133 StGB) is an offence whereby the perpetrator intentionally (and with additional intent for unjust enrichment) appropriates a certain good, entrusted to him (and, therefore, already in his possession).[15] The offence only covers factual appropriations (such as the appropriation of bank notes or jewellery out of a hotel's safe by the hotel manager), not (legal) acts of representation, which are covered by different provision of § 153 StGB.

*Fraud:* Fraud (§ 146 StGB) is a crime whereby the victim suffers harm based on false factual pretences. Its elements are as follows: The perpetrator deceives someone else causing the person who has thus been deceived to perform a certain act which is 'self-harming' in the sense that it effectively reduces that person's assets; fraud is an intentional crime that also requires intent for undue enrichment. The crime of 'fraud' has plentiful applications; because of its 'normative' wording, the boundaries of the offence are, however, often ambiguous. Typical cases of fraud are the exchange of 'good money' against 'bad merchandise' (such as the sale of adulterated wine) or the inverse constellation of 'good merchandise' against either 'bad money' (e.g., bad checks or counterfeit money) or 'no money' in the sense of the buyer's inability or unwillingness to pay. Bid rigging is also considered fraud if the companies fraudulently agree to raise the overall price level well above the market price so that the seemingly cheapest (but still overpriced) offer is chosen in the tendering procedure, the harm being the difference between the market price and sales price.

*Harmful abuse of powers of representation: 'Untreue'* (§ 153 StGB) always requires powers of representation. The offence is defined such that the perpetrator actually uses these powers of representation, but uses them in an undue manner:[16] he 'abuses' them, thereby causing financial harm to the party being represented. In terms of mental state, the wrongdoer has to act against better (positive) knowledge with regard to the breach of the internal constraints (= the abuse) and with *dolus eventualis* regarding the harm caused;[17] the offence does not require intent for undue enrichment. *'Untreue'* is the most important white-collar offence. Since all directors of companies hold (statutory) powers of representation, abusive acts of representation that harm the company (whether motivated by kick-backs or not) constitute *'Untreue'*. Whereas the Supreme Court has recently interpreted *'Untreue'* in a very broad manner, this development has sparked intense public debate[18]) on whether to reduce the scope of this offence by deliberate statutory amendment.

15. So that he behaves as if he were the 'free' (unencumbered) owner of this good.
16. This is generally assumed when the perpetrator violates 'internal constraints' that specify due behaviour in the interest of the principal. If no explicit or implicit internal constraints exist, the representative has to act in the best (assumed) interest of the principal.
17. There is no exact equivalent to this provision in the Anglo-American legal tradition..Other highly relevant provisions are 'receiving stolen goods' (*'Hehlerei'*, as defined in § 164 StGB) and – with a very wide scope – money laundering (*'Geldwäscherei'*, as defined in § 165 StGB), robbery (*'Raub'*, as defined in § 142), and blackmail (*'Erpressung'*, as defined in § 144 StGB).
18. Whereas not yet included in the current reform proposal, an amendment of § 153 StGB (defining the crime's core elements in a more restrictive manner) is likely to be introduced in the course of the further debates.

*Active repentance ('Tätige Reue', § 167 StGB):* Unlike most other jurisdictions, the Austrian Criminal Code grants the perpetrator of many offences against foreign property the possibility to relieve himself from criminal responsibility by fully compensating the victim. The requirements are: (i) the commission of a 'listed' offence against foreign property,[19] (ii) full compensation by the perpetrator of the criminally relevant damage (that may well be lower than full compensation under tort law), in (iii) due time (= before enforcement agencies have taken notice of the facts of the case), and (iv) without being (physically) forced.[20] This provision is of considerable practical relevance.[21]

*Bribery/Anti-Corruption:* Austria's Criminal Code has recently been amended on several occasions to toughen its provisions against corruption. These new provisions, now grouped together in a separate section (section 22) of the Code are quite detailed and technical. They cover the giving and taking of bribes with regard to state officials (broadly defined, including managers of state controlled enterprises) in various circumstances (unlawful, lawful = facilitation payments, and preparatory if performed with the intent of exerting an influence). There are separate bribery offences in the private sector with regard to the undue commission of legal acts (§ 309 StGB).

## §14.04 CRIMINAL PROCEDURE

### [A] Framework and Basic Principles

*Framework:* The Austrian criminal procedure follows the libertarian heritage of the nineteenth century. It has, thus, traditionally required the involvement of all three state powers to obtain a conviction, namely the involvement of the legislator to enact the criminal offence, the administrative branch of government ('the prosecutor') to prosecute a possible criminal act, and the judiciary to render a verdict. In principle this concept still underlies the Austrian criminal procedure, even though the prosecutor has been transformed, by means of a constitutional amendment (Article 90a Federal Constitution), to a functionary of the judiciary in the broad sense (with the peculiarity, however, of the Ministry of Justice remaining ultimately competent to decide on issues of criminal prosecution).

The basic principles of Austrian criminal procedure are enshrined in constitutional law, in particular in the Articles 82 et seq. of the Federal Constitution[22] and in the 'fair trial guarantees' of Article 6 of the ECHR. Over the past fifteen years, the Supreme

---

19. This list covers basically all relevant offences with the exception of offences committed by force or threat, such as robbery.
20. *'Tätige Reue'* is not precluded if the victim requests repayment of the damage, even when threatening to take legal action against the perpetrator or to ask the prosecutor to press charges.
21. Many offences against the property (namely those enumerated in § 166 StGB, under exclusion of crimes involving an element of force or threat) are only punishable by a very lenient punishment if they were committed against a family member (*'Begehung im Familienkreis'* as provided in § 166 StGB); these offences may then be enforced only by the victim.
22. See Grabenwarter, *Constitutional Law*, 5.a).

Court (in Civil and Criminal matters) has very actively developed the role of human rights in criminal procedure.

The core principles and characteristics of Austrian criminal procedure are:

- Accusation-based criminal trials; public prosecutors perform tasks of investigation and accusation in criminal proceedings.
- Lay participation (jury trials and mixed panel courts with lay assessors) for severe and political offences.
- Judicial independence.
- Immediate, oral, and public trials; appraisal of evidence by judge (based on his/her personal, trial-based conviction); presumption of innocence until final verdict.
- Two instances, the scope and intensity of the appeals procedure being inversely related to the thoroughness of fact-finding in the first instance.
- Additional instruments (outside of regular appeals) to address the Supreme Court for legal review of acts/decisions within the criminal justice system.
- Procedural 'rule of law': All procedural acts that interfere with the rights of individuals must be explicitly empowered by statutory law; all state acts in the realm of criminal law (in particular, also those by prosecutors) must ultimately be contestable before criminal courts.
- The principle of proportionality.

### [B] Role and Tasks of the Prosecutor

*Ex officio enforcement:* In Austria, as in most other countries, the public prosecutor enjoys a monopoly on the enforcement of criminal law; only in a few cases (such as the violation of intellectual property rights, defamation, or property crimes committed against family members) does substantive criminal law entrust the enforcement task exclusively to the victim. Criminal prosecution in Austria is ex officio, meaning the public prosecutor is obligated to enforce the law (§ 2 StPO); prosecutorial discretion only exists with regard to enforcement against legal persons (§ 18 VbVG).

There are two types of public prosecutor: (i) regular prosecutors at the Regional Courts and (ii) the 'Central Public Prosecutor's Office for White-Collar Crime and Corruption' ('*Zentrale Staatsanwaltschaft zur Verfolgung von Wirtschaftsstrafsachen und Korruption*', in short 'WKStA') located in Vienna, competent for all relevant cases in Austria.

*Procedural tasks:* Pursuant to the current Procedural Code, the prosecutor's position varies depending on the stage of the proceedings (preliminary or main proceedings). During the preliminary (investigative) phase, the prosecutor is 'the master of the proceedings'. He alone decides which lines of investigations should be followed and which evidence to collect. He is obligated to conduct the proceedings in a strictly objective manner, searching both for incriminating and exculpatory evidence. The prosecutor is also bound by objective criteria when it comes to his decision whether or not to indict the suspect (see *infra*).[23] After the investigative stage, the prosecutor switches into a 'party' of the main proceedings, pursuing the indictment against the accused as his adversarial opponent and seeking a guilty verdict.

*Legal remedies against prosecutorial decisions in the investigative proceedings:* Pursuant to § 106 StPO, all acts by the prosecutor (and the assisting police) during the preliminary proceedings may be challenged by a complaint (*'Einspruch wegen Rechtsverletzung'*), to be directed first to the prosecutor himself, and, upon his non-compliance, second, to the courts (namely to a single judge at the Regional Court, his decisions being appealable to a panel of three professional judges at the Higher Regional Courts of Appeals pursuant to the general rules). This judicial control of all prosecutorial action with regard to possible violations of subjective rights of the individual provides the 'golden cornerstone' of the rule of law with regard to the investigative phase of the proceedings.

Further to this general instrument, specific checks and balances apply with respect to the prosecutor's (ex officio) monopoly and duty to enforce criminal law, both protecting against an allegedly unjustified (or excessively long) investigation[24] and, inversely, from the (alleged) victim's standpoint, against unjustified or premature acquittal:

- The suspect may (when investigations exceed three months) request the prosecutor to close proceedings for either legal or factual reasons (§ 108 StPO); if the prosecutor declines acquittal, a judge has to decide on the request (this decision being appealable to a panel of three judges). Empirically, there are not too many such requests, and when they are made they are rarely successful. Typically, the suspect would seek closure of the case informally, outside of the formal instrument of this 'motion for closure of case'.
- In turn, if the prosecutor closes a case, the (alleged) victim may request its continuation (either on factual or legal grounds), again initially by motion to the prosecutor and, if unsuccessful, to the judge, who in this case takes a final decision (and either confirms that the case is to be closed or orders its continuation[25]). Motions by victims to reopen investigations have been plentiful and are still quite frequent, but they very rarely prevail.

*Decision to indict/not to indict:* Having regard for the checks and balances mentioned above, the prosecutor alone is competent to decide whether to close or to

23. It is commonly held that the prosecutor may only indict, if the probability of conviction exceeds 50%.
24. A recent amendment (§ 108a StPO) requires prosecutors to request judicial prolongation for preliminary investigations after three (and again after two more) years.
25. The respective motion is provided in § 193 StPO. Note that the decision only orders that preliminary proceedings be continued, but not that the suspect be indicted. The prosecutor may, therefore, continue investigations and subsequently close the case again, and the victim may challenge that acquittal by a new motion pursuant to § 193 StPO. The Procedural Code does not provide an instrument comparable to the German *'Anklageerzwingungsverfahren'* ('procedure to directly oblige the prosecutor to indict the suspect').

pursue a case at the end of the investigative stage. Various options exist. If the findings of the investigative phase have not fostered the original suspicion, the prosecutor has to acquit the suspect. For petty offences, the prosecutor also has the option of closing the case on a *de minimis* basis (§ 191 StPO). Otherwise, the prosecutor may file an indictment (which is appealable in cases of mixed panel or jury trials, but rarely appealed on a de facto basis). For offences of minor or lower-medium gravity (with the perpetrator's guilt not being severe) Austrian procedure, however, provides for diversionary dispositions, as an alternative to an indictment (*'Diversion'*, as provided for in §§ 198 et seq. StPO). In essence, these diversionary dispositions are a voluntary 'deal' between the suspect and the prosecutor, where the case is settled with non-stigmatic sanctions only. All diversionary dispositions do not lead to a criminal record ('third track'); because of the lack of a formal conviction, the suspect is still deemed innocent in the legal sense. Diversionary dispositions encompass a suspension of the proceedings, social work, 'victim-offender mediation', and pecuniary (but non-stigmatic) sanctions (§ 198 StPO). Even if the prosecutor declines a diversionary disposition, the trial judge may still approve it during trial (§ 209 StPO). Since the suspect is entitled to diversionary dispositions (but not a specific measure), a conviction rendered under the conditions required in the Procedural Code instead of a diversionary disposition may therefore be challenged by the suspect by an appeal for nullity.

*Searches, Seizures, and Arrest:* The Criminal Procedure provides for a wide range of procedural measures (§§ 109 et seq. StPO) that allow for the gathering of evidence with, without or against the will of the presumed holder of that evidence and/or the suspect and for the arrest of the suspect. Whereas these measures are also applicable during the main proceedings, their principal importance is during the investigative/preliminary phase. The competence for these measures varies depending on their sensitivity: Whereas the prosecutor is competent to decide on measures of minor importance, more sensitive measures require the approval of a judge. In some cases, such as where a person is remanded in custody pending trial (*'Untersuchungshaft'*),[26] the prosecutor may only apply for the respective measure, while the judge is competent to decide on this issue (§§ 173 et seq. StPO).

Decisions taken by the prosecutor alone may be challenged, according to the general rules, by complaint (*'Einspruch wegen Rechtsverletzung'*) pursuant to § 106 StPO. Measures that are approved or issued by a judge may, however, be contested, again according to the applicable general principles, by appealing to the panel of three judges at the Higher Regional Courts of Appeals. Only with regard to questions of arrest may decisions of the Higher Regional Court of Appeal in turn be challenged before the Supreme Court by virtue of a piece of special legislation (*'Grundrechtsbeschwerdegesetz'*).

26. A mere detention, however, may be ordered by the prosecutor with judicial approval or even performed by the police in exigent circumstances, as defined by law (§ 171 StPO).

### [C] The Austrian Court System

The Austrian Criminal Procedure provides two instances. In the first instance, there are two types of trials before single judges and two types of trials with lay participation, namely *'Schöffengerichte'* (mixed panel courts) and *'Geschworenengerichte'* (juries). In the second instance, (different) panels of three professional judges decide on appeals against rulings by single judges, while the Supreme Court considers appeals against rulings by courts with lay participation.

*Trials:* The Procedural Code provides for four different types of trial:

(1) Trials at District Courts (*'Bezirksgerichte'*) for petty offences with a maximum penalty of under one year imprisonment (with certain enumerated crimes being excluded).

(2) 'Single judge trials' (*'Einzelrichterverfahren'*) at the regional courts for cases with a maximum penalty of between one and five years (including the aforementioned enumerated crimes).

(3) Mixed panel courts competent to decide on criminal offences punishable with a maximum penalty of between five and ten years' imprisonment (plus certain 'sensitive' crimes, such as assisted suicide, abuse of state powers, etc.). Mixed panel courts consist of two lay assessors and one (in severe cases: two) professional judge(s); they decide together both on the question of guilt and on the penalty.

(4) As for the most severe crimes (minimum penalty exceeding five years, maximum penalty exceeding ten years) and enumerated political crimes, Austrian procedure provides for trial by jury. The jury consists of eight lay persons who decide alone by simple majority on the guilt of the accused (*'Wahrspruch'* = 'verdict') and, subsequently, together with a panel of three professional judges, on the sanction. Unlike the United States system, the Austrian jury system provides a complex interplay between jury and professional judges. At the end of the hearing, the professional judges prepare a 'schedule of questions', structuring the case in its legal dimensions, for answers by the jury. The professional judges may require an improvement of the verdict by the (same) jury if the verdict happens to be inconsistent or otherwise formally flawed and they may, by unanimous decision, suspend the verdict if they consider the verdict in substance 'erroneous' (wrong conviction, wrong acquittal). In the latter case, the Supreme Court will appoint a new jury; should the new jury concur with the old jury, the verdict cannot be suspended again. Suspensions of verdicts are rare (around 2% or less); however, most are to the detriment of the accused.

The main characteristics of the procedure of first instance are basically identical for all four types of trial. The Procedural Code's reference procedure is that for the mixed panel court; the Code refers to these rules also for the other types of trial, providing in addition only those special rules that are required for the particularities of these trials (say, rules on the question schedule in jury trials). Pursuant to Austrian criminal procedure, the judge is an active judge endowed with inquisitorial powers, not only a referee. Judicial passivity, however, can (for the most part) not be challenged successfully in an appeal.[27]

*Appeals:* The Austrian system of appeals is based on the concept that the criminal procedure must provide adequate overall fact-finding and control, but not in every instance. To the extent that thorough fact-finding occurs already in the first instance, there is no need to replicate such proceedings in the second instance. Moreover, with regard to (constitutionally guaranteed) lay participation in the first instance, it is obvious that a Court of Appeal cannot reverse factual questions unless – which would be a waste of resources – lay judge participation was also provided for in the second instance.

As to appeals, the Procedural Code provides a 'two track' system (confined to legal review in 'nullity appeals', and allowing additionally for a *trial de novo* in 'full appeals'):

- Appeals for nullity against rulings by mixed panel courts or juries go to the Supreme Court (for civil and criminal matters). The Supreme Court is a purely professional court without lay participation. The Supreme Court is not a trial court; it does not rehear the case nor does it reconsider any evidence. All factual questions are considered on the basis of the findings of the Court of First Instance. The scope of this appeals process is confined to a review of the ruling of first instance with regard to its compliance with procedural and substantive rules. The Supreme Court may confirm the first instance's ruling or it may repeal the ruling and either finally acquit the suspect or order a new hearing in the first instance. Appeals on the severity of the penalty go to the Supreme Court if combined with an appeal for nullity and to the Higher Regional Court of Appeals (*'Oberlandesgericht'*) if filed on a stand-alone basis.
- Appeals against judgments of single judges are much more encompassing (*'volle Berufung'* = 'full appeal'). All court rulings by single judges can be appealed both on the above grounds of nullity (*'Berufung wegen Nichtigkeit'*) and, in addition, because of the lesser degree of reliability of fact-finding in the first instance, with regard to its factual basis and appraisal of the evidence by the judge (*'Berufung wegen Schuld'*). The second type of appeal allows new evidence to be heard, new witnesses to be called, and even a completely new trial to be conducted before the Court of Appeal (*'trial de novo'*); the appeals court may, however, also on the occasion of such a full factual appeal, simply repeal the ruling and order a new hearing in the first instance. All appeals go to a panel of three professional judges. In case of an appeal against the ruling of a District Court, the Court of Appeal is a panel at the Regional Court, in case of an appeal against the ruling of the Single Judge at the Regional Court, the appeal goes to the Higher Regional Court of Appeal (*'Oberlandesgericht'*). There are four Higher Regional Courts of Appeals in Austria. The decision by

27. Successful appeals on procedural issues require (again for the most part) a respective motion by the defence counsel, and, hence, an 'active' lawyer.

the second instance cannot be challenged by regular appeal; there is no third instance.[28]

*Additional instruments of legal review by the Supreme Court outside regular appeals:* A Supreme Court is typically entrusted with the tasks of ensuring (i) the correct application of criminal law, (ii) its uniformity and, in particular, (iii) its development. Since the Austrian Supreme Court has only very limited competencies in the regular appeals process, namely only with regard to nullity appeals against rulings in trials with lay participation (i.e., a tiny fraction of all criminal cases), it needs further competencies to fulfil the aforementioned basic tasks:

- These competencies are (partly) provided by an additional control instrument outside of the regular appeals process where the Advocate General (not an individual party) may request, by means of a formal 'recourse' (*'Nichtigkeitsbeschwerde zur Wahrung des Gesetzes'* = 'Recourse for the preservation of the law', as provided in § 23 StPO), that the Supreme Court decide on any alleged violation of the law – not on factual mistakes[29] – committed in the course of criminal proceedings. Such a request is possible irrespective of whether the decision or act at stake is as such appealable or not. This instrument is, for obvious reasons, of paramount importance for the functioning of the criminal justice system as a whole. If the Supreme Court concurs with the Advocate General, it rules that the law has been violated in this concrete instance. If the error in law has been to the detriment of the accused, the Supreme Court may, in addition to the finding of the mistake, order the renewal of the trial or acquit the accused straightaway. If, however, the legal error has benefited the accused, the Supreme Court confines its decision to the finding of the mistake.
- Moreover, the Supreme Court has developed an additional instrument that allows the accused to directly address the Court with alleged violations of constitutional (or equivalent) rights, namely by making applicable for these cases a legal remedy, originally provided to repeal uncontestable domestic decisions to abide with a ruling of the European Court of Human Rights (§ 363a StPO). Whereas this instrument in principle requires, as a national follow-up instrument to an European Court of Human Rights ruling, a previous decision by this European Court (and not only the assertion of such a violation), the Supreme Court has, in a seminal ruling, opened up a 'shortcut', according to which the Supreme Court itself may rectify alleged violations of the ECHR under the same conditions that would apply for an application to the European Court of Human Rights (basically, within six months upon exhaustion of domestic remedies).[30] The extension of this instrument beyond its original

28. There is also no recourse to the Constitutional Court for a constitutional review of a final verdict by the regular courts, as provided under German law.
29. § 362 StPO provides the opportunity for the Supreme Court to repeal guilty verdicts in case of gross factual error under certain restrictive conditions.
30. See Supreme Court ruling 11 Os 132/06f, and subsequently 14 Os 133/13k, 11 Os 73/13i, and 17 Os 11/12i.

scope has turned out to be the single most important judicial development in criminal procedure within the past few decades. In essence, it allows the accused to directly challenge before the Supreme Court all final decisions by second instance courts on grounds of an alleged violation of 'human rights'. Whereas the Supreme Court has developed this line of rulings in the realm of the (technical) rights granted under the ECHR (and in particular its fair trial rights pursuant to its Article 6), it has further extended the scope of this instrument by allowing recourse based on alleged violations of all constitutional rights (namely of rights granted under the Federal Constitution and the Austrian Bill of Rights) and even of fundamental guarantees without constitutional rank (such as rights granted under EU law that do not formally have constitutional rank under Austrian law).[31] Hence, this extended application of § 363a StPO provides in some real sense the missing link for the completion of the criminal justice system according to the concept of the rule of law.

31. Moreover, the Supreme Court has opened this instrument also to challenge uncontestable decisions during the preliminary proceedings (say, against appeals on indictments or on procedural measures approved by the three judge panel of the Higher Regional Court of Appeals) to the extent that subsequent remedies in the main proceedings would not provide equal relief.

## CHAPTER 15

# Austrian Tax Law*

*Michael Lang & Erich Schaffer*

### §15.01 THE LEGAL FRAMEWORK IN AUSTRIAN TAX LAW

Austria is a federal country composed of the *federal state ('Bund')* and nine *provinces ('Länder')*. Moreover, the Federal Constitution grants a certain degree of financial autonomy to the *local communities ('Gemeinden')*. The right to levy taxes is allocated among these three territorial authorities. Other entities under public law are not entitled to levy taxes; therefore, for example social security contributions are not considered taxes in a legal sense. The constitutional basis of the financial equalisation between the different territorial authorities can be found in the Fiscal Constitution Act of 1948 (*Finanz-Verfassungsgesetz 1948*, 'FVG 1948'). The regulation of the details is subject to the Finance Equivalization Act (*Finanzausgleichsgesetz*, 'FAG'). The F-VG 1948 regulates two different types of taxes: First, *exclusive taxes* levied for the benefit of only one territorial authority (federal state, provinces or local communities) and second, *shared taxes*, whose revenues are distributed among the different territorial authorities.

Among the three territorial authorities the *predominant position is exercised by the federal state*. It is for the federal legislature to decide, whether a specific tax is an exclusive or a shared tax. In the latter case, the *federal legislature* also determines each territorial authority's proportion of the tax revenue. In addition, the predominance of the federal state in Austria's tax matters is also highlighted by the fact that the most important taxes, especially the individual income tax, the corporate income tax, and the value added tax (VAT) are regulated by the federal state. Municipal taxes are usually levied on basis of the laws passed by the legislators of the provinces. However,

* This Chapter was finalised as on 10 Mar. 2015. Changes in the law after that date are not taken into account.

regarding certain municipal taxes, federal legislature has retained its rights for standardised regulation, in order to prevent harmful tax competition. In this framework, the provinces have the legal competence to regulate the exclusive taxes allocated to them by the federal legislation and the exclusive taxes of the local communities. Additionally, according to case law of the Constitutional Court, the provinces also have the right to create new taxes, as long as the new tax is not similar to an existing federal tax. However, as federal law (FAG) regulates almost all important taxes on income and property, in practice there are only few ways for provinces to exercise the power to create new taxes.

The system of tax distribution among the territorial authorities is supplemented by financial transfer mechanisms. The federal government not only allocates the rights to levy taxes and tax revenues, but also general grants and grants for special purposes to the territorial authorities. Thus, Austria's fiscal system is often described as a tax sharing system.

## §15.02 INCOME TAXATION

### [A] Individual Income Tax Act (*Einkommensteuergesetz*, 'EStG')

#### *[1] Personal Scope: Unlimited and Limited Tax Liability*

Under Austrian legislation only individuals are subject to *individual income tax*. Corporations are subject to the *Corporate Income Tax Act*. However, *partnerships* are not treated as taxable entities. They are deemed to be *fiscally transparent* which means that income of partnerships is taxed *in the hands of the partners*. Consequently, corporate partners are subject to corporate income tax, individual partners are subject to individual income tax.

A person is subject to *unlimited taxation*, if he/she has either *residence or habitual abode* in Austria. In that case these persons are taxed on the basis of their *worldwide income*. A residence is constituted, if a person has a home possessed under circumstances that indicate that it will be maintained and not only used on a temporary basis. A home is considered to be possessed by a person, if this person actually uses it or has the right to use it for dwelling purposes. A residence in Austria in general is constituted, if the person, from the beginning of the stay in Austria, intends to maintain this place for more than six months. The habitual abode is the place, where a person is present under circumstances indicating that he/she will stay at that place not just temporarily. However, physical presence in Austria in excess of six months in any case establishes the habitual abode. This habitual abode is deemed to be established already in the beginning of the six-month period. The habitual abode ends at the time the person leaves Austria not just temporarily, also in this respect the six-month criterion is relevant.

EU and EEA citizens who obtain at least 90% of their income in Austria and whose total amount of income generated abroad is not higher than EUR 11,000 may exercise an *option for being subject to unlimited taxation*. The benefit of this option is that certain tax benefits, which are normally only granted to residents, now are also extended to non-residents (e.g., individual tax deductions such as the sole-earner deduction).

According to a regulation on *inland secondary residence* (BGBl II 2003/528) special rules apply if a taxpayer has his/her centre of vital interest outside Austria for more than five years. In this case, maintaining an Austrian secondary residence only triggers unlimited tax liability in Austria in these years, in which the taxpayer has used his secondary residence for more than seventy days. Otherwise the person is only subject to limited tax liability. The taxpayer has to keep records of the days, where the Austrian secondary residence has been used.

*Limited liability* applies to taxpayers who have neither a residence nor their place of habitual abode in Austria. They are subject to tax only on the part of their income from Austrian sources (see also section §15.02[A][7])

### *[2] Income Types*

According to § 2 paragraph 2 EStG taxable income is defined as the total amount of income aggregated from all seven categories of income, after utilisation of losses derived from the several categories and after deduction of special expenses (§ 18 EStG) and extraordinary charges (§§ 34 and 35 EStG) and after consideration of allowable deductions from §§ 104, 105 and 106a EStG.

§ 2 paragraph 3 EStG lists the following seven categories of income:

| | | |
|---|---|---|
| **Business income** | **1. Income from agriculture and forestry (§ 21)** | **Main categories of income** |
| | **2. Income from independent personal services (§ 22)** | |
| | **3. Income from commercial activities (§ 23)** | |
| **Non-business income** | **4. Income from employment (§ 25)** | |
| | **5. Income from capital investment (§ 27)** | **Ancillary categories of income** |
| | **6. Income from rental, leasing and royalties (§ 28)** | |
| | **7. Other specific income (§ 29)** | |

The distinction between *business income* and *non-business income* is of high relevance for the computation of the basis for taxation. Another distinction is made with regard to subsidiarity; the three *ancillary categories of income* are subsidiary to the four *main categories of income.*

The seven categories of income are further defined in the following way:

(1) *Income from agriculture and forestry* (§ 21 EStG): This category particularly consists of income earned by farmers, market-gardeners, winegrowers, stock-breeders, freshwater fishers as well as income from hunting in context with agriculture and forestry.

(2) *Income from independent personal services* (§ 22 EStG): This category comprises:
   - income from scientific, artistic, literary, teaching or educational activities.
   - professional activities from doctors, lawyers, tax advisors, notaries, architects, journalists, or interpreters.
   - income from the administration of property.
   - income as a member of the supervisory board of directors.
   - salaries or other forms of compensation of any kind granted to a company to substantial shareholder (a substantial shareholder is a person whose share amounts to more than 25% of the share capital of the company; see also income from employment).

(3) *Income from commercial activities* (§ 23 EStG): Income from commercial activities is defined as income from trade or business which is not considered as agricultural or forestry activity or as income from professional services.

(4) *Income from employment* (§§ 25 and 26 EStG): This category includes:
   - Any remuneration in cash or in kind derived by an employed person.
   - Pension income received by a retiree from social Security, from a pension fund or from the employer himself.
   - Salaries or other forms of compensation of any kind granted to a company to others than substantial shareholder (a shareholder which is not substantial is a person whose share amounts to less than or equal to 25% of the share capital of the company; see also income from independent personal services).

(5) *Income from capital investments* (§ 27 EStG): This category of income particularly comprises:
   - Income from dividends, as well as other distributions of profits by legal entities subject to corporate tax, as well as interest from all kind of obligations, whether or not guaranteed (paragraph 2).
   - Income from capital gains of investments, including capital gains of assets generating capital gains from investments (paragraph 3).
   - Income from derivative activities (paragraph 4).

(6) *Income from rental, leasing and royalties* (§ 28 EStG): This category consists of:
   - Income from renting or leasing out real estate.
   - Income from renting or leasing out conglomerations of assets, such as those of an enterprise.
   - Royalties from the license of the right to use works protected by the Austrian Federal Copyright Act, as well as royalties from the assignment of industrial property rights, patents and know-how.

(7) *Other specific income* (§§ 29 et seq. EStG): Other specific income exhaustively includes:
   - Recurring earnings (§ 29 No. 1 EStG).
   - Income from private alienation of real estate (§ 30 EStG) and from speculative gains (§ 31 EStG).

- Income from occasional services (§ 29 No. 3 EStG).
- Special office payments (§ 29 No. 4 EStG).

The seven categories of income are numbered *exhaustively* in § 2 paragraph 3 EStG. Within the seven categories the applicable types of income are again defined exhaustively. As a consequence of this, income which is not applicable to one of the seven categories of income is not subject to income taxation (e.g., income from lottery winnings, awards or compensation payments which are not paid in the form of annuities).

### *[3] Tax Exemptions*

Pursuant to § 3 paragraph 1 EStG exempt income particularly includes:

- Certain social distributions such as unemployment compensations, maternity allowances, parental-leave benefits, parental-leave assistance and child-care benefits.
- Payments received from foundations or public funds for the promotion of arts, science or research.
- Scholarships and grants for school children.
- Income from Austrian officials on duty in a foreign country.

### *[4] Determination of the Assessment Base for Taxation*

#### *[a] Dualism in the Computation of Taxable Income*

Depending on the relevant category of income, the computation of income has to be done according to different provisions. The first three categories of income are seen as *profit income*. Here, the income is determined as the profit arising from the commercial activities. The remaining four categories are seen as *surplus income* implying that income is determined as the excess of receipts over expenditure. The differentiation between profit income and surplus income leads to a *dualism in the computation of taxable income*. For profit income, the taxable income is computed by the *net equity comparison method*. Profit is the difference of net equity of the company at the end of the business year and the preceding business year. This also includes profits from the write-up of assets and the alienation of assets or even the alienation of operating units or the whole enterprise (§ 4 paragraph 1 EStG). Regarding surplus income, receipts and expenditure (§ 15 EStG) are compared by using the *cash method*. Changes in value or profits from the alienation of assets – apart from alienations of shareholdings or speculative gains – are not considered for tax reasons. The results of profit income as well as surplus income generally are net values. This means that not only the operating profits or receipts are taken into account, but also from these results operating expenses or expenditure have to be deducted. The result of this calculation – positive or negative – is the income which finally serves as assessment base for taxation.

### [b] *Different Methods for the Calculation of Income*

There are three different ways for calculating business income:

(1) Pursuant § *4 paragraph 1 EStG*, profit is the *difference between net equity* of the business at the end of the business year and the last preceding business year, increased by the value of withdrawals from capital and reduced by the value of contributions to capital during the business year. In short, taxable income is computed according to the general accounting principles. The determination of profit for tax purposes is similar to the determination of profits according to the Code of Enterprises (*Unternehmensgesetzbuch*, 'UGB'). Therefore, for tax purposes, for each fiscal year annual financial statements comprising balance sheet as well as profit and loss statement have to be presented.

(2) For taxpayers who are under the obligation to keep books and who derive income from commercial activities, the determination of income pursuant § 4 paragraph 1 is modified by the rule of § *5 paragraph 1 EStG*. Here, the valuation for commercial law purposes is also binding for tax purposes ('*Maßgeblichkeitsprinzip*').

(3) The third method is the simplified determination of business income according to § *4 paragraph 3 EStG*. If the taxpayer is not legally obliged to keep books, and does not keep them on a voluntary basis either, the cash method can be applied by determining the *surplus of business profits over expenses.*

In all these cases income is assessed separately for each *tax year* which usually equals the calendar year. However, taxpayers who are subject to the provision of § 5 paragraph 1 EStG are allowed to have a business year (= financial year) which deviates from the calendar year. In such a case taxable income from the business is computed for the calendar year, in which the financial year ends (§ 2 paragraph 5 EStG). Still, in any case the financial year must not exceed twelve months. It may only be shorter in case of the opening and termination of business, or in the period where the change from calendar year to the deviating calendar year actually takes place (§ 2 paragraph 6 EStG)

### [c] *Operating Expenses and Expenditure*

*Operating expenses* are defined as expenses which occur in the conduct of a trade or business (§ 4 paragraph 4 EStG). In comparison to that, *expenditure* is defined as costs or expenses for the reasons of generation, protection or preservation of the receipts (§ 16 EStG). The different wording may imply that the extent of these two notions for the deduction of expenses may be different. However, according to the prevailing opinion in Austria, the criteria for the deductibility of expenses are the same for both, operational expenses and expenditure. This result stems from the fact that first and foremost the distinction has to be made whether expenses are made for the *realisation of income* or whether they constitute *usage of income*. Consequently, operating expenses have to be distinguished from expenses which are made for private reasons and therefore not tax deductible.

#### *[d] Special Expenses and Extraordinary Burdens*

With allowing certain expenses to be deducted as *special expenses*, the legislator has followed social, cultural or economic goals. These expenses are in essence private expenses; however, the legislator has attributed to them an *income-reducing effect*. Section 18 EStG enumerates the special expenses and comprises, for example:

- Contributions to certain insurance funds.
- Expenses for construction and renovation of real estate and housing.
- Mandatory contributions to specific religious communities.
- Donations to entities that pursue charitable purposes, carry out development aid or disaster relief, or work in the field of animal protection.
- *Loss carry forward*: The possibility to carry forward losses attenuates the strictness of the *periodic principle*. It has to be distinguished from the notion *loss compensation*. While loss compensation balances positive and negative results within one tax period, loss carry forward works as compensation between subsequent tax periods. Basically, a loss carry forward is possible, if the losses are incurred in a *previous year*, but have not already been considered through loss compensation or loss carry forward in prior periods. Furthermore, the losses must stem from a source of business income, for non-business income a general possibility to carry forward losses does not exist (although certain extraordinary expenses from rentals, leasing and royalties can be spread over ten years pursuant to § 28 paragraph 2 EStG).

In addition to the deductibility of special expenses the legislator also allows taxpayers to deduct *extraordinary burdens*. § 34 EStG defines extraordinary burdens as expenditure accruing in an exceptional and unavoidable manner and significantly affecting the economic capacity of the taxpayer. These are for example catastrophic losses or medical expenses, if they are not covered by insurance.

### *[5] Calculation of Tax Burden: Tax Rates*

Taxable income is the total amount of income from all categories after setting of losses and after deducting special allowances and extraordinary burdens. If no final withholding tax regime is applicable the tax burden of a taxpayer is calculated by using the following formulas:

| *Income (EUR)* | *Formula pursuant to § 33 EStG* | *Marginal Tax Rate in %* |
|---|---|---|
| Up to 11,000.00 | 0.00 | 0.00 |
| > 11,000.00 to 25,000.00 | (income-11,000)*(5,110/14,000) | 36.50 |
| > 25,000.00 to 60,000.00 | (income-25,000)*(15,125/35,000) + 5,110 | 43.21 |
| > 60,000.00 | (income-60,000)*0.5 + 20,235 | 50.00 |

In general, the progressive tax rate affects the total income of a taxpayer and is thus applicable independent of the type of income. However, there are several exceptions to this rule:

- *Beneficial tax rates regarding income from employment for the salary of a 13th and 14th month* (§ 67 EStG): This benefit continuously has been subject to political controversies. This stems from the fact that the special tax rate for top income earners is even more beneficial than for low income earners, whose average tax rate was low to begin with. Thus, in the last years this provision has been subject to several amendments, in order to avoid inappropriate benefits for the top income earners.
- *Taxation at half the average rate* (§ 37 paragraph 1 EStG): This rate especially can be applied regarding capital gains derived by an individual on the sale or liquidation of a business, if a seven years period has elapsed and the taxpayer has died, becomes unable to carry on his business or is at least 60 years old and has gone out of business. Furthermore, also income from the exploitation of patent-protected inventions is subject to the preferential tax rate.
- *Spreading of specific income over three or five years* (§ 37 paragraphs 2 and 3): Also this preferential tax regime primarily can be applied upon request regarding the sale or liquidation of a business. Without this preferential regime gains accrued in the course of several years would all suddenly have to be taxed in one tax period. Especially with regard to the progressive tax rate this would lead to an inappropriately high tax burden. Therefore, the possibility of spreading income over several years – as well as taxation at half the average rate – aims at protecting the taxpayer from such exceptional burden.

Moreover, two important sources of income are totally excluded from calculation of the progressive tax rate as described above. Income from *capital gains* as well as income from *private alienation of real estate* is generally subject to a *flat tax rate of 25%* (§§ 27a and 30a EStG). Still, upon request the normal progressive tax rate instead of the special flat tax of 25% can be applied.

### *[6] Methods of Levying*

#### *[a] Assessment*

Income tax is generally levied by way of an *assessment procedure*. This means that the taxpayer is obliged to fill out a tax return after the end of the tax year. The tax authorities will then issue a tax assessment stating the amount of tax to pay. If the taxpayer assumes that the tax authorities have not computed the income correctly, or another error occurred during the assessment of the tax, the taxpayer may file an appeal. As the tax authorities would like to dispose of the tax as soon as possible, a taxpayer needs to pay *quarterly advance payments* during the calendar year. These payments correspond to the estimated amount of income or to the latest assessed income. The difference between the income tax as assessed by the tax authorities and the advance payments then leads to either a final payment or a repayment (§ 46 EStG). If no mandatory assessment is required, a voluntary assessment may be requested within a period of five years, in order to enjoy a lower progressive tax rate and to deduct expenses where applicable.

#### *[b] Wage Tax*

Taxes on income from employment are usually levied in the form of *wage withholding taxes*. One requirement is that the employer has a permanent establishment in Austria (§ 47 EStG). The wage tax generally corresponds with the income tax, especially regarding allowances and tax rates, which are adapted to the payment periods of wages. The wage tax does, however, have a series of special provisions, especially those regarding fringe benefits and other extra pay.

#### *[c] Capital Yields Tax*

Income tax on certain income from capital investment is levied by way of *withholding*. The debtor of the capital is obliged to withhold a tax of 25%. Such income from capital investment is subject to capital yields tax without the opportunity of any deductions. Capital yields tax is in particular levied on (§ 93 EStG):

- Domestic *dividends* from shares in a stock company, a limited liability company and shares in commercial cooperatives.
- Domestic *interest* from capital receivables with a credit institution.
- Capital gains from domestic bonds.
- Income from realised *increases in value* of assets generating investment income.
- Income from derivatives.

One speaks of domestic income from capital investment if the paying agent is *established in Austria* or if the debtor has his domicile, place of management or legal seat in Austria. With income from realised increases in value of capital and income from derivatives, the decisive question is whether the paying or depository office is *located in Austria*.

In many areas, the withholding tax has become an independent tax instead of merely a method of levying personal income tax. With certain types of income subject to capital yields tax, the levying of personal income tax is *finalised* by the deduction of 25% tax. Result of this effect is that this income does not have to be included in the tax return.

### [7] Limited Liability

Individuals who neither have their residence nor place of habitual abode in Austria are subject to *limited tax liability* in Austria. These individuals are only subject to Austrian income tax in respect of *income from domestic sources*. The relevant category of income has to be determined exclusively from an Austrian tax perspective, only the Austrian facts and circumstances have to be considered (isolation theory). The scope of the limited tax liability in Austria is determined by § *98 EStG*. However, the scope to define a 'domestic source' of income is rather different, depending on the category of income in question. For example regarding income from commercial activities not all activities which are actually performed in Austria are deemed to be Austrian income. Apart from a few exceptions (i.e., income from technical advisory services, income from leasing of personnel and income as a sportsman or artist), non-resident individuals are only subject to taxation from income from commercial activities if:

- A permanent establishment is maintained in Austria for such trade or business.
- A permanent agent is appointed in Austria.
- Immovable property is situated in Austria.

Whereas, regarding income from independent personal services and income from employment not only the inland exercise of such activities, but also the sole *exploitation* of these activities already constitutes an Austrian income source.

In general, non-residents' Austrian source income is taxed at the 'normal' rates; with the peculiarity that in the computation of the income tax liability an amount of EUR 9,000 must be added to the income of the none-resident taxpayer. However, for certain domestic income the legislator wants to assure the collection of taxes by introducing a *special withholding tax* at a flat rate of 20% which is levied on a gross basis. Persons resident in the EU or EEA may choose that the withholding tax is calculated on a net basis with a higher flat rate of 35%. Income subject to the special withholding tax particularly comprises (§ 99 EStG):

- Income from independent personal services as *author, lecturer, entertainer, architect, sportsman, artist or participant in an entertainment performance* if the activities are performed or exploited in Austria.
- Profits form a cross-border multi-tiered transparent partnership, if the recipients of the income are not disclosed.

- Royalties and fees for the use of know-how.
- Directors' fees.
- Income from commercial or technical consultancy activities.
- Income from cross-border hiring out of labour.
- Distributions or deemed distributions of real estate funds, if the real estate is located in Austria under the condition of public-placement.

## [B] Corporate Income Tax Act (*Körperschaftsteuergesetz*, 'KStG')

### *[1] Scope*

The Corporate Income Tax Act applies to the following taxable persons (§ 1 paragraph 1 KStG):

- Legal entities organised under private law (e.g., stock companies, limited liability companies, foundations, associations and cooperatives) and comparable foreign entities.
- Corporations under public law and businesses carried on by corporations under public law.
- Institutions and funds without independent legal existence and accumulations of property for a specific purpose.

Companies are subject to *unlimited taxation* (§ 1 paragraph 2 KStG), if they are *resident* in Austria. A company is resident in Austria, if it has its legal *seat or place of management* in Austria. The legal seat is defined as the place which is designated as such in the articles of association or other basic documents. The place of management is defined as the centre from which the activities of the company are effectively directed.

Companies are *subject to limited taxation* in Austria (§ 1 paragraph 3 KStG), if they neither have their seat nor their place of management in Austria. In such cases, similar to the principles in the EStG, they are only subject to tax on their income from domestic sources. However, a different tax regime applies for corporations under public law and tax exempt legal entities (e.g., charitable companies): They are only taxable with their income subject to withholding tax (capital yields tax) or comparable foreign income.

### *[2] Taxable Income*

#### *[a] Income Calculation According to the Rules of the EStG*

The Corporate Income Tax Act refers to the definition of taxable income as contained in the Income Tax Act (EStG). Consequently, in principal a company may derive income from all seven categories of income as defined pursuant to the EStG. However, § 7 paragraph 3 KStG explicitly determines that all income of legal companies, whose financial accounting has to be based on the double bookkeeping under commercial law only can fall under *one category of income*, namely *income from commercial activities*.

Also the computation of taxable income follows the rules of the EStG, if not otherwise determined by the KStG. The profit or loss of the company is defined by using the *net worth comparison method*. The profit or loss is the difference between the company's net assets at the beginning and the end of the tax year adjusted by contributions or withdrawals.

### *[b] Contributions and Withdrawals*

According to § 8 paragraph 1 KStG a *contribution* made to the capital of a company is not taken into account for determining the company's income. Conversely, this principle applies in the same way if a person withdraws capital from a company. This rule applies regardless of whether the person receives any shares or other membership rights in return for the contribution. A contribution can be made in cash or in kind. If a contribution occurs by way of transaction qualifying as capital contributions under general corporate law (e.g., formal capital increase), a contribution is deemed to be *'open'*, otherwise a contribution is deemed to be *'hidden'*. A hidden contribution occurs if a shareholder provides a benefit to the company either for no consideration or for consideration that is below the price that would have been paid to an *independent third person* in an *arm's length transaction*. For tax purposes, a hidden contribution shall be treated the same way as on open contribution. For example, if a shareholder sells an asset to the company below the market value, the company has to increase its tax basis in the assets to their market value and account for the difference between purchase price and market value as hidden contribution.

### *[c] Profit Distributions*

Also the *distribution of profits* to the shareholders is deemed to be a tax neutral event on company level. In this respect, it is irrelevant, whether the profit distribution is performed by way of *an open dividend* or *hidden dividend* (§ 8 paragraph 2 EStG). An open dividend occurs if it is based on a formal shareholder's resolution of the distributing company. However, if a company grants a benefit to its shareholders, which would not have been granted to an independent third person, this transaction occurs *'causa societatis'* and therefore is treated as hidden dividend. This for example is the case, if a company pays a price above the market price for services of a shareholder. In such a case, only the arm's length part of the payment is tax deductible, the exceeding part is deemed to be a hidden distribution and thus tax neutral on company level.

### *[d] Deductions and Special Expenses*

In general, all *expenses* caused by the conduct of the business are *tax deductible* (§ 11 KStG for deductible expenses and § 12 KStG for non-deductible expenses). As regards *special expenses*, only the following may be taken into account (§ 8 paragraph 4 KStG with reference to the EStG):

- Annuities and permanent charges.
- Expenses for certified tax advisors.
- Special donations.
- Loss carry forwards.

### *[3] Group Taxation*

#### *[a] General Information and Requirements*

Companies by law are separate and independent legal entities. However, within a group of companies, they can be *economically dependent and linked to each other*. Thus, in the year 2005 the Austrian legislator has introduced a new regime for group taxation by replacing the provisions of the old '*Organschaft*' regime. The '*Organschaft*' only remains relevant for VAT purposes (VAT grouping).

The relevant provisions for group taxation can be found in § 9 KStG. Under certain conditions this new group taxation regime allows the *formation of a group*, where certain profits and losses can be transferred from a subsidiary to the parent:

- The *parent company* is a domestic company (stock company, limited liability company, cooperative, insurance company or bank) or a foreign company that is either comparable to a domestic company or listed in the annex of the EU Parent Subsidiary Directive. Additionally, a foreign company needs to have a permanent establishment in Austria, to which the participations are attributed.
- The *group subsidiaries* may be domestic or comparable foreign companies. However, only first-tier foreign members may be included into the group.
- Group taxation requires a group-member *participation* (directly or indirectly) *of more than 50%* in the statutory capital and the voting rights of a group subsidiary.
- A *formal application* must be filed with the tax authorities. Moreover, a minimum group taxation *period of three years* is required. If the group breaks up within the three-year period, all tax effects resulting from the group are retroactively neutralised.

#### *[b] Consolidation of Income*

The main consequences of the formation of the group can be described as follows:

- *Total profits or losses* of a domestic group subsidiary are *attributed to the parent*. For this attribution the participation degree is irrelevant. Even if the participation is less than 100%, the total profits or losses are attributed to the parent.

- In case of *foreign group members* profits are not attributed to the parent. Only *losses* are attributed to the parent according to the *percentage of the participation*. However, a *recapture* of taxes in Austria takes place, if the losses may be set off against profits abroad in the subsequent years. Also the exit of foreign group-members triggers the recapture of losses, unless the exit is due to liquidation or insolvency of the foreign member.
- *Write-offs* in respect of participations in group-members are *not deductible*, as by means of income consolidation the parent makes direct use of the subsidiary's losses.

### *[4] Participation Exemption*

#### *[a] General Information and National Participation Exemption*

The *participation exemption* in § *10 KStG* in a national as well as in an international context is one of the key features of the Austrian Corporate Income Tax Act. Its aim is the prevention of double taxation resulting from a profit distribution by a subsidiary to its parent. Such *economic double* or even *multiple taxation* would arise because of the taxation of profits on the level of the subsidiary and the taxation on the level of the receiving parent company, whenever this profit is distributed further up.

Under the *national participation exemption* any dividends from a participation received by a resident company from another resident company or cooperative is exempt from corporate taxation. This exemption also applies to similar participation rights or participation capital. There is no minimum participation requirement or minimum holding requirement. However, gains from the alienation of domestic shares are tax effective.

#### *[b] International Participation Exemption (Participation of 10% or More)*

Dividends from a participation in a foreign company *of 10% or more* are exempt from corporation tax under the following conditions:

- The parent company is legally required to keep books and records according to the Austrian Commercial Code or the parent company is a foreign company that qualifies as a resident of Austria for corporation tax purposes.
- The participation is held for at least a *one-year period* incessantly.
- The foreign subsidiary has a legal form listed in the Parent Subsidiary Directive or is comparable to a domestic company.

*Capital gains and losses* from such participations in foreign companies are deemed to be *tax neutral* as well. However, the taxpayer may opt to treat potential capital gains as taxable income; conversely, occurring losses are tax deductible. This *option* has to be exercised in the year of the acquisition of the participation and is irrevocable.

A *switch-over from the exemption to the credit method* takes place if:

- Foreign-source income is subject to taxation which is *not comparable to the Austrian corporation tax* (if the foreign tax does not exceed 15%).
- The *main aim* of the business of the foreign company is to directly or indirectly derive interest, income from leasing of movable or intangible assets or the alienation of participations (passive income).

##### [c] International Exemption for Minor Shareholdings (Share of Less than 10%)

Dividends from a share in a foreign company *of less than 10%* are exempt from corporation tax under the following conditions:

- The foreign subsidiary has to have a legal form which is listed in the Parent Subsidiary Directive (90/435/CEE).
- The foreign subsidiary has to be a company of an EEA Member State, it has to be comparable to a domestic company and there has to be an extensive exchange of information and administrative assistance in the recovery of taxes with the foreign country in which the company is a resident.

In order to avoid non-taxation or under-taxation *a switch-over from the exemption to the credit method* takes place if one of the following requirements is met:

- The foreign company is actually not subject to a tax which is *comparable to the Austrian corporation tax*, neither directly or indirectly.
- The profits of the foreign company are subject to a tax which is comparable to the Austrian corporation tax, but the rate applicable is less than 15%.
- The foreign company benefits from an *extensive exemption* from tax (except exemptions for domestic dividends).

## §15.03 AVOIDANCE OF DOUBLE TAXATION AND TAX TREATY POLICY

### [A] Unilateral Measures

*Unilateral relief* is granted either by an exemption or a foreign tax credit. The main purpose of this relief regulated in § *48 Fedaral Fiscal Code* (*Bundesabgabenordnung*, 'BAO') is to achieve a balance between the domestic and the foreign tax liability or to provide a tax treatment in accordance with the principle of reciprocity. Tax exemption is granted under the condition that the income is subject to an average tax burden of at least 15% in the source state. The *exemption* only concerns positive income, foreign losses can be included into the Austrian tax base, provided that no double utilisation of losses occurs in the succeeding years. Basically, the following categories of income may be tax exempt:

- Income from immovable property located abroad.
- Business profits derived by a foreign permanent establishment.
- Income from a foreign building site or construction project.

In case that the average tax burden of these categories of income is below 15%, double taxation is avoided by a *foreign tax credit*. A credit is also granted with respect to other categories of income as mentioned above (e.g., dividends, capital gains, interest and royalties). In all cases unilateral relief is subject to several documentary requirements; the taxpayer for example is obliged to keep records providing information about the source state, the category of income, as well as the amount of income and the effective tax rate in the source state.

### [B] Tax Treaties

Austria has concluded more than ninety conventions to *avoid double taxation* (*Double Taxation Conventions*, 'DTCs'). These treaties cover individual income tax, corporate income tax and in certain cases also net worth tax and business tax. However, business tax and net worth tax have been abolished effective the year 1993. According to a DTC, the resident state of the taxpayer is defined and the taxing rights are allocated to the two contracting states. If the *allocation rule* still leaves taxation rights for both states, finally the *method article* defines the method of avoiding double taxation (exemption or credit method). At the end of a DTC, non-discrimination provisions, provisions on the exchange of information, on the collection of taxes and on arbitration are included.

The aim of the *Austrian tax treaty policy* is to go beyond merely avoiding double taxation. When Austria enters into treaty negotiations, the treaty is expected to meet three requirements: (i) *promotion of economic development*, (ii) *prevention of international tax avoidance* and (iii) *guarantee of legal certainty*. By taking into account these basic principles the fair sharing of profits and losses between two countries should be ensured with a focus on the reciprocity principle. Under most of the Austrian treaties, double taxation is eliminated by using the *exemption method*. However, as a general rule, double taxation of dividends, interest and royalties is eliminated by using the *credit method*. To a large extent, the Austrian model follows the *OECD Model Tax Convention*. Some of the highlights of the Austrian tax treaty policy explicitly can be described as follows:

- No withholding taxes on interest, royalties and inter-company dividends.
- Application of the Commentary to the OECD Model Convention for interpretation purposes.
- Avoidance of discriminatory treatment with regard to other EU Member States.

## §15.04 OTHER TAXES[1]

### [A] Value Added Tax (VAT)

After Austria's accession to the European Union on 1 January 1995, the VAT system had to be amended to be in conformity with the EU law provisions. A completely new VAT Act (*Umsatzsteuergesetz*, 'UStG') was enacted together with a Single Market Regulation. Consequently, as within the EU indirect taxation is widely harmonised, the Austrian UStG – which was implemented on basis of the 'VAT Directive' (2006/112/EC) and the former '6th VAT Directive' (77/388/EEC) – is rather similar to the VAT systems in other countries.

VAT is levied at all levels of the supply of goods and services. The entrepreneur deducts the VAT he paid on purchases and services (input VAT deduction) during the taxable period against the VAT he charged on the supply of goods or services during the same period. Thus, he pays VAT only on the value added by him, i.e., the increment in price. The number of transactions through which a product passes on its way to the consumer is normally irrelevant, and the total tax burden passed on at the retail stage is always the same, namely the statutory rates which apply to the retail price before tax. VAT is not an element of cost for the entrepreneur (except in certain cases of non-deductibility). For VAT purposes, it is decisive that the transaction needs to be carried out in Austria. However, it is not relevant whether the entrepreneur is a national or resident of Austria or has its legal seat, place of management or a permanent establishment inland.

### [B] Real Estate Transfer Tax (*Grunderwerbsteuergesetz*, 'GrEStG')

The *transfer of the title to immovable property* located in Austria is subject to real estate transfer tax. The term immovable property includes land and buildings. It does not include machinery and equipment forming part of an industrial plant or industrial or commercial franchises. The GrEStG also provides for a number of supplementary and substitutive rules to prevent taxpayers from circumventing the tax liability by choosing legal forms which are not covered by the GrEStG but have the same economic result (e.g., in case that all shares of a company owning immovable property are united). The taxable base normally is the *value of the consideration* given to the transfer. The tax rate is 3.5%. If the property is transferred between husband and wife or parents or children, the tax rate only amounts to 2%.

### [C] Transaction Duties

The Act on Transaction Duties (*Gebührengesetz*, 'GebG') stipulates duties for certain *written authenticated transactions* (§§ 15 et seq. GebG). Duties become due if they are

1. This section gives an exemplary overview about specific other taxes important in Austrian Tax Law.

covered by so called *fee items* (enumeration principle). Transactions are only then subject to tax if a *certificate* is drawn up (so called principle of certificate, § 15 GebG), unless the GebG specifies something different. A certificate is every document on which characters are put and which authenticates the conclusion of a transaction. Subject to duties is the *transaction* itself. The documentation itself is only the condition for taxability. Therefore, the economic view which prevails in tax law normally does not apply for the GebG.

### [D] Inheritance and Gift Taxes (*Erbschafts- und Schenkungssteuergesetz,* 'ErbStG')

Since 1 August 2008, the inheritance and gift taxes have been *abolished*. Gifts now have to been notified to the local tax authorities.

## §15.05 PROCEDURAL ASPECTS

### [A] From Filing the Tax Return to the Administrative Act

Tax returns for income tax, corporate income tax, VAT and for the determination of income from a co-entrepreneurship are to be filed until the end of April of the subsequent year. If the tax return is filed electronically, the deadline can be extended to the end of July. A general extension of maturity is granted to taxpayers who are represented by professional representatives (e.g., tax advisors).

Persons subject to *unlimited tax liability* in Austria must *file an income tax return* for the relevant year (§ 42 paragraph 1 EStG), if:

- So required by the tax office.
- The income entirely or partly consists of business income and the profit had to be or was computed by way of accounting.
- The income not including income from employment exceeds EUR 11,000. Under certain circumstances, in particular if the employee receives income from two or more employers or from other sources of income exceeding a total amount of EUR 730, the employee must file a tax return (§§ 41 et seq. EStG).
- The income is subject to the special tax rate pursuant § 27a EStG, but no capital yields taxes were levied.

Persons subject to limited tax liability in Austria must *file an income tax return* for Austrian income (§ 42 paragraph 2 EStG), if:

- So required by the tax office.
- The total amount of Austrian Income which has to be assessed according to § 102 EStG exceeds EUR 2,000.

In practice, about 80% of the tax returns are electronically saved and processed by the tax authorities without additional evaluation of the content of the tax return.

Specific cases which seem to require extended evaluation are evaluated by using computer-based standard evaluation criteria such as the total amount of income, significant changes compared to the previous years, etc. All various types of *evidence* can be used in this context (e.g., official and private certificates, witnesses, consult experts, legal inspections...). At the end of the investigation of the tax office when the amount of taxes to be paid is determined, an *administrative act* is issued.

A tax *falls under the statute of limitation*, when it is not executed for a specific period. The statute of limitations has to be claimed ex officio. If a tax is assessed although it does already fall under the statute of limitation, the taxpayer may appeal against the assessment. In tax law it has to be differed between the *statute of limitations for assessment* and the *statute of limitations for collection*. A tax may no longer be levied ten years after the tax triggering event (*'absolute statute of limitations'*).

### [B] Protection of Taxpayers' Rights

#### *[1] Appeals against Assessments*

If the taxpayer does not agree with the assessment issued in the administrative act of the tax authorities, he/she may file an *appeal against assessment* within *one month* with the relevant tax office. To facilitate the procedure, in general the tax administration at first has to issue a decision on its own. If the taxpayer still is not satisfied with the assessment, he may request the appeal to be forwarded to the *Federal Financial Court (Bundesfinanzgericht, 'BFG')*. The Federal Financial Court may decide to amend the administrative act in any way. This could be to the advantage or detriment of the taxpayer. Against the decision of the Federal Financial Court, the taxpayer may file an appeal with the *Supreme Administrative Court*; a constitutional issue may be raised by appealing to the *Constitutional Court*. The decisions of these two courts are final, against those decisions there is no judicial remedy.

#### *[2] Federal Financial Court* **(Bundesfinanzgericht, *'BFG'*)**

The BFG has been newly established with effect of 1 January 2014. As a result of a total reform on the organisation of administrative courts in Austria, it is replacing the former Independent Fiscal Senate (*Unabhängiger Finanzsenat*, 'UFS'). The BFG is an authority independent from the ordinary tax administration. It handles appellate procedures comprising taxes, as well as less serious penal proceedings in tax matters. The court is entitled to amend the administrative act in any way and to hand down a new judgment on the merits. Alternatively, the decision can also be remand for reappraisal to the competent tax authority. In addition, in all of its judgments the BFG also has to decide on whether against this judgment an ordinary appeal to the VwGH shall be possible or not. If the ordinary appeal is denied, the taxpayer is entitled to file an extraordinary appeal stating why – contrarily to the reasoning of the BFG – the taxpayer is of the opinion that an appeal to the VwGH shall be possible.

### *[3] Supreme Administrative Court* (Verwaltungsgerichtshof, *'VwGH'*)

Similar to administrative law issues also regarding tax law cases the VwGH acts as Supreme Court. For this purpose specialised tax law senates have been established. They mainly deal with the illegality of administrative acts (*'Bescheidbeschwerden'*) and appeals claiming a breach of the obligation to reach a timely decision (*'Säumnisbeschwerden'*). Regarding appeals *against the illegality of an administrative act* the VwGH may not only *abolish or confirm* the administrative act of prior instance (mostly the BFG), but also, under certain conditions, is entitled to hand down a new *judgment on the merits*. If an administrative authority completely fails to make a decision within a given period (mostly six months), the petitioner may first request that a higher authority deals with this issue. If this motion fails too, the taxpayer may lodge an *appeal claiming a breach of the obligation to reach a timely decision* and bring the case before the VwGH.

### *[4] Constitutional Court* (Verfassungsgerichtshof, *'VfGH'*)

The VfGH acts as a Supreme Court with special administrative jurisdiction if the constitutional rights of a taxpayer are infringed. This particularly is the case if tax authorities apply the law in an inconceivable way in legal terms. Such *'inconceivable'* application of the law is a violation of the constitutionally granted *principle of equality*. Moreover, the VfGH has the authority to annul the application of *unconstitutional statutes* as well as of *unlawful regulations*. In addition, in ordinary tax cases the court also has competences regarding certain conflicts of jurisdiction.

## SELECTED BIBLIOGRAPHY

Althuber/Vondrak, *Steuerrecht für Juristen* (2012).
Beiser, *Steuern*, 12th edition (2014).
Doralt, *Steuerrecht* 2014/15, 16th edition (2014).
Doralt/Ruppe, *Grundriss des österreichischen Steuerrecht I*, 11th edition (2013).
Doralt/Ruppe, *Grundriss des österreichischen Steuerrechts II*, 7th edition (2014).
Lang/Schuch/Staringer, *Einführung in das Steuerrecht*, 14th edition (2014).
Tumpel, *Steuern kompakt* 2015 (2015).
Unger/Vock, *Casebook Steuerrecht*, 6th edition (2014).
Buzanich, *Austria – Individual Taxation 2014*, IBFD Country Analyses.
Jann/Schuch/Toifl, *Austria – Corporate Taxation 2014*, IBFD Country Analyses
Ruppe et al, *58th IfA Congress Vienna 2004*, Bulletin for International Fiscal Documentation 2004, Volume 58, Number 8/9.
Ubelhoer/Pfeiffer/Huisman/Schaffer, Introduction to Austrian Tax Law (2014).